NEW ACCENTS

General editor: TERENCE HAWKES

Post-Colonial Shakespeares

This collection of new essays explores the multiple possibilities for the study of Shakespeare in an emerging post-colonial period. *Post-Colonial Shakespeares* examines the extent to which our assumption about such key terms as 'colonization', 'race' and 'nation' derive from early modern English culture. It also looks at how such terms are themselves affected by what were established subsequently as 'colonial' forms of knowledge.

The volume features original work by some of the leading critics within the field of Shakespearean studies. It is the most authoritative collection on this topic to date and represents an exciting step forward for post-colonial studies.

Ania Loomba is the author of *Gender, Race, Renaissance Drama* (1989) and *Colonialism / Post-Colonialism* (1998). She is Associate Professor of English at Jawaharlal Nehru University, New Delhi, India.

Martin Orkin is the author of *Shakespeare Against Apartheid* (1987) and *Drama and the South African State* (1991). He is currently Associate Professor in the Departments of English and Theatre at the University of Haifa, Israel

NEW ACCENTS

General Editor: TERENCE HAWKES

Post-Colonial Shakespeares

Edited by
ANIA LOOMBA and MARTIN ORKIN

London and New York

822·33
3 who·

First published 1998
by Routledge
11 New Fetter Lane,
London EC4P 4EE

Simultaneously published in
the USA and Canada
by Routledge
29 West 35th Street,
New York, NY 10001

© 1998 selection and editorial matter, Ania
Loomba and Martin Orkin; individual
chapters, the contributors

Typeset in Baskerville by
Ponting–Green Publishing Services,
Chesham, Buckinghamshire
Printed and bound in Great Britain by
Clays Ltd, St Ives PLC

British Library Cataloguing in
Publication Data

A catalogue record for this book is available
from the British Library

Library of Congress Cataloguing in
Publication Data

A catalogue record for this book has been
requested

ISBN 0–415–17386–8 (hbk)
ISBN 0–415–17387–6 (pbk)

Contents

General editor's preface

How can we recognize or deal with the new? Any equipment we bring to the task will have been designed to engage with the old: it will look for and identify extensions and developments of what we already know. To some degree the unprecedented will always be unthinkable.

The *New Accents* series has made its own wary negotiation around that paradox, turning it, over the years, into the central concern of a continuing project. We are obliged, of course, to be bold. Change is our proclaimed business, innovation our announced quarry, the accents of the future the language in which we deal. So we have sought, and still seek, to confront and respond to those developments in literary studies that seem crucial aspects of the tidal waves of transformation that continue to sweep across our culture. Areas such as structuralism, post-structuralism, feminism, Marxism, semiotics, subculture, deconstruction, dialogism, post-modernism, and the new attention to the nature and modes of language, politics and way of life that these bring, have already been the primary concern of a large number of our volumes. Their 'nuts and bolts' exposition of the issues at stake in new ways of writing texts and new ways of reading them has proved an effective stratagem against perplexity.

But the questions of what 'texts' are or may be has also become more and more complex. It is not just the impact of electronic modes of communication, such as computer networks and data banks, that has forced us to revise our sense of the sort of material to which the process called 'reading' may apply. Satellite television and supersonic travel have eroded the traditional capacities of time and space to confirm prejudice, reinforce ignorance, and conceal significant difference. Ways of life and cultural practices of which we had barely heard can now be set compellingly beside – can even confront – our own. The effect is to make us ponder the culture we have inherited; to see it, perhaps for the first time, as an intricate, continuing construction. And that means that we can also begin to see, and to question, those arrangements of foregrounding and backgrounding, of stressing and repressing, of placing at the centre and of restricting to the periphery, that give our own way of life its distinctive character.

Small wonder if, nowadays, we frequently find ourselves at the boundaries of the precedented and at the limit of the thinkable: peering into an abyss out of which there begin to lurch awkwardly formed monsters with unaccountable – yet unavoidable – demands on our attention. These may involve unnerving styles of narrative, unsettling notions of 'history', unphilosophical ideas about 'philosophy', even unchildish views of 'comics', to say nothing of a host of barely respectable activities for which we have no reassuring names.

In this situation, straightforward elucidation, careful unpicking, informative bibliographies, can offer positive help, and each *New Accents* volume will continue to include these. But if the project of closely scrutinizing the new remains none the less a disconcernting one, there are still overwhelming reasons for giving it all the consideration we can muster. The unthinkable, after all, is that which covertly shapes our thoughts.

TERENCE HAWKES

Contributors

Andreas Bertoldi, Research Student, Department of Comparative Literature, University of the Witwatersrand, Johannesburg

Jerry Brotton, Research Fellow, School of English, University of Leeds, UK

Jonathan Burton, Adjunct Lecturer in English, Baruch College of the City University of New York

Jonathan Dollimore, Professor of English, Humanities Graduate Research Centre, University of Sussex, UK

Kim F. Hall, Associate Professor of English, Georgetown University

Terence Hawkes, Professor of English, University of Wales, Cardiff

Margo Hendricks, Associate Professor of Literature, University of California, Santa Cruz

David Johnson, Lecturer in English, University of Natal, Durban

Ania Loomba, Associate Professor of English, Jawaharlal Nehru University, New Delhi

Michael Neill, Professor of English, University of Auckland, New Zealand

Martin Orkin, Associate Professor of English, University of Haifa

Avraham Oz, Head of Department of Theatre, University of Haifa; also Lecturer in the Department of Poetics and Comparative Literature, Tel Aviv University

Nicholas Visser, Associate Professor of English, University of Cape Town

Acknowledgements

This volume contains only a small number of the presentations that were first given at the 'Shakespeare–Post-coloniality–Johnanesburg, 1996' conference. We thank every participant for making both post-coloniality and Shakespeare vital living issues and problems. There were many more papers we should have liked to include. We express warmest thanks to Terence Hawkes for his suggestions, his firm support and his always good-humoured encouragement. John Drakakis helped us with the planning of the volume and Jean Howard, as reader, gave us invaluable advice. In addition, Ania Loomba would like to thank Suvir Kaul and Tariq Tachil. Martin Orkin thanks Joan Orkin for making everything possible, Mikhail Orkin for his love and support, and Chloë Orkin for her tenacity.

As this book went to press we were deeply saddened to hear of the untimely passing of one of our contributors, Nick Visser (1943–1998), to whose memory we dedicate this volume.

1
Introduction
Shakespeare and the post-colonial question
ANIA LOOMBA AND MARTIN ORKIN

Shakespeare lived and wrote at a time when English mercantile and colonial enterprises were just germinating. Although the Portuguese, Spanish and Dutch ventures began earlier, European colonialism as a whole was still in its infancy. But this infancy was also an aggressive ascendancy: four hundred years later, both Shakespeare and colonialism have left their imprint on cultures across the globe. The nature of their global presence, and the historical interactions between 'Shakespeare' and colonialism, have been, in the last decade, subjected to new and exciting critiques. Such critiques have shown how Anglo-American literary scholarship of the last two centuries offered a Shakespeare who celebrated the superiority of the 'civilized races', and, further, that colonial educationists and administrators used this Shakespeare to reinforce cultural and racial hierarchies. Shakespeare was made to perform such ideological work both by interpreting his plays in highly conservative ways (so that they were seen as endorsing existing racial, gender and other hierarchies, never as questioning or destabilizing them) and by constructing him as one of the best, if not 'the best', writer in the whole world. He became, during the colonial period, the quintessence of Englishness and a measure of humanity itself. Thus the meanings of Shakespeare's plays were both derived from and used to establish colonial authority.

Intellectuals and artists from the colonized world responded to such a Shakespeare in a variety of ways: sometimes they mimicked their colonial masters and echoed their praise of Shakespeare; at other times they challenged the cultural authority of both Shakespeare and colonial regimes by turning to their own bards as sources of alternative wisdom and beauty. In yet other instances, they appropriated Shakespeare as their comrade in anti-colonial arms by offering new interpretations and adaptations of his work. In recent years, both Shakespearean scholars and critics working within postcolonial studies have increasingly begun to scrutinize the ways in which the colonial and racial discourses of early modern England might have shaped Shakespeare's work, and also the processes by which Shakespeare (in performance and study) later became a colonial battlefield. The overlaps, tensions, as well as possibilities of a dialogue, between Shakespearean and post-colonial studies is the subject of *Post-Colonial Shakespeares*. In this introductory essay, we would like briefly to map the intellectual histories and contours of this dialogue, and gesture at its potential problems as well as enormous possibilities.

The collapse of formal empires accelerated critiques of imperial and colonial philosophies, ideologies and aesthetics, both from within so-called metropolitan societies and, most vitally, from once-colonized ones. Anti-colonial struggles and individuals in both places challenged established colonialist readings of history, culture and literature. So did some of the critical vocabularies that developed within Western intellectual and political traditions such as Marxism, feminism, post-structuralism, psychoanalysis and linguistics. There are enormous differences between and within these various perspectives, but also important areas of overlap and dialogue. All of them challenged the 'meta-narratives' (or dominant writings on philosophy, language, history, culture and aesthetics) that had excluded and marginalized the experience and cultures of the under-privileged – the lower classes and castes, women, colonized people, homosexuals and others. The interests of these subordinated groups did not always overlap, but all of them, in rewriting dominant intellectual and political traditions, insisted that ideological and social practices are interconnected, indeed that they constitute each other. The decentring of the human subject was important to all of them because such a subject had been theorized by European imperialist discourses as male and white. Again, various oppositional movements (particularly anti-colonial and feminist struggles) as well as the new critical perspectives have all emphasized culture and literature as a site of conflict between the oppressors and the oppressed. They also paid new attention to language as a tool of domination and as a means of constructing identity.

Of course, there have also been disagreements on these questions, as anti-colonial feminists and other activists are involved not only in questioning totalizing frameworks but also in the possibility of social change. But together, they have made possible a new kind of literary criticism, where history does not just provide a background to the study of texts, but forms an essential part of textual meaning; conversely, texts or representations are seen as fundamental to the creation of history and culture. Within Anglo-American academic institutions, such critical vocabularies, as is well known by now, were in part developed via studies of Shakespeare and early modern culture. During the 1980s and 1990s cultural materialists, new historicists and feminists utilized the insights of Marxism, feminism, post-structuralism, psychoanalysis and semiotics to reinterpret class, gender and sexual relations in early modern Europe and to reflect on the dynamic interrelation between cultural forms (including literature) and social power. Most importantly, some of these new analyses also considered the ways in which these earlier cultural, social and literary heritages shape our contemporary world. Thus, reintepreting Shakespeare's plays became, at least for some critics, part of the business of reinterpreting and changing our own world. How 'Shakespeare' functioned in contemporary classrooms, in films, television, theatre and the tourist trade, and how his cultural authority was built up over the past four hundred years, became the subject of new critiques.

These re-readings of Renaissance culture and power opened up, in at least two important ways, questions of colonialism and race in relation to Shakespeare. First, scholars began to examine emergent colonial discourses and relations during the early modern period and their impact on different aspects of English history, culture and representations. Of course, there had been pioneering scholarship in these areas earlier – books such as Samuel Chew's *The Crescent and the Rose* (1937), which examined views and representations of Islam in Elizabethan and Jacobean England; Eldred Jones's *Othello's Countrymen* (1965) and *The Elizabethan Image of Africa* (1971), both of which focused on images of black Africans in the period and its literature; and G. K. Hunter's *Dramatic Identities and Cultural Tradition* (1978), which examined racial discourses and the status of foreigners during the period and in Shakespeare's plays, must all be acknowledged as important progenitors for current scholarship on these matters.

However, the latter brings new critical perspectives on language, literature and culture to bear upon its understanding of racial identities, colonial discourses and the Shakespearean text. As Francis Barker and Peter Hulme argued in a revisionist essay on *The Tempest*, English colonialism had previously been acknowledged only as source material or backdrop for Shakespeare's play; they showed instead how colonial discourse was central to the play's thematic as well as formal concerns, forming not a background but rather one of its 'dominant discursive con-texts' (Barker and Hulme 1985: 198).

Current scholarship has offered sophisticated readings of the webbed relations between state power, the emergence of new classes and ideologies, the reshaping of patriarchal authority, the development of the idea of an English nation, sexual practices and discourses, and the real and imaginary experiences of English people in the Americas, Africa and Asia. These experiences built upon and transformed ideologies about 'others' which filtered down from earlier times, particularly the experience of the Crusades, or which emerged in interactions with other Europeans such as the Spanish, the Italians and the Dutch, or, most importantly, those that were developed in relation to those living on the margins of English society – Jews, gypsies, the Irish, the Welsh and the Scots. Political criticism of Shakespeare as well as of early modern England has begun to show, with increasing detail and sophistication, that it is virtually impossible to seal off any meaningful analysis of English culture and literature from considerations of racial and cultural difference, and from the dynamics of emergent colonialisms.

Second, the newer critical vocabularies make possible an examination of the complex relationship between these earlier histories and subsequent developments of colonial and racial vocabularies. One of our most difficult tasks may be to balance our search for early modern meanings of race, colonialism and cultural difference while also exploring the contemporary imperatives of these terms. How do our attitudes to 'race' differ from those of Shakespeare's contemporaries, and to what extent have our views been shaped by early modern histories and ideologies? And most crucially, what part do Shakespeare's plays and poems play in the transmission of ideas about race and cultural difference? Literary texts that were written a long time ago but which circulate powerfully in our own lives constantly mediate between the 'then' and the 'now'. As we have mentioned earlier, stage as well as classroom histories of Shake-speare's plays reveal how racial ideologies continued to shape the ways the plays were interpreted, taught and produced, but also re-veal oppositional practices, appropriations of Shakespeare and contests over the meaning of the plays. These two important aspects of Shakespeare and the colonial question – we can, for the sake of convenience, call them colonial and post-colonial Shakespeares – are often examined independently of each other, or at least their relationship is often implied rather than explicitly considered.

For example, new historicist critics have offered some incisive readings of early modern colonialisms and the gendered and sexualized nature of these operations. As has been widely noted, they have not engaged directly with contemporary pedagogical or institutional dynamics, or with the forms and circulation of issues of colonial-ism and racism today. Despite this, the best of new historicist work has advanced theories of intracultural contact and the workings of colonial discourse, some of which have been influential far beyond Shakespearean or English studies. Essays on South Asian history and anthropology may now invoke Stephen Greenblatt's analysis of the relationship between power and subversion in early modern culture and apply it to contemporary 'Third World' societies (Haynes and Prakash 1991). Greenblatt's work has itself been inspired by revisionist anthropological work on 'Third World' cultures. But these evocative and often illuminating movements between time and space do not include any sustained reflection on the power relations that shape our contemporary world – for example, those between con-temporary Indonesia and America. Neither Shakespeareans nor post-colonial critics have so far considered in any significant detail the implications of analysing sixteenth-century Europe from mod-els derived from contemporary culture or vice versa.

Very recently, however, this relationship between past and present has come under scrutiny. Several critics have suggested that present-day meanings of 'race' and 'colonialism' cannot be applied to the past. It is possible, for example, that blackness may not have been the most outstanding marker of race in early modern Europe. One critic has recently argued that post-colonial criticism emphasizes European domination and the victimization of colonized subjects to the extent that it misleads Shakespeareans into assuming that the same inequities between Europeans and others existed in early modern England (Bartels 1997). It is certainly true that we must not flatten the past by viewing it entirely through the lens of our own assumptions and imperatives. However, neither is it desirable, or even possible, entirely to unhook the past from the present. Early modern Europe was the crucible for the genesis of many modern European institutions and practices, and later, via colonial regimes, of many modern non-European ones as well. We read the past to understand our own lives, and equally, our own commitments direct us to the 'truth' about the past. The relationship between societies separated in time is as complex as the one between societies that are spatially and culturally apart – in both cases 'difference' is a category that should be neither erased nor valorized.

We hope the present volume will provoke fresh thinking on these issues. It brings together essays that deal with early modern Europe and with our contemporary world, as its two-part structure makes evident. The first part foregrounds considerations of the Shakespearean text 'then' and the second part concentrates on later histories of Shakespeare. However, the two parts are not sealed off from each other – most of our contributors in fact move both between different times and between different cultures: thus Terence Hawkes's essay details, via Shakespeare's *Henry IV*, English impulses to anglicize and assimilate Wales, but he constantly places these attempts within the later reverberations of such a project; Avraham Oz attempts to address early modern English nationalism and its relationship with Jerusalem partly from the perspective of his location within late twentieth-century Israel; Margo Hendricks draws attention to racial discourses in *The Rape of Lucrece* and its connections with her understanding of 'hybridity' in the United States and South Africa; Nicholas Visser approaches the question of land ownership in the text of *King Lear* and in early modern England from the perspective of current South African attempts to redistribute land and wealth; and Kim Hall finds Toni Morrison helpful in decoding early modern mythologies of colour, and in the process she unearths, in Shakespeare's sonnets and other representations of the period, the germs of our contemporary colour-consciousness. In each case, these essays do not counterpose our own investments in the present against the search for truths about the past.

For the purposes of our discussion it is significant that Bartels holds 'post-colonial' critiques responsible for imprisoning us in an ahistorical model of European domination and non-European subjection. Various critics and historians have suggested that 'colonial discourse theories' overemphasize the power of colonialism, or erase the prior histories of colonized societies. However, this criticism has often come from within post-colonial studies, which is not, it may be helpful to remember, a homogeneous body of writing, or a single way of approaching the question of colonial power relations. Rather, there is sharp disagreement over the extent to which colonial regimes succeeded in silencing the people over whom they ruled. Some scholars think it is important to emphasize the power and violence of colonial rule and argue that it is both naïve and romantic to suggest that most colonized peoples had any manoeuvring power at all. Others find it imperative to highlight the agency of colonized peoples and usually argue that even the most coercive colonial hegemony was achieved in part through the 'consent' of the local peoples, or that even the most oppressed people create spaces from which they can 'speak'. Of course, the question that still remains is, in what voices do the colonized speak – their own, or in accents borrowed from their masters?

Revisionist studies of Shakespeare need to be concerned with these questions both when they reinvestigate the past and when they analyse the present. The negotiations and contestations of culture, and the battles for agency mentioned above, were often enacted via Shakespeare's work and reputation. Colonial masters imposed their value system through Shakespeare, and in response colonized peoples often answered back in Shakespearean accents. The study of Shakespeare made them 'hybrid' subjects, to use a term that has become central to post-colonial criticism and which is increasingly used to characterize the range of psychological as well as physiological mixings generated by colonial encounters. Many post-colonial critics regard the hybridity of colonial and post-colonial subjects as a potentially radical state, one that enables such subjects to elude, or even subvert the binaries, oppositions and rigid demarcations imposed by colonial discourses.

As Michael Neill's essay in this volume argues, Anglophone cultures the world over have been 'saturated with Shakespeare'. Indeed, Shakespeare has also penetrated much of the non-English-speaking world – he is today the most performed playwright in the world, a fact that is often taken as testimony of Shakespeare's 'universal genius'. Instead, we might suggest that such a phenomenon reveals not just the spread of imperial networks in education and culture but also the fact that there is no single 'Shakespeare' that is simply reproduced globally. Rather, as Denis Kennedy puts it, 'almost from the start of his importance as the idealized English dramatist there have been other Shakespeares, Shakespeares not dependent upon English and often at odds with it' (Kennedy 1993: 2). Thus Shakespeare's work not only engenders 'hybrid' subjects, but is itself hybridized by the various performances, mutilations and appropriations of his work. Indeed, from the perspective of this volume it could be argued that any act of reading and performing Shakespeare in the later twentieth century generates multiple levels of hybridity.

Not surprisingly, certain Shakespearean characters have circulated as symbols for intercultural mixings. For example, in a landmark essay, the Cuban writer Roberto Fernández Retamar invoked Caliban as a symbol of 'our *mestizo* America'. America, Retamar suggested, is unique in the colonial world because the majority of its population is racially mixed, it continues to use 'the languages of our colonizers', and 'so many of their conceptual tools ... are also now *our* conceptual tools' (Retamar 1974: 9–11). Caliban is the most appropriate symbol for this hybridity, although

> I am aware that it is not entirely ours, that it is also an alien elaboration, although in our case based on our concrete realities. But how can this alien quality be entirely avoided? The most venerated word in Cuba – *mambí* – was disparagingly imposed on us by our enemies at the time of the war for independence, and we still have not totally deciphered its meaning. It seems to have an African root, and in the mouth of the Spanish colonists implied the idea that all *independentistas* were so many black slaves – emancipated by the very war for independence – who of course constituted the bulk of the liberation army. The *independentistas*, white and black, adopted with honor something that colonialism meant as an insult. This is the dialectic of Caliban.
>
> (Ibid.: 27)

For Retamar, 'hybridity' becomes a radical, subversive condition, and the appropriation of the master culture a viable political method. But other anti-colonial intellectuals have argued (as have many feminists and Marxists) that the master's tools cannot be easily appropriated to dismantle the master's house. They view hybridity as a condition that marks the alienation of subordinated people from their own cultures. However, because colonial encounters varied so hugely in different parts of the world and at different points of time, any generalization about the hybridities they engendered cannot be universally valid. Although some post-colonial theorists may tend to flatten historically and politically variable conditions of mixings, crossovers and creolizations, they cannot all be considered radical or conservative in the same way, as Ania Loomba's essay in this volume argues. Loomba illustrates her discussion of post-colonial theories by considering the differences between Salman Rushdie's *The Moor's Last Sigh* and a recent adaptation of *Othello* in the Kathakali dance-drama form of Kerala. Michael Neill also discusses Rushdie's novel, and several other invocations, appropriations and adaptations of Shakespeare in Africa and the South Pacific, and he too assesses their different relationships to both Shakespeare and their own contexts. While he finds that, so far 'the decentring of Shakespeare has been more rhetorical than real', Neill nevertheless argues that the 'rehistoricization of Shakespeare that has taken place over the last two decades ought to make the study of his work in an antipodean context a *more* rather than less urgent priority'. Martin Orkin's essay similarly registers the extent to which Shakespeare is imbricated within South African education, and he too endorses the radical potential of the hybrid Shakespeare text in this situation. For him, the plays can be used to engender a hybridity among students and others which would be radical and subversive of the effects of apartheid. On the other hand, Margo Hendricks celebrates the possible connections between the '*mestizaje*' conditions of both US and South African subjects. But Hendricks also traces some of the anxieties surrounding race and ethnicity in our own times to Shakespeare's *The Rape of Lucrece*, reminding us of the persistent connections between our own and past figurations of both authenticity and creolization. Postcolonial debates about hybridity, then, are useful not only for thinking about encounters with Shakespeare the world over, but also about the encounters between races and cultures that were enacted in his own work and time.

Not just Caliban, whom Retamar appropriates, but also Othello and Shylock enact the tensions of intercultural interracial, or interreligious encounters. Race, culture and religion, and indeed nationality, are interlocking concepts that always derive their meaning from one another. Jonathan Burton contends in this volume that critics have not paid sufficient attention to how religious difference, especially Islam, shaped early modern discourses of race and culture. Burton places both *Othello*, and Leo Africanus's *Geographical Historie of Africa*, the text which supplied early modern English readers with most of their information on Africa, into this history. Othello is often said to invoke Africanus himself, a converted Moor. But Burton argues that the two texts exemplify the divergent effects of colonial mimicry or hybridity – the *Historie* strategically reproduces anti-Islamic and anti-African discourses in order to undermine them, whereas Othello's relationship to European Christianity allows him less space for the subversion of its ideologies, and the play 'produces a troubled and troubling fantasy of containment for a society frightened by the idea of cultural integration'. Thus, both in early modern times and later, the meeting of Europe and its 'others' generates a wide and complex spectrum of relationships, partly because 'subaltern' subjects, to use yet another term that has been made fashionable by post-colonial theories, differ in class provenance, gender, sexuality, caste and their proximity to colonial power structures, which are also not the same at all places and at all times.

Shakespeare's plays overlap with post-colonial concerns in a third important way – they regularly provided a vocabulary for theorizing the colonial encounter and psyches. We can glimpse this in the work of three people writing across a wide political spectrum – Octavio Mannoni, who used the relationship between Prospero and Caliban to suggest (via a study of anti-colonial revolts in Madagascar) that there are irreducible psychological differences between the colonizers and the colonized; the South African psychoanalyst Wulf Sachs who, in 1937, used Freud's concept of 'Hamletism' (a mental state of indecision and hesitancy when action is demanded) to suggest that there are no differences between black and white psyches; and Roberto Fernandez Retamar who, as has already been mentioned, appropriated Caliban as a symbol for a Latin American *mestizaje* or hybridity. Thus Shakespeare provides the language for expressing racial difference and human sameness as well as colonial hybridities. In the case of Mannoni, Sachs, Retamar and several others, new meanings of the plays, or their relation to early modern colonialism were incidental, and their value lay in providing metaphors for the understanding of colonialism and contemporary culture.

Andreas Bertoldi's essay charts Sachs's extraordinary analysis of John Chavafambira. In *Black Hamlet: The Mind of an African Negro Revealed by Psychoanalysis* (1937), Sachs suggested that his patient was suffering from 'Hamletism'. Sachs follows Freud in suggesting that Hamlet is unable to act because of an unresolved Oedipus complex. 'Hamletism' is, accordingly, a 'universal phenomenon symbolizing indecision and hesitancy when action is required' (Sachs

1947: 176). Bertoldi analyses the process by which Sachs came to this conclusion. Given the context in which 'the African mind' was slotted into a permanent and fixed difference from the European, Sachs's suggestion that Chavafambira's mental processes are part of a universally applicable framework can be seen as a progressive move. But in arguing for a fundamental sameness between black and white psychic structures, Sachs also suggests that Freudian categories such as the Oedipus complex are universally valid. Bertoldi reminds us of the part played by Shakespeare in the enormously complex encounter between psychoanalysis and colonialism, a role that needs more critical attention than it has hitherto received.

We have suggested that although revisionist early modern scholarship has not reflected sufficiently on its relationship with post-colonial theory, there is a shared intellectual history that has revitalized both areas. Although Shakespeare studies and post-colonial criticism are poised to interact productively with one another, such interactions cannot be simply invoked in the name of a politically invested critique of Shakespeare. If they are to come together, like two ends of a tweezer, to unpick Shakespeare from a colonial past and place him more meaningfully in a post-colonial world, then Shakespeareans need to engage critically and at some depth with post-colonial criticism and the controversies that energize it.

One such area of sharp controversy is the question of location. Various critics have complained that not enough attention is paid within post-colonial studies and theories to specific locations and institutions. Thus 'post-coloniality' verges on becoming a rather vague condition of people anywhere and everywhere. Arif Dirlik points out that whatever its other problems, the much discredited term 'Third World' permitted a certain 'concreteness of places of origin': 'postcolonial does not permit such identification … Now that postcoloniality has been released from the fixity of a Third World location, the identity of the postcolonial is no longer structural but discursive.' Thus, he argues, post-colonial studies construct a 'seemingly shapeless world', in which contemporary inequities are kept at bay (Dirlik 1994: 332, 355). At the same time, as Anne McClintock and others have argued, the term 'post-colonial', if used as *the* definitive adjective for so many different societies around the world, threatens to wipe out the varied histories of these places before the arrival of Europeans. These distinct histories and institutions also shaped colonial relations in each place – thus nomadic peoples were displaced differently from the residents of permanent settlement, and places where the Europeans desperately wanted to gain a trading foothold generated a dynamic distinct from areas where they tried to settle and plant colonies. Thus, as other scholars have also argued, English experiences in the Levant, Africa and India in the sixteenth century were quite different from one another and from those in the Americas.

Jerry Brotton takes this as the starting-point of his analysis of *The Tempest*, pointing out that readings of the play concentrate on New World materials, perhaps because American new historicists 'overinvest something of their own peculiarly post-colonial identities' into this play. The significance of the Mediterranean and the North African coast which played an important part in early modern commerce and politics is thus erased. According to Brotton, reading the play through these neglected histories shows that Prospero is not the prototype of the nineteenth-century English imperialist that he is made out to be, and that the play reflects 'the belatedness and subsequent subordination of English forays into the Mediterranean, and not the rise of English colonialism'. Jonathan Burton's account of Othello and Africanus shares this desire to highlight the place of the 'Old World' within the critical map of early modern England. And in his essay on the representation of Jerusalem as an English 'national preoccupation', Avraham Oz explores the extent to which territories which were not necessarily occupied or conquered may also play a role in the enunciation of nationhood: the locus of Jerusalem 'figures as a notable presence behind the dynastic procedures and national consolidation accounted for in Shakespeare's history plays'. If Oz's essay draws attention to emergent English nationalism's engagements with a symbolically crucial 'foreign' territory, Terence Hawkes examines how the English conquest of Wales is as much an 'imaginary' project as a material one, a project that rewrites Wales as English, and in so doing contributes to a further writing of the text called 'Great Britain'.

These essays all detail the multiplicities of early modern 'contact' histories. They also help us not to read early modern colonial and mercantile ventures solely in terms of what happened later in history. The connections between past and present, then, are better uncovered by keeping in mind the heterogeneity within each period. Representations of various 'others' in Renaissance theatre, travelogues and other writings are derived from specific histories of contact, but these texts also blur these histories and posit stereotypes that amalgamate suppositions about diverse peoples. In the theatre, including that of Shakespeare, the Irish, Jews, 'Moors', the Welsh, Turks, 'Savages', Africans, 'Indians' (from India as well as from the Americas) are shown as distinct from one another, and yet as sharing characteristic differences from the English. Moors as Muslims, for example, are shown by Renaissance writings in Africa, Turkey, India, Persia and the Moluccas, but their stereotypes collapse these various locations. Although 'white Moors' and Moors who have converted to Christianity abound in writings of the period, and although not all Muslims are seen as black, the association of blackness and Moorishness becomes increasingly pervasive, as does the association of Moors and Islam. Maybe because of this, Islam and blackness are often regarded as markers of similar qualities, such as lasciviousness and depravity. At other times, distinctions are strenuously traced between Turks (who are Muslims but not regarded as black) and black Africans (who are only sometimes Muslims).

Thus Othello the Moor clearly has an African past and yet is also identified with the very Turks he goes to fight. Thus, too, *The Tempest* brings together histories of New as well as Old World contact, and in John Webster's play *The White Devil*, Francisco tells the black servant girl Zanche that he dreamt of covering her nakedness 'with this Irish mantle' (V. iv. 203). The mantle, like blackness more generally, was the object of English ridicule, fear and censure, and Anne Jones calls Zanche the 'Irish Mooress' (Jones 1991: 258). Sometimes critics have invoked the Irish dimension to downgrade the significance of blackness as a marker of inferiority in the Renaissance. But Kim Hall's book, *Things of Darkness*, has traced the growing centrality of colour-consciousness in the period for the construction of Englishness, and for the shaping of gender identities. In her essay here, she argues that if whiteness began as a sign of class privilege, leisure and the ownership of property, it develops increasingly as a marker of gender and of racial difference. In fact all the discourses of racial difference are also gendered – James Shapiro's important recent book, *Shakespeare and the Jews* argues that 'Jewish usury was likened to the practice of female prostitution' (Shapiro 1996: 99).

Of course, the concept of 'race' not only shifts in meaning over the past four hundred years, but its connotations also vary *within* each historical context. Any simple equation of whiteness with racial superiority is indeed disturbed by Irish and Welsh peoples, while Jews trouble any easy congruence of religion and nationality. Both religion and colour can be understood as central but fluctuating markers of racial, national and cultural difference – religion seems to assume greater importance with respect to Turks, for example, and colour with respect to Africans. Cannibalism, as Peter Hulme (1986) has shown, becomes yet another potent construct that places various non-Europeans on the borders of humanity. While discourses of cannibalism gathered their meaning from and were directed primarily at inhabitants of the Caribbean and other parts of the 'New World' (and later the Pacific islands), various others, such as the Jews, were also accused of cannibalizing their victims (Shapiro 1996: 109). Histories of 'race' and of 'colonialism' are connected but not identical, as Ania Loomba points out in her essay for this volume. Ideologies of colour were made more rigid as well as more powerful by colonialism, but there were pre-histories in place here too. Prejudice against blacks certainly predated colonial contact, although the specific forms and effects of that prejudice were transformed by colonial relations.

Our contemporary spaces need to be charted with equal precision, for, as Martin Orkin puts it, 'different locations cannot be homogenized'. Michael Neill points out that the

> 'post-colonial condition' ... of former colonizers differs in significant ways from that of the formerly colonized; that of Third World societies from that of 'Fourth World' indigenes who have become minorities in their own countries; that of diasporic peoples from that of the metropolitans with whom they uneasily cohabit.

Most contributors to this volume share this concern to locate both themselves and the Shakespeares they analyse. Moreover, as Nicholas Visser soberly observes,

> it is worth remembering, as we grapple with the dilemma of what, if anything, should be the nature and role of Shakespeare studies in a 'post-colonial' South Africa, that South Africa's colonial legacy has not in fact ended with the installation of a post-apartheid government, no matter how welcome that is.

In fact, the very popularity of the term 'post-colonial' has become fairly controversial. Because the hierarchies of colonial rule are reinscribed in the contemporary imbalances between 'First' and 'Third' World nations, it is debatable whether once-colonized countries can be seen as properly 'post-colonial' (see McClintock 1992).

Some critics have suggested that it helps to think of post-colonialism not just as coming literally after colonialism and signifying its demise, but as an oppositional stance, that is, as the contesting of colonialism and its legacies. Jorge de Alva, for example, suggests that we should 'remove post-coloniality from a dependence on an antecedent colonial condition' and 'tether the term to a post-structuralist stake that marks its appearance' (de Alva 1995: 245). But in fact most critics of post-colonial theory blame it for too much dependence upon post-structuralist or post-modern perspectives. Arif Dirlik calls post-colonialism a 'child of post-modernism', which is born not out of new perspectives on history and culture but because of 'the increased visibility of academic intellectuals of Third World origin as pacesetters in cultural criticism' (Dirlik 1994: 330). Dirlik echoes an earlier essay by Kwame Anthony Appiah, which had pronounced that:

> Post-coloniality is the condition of what we might ungenerously call a comprador intellegentsia: a relatively small, Western-style, Western-trained group of writers and thinkers, who mediate the trade in cultural commodities of world capitalism at the periphery. In the West they are known through the Africa they offer; their compatriots know them both through the West they present to Africa and through an Africa they have invented for the world, for each other, and for Africa.
>
> (Appiah 1991: 63)

These critics argue that the insistence on multiple histories and fragmentation within these perspectives has been detrimental to thinking about the global operation of capitalism both today and in the past. The term 'post-colonial' has become acceptable within the Western academy precisely because it serves to keep at bay more sharply political terms such as 'imperialism' or 'geopolitics' (Shohat 1993: 99). Thus, the global imbalances of power are glossed over, and the world rendered 'seemingly shapeless' (Dirlik 1994: 355).

Critics writing from Western as well as 'Third World' locations often connect post-colonial theory's shortcomings to its currently fashionable status within the Euro-American academy. Aijaz Ahmed's work, for example, attributes a post-modern outlook and sensibility to what he calls 'literary post-coloniality', and contrasts this unfavourably with a Third World Marxist radicalism. Feminists had already pointed out that post-structuralist theories of split and agonistic subjectivity came into vogue just at the moment when marginalized subjects were finding a more powerful collective voice (Hartsock 1987). Critics of post-colonial studies also ask how one can conceptualize the agency of the colonized subject if human subjectivity is understood as always split, contradictory and unstable. Is the 'disintegration of the subject' the latest ideological strategy of Western colonialism? As Denis Epko puts it:

> nothing stops the African from viewing the celebrated postmodern condition ... as nothing but the hypocritical self-flattering cry of overfed and spoilt children of hypercapitalism. So what has hungry Africa got to do with the post-material disgust ... of the bored and the overfed?
>
> (Epko 1995: 122)

While these critiques cannot be dismissed lightly, often the divide between a post-modern 'West' and a more focused and radical 'Rest of the World' operates as a reductive binary opposition which glosses over the complexity of issues at stake. As Annabel Carusi cautions,

> while the usefulness of Marxist strategies for opposition movements should not be minimized, their terms need to be looked at more closely. ... [the] critique of humanism cannot simply be brushed away; one cannot continue as though it had never been.
>
> (Carusi 1989: 88)

And although each side usually tries to enlist feminists, considerations of gender are always sidelined if the battle is configured as one between post-modernism and Marxism, or between post-colonial intellectuals inside and outside the Western academy. Feminist politics in the Third World has always had to negotiate a complex relationship with nationalist as well as left-wing movements at home, as well as with women's movements in the West.

Jonathan Dollimore begins his essay in this volume by acknowledging the 'distrust of "metropolitan" theory' which he found in South Africa, 'a sense that this theory, which gestured so much towards difference as a fundamental philosophical premise, disregarded its material realities.' Dollimore found that 'the most hostile divide of all' seemed to be between 'a materialist tradition of criticism and subsequent developments conveniently (though again reductively) lumped together as "the" post-modern'. His essay maps an intellectual history of these traditions, a history that questions any absolute opposition between a right-wing pessimism and a leftist optimism, or between 'the West' and 'Africa. By mapping the crucial crossovers between anti-humanist critiques and a radical commitment to social change, Dollimore reiterates the contemporary significance of Gramsci's maxim: 'pessimism of the intellect, optimism of the will'.

Dollimore makes the important point that 'it's the aestheticizing of politics, rather than the aesthetic escape from it, that post-modernism is making attractive once again'. Within post-colonial studies, there is a similar concern that 'in calling for the study of the aesthetics of colonialism, we might end up aestheticizing co-lonialism, producing a radical chic version of raj nostalgia' (Dirks 1992: 5). Abdul JanMohamed (1985), Benita Parry (1987) and other critics find that post-colonial theorists are often guilty of neglecting the material conditions of colonial rule by concentrat-ing on colonial representations. The meaning of 'discourse' thus often shrinks to 'text', and from there to 'literary text', and from there to texts written in English, because that is the corpus most familiar to these critics. Shakespeare is the site for colonial and post-colonial encounters, but these encounters cannot be under-stood without reference to specific social, political and institu-tional histories. In this context it is remarkable how pedagogical or institutional aspects of the questions of race, colonialism and Shakespeare have taken a backseat in recent years, or have been relocated outside the metropolis. As we both found at a seminar in Chicago a couple of years ago, we are always asked questions about Shakespeare and race in the Indian or South African class-room, but were told very little about similar issues in the Ameri-can or European classroom.

David Johnson's essay in the present volume juxtaposes Shake-spearean critics with education policy-makers for Africa. Johnson reads a congruence between eminent English critics of the 1930s, such as G. Wilson Knight, and colonial administrators of the pe-riod who 'were trying to spread the word of Shakespeare in Africa'. But in the post-colonial world he points to the dissonance between a critic such as Greenblatt and World Bank policy-makers who fa-vour a 'vocational or technical' education for Africa rather than a 'literary one'. Thus, in the so-called post-colonial world, there may be no Shakespeare at all! Johnson's essay is, he says, 'an appeal to remember the post-colonial world beyond the academy, in which "progress", particularly since 1980, has been celebrated not by the majority of the people living in Third World countries, but by the Western powers and their agencies.'

Prompted by such enquiries, we might ask how both 'metropoli-tan' and 'Third World' critics can interrogate the limits of their present position and function within institutions established during the period of colonization and imperialism and powerfully inflected by what became, over the centuries, colonial epistemologies. To what extent are the relationships between these two sets of academics structured by global imbalances? And to what extent is imbalance inherent in the very structure of our knowledge-systems and the institutions in which they are housed? In an influential article, Dipesh Chakrabarty suggests that in so far as the academic discourse of history – that is, 'history' as a discourse produced at the institutional site of the university is concerned,

> 'Europe' remains the sovereign, theoretical subject of all histories, including the ones we call 'Indian', 'Chinese', 'Kenyan' and so on … Third-world historians feel a need to refer to works in European history, historians of Europe do not feel any need to reciprocate … The everyday paradox of third-world social science is that we find these theories, in spite of their inherent ignorance of 'us' eminently useful in understanding our societies. What allowed the modern European sages to develop such clairvoyance with regard to societies of which they were empirically ignorant? Why cannot we, once again, return the gaze?
>
> (Chakrabarty 1992: 1–3)

Chakrabarty's declared project is to return the gaze by ' provincializing Europe'. Can we manage this within Shakespeare studies, where the terms of discussion are still drawn from the Western academy? What are the critical vocabularies and methods which might make it possible for us to perform such a task? As Chakrabarty comments upon his own project, the task of provincializing Europe often encodes within it a sense of its own failure, or at least of its limits.

In countries like South Africa and India, the very future of Shakespeare studies, including any political, radical, alternative Shakespeares, is uncertain. Apart from the general shortages of resources faced by the humanities, there are sharp debates on the continued usefulness of Western icons like Shakespeare or indeed of Western theories, post-structuralist or otherwise, to any truly 'post-colonial agenda'. These debates were evident at the conference 'Shakespeare–Postcoloniality–Johannesburg, 1996' at which all the papers included here were first presented. (Unfortunately, we have not been able to include, for logistical reasons, other excellent presentations and interventions.) The conference took place in Johannesburg, after the first democratic elections had been held in 1994, when South Africa was under an ANC government and during what is optimistically regarded as a transitional period in the move away from apartheid. Yet it is noteworthy that while Witwatersrand University supported it, the conference was organized not by the University's English Department, but by a self-generating group, consisting of one member each from the Departments of Sociology, African Literature, Theatre and Drama, Comparative Literature and English, which called itself the Africa/Shakespeare Committee.

This is perhaps as good an indication as any that in so many 'non-metropolitan' contexts, Shakespeare takes on a vitality outside of English departments, whose members are more prone than others to present a moribund, ossified version of the 'Bard of Avon' and his high-cultural legacy. At Johannesburg, every word in the title of the conference was debated, apart perhaps from '1996'. But as people living through an extraordinary moment in South African history (or as visitors privileged to share that experience), we noticed that no one had to strain to establish that 'Shakespeare' is a political issue. Shakespeare was political, whether one wanted to celebrate him, appropriate his work or throw it out of the classroom, the academy or the theatre. Discussions on Shakespeare inevitably led to impassioned debates on the nature of subaltern agency, post-structuralist theory, the possible connections between South Asian and South African historiography, or indeed ANC policies on land ownership; all with an urgency and an energy that is not often found in academic conferences. This could be a tribute to an extraordinary time and place, or it could point to the intellectual conjuncture that the essays in this volume address. The Shakespearean text, which for so long helped anchor a disciplinary formation called 'English studies', can become a means for discussing the nature of our diverse post-colonialities. The 'post-colonial Shakespeares' debated in this volume, as well as the recognition that post-coloniality cannot be debated solely through Shakespeare, may together allow us to contribute to the task of 'provincializing Europe'.

Part 1

2

'This Tunis, sir, was Carthage'
Contesting colonialism in
The Tempest

JERRY BROTTON

Gonzalo: Methinks our garments are now as fresh as when we
    put them on first in Afric, at the marriage of the King's fair
    daughter Claribel to the King of Tunis.
Sebastian: 'Twas a sweet marriage, and we prosper well in our
    return.
Adrian: Tunis was never graced before with such a paragon to
    their queen.
Gonzalo: Not since widow Dido's time.
Antonio: Widow? A pox o'that! How came that widow in? Widow
    Dido!
Sebastian: What if he had said 'widower Aeneas' too? Good lord,
    how you take it!
Adrian: 'Widow Dido' said you? You make me study of that. She
    was of Carthage, not of Tunis.
Gonzalo: This Tunis, sir, was Carthage.
Adrian: Carthage?
Gonzalo: I assure you, Carthage.

(II. i. 68–84)[1]

The exchange between Alonso's retinue concerning 'widow Dido'
and the historical geography of Carthage has consistently perplexed
modern critics and editors of *The Tempest*.[2] In his notes to the Oxford edition of the play published in 1987, Stephen Orgel has observed that the dispute 'has proved baffling to editors' (Shakespeare
1987: 40), while in her Penguin edition of the play published in
1968, Anne Barton noted that 'the whole passage may well have
held a meaning for Shakespeare's contemporaries that is lost to
us' (Shakespeare 1968: 153). Perhaps one of the most suggestive

comments on the scene can be found in Frank Kermode's still highly influential Arden edition of the play, published in 1954. In his notes on the exchange, Kermode suggested that '[i]t is a possible inference that our frame of reference is badly adjusted, or incomplete, and that an understanding of this passage will modify our image of the whole play' (Shakespeare 1954: 47).

Despite such allusive comments, critics have nevertheless continued to dismiss the significance of the exchange as either a piece of obscure ribaldry or a laboured and pedantic allusion to the narratives and geography of the Mediterranean, or the so-called 'Old World'[3] represented in Virgil's epic poem *The Aeneid*.[4] The exchange has also by and large been ignored by more recent readings of the play which have sought to stress the extent to which, as Paul Brown amongst many others has argued, '*The Tempest* bears traces of the contemporary British investment in colonial expansion' (Brown, P. 1985: 48)[5] in the Americas at the beginning of the seventeenth century. Despite the success which this approach has had in politicizing interpretations of the play and Shakespearean drama more generally in the last two decades, I want to suggest that in dismissing the significance of the Mediterranean, or Old World references in *The Tempest*, colonial readings have offered a historically anachronistic and geographically restrictive view of the play, which have overemphasized the scale and significance of English involvement in the colonization of the Americas in the early decades of the seventeenth century.[6] The presence of a more definable Mediterranean geography which runs throughout the play, and which emanates outwards from the disputation over contemporary Tunis and classical Carthage, suggests that *The Tempest* is much more of a politically and geographically bifurcated play in the negotiation between its Mediterranean and Atlantic contexts than critics have recently been prepared to concede.[7]

In seeking to redress the marginalization of the Mediterranean contexts of *The Tempest*, I would argue that if it carries traces of England's earliest encounters with the Americas, then it is also concomitantly and crucially inflected with English involvement in the trade and diplomacy of the Mediterranean World. Reading *The Tempest* in relation to this particular history offers a significantly different perspective on both the play itself and wider presumptions concerning the development of early seventeenth-century England as a colonial power of some significance within the early modern world. This essay is therefore offered as not only an intervention within critical readings of *The Tempest*, but also prevailing critical practice, which has been too quick to insist on the validity of claiming a direct relation between what it terms early English colonialist discourse and the play itself.

I

Whatever the pitfalls and theoretical problems currently associated with the application of the term 'post-colonialism', I would argue that it is important to stress the positive impact that much criticism which comes under the rubric of 'post-colonialism' has started to make upon a wide range of related areas of intellectual enquiry, and in particular disciplines which have on the whole lacked sufficient sensitivity to issues of colonialism and racial difference, namely, in this instance, Shakespearean studies and Renaissance studies more generally.[8] The emergence of *post*-colonialism within recent critical vocabularies has alerted critics working in related fields to question their historical and cultural application of terms like 'colonialism' and 'colonialist discourse'. Anne McClintock has recently argued that 'post-colonialism' is itself a potentially prescriptive theoretical and historical term, which 'reduces the cultures of peoples beyond colonialism to prepositional time. The term confers on colonialism the prestige of history proper; colonialism is the determining marker of history' (McClintock 1995: 11).[9] McClintock's observation is a particularly valuable one for critics of the early modern period, in cautioning against accepting the view that the historical logic implied within colonialist discourse is a monolithic entity which comes to shape all subjective and political relationships developed in the activities of travel and commercial expansion from the late fifteenth century onwards. Such a monolithic model of colonial discourse is, as McClintock points out, not necessarily a historically continuous model of global relations, but one that emerged within a highly specific historical and cultural context, that of the body of scientific, medical, sexological, commercial and philosophical justifications, which were created to underpin the expansion and ideological naturalization of nineteenth-century European imperialism (ibid.: 13).[10]

McClintock's reminder that much recent theory and criticism is imbued with this nineteenth-century model of colonial relations, is particularly valuable in contesting critically dominant colonial readings of *The Tempest*.[11] While a spate of articles throughout the 1980s successfully 'politicized' readings of not only *The Tempest* but Shake-spearean drama more generally, I would suggest that they nevertheless ultimately reproduced the discursive logic of a colonialist discourse which they ostensibly sought to critique. To take one example: in what remains one of the most highly influential essays published on the play in recent years, Paul Brown argued in 1985 that 'a sustained historical and theoretical analysis of the play's involvement in the colonialist project has yet to be undertaken' (Brown 1985: 48). How-ever, in his subsequent analysis of the play, which drew on a range of historical and theoretical positions, Brown concluded that *The Tem-pest* 'serves as a limit text in which the characteristic operations of colonialist discourse may be discerned' (ibid.: 68). In this respect Brown's conclusions were noticeably similar to those reached by Francis Barker and Peter Hulme in their discussion of the play, also published in 1985. Barker and Hulme argued that *The Tempest* was 'imbricated within the discourse of colonialism' (Barker and Hulme 1985: 204). Yet both arguments explicitly relied upon the acceptance of a histori-cally and geographically monolithic concept of 'the' discourse of colonialism, as opposed to the possibilities of a more diverse range of historically and regionally distinct discourses and effects of cultural encounter and exchange. This was partly a result of their exclusive focus upon the play's supposed relation to a range of 'New World' contexts, and in particular the development of England's first settle-ment in the Americas in Virginia in the first decades of the seventeenth century (Quinn 1979), a point to which I shall return in a moment.

It is significant that the subsequent perception of the play pro-duced by both Brown and Barker and Hulme is very much in keeping with the critical concerns of materialist criticism of the early 1980s. Much of the analytical energy of criticism which emerged from the impact of critical theory upon English studies from the 1970s on-wards was directed towards offering an intellectual critique of the supposed racial and cultural superiority of the nineteenth-century British Empire (Barker *et al.* 1984). It therefore comes as no surprise that the singular perception of 'colonial discourse' adopted by these critics in their reading of the play is one that is in accordance with the contours of nineteenth-century British imperial history, whereby, somewhat understandably, Prospero is perceived as a figure more akin to Cecil Rhodes and Henry Stanley than a Jacobean magus.[12]

While accounts of the play which emerged from the perspective of British cultural materialism tended to reproduce a reading of *The Tempest* inflected through the lens of nineteenth-century impe-

rial history, the equally influential accounts of the play which ema-
nated from the critical perspective of American new historicism
since the 1980s also invested something of their own complex relation to nineteenth-century colonial history in their readings of *The
Tempest*. Critics like Greenblatt (1988) and Knapp (1992) have produced a series of homologous readings which have argued, most
recently in the words of John Gillies, that, with differing levels of
intensity, *The Tempest* 'is vitally rather than casually implicated in
the discourses of America and the Virginia colony' (Gillies 1994:
149). However, while the political attitude of these critics has been
generally hostile to the perceived colonial politics of the play, their
concern to situate *The Tempest* in relation to the earliest moments of
Anglo-American relations has a significantly longer lineage, stretching
back as far as the late nineteenth century. As Alden T. Vaughan has
persuasively argued, '[t]he trend toward an American-focused interpretation of *The Tempest* by scholars on both sides of the Atlantic
drew much of its inspiration from a concurrent cultural and political rapprochement between England and the United States' (Vaughan,
A. 1988: 142) which began to develop towards the end of the nineteenth century. The emergence of increasingly amicable diplomatic
and economic relations between England and one of its most important former colonies towards the end of the nineteenth century
was matched throughout this period by the creation of intellectual
initiatives which sought to situate *The Tempest* as a key text of 'early
Anglo-American history' (ibid.: 140).

Subsequent studies of the play by twentieth-century American critics
such as Cawley, Marx and Fiedler utilized the text as an exemplary
bridge between early English culture and American letters, to the
point that in 1960 Leo Marx even referred to the play as 'a prologue
to American literature' (cited in ibid.: 146). More recent new
historicists, eager to emphasize the 'American' contexts of *The
Tempest*, while distancing themselves from the morally prescriptive
nature of its supposed colonial politics, nevertheless reproduce a long-
held preoccupation defining the play as part of America's own cultural
heritage and abiding relationship with one of its colonial creators,
early modern England. In claiming an exclusively American context
for the play's production, American new historicist critics overinvest
something of their own peculiarly post-colonial identities as American intellectuals within the one text that purports to establish a firm
connection between America and the culture which these critics analyse with such intensity: early modern England.[13] One consequence

of this is that, in their criticism of the colonially expansive initiatives of the early modern English crown, American new historicism tends to give too much credence to a presumption of the importance of English commercial and territorial expansion within the more global contexts of the early seventeenth-century world. As a result, their critique of the supposedly 'colonial' politics of a play like *The Tempest* tends to reinvest early seventeenth-century England with a politically and territorially dynamic expansionism which has been questioned by more recent historical studies of the period.[14]

One particular consequence of the reproduction of certain aspects of nineteenth-century imperial discourse on the part of both cultural materialist and new historicist readings of *The Tempest* has led to a particularly predominant perception of the play's central protagonist, Prospero, and in particular his relationship to Caliban. In politicizing older humanist perceptions of Prospero as a benevolent and, in the words of Hazlitt, 'stately magician' (cited in Shakespeare 1987: 7), critics have defined Prospero as the archetypally paternal figure of colonial domination and authority, and his treatment of Caliban as a colonized subject 'a foundational paradigm in the history of European colonialism' (Cartelli 1987: 101). In seeking to question this colonial reading of the play, immersed as it is in the legacy of nineteenth-century colonial discourses, I would suggest a more historically situated reading of Prospero, more in keeping with late sixteenth-century perceptions of figures who experience long-distance travel and cultural encounters.

In her study of the relations between power, knowledge and the experience of geographical distance in pre-industrial societies, the cultural anthropologist Mary Helms has analysed the ways in which social and political authority accrues to those who experience geographical and cultural difference, in terms which are strikingly similar to those that define Prospero's quasi-magical identity:

> To the extent (and it varies greatly among societies) that geographically distant places, peoples and experiences are perceived (either at first hand or by some manner of extrapolation) within essentially supernatural or cosmological contexts, then knowledge of, or acquaintance with, geographically distant places, peoples, and things rightfully falls within the domain of political-religious specialists whose job it is to deal with mysteries. Knowledge of geographically distant phenomena, whether acquired directly or indirectly, may be expected to form part of the corpus of esoteric knowledge

controlled by these traditional specialists … the select few who are either able or expected to become familiar with geographically distant phenomena may be accorded an aura of prestige and awe approaching the same order, if not always the same magnitude, as that accorded political-religious specialists or elites in general. In fact, those with direct experience of such distant matters are themselves likely either to be political-religious specialists or elites.

(Helms 1988: 5)

The play makes quite clear that Prospero is just such a 'political-religious specialist', who brings together his status as an exiled leader of a ruling political elite (as Duke of Milan) with his experience of 'geographically distant places'. His immersion in 'the liberal arts' (I. ii. 73) allows him unprecedented access to the arcane mysteries of the elements most feared and respected by early modern cosmographers and travellers – the sea and the stars.[15] Throughout the play Prospero's esoteric learning is constantly emphasized, from the recollection of his banishment from Milan, forsaking 'worldly ends' (I. ii. 89) on the basis that 'my library / Was dukedom enough' (I. ii. 109–10), to Caliban's reminder to Stephano and Trinculo in attempting to repeat Prospero's overthrow: 'Remember / First to possess his books' (III. ii. 89–90).

To read this aspect of the play as a seamless representation of nascent colonial power and authority appears anachronistic and at odds with the deeply ambivalent nature of contemporary concerns with the perceived effects of travel and the status of the elite traveller. From the end of the fifteenth century long-distance travel was regarded with fear and suspicion by many people. As Richard Marienstras has pointed out in his discussion of the relations between *The Tempest* and contemporary travel writing, '[w]hen man travels, he exposes himself to the unpredictable, is at the mercy of accidents, the hazards of chance, the interplay of circumstances; he lays his symbolic universe open to the test of fortune' (Marienstras 1985: 166). Within the context of the personal danger and logistical complexity of early modern travel, allied to the fear of the still relatively unknown size and scope of the world, travellers evoked a persistent anxiety amongst the members of the culture which they left behind, in terms of where they were going, what they might experience, and, if they managed to return, how they had been affected by the experience of contact with cultural and geographical difference.[16] One response to such a perception was self-consciously to create an aura of wonder and mystery around the figure of the traveller, precisely along the lines expressed by Helms. It is this curiously ambivalent situation which defines Prospero; he is the subject of both admiration *and* suspicion throughout the play. This is not an effect of the play's ambivalence concerning the morality of any colonial project which Prospero's actions may or may not symbolize, but rather an ambivalence regarding the status of his identity and actions as an elite traveller.

Two crucial factors add to Prospero's ambivalent and liminal status as an elite traveller, neither of which has been adequately accounted for in colonial readings of the play; Prospero is both an Italian and a magician. Colonial readings have persistently elided Prospero's Italian identity, conflating *The Tempest*'s apparent engagement with 'English colonialism' (Barker and Hulme 1985: 198) with Prospero as a prototypical English colonizer.[17] This approach elides the play's highly specific Italian contexts, and the extent to which Prospero's magical activities are aimed at exposing his political deposition as rightful Duke of Milan, and ensuring his ultimate return to Italy from enforced exile. Consequently, the Italian aspects of the play effect a distancing of audience identification with Prospero, a distance that is appropriate to his ambivalent status as an elite traveller with whom an English audience would arguably feel fascination, but also unease.

Such unease is also reflected in Prospero's status as a magician. Despite the fact that Prospero's magic is contrasted with the 'evil' magic of Sycorax, there remain anxieties concerning the exact status of Prospero's 'rough magic' (V. i. 50). As William Sherman has pointed out in his study of the Elizabethan scholar and 'intelligencer' John Dee (who was in fact perceived by Frances Yates as Shakespeare's model for Prospero), magic and the secretive, closeted scholarship which it entailed were deeply suspect activities, precisely because of the difficulty of establishing just what the scholar was doing behind closed doors:

> Knowledge was magical, and sometimes even entailed magic. But the attacks on libraries, the condemnations for conjuring, and the polemical complaints betray a deeper and more significant phenomenon: there were in early modern England dramatic uncertainties about the power of information and those who possessed it.

> (Cited in Jardine 1996: 105)[18]

Like the traveller, the magus or 'intelligencer' inspired unease precisely because of the difficulty of situating his activities within a comprehensible frame of cultural reference, where his activities could be seen and understood. Prospero unites the fields of travel and scholarship, a situation made even more problematic by the fact that, as John Gillies has pointed out, the figure of the magician was often associated with the mysteries of the East, and more specifically with Egypt (Gillies 1994: 29).[19]

II

The identification of Prospero's magic with an apparently exoticized East is symptomatic of the extent to which the play carries resonances of different geographical trajectories which have been marginalized within its more recent critical reception. In re-addressing these geographical traces of the 'Old World', I would suggest that a different perception of *The Tempest* emerges, one that appears deeply at odds with colonial, 'New World' readings. One of the difficulties in addressing this Mediterranean, or 'Old World' geography is the extent to which such critical considerations have been dismissed as part of an older, romantic-conservative appreciation of *The Tempest*, which invokes the pastoral and Virgilian parallels of the play at the expense of its 'New World', and hence colonial, contexts.[20] However, in dismissing the significance of the Mediterranean geography of the play, colonial criticism of *The Tempest* leaves the play curiously one-dimensional, implying that the eastern frontier of the play's geography is politically inert, thus suggesting that significant contemporary English expansion was confined to a western horizon encompassing the Atlantic and the Americas. Such an assumption is significant and troubling in its implicit reproduction of an orientalizing discourse which occludes any possible traces of English involvement with the eastern Mediterranean and North Africa. Critical controversy over the imprecision of the geography of the play is infamous, and while not wishing to simplify these debates and offer a positivist account of the 'meaning' of the geography of *The Tempest*, I would like to investigate the play's potential for disclosing traces of England's encounter with other, specifically eastern territories in its early, tentative steps towards commercial and maritime expansion.

While *The Tempest*'s geographical frame of reference is infamously allusive, its interrogation of geographical specification is intriguingly precise. Alonso's entourage chart with some exactitude their voyage from Naples to Tunis on the African coast, in honour of 'the marriage of the King's fair daughter Claribel to the King of Tunis' (II. i. 69–70), a direct inversion of Aeneas' voyage to Carthage *en route* to Italy portrayed in Virgil's *Aeneid*. Prospero rhetorically demands of Ariel that he disclose the birthplace of Caliban's mother, Sycorax, which turns out to be Tunis's neighbouring port of 'Algiers' (I. ii. 261). That Caliban's mother arrived on the island from Algiers 'with child' (I. ii. 269) gives Caliban a specifically African lineage, something that has been inadequately addressed in recent accounts of the play (Vaughan and Vaughan 1991: 51).[21]

But perhaps the most suggestive Mediterranean dimension of the play is the Carthage/Tunis debate between Gonzalo and Alonso's retinue. With its echoes of *The Aeneid* and contemporary invocations of Tunis, Gonzalo's comments run against the grain of New World readings of the play, which remain, on the whole, unable to accommodate the scene. One notable exception is Peter Hulme's excellent analysis of the exchange (Hulme 1986: 109–15). In resisting critical dismissal of the scene, Hulme argues that Gonzalo's discussion of 'widow Dido', and his claim that ancient Carthage is coterminous with contemporary Carthage, are symptomatic of 'the scholar who sees a pattern of classical repetition: Claribel, Queen of Tunis, is the new Dido, just as Tunis itself is the new Carthage' (ibid.: 111). As Hulme points out, Gonzalo's analogies are of greater significance than the sceptical courtiers appreciate. While ancient Carthage had been destroyed in the aftermath of the Punic Wars, the city of Tunis had grown up literally in the ruins of its famous neighbour, close enough to produce (and probably encourage) a level of geographical conflation of the type offered by Gonzalo.[22] Similarly, as both Hulme and Orgel point out, the dismissal of Gonzalo's reference to 'widow Dido' as a travesty of Virgil's account of the Queen of Carthage is historically inaccurate. An older version of the Dido story, predating Virgil, portrays Dido as an honourable and chaste widow, who founds Carthage and subsequently kills herself to avoid enforced marriage to an African king (Shakespeare 1987: 41). As Hulme stresses, Gonzalo's scholarly attempt to situate the dynastic politics of the contemporary situation within a more grand classical narrative backfires upon closer inspection; if Dido is invoked as a chaste figure to be compared favourably to Claribel, it should be remembered that Dido kills herself rather than marry an *African* king; yet Claribel has herself married just such 'an African' (II. i. 123), much to the consternation of Alonso's retinue. Similarly, to invoke Carthage is, as Hulme emphasizes, painfully to recall 'several centuries of punishing wars with Italy' (Hulme 1986: 111).

Before moving on to pursue the New World contexts of the play, Hulme concludes his discussion of the Carthage/Tunis scene by arguing that 'It is perhaps no longer possible – if it ever was – to fully disentangle the skeins of this Mediterranean labyrinth' (ibid.: 112). My problem with this conclusion is that it offers an inadequate account of the contemporary significance of the play's eastern Mediterranean geography for English diplomats and merchants. It also fails to question the extent to which contemporary encounters and accounts of this geography – Tunis, Algiers and Naples – were negotiated through the deployment of classical parallels, of the type that Gonzalo attempts to provide in his historically comparative geography of Carthage and Tunis. The eastern Mediterranean and the North African coast in particular played a highly significant part in the political and commercial world of sixteenth- and early seventeenth-century Europe; one that has been persistently downplayed in subsequent narratives of the historical ascendancy of the Atlantic World. As Andrew Hess has pointed out, the contact zone of the eastern Mediterranean and the African coastline has become the 'forgotten frontier' (Hess 1978) within accounts of the international relations of the early modern period. I would suggest that in reading such territories and their political significance back into *The Tempest*, it becomes possible to look at the play in a significantly new light.

Throughout the early sixteenth century North Africa was one of the main arenas within which the two largest empires of the early modern world vied for political and commercial dominance – the Habsburg Empire of Charles V and the Ottoman Empire of Sultan Süleyman the Magnificent. As both of their extensive empires stretched downwards from Western Europe and Central Asia respectively, North Africa became the geographical point of military and political confrontation between the two empires. Strategically, the North African coastline, and the city of Tunis in particular, was highly contested territory. The narrow strip of sea which divided Tunis from Italy not only separated Italy from Africa, but also marked the boundary between the western and eastern Mediterranean. As a result it was of particular military and commercial significance, as whoever possessed Tunis controlled the flow of traffic between the two halves of the Mediterranean. Thus, the voyage undertaken by Alonso and his retinue from Naples to Tunis in *The Tempest* was a voyage that traversed one of the most contested stretches of water within the Mediterranean World.

In 1534 Ottoman forces took Tunis, much to the alarm of the Emperor Charles V, who sent an enormous force to retake the city in 1535 (Hess 1978: 73). Modelling himself as a crusading Christian emperor, Charles justified his assault by looking to the past; he wrapped himself in the classical mantle of the Roman Scipio Africanus, who had decisively defeated the Carthaginians at the climax of the second Punic War at the Battle of Zama in 202 BC. In a remarkable series of tapestries entitled *The Conquest of Tunis*, which Charles had designed to commemorate his victory, descriptions were offered of Charles's taking of Tunis in terms which adumbrated Gonzalo's discussion of the historical topography of Tunis. In describing the landing of Charles's triumphant troops, the descriptive cartouche of one of the tapestries announces:

> Here they enter the port of Utica; *ancient Carthage receives them in her ruins*. Caesar [Charles V] goes with a small body-guard to explore Goleta … He pitches camp beside the walls of *Carthage once illustrious*, today again a village of small cottages.
>
> (Horn 1989, vol. 1: 289)[23]

This invocation of classical Carthage in the midst of the capture of present-day Tunis situated Charles's victory within a classical-heroical tradition which added historical weight to his conquest. Even more specifically, the analogy located Charles's victory within the larger dimensions of Roman imperialism to which, as the officially titled 'Holy Roman Emperor', Charles hoped to emulate.[24] However, Charles's triumph was short-lived; in 1541 his forces were routed by the Ottomans in Algiers, and Tunis remained an isolated Habsburg presence in an Ottoman-dominated North Africa. In 1569 the city was retaken by the Ottoman forces, only to be briefly retaken by Charles V's son, Don John of Austria in 1573, whose first action after taking the city was to ride out to the site of classical Carthage (Braudel 1995: 295), thus invoking a line of imperial descent which stretched through his own father's triumph and Scipio Africanus, right back to Aeneas. Just one year later the city was recaptured by the Ottomans, a final development in the struggle over North Africa and the eastern Mediterranean which saw the

Habsburg authorities disengage to pursue more fruitful expansion in the Americas, while the Ottomans concentrated on their eastern frontier in Asia (Hess 1972).

It was precisely at this point of imperial disengagement within the region that the first organized English forays into the eastern Mediterranean took place. In 1578 Francis Walsingham ordered the merchant and diplomat William Harborne to establish commercial relations with the Ottoman Empire, allowing English merchants to establish a foothold in the commerce of the eastern Mediterranean (Skilliter 1977). By the end of the decade Harborne had established trading consuls throughout the Ottoman Empire and North Africa, which allowed him to appoint English consuls in a series of locations which echoed the topography of *The Tempest* – Istanbul, Cairo, Alexandria, Aleppo, Algiers and Tunis (Andrews 1984: 92). England's trade with the Ottomans included the shipment of munitions to Istanbul, as English merchants took advantage of the fact that, as Protestants, they were not beholden to papal edicts which forbade trade with the Ottomans (Skilliter 1977: 22). By 1606 an outraged Venetian ambassador in Istanbul reported that an English ship had arrived with 'a cargo of kerseys, tin, gunpowder, etc., and had touched at Barbary and Tunis, having on board many Turks and Jews' (Brown, R. 1871: 57). English privateering in the region became a source of acute diplomatic tension throughout the first two decades of the seventeenth century. As early as 1603 the Venetian ambassador claimed that 'the Beglierbey of Tunis has made vast gains by keeping well with English privateers' (ibid.: 312).

Such accounts emphasize that, for English diplomats, merchants and sailors, the eastern Mediterranean and North Africa were not the distant and exotic locations which *The Tempest* might at first suggest. The English crown (and a whole range of freelance merchants and privateers) established an amicable, if politically subordinate relationship with the Ottoman Porte in Istanbul, eager to exploit the commercial possibilities offered by extensive trading relations with the Ottoman-controlled regions of the eastern Mediterranean, which became known as the Levant. Assuming an absolute distance between English expansion and territories to the east of Europe under Ottoman influence, criticism has consistently downplayed the presence of eastern territories and references to Ottoman authority which recur throughout late Elizabethan and Jacobean drama, including the shadowy presence of the

Ottomans in *Othello*, and the extensive eastern panorama of Marlowe's *Tamburlaine the Great*.[25] However, in *The Tempest* the Ottomans have disappeared. The eastern Mediterranean is instead peopled by Italian courtiers disputing the appropriateness of defining their activities in relation to classical myths of travel and displacement. What has happened?

I would suggest that the play discloses a deep ambivalence regarding the nature of early English maritime encounters with territories over which it could exercise little or no political control. Even more problematically, these encounters placed the English crown in a position of political amity and diplomatic subservience to the publicly demonized 'infidel', the Ottoman Empire. In its occlusion of any traces of the controlling presence of the Ottomans, *The Tempest* offers a conveniently imprecise but sanitized version of the Mediterranean World, imbued with an aura of suitably familiar and assimilable myths of classical imperial travel and conquest, personified in its overdetermined references to Virgil's *Aeneid*.[26] Ironically, the critical power of Edward Said's thesis in *Orientalism* concerning Western Europe's cultural and geographical distancing of the East has in many respects been taken too literally by literary critics of the early modern period,[27] who read the Mediterranean geography of a play like *The Tempest* as ambiguous due to the hazy exoticism of Shakespeare's, and hence early England's, awareness of the mysterious Orient. Such an argument reproduces the discursive pattern of orientalist discourse in failing to explore the historical complexities of English engagements with the East throughout this period, engagements which disclose extensive and politically compromising transactions between England and the territories throughout the eastern Mediterranean. If this history is read back into *The Tempest*, it allows for a repositioning of the New World coordinates of the play, whereby a turning to England's western horizons in the Americas appears as a much more promising avenue of exploration than the diplomatically belated and compromised encounters of the English crown in the eastern Mediterranean.

The preceding discussion of *The Tempest* suggests several ways of reconsidering the play in terms of both its historical contexts and its critical reception. First, to re-read *The Tempest* within its neglected Mediterranean context questions the extent to which it is appropriate to talk about the play disclosing a discourse of 'colonialism'. As Kenneth Andrews has pointed out in his study of the origins of the

English maritime empire, not only was the Mediterranean trade throughout the Tudor and early Jacobean period one of the most economically important for the English economy, but it also 'did not lead directly to empire in the conventional sense of territorial possessions overseas, nor even to the kind of domination that was later associated with imperial "spheres of influence" ' (Andrews 1984: 99).

Both the focus on the New World and the emplotment of nineteenth-century models of imperial authority on to the play have distorted the historically specific relations of travel, commerce, diplomacy and imperial aspiration which more directly inform its production.[28] To interrogate the specificities of *The Tempest*'s complex negotiation of its Mediterranean contexts does not simply call for a rejection of its New World readings in favour of its Old World resonances. Such an argument would only reinstall the problematic binaries and exclusions which so much *Tempest* criticism has reproduced over recent years. Instead, I would argue that the play is precisely situated at the *geopolitical bifurcation* between the Old World and the New, at the point at which the English realized both the compromised and subordinated position within which they found themselves in the Mediterranean, and the possibility of pursuing a significantly different commercial and maritime initiative in the Americas. As the economic historian James Boyajian has argued more recently:

> The much-talked-about shift from Europe's narrow Mediterranean-based economy to an expanded Atlantic-based economy in fact took a long time to complete; for what the Portuguese began in the sixteenth century, the Dutch and the English completed in the second half of the seventeenth century.
>
> (Boyajian 1993: 17)

Literary critics have tended to claim the pre-eminence of the Atlantic World as emerging far too early in their literary histories, ascribing an awareness and confidence in New World issues to texts that were only just beginning to come to terms with the colonial possibilities to the west of Europe. As far as readings of *The Tempest* are concerned, refracted through the lens of recent developments within the field of post-colonial theory, what begins to emerge is a play that ultimately reflects the belatedness and subsequent subordination of English forays into the Mediterranean, and not the rise of English colonialism.

Notes

1 All quotations are from Stephen Orgel's Oxford edition of the play (Shakespeare 1987).

2 On presenting this paper at a research seminar recently, a current editor of *The Tempest* dismissed this scene's relevance to the play as a whole, and suggested that it was textually corrupt. As there is very little basis to support such claims, this response appears to be symptomatic of a continuing critical reluctance to countenance other cultural and geographical perspectives on the play based on this particular scene.

3 The Mediterranean World formed the basis from which definitions of the 'Old World' emerged. For a discussion of the Greek notion of the Mediterranean World, or *oikumene*, see Braudel (1995) and Gillies (1994: 5–12).

4 On the Virgilian parallels in the play, see Kott (1976) and Pitcher (1984).

5 The most influential interventions within this field include Barker and Hulme (1985), Brown (1985), Greenblatt (1988), Willis (1989) and Skura (1989). More recently see Knapp (1992) and Gillies (1994).

6 For a more balanced and historically specific account of seventeenth-century English overseas interests, see Andrews (1984) and Brenner (1993).

7 There are some notable exceptions. Hulme (1986) remains one of the most sensitive responses to the play's Old and New World references; Norbrook (1992) is also alive to the significance of the Carthage/Tunis debate; Salingar (1994) makes some interesting points questioning the 'New World' material. Most recently Wilson (1997) has reconsidered the Mediterranean contexts of the play. Wilson offers a lively account of the play's relation to the history of piracy and slavery along the coast of North Africa, reading Sir Robert Dudley as a prototype for the figure of Prospero. While in general agreement with Wilson's perspective, my own concerns are less positivist.

8 For two excellent attempts to redress this situation, see Hendricks and Parker (1994) and Hall (1995).

9 See a range of other critics, including Appiah (1992: 7), who argues that the experience of the majority of 'Europe's African colonies [prior to the twentieth century] was one of an essentially shallow penetration by the colonizer'.

10 On the fashioning of racial and sexual myths and narratives which underpinned the machinations of nineteenth-century European imperialism, see Young (1995).

11 For accounts that question the colonial reading, but which lack historical contextualization, see Willis (1989) and Skura (1989).

12 Both articles draw on a significant body of earlier critical and fictional studies which had utilized *The Tempest* as a way of exploring

colonial relations, most famously Césaire (1969), Lamming (1960) and Mannoni (1964). However, both Césaire and Lamming are explicit about their utilization of *The Tempest* in relation to their own colonial contexts, while Brown and Barker and Hulme produce a more hypostatized notion of the play's relation to 'colonial discourse'. For two excellent critical accounts of these earlier engagements with the play, see Cartelli (1987) and Nixon (1987).

13 One of the few points at which such personal investments are acknowledged is in Greenblatt (1991), where he recalls that following one of his lectures, 'a student challenged me to account for my own position. How can I avoid the implication, she asked, that I have situated myself at a very safe distance from the Europeans about whom I write … The answer is that I do not claim such protection nor do I imagine myself situated at a safe distance. On the contrary, I have tried … to register within the very texture of my scholarship a critique of the Zionism in which I was raised' (viii–ix). It is significant that such searching interrogation is rarely carried out around the intellectual investments made in early modern *English* culture by such scholars.

14 See for instance Andrews (1984) and Brotton (1997).

15 Prospero repeatedly emphasizes his control over the elements (I. i. 1–5; V. i. 41–3). Caliban is similarly awed by Prospero's cosmographical abilities; when Prospero first arrived on the island he taught Caliban 'how / To name the bigger light and how the less, / That burn by day and night (I. ii. 334–6). Caliban's 'horizontal' engagement with the island, living from what the surface of the island yields (II. ii. 161–6), is repeatedly contrasted with Prospero's 'vertical' power and authority. I am grateful to Professor Shirley Chew for highlighting this aspect of the play.

16 For an anthropological account of the perception of travellers as breaching the perceived boundaries of their cultures, see Douglas (1979). For a more historically specific account, see Pagden (1993).

17 Both Hawkes (1985) and Barker and Hulme (1985) unproblematically read both Prospero and the play more generally in relation to English national expansion, regardless of the Italian elements of the play. For a critique of this position, see Norbrook (1992: 34): 'later Shakespeare, and Jacobeans in general, were tending to give more and more sociological specificity to Italian settings'.

18 On Dee, see Sherman (1995); for Yates's reading of Prospero as Dee, see Yates (1975).

19 As Gillies (1994: 29) points out in his investigation of the impact of Herodotus upon Renaissance ethnography, 'The association of magic with Egypt is also Herodotean. As the oldest and wisest of nations, the Egyptians are portrayed by Herodotus as the ultimate magicians'. His magical powers are thus not necessarily 'colonial'.

20 As Hulme argues, 'For a long time conventional readings of the play worked exclusively within this [Mediterranean] frame of reference. Generically the play was seen as a pastoral tragicomedy with the themes of nature and art at its centre, fully and confidently Mediterranean, as its title would suggest, a play moving majestically to its reconciliatory climax with hardly a ripple to disturb its surface' (Hulme 1986: 105).

21 Vaughan and Vaughan (1991: 32–3) also note that the town of 'Calibia' on the African coastline had featured prominently on maps and atlases of the period since 1529.

22 Contemporary geographical dispute surrounding this issue also suggests that Gonzalo's analogy was far from spurious, but formed the basis for serious scholarly debate. Abraham Ortelius (1968) felt the issue important enough to discuss at great length in the appendix to his *Theatrum Orbis Terrarum*, entitled the *Parergon*, and translated into English in 1606, which mapped the geography of the classical world, including that of ancient Carthage (112–13). Leo Africanus also suggests the geographical and historical convergence of the two locations in his account of the historical topography of Tunis, arguing that 'it was a small towne built by the Africans upon a certaine lake, about twelve miles distant from the Mediterran sea. And upon the decay of Carthage Tunis began to increase both in buildings and inhabitants' (Africanus 1969 [1600]: 246). The debate over Carthage/Tunis was apparently not as clear-cut as Sebastian and Adrian suggest.

23 As Horn notes (1989), maps of the campaign repeatedly emphasized the topographical relationship between the modern city and its classical predecessor (vol. 2, fig. C 87), thus further foregrounding the 'historic' nature of Charles's achievements.

24 The Habsburg retinue also possessed an earlier series of tapestries depicting *The Triumph of Scipio*, which appear to have inspired the *Tunis* tapestries (Ortiz 1991). Charles V's naval commander Andrea Doria also commissioned a series of tapestries in the aftermath of the victory at Tunis entitled *Navigatione d'Enea* (Davidson 1990). The classical-heroic concerns of all these tapestries appear to have offered a convenient space within which to rehearse a series of imperial postures on the part of their owners, all themselves 'elite travellers' in some form or another.

25 There are signs that this position is beginning to change. Most importantly see Loomba (1996), as well as Lupton (1997) and Vitkus (1997). Contemporary diplomatic reports concerning English commercial involvement with the Levantine regions suggests that more was at stake in, for example, Marlowe's eastern geography than simply local, exotic colour. In 1582 Cecil, Lord Burghley, traced a commercial itinerary which not only invoked classical analogies not dissimilar to those in *The Tempest*, but also charted with precision the

territories across which Tamburlaine moves; '[F]rom *Aleppo* to *Rasslea* upon *Euphrates*, which is 3 days journey by land then down by water to *Bagdett* [Baghdad] which anciently was Babylon, which is about 12 days sailing. From thence into ye *Tygris* and so to *Balszara* [Basra] where ye best baulm is made. From *Balsara* to *Ormus* in 15 days sailing. From thence to *Goa* where ye viceroy for portyngall [Portugal] resideth' (Skilliter 1977: 17; spelling modified). For the ways in which this classical/contemporary doubling mediated a range of contemporary political and diplomatic situations, see Spencer (1954: 59–60). I am deeply grateful to Professor Kenneth Parker for drawing my attention to this, and for his consistently astute comments on my argument more generally.

26 Critics of the play who have acknowledged the importance of the play's Virgilian references have failed to locate such references within the contemporary context of the reception, translation and distribution of such texts. Recent scholarship on the reception and translation of classical texts has stressed how they were 'studied for action' (Grafton and Jardine 1990). Classical authors like Virgil, Livy and Xenophon were read and translated in the light of contemporary political, military, geographical and commercial issues. Sixteenth-century translations of *The Aeneid* offer a range of marginal glosses on the text, which clearly places it within the context of contemporary North African events, particularly Thomas Phaer's highly influential translation of *The Aeneid* (Phaer 1573); in Phaer's text Dido is perceived as 'a Moore among the Moores' (ibid.: sig. k.ii^r), and Iarbas is compared to 'the Turkes' (ibid., sig. k^r). Such glosses reflect English anxieties concerning the fact that the classical world valorized by English humanist scholarship was, by the end of the sixteenth century, almost exclusively in the hands of the Ottoman Empire.

27 Said has recently revised his position, arguing that what is now required is a process of 'rethinking and reformulating historical experiences which had once been based on the geographical separation of peoples and cultures' (Said 1995: 6).

28 The relations that defined European contact with the Americas was, even towards the end of the sixteenth century, one among many, and the commercial and political significance of the Mediterranean World remained the focus for most merchants and diplomats within the period. It also disclosed a specific model of possession and control, which as Palmira Brummett has pointed out, was significantly different from historically later models of imperial possession; 'Conquest was defined not in terms of chunks of territory but in terms of routes defended and fortresses garrisoned. It meant the occupying of towns, the setting up of customs posts, and the sending of central government agents ... Sixteenth-century monarchs were not preoccupied with drawing boundaries so much as they were with

controlling agricultural and mineral resources, taxing trade, and demanding the submission of subordinates and opponents' (Brummett 1994: 12–13).

3

'A most wily bird'
Leo Africanus, *Othello* and the trafficking in difference

JONATHAN BURTON

I

Animated by the politically charged quincentennial of Columbus's American landfall, Anglo-American literary critics of the past twenty years have been fascinated by early modern English relations with the New World. Recently, this interest has been subject to an important line of criticism. John Archer reminds us that 'during the late sixteenth and early seventeenth centuries, England remained captivated by the Old World even as it turned with the rest of Europe toward America' (Archer 1997: 15). Similarly, Ania Loomba has suggested that 'critical studies of "race" or "culture" in Shakespeare should reconsider the existing paradigms of colonial relations' that have been primarily shaped by a New World archive (Loomba 1996: 190). Loomba indicates how the relative subordination of Eastern materials produces a monolithic picture of non-European peoples as linguistically and materially overpowered. That picture becomes more intricate and heterogeneous when historical and theatrical materials concerning Africa and the East supplement the current New World bias.

As I survey the conjuncture of Shakespeare's *Othello* and Leo Africanus's *Geographical Historie of Africa*, I hope to take up Loomba's challenge and illustrate the ways in which turning to the 'Old World' can affect our readings of early modern culture. More specifically,

I shall propose a paradigm for cultural intercourse that takes into account the ways in which cultural production occurs at an axis of various and even conflicting forces, an entrepôt as it were, from which those forces invariably come away changed. Such a model begins from the recognition that 'conquest did not necessarily provide the order of the day, at least not the only order' (Bartels 1997: 48). In many cases – England's traffic with the Ottoman Empire, for example – conquest and conversion were distinct impossibilities in the face of tenacious and/or imposing military and religious establishments. England's jerry-built military would have been no match for Mughal, Ottoman or Persian forces,[1] and what religious conversions did come out of English contact with the East more often than not involved Christians embracing Islam. But cultural intercourse could also come in less macroscopic and institutional forms. When disentangled from Othello, Leo Africanus and his *Geographical Historie* emerge as a less obvious, but no less important example of how Eurocentric principles such as European Christian superiority and entitlement were challenged and even reshaped by their non-Western counterparts.

Apart from a few recent exceptions, the interest of literary scholars in the sixteenth-century Moorish traveler and author has followed Shakespeare's lead, discussing little more than those passages of his *Geographical Historie* that resonate with others in *Othello*. When examined in the context of 'race' in the early modern period, passages are again carefully mined to support claims like Emily Bartels' that 'the text produces an author who seems … to be securing his Christian, European self at the expense of his "Other" identity as a Moor' (Bartels 1990: 435). While this is a rather unfair summary of Africanus's considerable work, it is, nevertheless, the abstract that has emerged from an interest that rarely reads Africanus outside of the empire of Shakespeare studies.[2]

I want to argue that Africanus, unlike Othello, reveals the instability of European discourse about difference by undermining many of those anti-African and anti-Islamic shibboleths which, ironically, gain him admission to the ranks of authoritative European historians. I believe the *Geographical Historie* reproduces some of the fantastical and anti-Islamic tendencies of earlier works on Africa as a strategic form of textual mimicry. In other words, Africanus engages in a form of discursive negotiation that Mary Louise Pratt has identified as 'autoethnography.' In autoethnography, 'colonized subjects undertake to represent themselves in ways that engage with the

colonizer's own terms; … autoethnography involves partial collaboration with and appropriation of the idioms of the conqueror' (Pratt
1992: 7). My essay will attempt to identify the *Geographical Historie*'s
vexed collaboration with European histories of Africa in order to
dis-entangle Africanus and Othello from a coupling that obscures
religious concerns operating in Shakespeare's play as well as the
subversive nature of Africanus. When extricated from the umbra
of Shakespeare studies, Africanus emerges as a critical exponent of
African social, political and religious history that can inform our
post-colonial assessments of early modern texts like *Othello* with a
greater and more fruitful complexity.

II

Othello's 'travells history' (I. iii. 139), including the story of his
captivity before coming to prominence in Venice, has led numerous
critics to examine him alongside the Moorish traveler John Leo
Africanus, whose own travel history relates similar events and observations. While it has been some time since the *Geographical Historie*
has been treated as a source for *Othello*,[3] or Africanus himself for
Shakespeare's 'extravagant and wheeling stranger' (I. i. 135), the
two continue to be intertwined, often rendering Africanus ideologically conformist and innocuous. In separate examinations concerned
with Othello's relationship to Africanus, Emily Bartels and Jack
D'Amico each describe an Africanus who willingly slanders his racial and religious origins in like manner to Othello's anxiety-laden
denigration of Turks and blackness. Bartels argues that 'while
[Africanus] insists that his intention is to valorize his African subjects and to affirm and display his loyalty to his African heritage, his
strategies work to the opposite effect' since their author is more
concerned with his admission into Christendom (Bartels 1990: 436).
D'Amico similarly finds that 'whatever his personal opinions,
[Africanus] echoed the assumptions and expectations of his reader'
(D'Amico 1991: 53).[4]

More recently, Kim Hall has likened Africanus to the text his
English editor, John Pory, produced in 1600, calling each 'a safe
conduit through which readers become protected tourists, enjoying
the wonders and promised wealth of Africa while safely distanced
from its more ominous and seductive cultural practices' (Hall 1995:
30). While Hall treats Africanus quite separate from Othello, her
understanding of him seems nevertheless informed by the same

idea of a conforming alien-insider which holds sway in *Othello* criticism. Her specific interest in the relationship between race and gender leads her to consider only a small portion of Africanus's text, from which she draws fascinating conclusions about early modern constructions of race, gender and beauty, but from which Africanus emerges as a toady for European ideology and a historian of nothing more than anecdotal material. She attributes Africanus's censure of the 'base' inhabitants of Barbary, and particularly 'the failure of the patriarchal family to restrict sexual relations before marriage,' to his 'imposition of European values of family and marriage' (ibid.: 34). Why should Hall assume that bridal virginity is an exclusively European value? Similarly, her contention that the '*Geographical Historie* gives the reader a sense of Africa as a chaotic and disordered land, one badly in need of a sense of order,' evidences the same tendency to read Africanus as conformingly anti-African, despite the text's generous treatment of African accomplishments and interest in Islam, a treatment so prevailing that it leads Pory to surround the text with an introduction and appendices focused on African Christianity.

The author of the *Geographical Historie* is, like Othello, 'doubly tainted' and thus he needs to establish the credibility of his adopted subject-position as John Leo Africanus, an objective, converted-Christian historian for a European readership. For this reason, Africanus declares himself by 'the streit law of historie enforced' (L6r) to catalog the ills of an Africa he describes as 'infected with the Mahumetan lawe' (A4v), while likening his task to that of an executioner who dutifully beats a censurable old acquaintance.[5] Nevertheless, a non-archeological reading of the *Geographical Historie* reveals that Africanus's text must be set apart from the Eurocentric travelers' accounts among which it is often discussed. What distinguishes Africanus's text from other accounts of Africa is that which has occasioned his comparison to Othello – the ability substantially to add to and transform contemporary discourses about Africa. What distinguishes Africanus from Othello is his ability successfully to employ hybridity as a strategy to maintain the resulting compound.

Whereas most travelers' accounts of Africa tell far more of the traveler than his supposed subject, Africanus's far-ranging work of 1523 generally concerns itself with the history, geography and culture of Africans, thereby populating what had previously been an ideascape or, at best, a landscape. Furthermore, unlike other travelers of the period, Africanus refuses to rehearse the fantastic and pre-

posterous material African historiography had inherited from
Herodotus, Pliny and Mandeville.[6] Where Africanus does describe
the vices of Africans, he affords equal attention to their 'commendable actions and vertues.' Indeed, lists of virtues often directly follow
lists of vices in oddly ambivalent narratives of various African peoples. This ambivalence, further evidenced in various moments of
autobiography and meta-narration, suggests that Africanus and his
work merit re-examination in terms of strategic mimicry and the
supplementation of African history. As Homi Bhabha has shown
for the post/colonial era, such mimicry is Janus-faced, 'at once resemblance and menace' (Bhabha 1994a: 86). The menace of the
Geographical Historie, enabled by its textual mimicry, lies in the supplementing threat it poses to those accounts of Africa that erased its
histories and inhabitants in the project of European self-making.

   In a discussion of minority discourse within 'the nation,' Bhabha
adapts Jacques Derrida's theory of the supplement to the issue of
discursive negotiation. For Bhabha, the supplement is that addition
which is simultaneously disruptive and disrupted as it is accommodated into a discourse. Bhabha explains that by '[i]nsinuating itself
into the terms of reference of the dominant discourse, the supplementary antagonizes the implicit power to generalize, to produce
the sociological solidity.' Thus, the supplement poses as a belated,
missing piece, while occasioning a 'renegotiation of those times,
terms and traditions through which we turn our uncertain, passing
contemporaneity into the signs of history' (ibid.: 155). A version of
this same supplementary strategy is at work in Leo Africanus's trafficking in the intromissive discourse on Africa.

   One indication of permeability and exchange in the discourse
on Africa lies in Giambattista Ramusio's decision to place the *Geographical Historie* first in his *Delle Navigationi et Viaggi* (1550). As
Oumelbanine Zhiri has pointed out, Ramusio's anthology was expressly intended to correct old errors and misunderstandings (Zhiri
1991: 52). The placement of a non-European at the head of such
a text speaks to a certain discursive openness. A second indication
of the potential for discursive revision appears in Ramusio's preface to the first edition, which predicted of its readers that 'having
once read this book of John Leo, and thoroughly considered the
matters therein contained and declared, they will esteem the relations of all others, in comparison of this, to be but brief, unperfect,
and of little moment' (e5v–6r).

   We cannot be certain whether Africanus was commissioned to

write the *Geographical Historie* for a readership aware of the obsolescence Ramusio describes, or one that expected a confirmation of
the prevailing discourse. (Of course, the very impulse to buttress
the status quo suggests at least some recognition of obsolescence.)
In either case, Ramusio's comment indicates that increasing European contact with Africa and Africans put new pressures on the
prevailing discourse, raising doubts about its ability to stand in the
place of 'Africa.' As this occurred, the *Geographical Historie* emerged
as a 'supplement' that, in Derridean terms, 'intervenes or insinuates itself in-the-place-of; if it fills, it is by the anterior default of a
presence' (Derrida 1976: 145). As is the case with any supplement
that issues new claims of an absolute ground, Africanus's text will
also fail adequately to represent its subject due to its various elisions.
I shall, for the moment, pass over those elisions, exploring first the
way in which, in its over two-hundred-year tenure as Europe's principal source of information about Africa, the *Geographical Historie*
'passes as the sign' and thereby reconfigures the discourse through
a process of sanctioned antagonism. In short, textual mimicry allows Africanus to move into a restricted position from which he
may supplement a wanting discourse. In Bhabha's terms, 'The supplementary strategy suggests that adding "to" need not "add up"
but may disturb the calculation' (Bhabha 1994a: 155).

By the early sixteenth century, few works had joined Pliny's *Natural
History* atop the hierarchy of authorities supporting the dominant
European discourse on Africa. Pliny's work emphasizes features of
the landscape and vast multitudes of wild beasts and monstrous hybrids. For most of the text, the African peoples are merely landmarks,
described by little more than their location.[7] Pliny's bestial Africans
were reproduced, embellished upon and further circulated in that
enormously popular amalgam of travelers' tales, *The Book of John
Mandeville*. This polyphonic text passes through several narrative strategies. One voice seems concerned with one-upping Pliny's oddities
with dragons, cyclopes, ape-men, hound-headed men, mouthless dwarfs,
man-eating giants, basilisk-men, incestuous cannibals, blood-drink-
ers and Amazons. Another of 'Mandeville's' voices more clearly
distinguishes itself from Plinian conventions in its concerned awareness of the spread of Islam across North Africa. This voice, therefore,
engages in the construction of a religious ideascape threatened by
'heathen' occupation. For this 'Mandeville,' North Africa is the land
of the Old and New Testaments, and his text is an appendix to those
works, leading the Christian pilgrim through the sites of Judeo-Christian

parables, where little or no trace of modern Africans is made apparent. When those 'foul peoples' are presented, it is generally in terms of corrupt religious practice and the fact that 'because they go so nigh our faith they be lightly converted to Christian law.' This textual confirmation of crusader-rhetoric was, arguably, Mandeville's most influential contribution to the European discourse on Africa since virtually every account of Africa that followed produced its own avatar of a developing anti-Islamicism.

Europe's anti-Islamic heritage may help explain why, when introducing his 1600 translation of Africanus to English readers, John Pory feels compelled to begin with a defense of the culturally and theologically suspect author,

Who albeit by birth a More, and by religion for many yeeres a Mahumetan: yet if you consider his Parentage, Witte, Education, Learning, Emploiments, Trauels, and his conuersion to Christianitie; you shall finde him not altogither vnfit to vndertake such an enterprize; nor unwoorthy to be regarded.

(Unsigned2)

Pory's defense indicates that, should Africanus have wished to publish a text that openly controverted Eurocentrism and anti-Islamicism, he could not have done so: an alien author like Africanus would have found himself in a position requiring a degree of ideological conformity toward his audience. Furthermore, he was in either the custody or employ of Giovanni de' Medici, Pope Leo X. In either case, it would, most likely, have been fatal directly to confront certain aspects of a discourse by means of which European Christendom affirmed its own sanctity. It therefore comes as little surprise to find Africanus affirming the descent of Africa's 'savage,' 'wild,' and 'rude' inhabitants from Ham, or assigning responsibility for architectural, intellectual and moral decay to the spread of 'the Mahumetan superstition … [when] certaine of *Mahomet's* disciples so bewitched [Africans] with eloquent and deceiueable speeches, that they allured their weake minds to consent vnto their opinion' (C2r). Of equal import, however, is the way in which Africanus undermines the very statements, such as these, which gain him admission to the ranks of authoritative European historians. Beginning then from the suspicion that contradictions demand closer investigation, I will now turn a critical eye to those antinomies in the *Geographical Historie* that suggest an authorial parallax.

Often, the places where texts make their proclamations of objectivity are the very places that provide us with our clearest insights into their ideological paradoxes. The very inclination to assert impartiality suggests a point of view under suspicion and obliged to rhetorical strategies of substantiation. It is particularly telling that Africanus makes his first objectivity claims immediately following consecutive sections of the *Geographical Historie* that Ramusio headed, 'The commendable actions and vertues of the Africans' (D2r) and 'What vices the foresaid Africans are subiect vnto' (D3r). Because they so neatly parallel and contradict each other as they catalog both urban and rural Africans, these passages are worth quoting at considerable length. In the first we learn that the people of Barbary are

> greatly addicted vnto the studie of good artes and sciences: and those things which concerne their law and religion are esteemed by them in the first place ... The inhabitants of cities doe most religiously obserue and reuerence those things which appertaine vnto their religion: yea they honour those doctours and priests, of whom they learne their law, as if they were petie-gods. Their Churches they frequent verie diligently, to the ende they may repeat certaine prescript and formal prayers ... Most honest people they are, and destitute of all fraud and guile; not onely imbracing all simplicitie and truth, but also practising the same throughout the whole course of their liues: albeit certaine Latine authors, which haue written of the same regions, are farre otherwise of opinion ... They keepe their couenant most faithfully; insomuch that they had rather die then breake promise ... They trauell in a manner ouer the whole world to exercise traffique ... and whithersoeuer they goe, they are most honorably esteemed of: for none of them will professe any art, vnlesse hee hath attained vnto great exactnes and perfection therein. They haue alwaies been much delighted with all kinde of ciuilitie and modest behauior: and it is accounted heinous among them for any man to vtter in company, any bawdie or vnseemly worde. They haue alwaies in minde this sentence of a graue author; Giue place to thy superiour.

(D2r–v)

As Africanus's description proceeds, the picture of an intelligent, courteous, hospitable and industrious people of outstanding modesty, piety and honesty emerges in overt contradistinction to what, accordingly, become the misrepresentations of 'certaine Latine authors.' Likewise, despite the author's urban prejudices (which are elsewhere more prominent), rural peoples are here described as 'of a more liberall and ciuill disposition: to wit, they are in their kinde as deuout, valiant, patient, courteous, hospita[ble], and as honest in life and conuersation as any other people' (D2v). This portrait is immediately and paradoxically contradicted in its particulars in the section that follows:

> Those which we named the inhabitants of the cities of Barbarie are somewhat needie and couetous, being also very proud and high minded and woonderfully addicted vnto wrath … So rusticall they are & void of good manners, that scarcely can any stranger obtaine their familiaritie and friendship … So ignorant are they of naturall philosophie, that they imagine all the effects and operations of nature to be extraordinarie and diuine. They obserue no certaine order of liuing nor of lawes … By nature they are a vile and base people, being no better accounted of by their gouernours then if they were dogs … They are vtterly vnskilfull in trades … neither is there (I thinke) to bee found among them one of an hundred, who for courtesie, humanitie, or deuotion's sake, will vouchsafe any entertainment vpon a stranger … Their minds are perpetually possessed with vexation and strife, so that they will seldom or never shew themselves tractable to any man … The shepherds of that region … are a rude people, and (as a man may say) borne and bred to theft, deceit, and brutish manners … Concerning their religion, the greater part of these people are neither Mahumetans, Iewes, nor Christians; and hardly shall you finde so much as a sparke of pietie in any of them. They have no churches at all, nor any kinde of prayers, but being vtterly estranged from all godly deuotion, they leade a sauage and beastly life.
>
> (D3r–v)

Africanus allows these two descriptions to coexist, indicating no concern with either reconciliation or explanation. Instead, the text takes its first autobiographical turn at this point, anticipating a separate but related concern:

> Neither am I ignorant, how much mine owne credit is impeached, when I my selfe write so homely of Africa, vnto which countrie I stand indebted both for my birth, and also for the best part of my education: Howbeit in this regarde I seeke not to excuse my

selfe, but only to appeale vnto the dutie of an historiographer,
who is to set downe the plain truth in all places, and is blame-
woorthie for flattering or fauoring of any person. And this is the
cause that hath mooued me to describe all things plainly without
glossing or dissimulation.

(D4r)

Evidently it is not the contradictions in a text about Africa which
must be justified, but rather the apparent contradiction in an African
author's revealing African corruption to a European readership. Thus,
Africanus sets about legitimizing his position among European
geographers and historians by relating the tale of a dutiful executioner. Suggesting that the story illustrates 'how indifferent and sincere
I haue shewed my selfe' (D3v), Africanus figures himself as an executioner and Islamic Africa the 'lewd countriman' whose sentence must
be impartially dealt. Yet, if the dutiful executioner/historian here
confirms Eurocentric prejudices and publicly shames his 'lewd
countriman' (D3v), as he does at other points in the text, his 'impartiality' also enables him to supplement those prejudices with notions
of African nobility and the possibility of European fallibility.

Could Africanus have asserted African nobility and European
fallibility without the consolation of anti-African prejudice? The
text promptly supplies an answer to this question in the form of a
second 'resemblance, or similitude' (D4r), whose protagonist is
immediately recognizable as a figure of the author. The tale, ostensibly included to reconfirm the author's *European impartiality*, suggests
that Africanus's narrative strategy may be alternatively mimetic and
subversive, to the end of producing a supplement, a disruptive yet
sanctioned counternarrative of Africa. Thus, after once more pro-
nouncing his position *vis-à-vis* Africa and Africans, he begins,

There was vpon a time a most wily bird, so indued by nature that
she could liue as well with the fishes of the sea, as with the fowles
of the aire; wherefore she was rightly called Amphibia. This bird
being sommoned before the king of birds to pay her yeerely tribute, determined foorthwith to change her element, and to delude
the king; and so flying out of the aire, she drencht herself in the
Ocean sea. Which strange accident the fishes woondring at, came
flocking about Amphibia, saluting her, and asking her the cause
of her comming. Good fishes (quoth the bird) know you not, that
all things are turned so vpside downe, that we wot not how to liue
securely in the aire? Our tyrannicall king (what furie haunts him,

I know not) commanded me to be cruelly put to death, whereas no silly bird respected euer his commoditie as I haue done. Which most uniust edict I no sooner heard of, but presently (gentle fishes) I came to you for refuge … With this speech the fishes were so perswaded, that Amphibia staied a whole yeere among them, not paying one penie or halfepenie. At the yeeres ende the king of fishes began to demand his tribute, insomuch that at last the bird was fessed to pay … but she suddenly spred her wings, and vp she mounted into the aire. And so this bird, to auoide yeerely exactions and tributes, woulde eftsoones change her element.

(D4r)

The Amphibia fable, adapted from Aesop's fable of the bat, serves as a peculiar and telling example of the impartiality Africanus first claims it will illustrate. Clearly, the migrant creature of the fable resembles the wayfaring Africanus, who found he could live as well with the Europeans who flocked about him in curiosity. Yet, rather than illustrating impartiality, Amphibia displays a wily mimeticism designed to further her own ends. By taking on the form of her patrons and flattering, even ennobling, them ('gentle fishes') in contrast to herself ('silly bird') and her former 'uniust' and 'tyrannicall' acquaintances, Amphibia submits the alien's necessity of deluding fabrications and an ingratiating manner, not an unmitigated candor. Furthermore, the tale suggests the ease with which the outsider may assume and manipulate a pose of impartiality. In other words, Africanus employs a fable drawn from Aesop – whose tales represent a sort of crossroads of European and African culture – to offer a fable of successful hybridity. Amphibia's doubleness allows her to thrive in two different cultures and avoid subjection in either.[8] Africanus unabashedly admits that this has always been his own experience:

Out of this fable I will infer no other moral but that all men do most affect that place, where they find least damage and inconvenience. For mine own part, when I hear the Africans evil spoken of, I will affirm my self to be one of Granada: and when I perceive the nation of Granada to be discommended, then I will profess my self to be an African.

(D4v)

That Africanus, like Amphibia, may pass as an objective narrator of alien places and events, and maintain a parallax view of his homeland, may explain the sustained contradictions in his text. As Amphibia promotes her own ends by 'chang[ing] her element,' Africanus punishes his 'lewd countriman' before all Europe in order to distinguish this man from himself and his worthy, but overlooked, compatriots. Furthermore, like the unusual hybrid that finally takes flight, Africanus's allegiance to European Christendom ultimately betrays its strategic ends. As Amphibia reveals that she really is a bird passing as a fish, Africanus tells of his plans for further books to be written upon his 'being returned forth of Europe into *mine own country*' (Ff2v; emphasis mine). His plans, repeatedly punctuated with locutions recognizing his fortune's deference to the will of God (common in both Islamic and Christian texts), include a work 'touching the patrons of the Mahumetan law, and likewise concerning the difference in religion between the Mahumetans of Africa, and of Asia, [which] we will (by God's grace) write more in another several volumes' (C2v). Thus, while mimetically conforming to European views of the corruptions of Islam, Africanus seeks to supplement and redirect those views by assigning corruptions to sects of 'heretiks' (N4r). In addition to the inclusion of his plans and a brief history of Islam, Africanus urges his reader to take up Elefacni's discourse on the seventy-two distinct sects of Islam, thereby insisting on a European ignorance in obvious need of remedy. Thus by insinuating himself into a Eurocentric idiom, Africanus manages to deflect and interrogate the tendency toward ill- or uninformed generalization in that same idiom.

Africanus's reference to the work of Elefacni is only one among many bibliographic supplements to the early modern discourse on Africa hitherto dominated by Europeans like Pliny, Mandeville and Johannes Boemus. The *Geographical Historie* cites numerous African poets, cosmographers and historiographers (e.g. Ibn Battuta, Ibn Rachich and Ibn Khaldoun), simultaneously indicating a space in the discourse requiring antagonistic supplementation and the existence of a rich, lettered culture where foul hybrids and corrupt Muslims had previously been imagined inhabiting geographic and intellectual deserts. The many conquerors of North Africa had, Africanus suggests, rooted out histories before them to spread their own glory and histories (C3r–v). Thus, the *Geographical Historie* sets about restoring African histories as well as humanizing the Africa bequeathed to Europe by Herodotus and Pliny. It contains none of the hybrids or Amazons his readers would expect, and respectfully but pointedly admits to omitting many things reported by Pliny, who was doubtless a man of rare and singular learning, notwithstanding by the default and negligence of certain authors which wrote before him, he erred a little in some small matters concerning Africa: howbeit a little blemish ought not quite to disgrace all the beautie of a faire and amiable body.

(Ff6v)

Instead, regions are described in terms of both their histories and present states, highlighting a continuity of traditions and a socio-economically complex and diverse civilization featuring governments, educational institutions, juridical systems, free markets, hospitals and various civic projects. Furthermore, Africanus describes peoples of widely disparate characters and customs, resisting the tendency toward generalization and demonstrating 'that even Africa is not destitute of courteous and bountiful persons' (I1r), while respectfully permitting some prejudices to stand. Indeed, Africanus was so skilled at respectfully but radically supplementing the prevailing discourse that Jean Bodin would reassess the terms of Eurocentrism and call him 'the only man by whom Africa, which for a thousand years before had lien buried in the *barbarous and gross ignorance of our people*, is now plainly discovered and laid open to the view of all beholders' (e6v; emphasis mine).[9]

III

When early modern voyagers encountered non-Europeans in their peregrinations, they tended to describe them according to one of two models. Either they found docile and noble savages eager to embrace the Christian empire, or menacing agents of deception irrevocably steeped in, and tempting Christians toward, satanic error. Typically (though not exclusively), the first model was deployed in New World encounters, whereas the second was reserved for the various Moors, Turks and Jews of Africa and Asia.[10] Europe's relative familiarity and antagonistic history with Islamic and Hebraic cultures rendered them less easily dismissed or overwritten.[11] Instead they had to be engaged and refuted in a Christianized version of their own terms. Thus various scholars and travelers 'explained' Islam to their compatriots, basing their exegeses upon their inheritance of a Christian tradition aimed toward delegitimation. As Norman Daniel has argued, 'The polemical purpose was to attack the Islamic claim to be the true revelation of God, and to this end it was essential that the character of Mohammed be shown to be wholly and unquestionably incompatible with religion' (Daniel 1960: 244). As a result, writers created a necromancing Mohammed inspired by the devil to found Islam as a license for his own sexual indulgence. Furthermore, lechery was used to explain Christian conversion to Islam, and in justifying the fervor and successes of 'fanatical' Turkish armies who, they explained, believed themselves rewarded with sensual afterlives.[12] Thus, whereas the inhabitants of the Americas were most often seen in terms of pre-Christian innocence, European Christendom figured Islam as a religion of sorcery and carnality.

Across the five acts of Shakespeare's play, Othello's contested identity is bandied between these two discourses as Iago locates and activates his community's fears and his master's insecurities as stranger, proselyte and racial Other. In a reading of the play whose insights make superfluous my close examination of the same scenes, Ania Loomba concludes that Othello's 'political colour rather than precise shade of non-whiteness is what matters' (Loomba 1989: 50). Peter Stallybrass similarly argues that, '[f]or Othello to "gain" ... there must be a mark against him that will be overcome by his marriage. That mark can be located in the construction of Othello as "black" ' (Stallybrass 1986: 135). Without contesting Stallybrass's and Loomba's assertions concerning the significance of race, I would add that a significant part of the politics of race is to mark religious difference. Indeed, race often functions as a marker of religious difference in the early modern period, as indicated by Queen Elizabeth's notorious warrant of 1596 calling for the deportation of eighty-nine black people. Here Elizabeth places 'those kinde of people' in contradistinction to her Christian subjects.

In the first scenes of *Othello*, race similarly functions as a marker of religious difference, subtly indicated by Iago's vilification of a cunning, sexualized Othello, and Brabantio's imagination of a conjuring Othello. Thus, even before he appears on stage, Othello's irrevocably non-Christian origins are foregrounded in the terms of Christianity's narrative of Islamic error.[13] Yet, when Othello first appears before the audience, his impeccable behavior reveals him to be, in some ways, more like the idealized New World savage (tractable but noble) who gratefully embraces Christianity. Indeed, he has become a Christian and defends his adopted world 'against the general enemy Ottoman' (I. iii. 49) with loyalty apparent enough to convince the Duke to counsel a distraught Brabantio, 'Your son-in-law is far more fair than black' (I. iii. 290).[14] Thus an initially confident and confidence-inspiring Othello successfully enrolls in and simultaneously calibrates the white Christian culture from which he would normally be excluded on the basis of race, religion and citizenship.

Given his trebly suspicious position as stranger, proselyte and racial Other, Othello's confidence and the confidence of the community are tragically susceptible to Iago's insidious narrative.[15] With recourse to Frantz Fanon, Loomba has illustrated how

> Othello moves from being a colonized subject on the terms of a white Venetian society and trying to internalize its ideology, toward being marginalized, outcast and alienated from it in every way until he occupies his 'true' position as its other.
>
> (Loomba 1989: 48)

Yet Loomba's eagerness to refute Stephen Greenblatt's location of Othello's vulnerability in doctrinal guilt for passion or sexual pleasure, by relocating his sexual guilt in color-consciousness, creates a historically incongruous division between two linked discourses. For both Greenblatt and Loomba underestimate the significance of Renaissance Christianity's sexualized and racialized vision of Islam. As a Christian, Othello is taught the tripartite equation of dark skin, religious error and sexual excess.[16] As a man of color in a white-dominated society, he is consequently prone to a brand of self-doubt founded in what Fanon terms 'affiliation neuroses.'[17]

The notion of an affiliation neurosis may help explain Othello's purple speech, his position at the vanguard of Christendom's forces against the Turks (and verbal positioning as part of the Christian 'we' in his question, 'Are we turn'd Turks?') and his marriage to Desdemona. These actions linguistically, religiously, socially and politically authorize his place in the Venetian community by supplementing the pejorative discourse about the Other. Yet, while confirming his place before the community, the very decision to take such actions simultaneously indicates the profundity of Othello's self-doubt. Thus, Othello is liable to imagine a sexually excessive Desdemona, whereas he may thereby displace questions of his own lascivious 'appetite' (I. iii. 258) raised by the *religious color* of his skin. The ideological incompatibility of his dark skin and Christian faith makes Othello susceptible to a vision of himself as the tainted other for whom no white, Christian woman's affection can last. Desdemona's love thus seems to him 'nature erring from itself' and he speculates that she is untrue '[h]aply for I am black' (III. iii. 229, 265).

As Othello begins to suspect his own irredeemable difference, he is gradually stripped of his ability to supplement the discourse, modify the community and sustain his place therein. Perhaps this is most apparent in his failure to continue seeing Desdemona in supplementary terms. Through the first half of the play he presents her with an Africanus-like ambivalence. In his defense before the Duke, he figures Desdemona as a sly seductress who coyly invites his love and 'with a greedy ear / Devour[s] up [his] discourse' (I. iii. 150–1). But he is also prepared to wager his 'life upon her faith' (I. iii. 295) and finds virtue in the fact that she 'feeds well, loves company, / [and] Is free of speech' (III. iii. 186–7). In the last two acts of the play, however, Othello sees his wife only in Iago's terms, as 'false,' a 'devil' and 'whore.'

As Othello embraces (and ceases to supplement) the discourse of misogyny, the composure with which he supplemented the discourse of the Moorish Other also melts away. Lodovico is led to wonder, 'Is this the noble Moor whom our full Senate / Call all in all sufficient?' (IV. i. 264–5). Emilia's accusations answer by returning him to the religious calumny of Act I as he is considered a 'blacker devil' (V. ii. 129), and 'no more worthy heaven / Than thou wast [Desdemona]' (V. ii. 160–1). Finally, the discovery of Iago as 'devil' confirms Othello's religious Otherness as he comes to understand that the devil has 'ensnar'd his soul and body' (V. ii. 299). He is accordingly stripped of 'power and command' (V. ii. 329) and condemned to prison like an enemy of the state. Consequently, in a simultaneous affirmation of his Otherness and desperate attempt to reclaim his standing, a forlorn Othello delivers his schizophrenic final soliloquy, within which he inhabits the dual role of 'a malignant and a turban'd Turk' and the redeeming Crusader who 'smote him' (V. ii. 354–6). Thus, Othello's insecurity leads him to confirm the Christian reading of his skin, but in a way that illustrates the misprision inherent in those semiotics. For Othello's susceptibility to Christian dogma and consequent inability to continue unsettling the meaning of his skin is, finally, evidence of his faith. 'In short,' Walter Cohen argues, 'with the passion of the recently converted, Othello is driven to murder not by reversion to African barbarism but by the adherence to an extreme, perverse version of the logic of Christian society' (Shakespeare 1997: 2095).

To win Desdemona and the inclusion she represents, Othello willingly places his 'unhoused free condition … into [the] circumscription and confine' (I. ii. 26–7) of what Cohen (ibid.: 2094) calls 'Christian civilization's secular mores.' In this Othello differs distinctly from Africanus's fabulous creation: Amphibia changes her element for 'the sea's worth' (I. ii. 28) Othello rejects, but continues to enjoy an 'unhoused free condition' by putting her hybridity to use. Where Othello's faith renders him unable to 'affect that place, where [he would] find least damage and inconvenience' (Africanus: D3v), Amphibia, and by extension Africanus, succeed because of their ability to 'change [their] element' and elude absolute subjection to either realm they inhabit.

IV

It may be fair to conclude that Shakespeare's play produces a troubled and troubling fantasy of containment for a society frightened by the idea of cultural integration. But if *Othello* illustrates the violence with which supplementary strategies could be disarmed and contained, Africanus illustrates the ways in which they could successfully unsettle the defining fictions of European Christendom. For Othello's attempt to supplement the *religious meaning* of his skin is ultimately contained by his inability to recognize ideology as such. What distinguishes Africanus is his ability to apprehend the workings of ideology and redirect its tools to supplement European discourse, despite the containment strategies of editors like John Pory. Africanus fashions himself as, at once, both reassurance and menace. Yet his conflation with Othello has obscured the menace and consequently the fact that European discourse was not a stable, unidirectional and totalizing system, but rather one whose growing coerciveness was never absolutely free from renegotiation and foreign materials.[18] In short, the silks and spices imported into Europe's mercantile economy were accompanied by less tangible cultural commodities which found their way into Europe's intellectual economy.

Works like the *Geographical Historie* suggest that we should consider thinking of early modern cultural intercourse not only in terms of dominating colonialism, but also in terms of *trafficking*, a term used at the time to describe mercantile enterprises and one that more clearly recognizes the exchanges and negotiations (ushered in by individuals like Africanus) that forever changed both European and non-European cultures. While etymologists agree that the term 'trafficking' arose in the context of Mediterranean commerce, there are equally reasonable arguments for a Latin derivation from *tra/trans* (across) and *facere* (to do or make), and an Arabic origin from *traffaqa*, which can mean 'to seek profit'[19] or *tafriq*, signifying distribution.[20] This divided etymology makes 'trafficking' all the more attractive as a descriptive term aimed to displace unidirectional models of early modern cross-cultural encounters.

Any acknowledgment of Africanus's achievement in supplementing early modern discourse on Africa must be qualified by the recognition of *which* 'Africa' is 'plainly discovered.' The historical and cultural Africa restored by the *Geographical Historie* to 'pass as the sign' is by no means complete. Restoration prerequires an act of selection based on some hierarchical principles that invariably produce a new set of exclusions or misrepresentations in the service of the new discourse. For some, then, Africanus's supplement provided no better representation than what preceded it. First, the *Geographical Historie*'s 'Africa' includes only Islamic Africa, excluding the southern half of the continent from African history. Second, though the women of Africa are no longer simply Amazons or non-existent, they are instead most vividly represented as unbridled witches whose sexual perversities and control over their husbands produced a troubling inversion of gender roles.[21] Finally, though Africanus carefully distinguishes between Africans of various religious sects and pigmentary shades to disable religious and national generalizations, his distinctions, in effect, erect and/or enforce a set of racial generalizations: '[W]hite, or tawny Moors' are described as steadfast and honorable. The 'Negros,' on the other hand, 'lead a beastly kind of life, being utterly destitute of the use of reason, of dexterity of wit, and of all arts' (D3v). Furthermore, the 'land of the Negros,' described in Book VII, is characterized by unequaled crudity, disorder, paganism and promiscuity.[22]

Ultimately, Africanus's supplement benefits the image of Africanus's Africa, an Africa of lighter-skinned Muslim men whose nobility and sophistication are authorized through both linguistic and methodological mimesis. Like Othello in his vilification of Turks, Africanus insinuates himself into the idiom of Eurocentrism and thereby positions himself as a legitimate and objective historian. Unlike Othello, he successfully maintains his position (for over two centuries) and from it proves his contentiousness as a historian, challenging the established discourse, but reproducing its method of elision and misrepresentation through the establishment of women and dark-skinned Africans as a 'more other' to nullify the otherness of the lighter-skinned Muslim man.[23]

Notes

1 England possessed no capacity for siege warfare or initiating any kind of advance that would result in a significant shift of territorial control. At a time when Mehmet III was leading a force of 100,000 into Austria, England's army was only 30,000 strong. Among the European powers, Spain alone could match Ottoman forces in the field, with an army of 200,000. For a fuller discussion of comparative military strength in the early modern period, see Kennedy (1997) and Black (1996).

2 For a historian's account of Africanus's contribution to the geographical knowledge of his age, see Hallett (1965).

3 The first critic to argue for Africanus as a source for Othello was Whitney (1922). See also Johnson (1986) and Jones (1971).

4 See also Tokson (1982).

5 When quoting from Africanus I am using John Pory's 1600 English translation because of its temporal proximity to Shakespeare's Othello. The transmission history of this text is admittedly dubious: No manuscript has been confidently identified as an original, and Pory worked from Jean Florian's 1556 Latin translation of Ramusio's 1550 Italian edition. Zhiri (1991) illustrates that the various translators tended to omit details of African history and Arab culture, suggesting that Africanus's original supplement to Europe's knowledge of Africa was even greater than what I will identify.

6 Some material of this sort, including descriptions of dragons and hydras, was later inserted into the text by Pory.

7 Pliny's descriptions of Europe also evince a lack of interest toward human subjects, but to a lesser extent. Rather than landmarks, they are described in the more human terms of their genealogical ancestry.

8 In *The Arte of English Poesie* (1589), George Puttenham transforms the same fable into an analogue to women's simultaneous occupation of the roles of *virgo* and *mulier*. In Puttenham's version of the story, a 'Rattlemouse who in the warres proclaimed betweene the foure footed beasts and the birdes, beyng sent for by the Lyon to be at his musters, excused himself for that he was a foule and flew with winges: and beyng sent for by the Eagle to serue him, sayd that he was a foure footed beast, and by that craftie cauill escaped the danger of the warres, and shunned the seruice of both princes' (Puttenham 1936: 135–6). Rosemary Kegle has argued that the rattlemouse's evasion of service

marks his ability to do what women might if they were not kept from an 'awareness of oppression'. He converts his 'lack of any coherent position into a simultaneously held multiplicity of positions' (Kegle 1994: 26). Like Africanus then, Puttenham uses the tale of the hybrid to illustrate how doubleness can be used to destabilize certain subject positions, shore up others, and thus advance its own ends.

9   See Parker and Hendricks (1994) for an acute discussion of discovery and the sexualized rhetoric of 'laying open.'

10 See, for example, Richard Eden's preface to The *Decades of the New World* (Eden 1971: 57) which argues for New World conversion by contrasting those 'Jews and Turks who are already drowned in their confirmed error' to 'these simple gentiles living only after the law of nature, [who] may be well likened to a smooth and bare table unpainted.'

11 See Todorov (1982), Hulme (1986) and Greenblatt (1991) for discussions of the dismissal and overwriting of native American culture.

12 See Matar (1994) on conversion to Islam in English Renaissance thought.

13 My argument has much in common with Daniel Vitkus, 'Turning Turk in *Othello*: The Conversion and Damnation of the Moor' (1997), who argues for Othello as an apostate who loses his faith. My argument does not, however, depend upon Othello's having an Islamic past. What is more important is that Othello can be constituted as *Mahumetan* (and can know it) because of his skin color. The extensive signifying range of the Renaissance term 'moor' included, among its primary meanings, an individual of the Islamic faith. Indeed, the terms were used interchangeably, as in one traveler's account that explains, 'whereas I speake of Moores I meane Mahomet's sect.'

14 For an indispensable discussion of dark/light polarity and the significance of fairness, see Hall (1995).

15 Bartels (1997: 61–2) argues that in Othello we have 'neither an alienated nor an assimilated subject, but a figure defined by two worlds.' She argues that whereas Moors lived in England in the early modern period, for Othello 'to have a dual, rather than divided identity – is finally not so strange, so suspect or so charged.' Studies of Moors in England during the early modern period have, however, revealed that their lives *were* more often than not strange, suspect and charged; see, for example, Tokson (1982) and D'Amico (1991).

16 The Medieval tradition of Prester John bears witness to the European awareness of non-white Christians in Africa and Asia. In the early modern period, however, European reports (including Pory's appendix on the Christians of Africa) invariably pointed out the practice of concubinage, circumcision and various heresies among non-European Christians, including the kingdom of Prester John, thus characterizing their beliefs as somehow debased.

17 As my discussion of Africanus will indicate, I find Fanon's notion of the black man's affiliation neurosis useful only in certain cases, not as a rule.

18 I am not implying here that European discourse grew more benign and tolerant. On the contrary, I am suggesting that the discourse about racial and cultural difference may have grown more rigid in an effort to deny its initial and unavoidable porousness.

19 *The Oxford English Dictionary*, 2nd edn., s.v. 'traffic.'

20 Arnold (1931: 105).

21 For an acute discussion of Africanus's representations of African women, see Hall (1995).

22 Zhiri (1991: 37) argues similarly: 'De l'Afrique qu'il décrit, la partie qui l'intéresse le plus et qui le retient le plus longtemps est l'Afrique arabe et musulmane. Tous les compléments qu'il cite la concernent seule. L'Afrique noire, ou du moins les quelques régions que Léon décrit, n'est intéressée par ces textes que dans la mesure où elle est touchée par l'islam.' See also Alden T. Vaughan and Virginia Mason Vaughan, 'Before Othello: Elizabethan Representations of Sub-Saharan Africans' (1997).

23 I would like to thank Ania Loomba, Richard McCoy and especially Barbara Bowen, whose generous suggestions are apparent in any place this paper succeeds.

4

'These bastard signs of fair'
Literary whiteness in Shakespeare's sonnets

KIM F. HALL

> More white then whitest Lillies far,
> Or Snow, or whitest Swans you are:
> More white then are the Whitest Creams,
> Or Moone-light tinselling the streames:
> More white then *Pearls* or *Juno's* thigh;
> Or *Pelops* Arme of *Yvorie*.
> True, I confesse; such Whites as these
> May me delight, not fully please:
> Till, like *Ixion's* Cloud you be
> White, warme, and soft to lye with me.
> Robert Herrick, 'To Electra'

Whiteness is currently enjoying a certain vogue, particularly in American studies. Invigorated by Toni Morrison's call in *Playing in the Dark* to 'discover, through a close look at literary "blackness," the nature – even the cause – of literary "whiteness" ' (Morrison 1992: 9), scholars have been examining the ways in which an Africanist presence in the texts of American culture has been used to create white subjects. Likewise, some post-colonial theorists suggest how gender relations and cultural interactions dominated by the West are shaped by the need both to establish white hegemony and to deflect attention from whiteness as a source of power. However, despite liberal borrowing from other theoretical schools and periods, the study of whiteness *per se* has generally not been part of early modern scholarship.[1] On the one hand, there are logical reasons for this: the study of race has only belatedly reached the period and most work on whiteness in other arenas has pointed out that the most salient quality of whiteness is that it tends to be rendered invisible through being 'natural-ized in dominant ideologies' (Mercer 1991: 206). On the other hand, since neither 'race' nor white supremacy are dominant ideologies at this time, whiteness should in fact be more visible and open to analy-sis than it has been in early modern scholarship.[2] While not much is known about the presence of certain ethnic and religious minorities in England, one can say with some certainty and (only slightly face-tiously) that England was inhabited by a large population that came to be seen as 'white' and yet we have not uncovered ways of discuss-ing this as a factor in English identity formation. Even as scholars examine the social, political and imaginative construction of white-ness, whiteness still becomes normative so long as we assume that its viability as a racial signifier is self-evident. More bluntly, they do not address the more basic question: why is whiteness the mark of racial privilege at all?

The poem I cited above from Robert Herrick's *Hesperides* (1648) demonstrates an excess that is typical of evocations of whiteness in the period and thus is a vivid reminder that whiteness is an ubiqui-tous albeit little noted facet of early modern lyric and beauty culture. Through excessive comparisons the poet strains to find a 'white' that fulfills his poetic needs and desires as much as he anticipates that his beloved's body will. In this he is not alone, such idealized figures are almost always characterized by 'blondness' and spar-kling whiteness (Vickers 1982: 96). For example, Imogen in Shakespeare's *Cymbeline* is white on white: a 'fresh lily, / And whiter than the sheets!' (II. ii. 15).[3] While the praise of white beauty is by no means new in the early modern period and can be seen in clas-sical and medieval verse (Ogle), I am drawing on Roland Greene's recent assertion that the 'Petrarchan subjectivity' related to lyric whiteness is an important adjunct to European colonialist practices (Greene 1995: 130–3).

Whiteness often appears in hyperbolic comparison, as seen in Herrick, and in juxtaposition with references to African black-ness. For example, in *A Winter's Tale*, Florizel claims that Perdita's hand is 'As soft as dove's down and as white as it, / Or Ethiopian's tooth, or the fann'd snow that's bolted / By th' Northern blasts twice o'er' (IV. iv. 362–5). Just as it interrupts the ongoing simile, the use of 'Ethiope' 'interrupts' or perhaps energizes a poetic tra-dition that was increasingly being satirized. (Polixenes mockingly comments 'How prettily th' young swain seems to wash / The hand that was fair before!' (366–7)). This Africanist presence becomes a crucial part of a larger economy of whiteness in early modern England.[4] Color is one of the categories much pressured as the result of European colonialism (Greene 1995: 148) and the signs of this economy can be seen in the many 'eruptions of white-ness' that occur in early modern texts. So too, the appearance of references to African blackness suggests that the sense of white-ness is being reconfigured by England's expanding trade and colonial ambitions. Importantly, the linkage of white/fairness with these economic practices make lyric whiteness a key component of white supremacy. The desirability and overvaluation of a seemingly abstract whiteness in conjunction with images linking blood, fam-ily and property interests then has material effects in that it upholds a system of power which increasingly licenses the exploitation of people perceived as nonwhite.

Critical practice has also tended to make early modern whiteness even more impervious to critique because most of the earliest terms employed to avoid the anachronism (or the politics) of the term 'race' all tend to refer to people of color (a phrase that also normal-izes white people). The 'exotic,' the 'outsider,' the 'other' and 'the stranger' all shift attention away from the center that uses these strategies and categories to establish dominance (see Fiedler 1972; Hunter 1978).[5] Like the general focus on Africans, Indians and other non-Europeans, such discursive practices assume that 'race' somehow only accrues to minoritized peoples. More importantly, they provide no conceptual clues for thinking about whiteness as a developing identity with potentially racialized meanings. If white-ness buries itself in dominant ideologies, then theoretically at least, looking at whiteness in texts produced while those ideologies are in flux should give us a better idea of how 'race' becomes part of a social heritage.

Herrick's poem should demonstrate that Shakespeare's sonnets are not the privileged site of whiteness in the culture. However, they do seem an obvious choice for such an investigation; they have for a long time now been haunted by the specter of a possible Africanist presence (the dark lady)[6] and they begin with a recognition of a dominant sexual ideology articulated in relation to a 'fair' beauty.[7] The poetic sequence foregrounds the contrast of dark and light that Winthrop Jordan sees as a crucial pre-text for modern racial ideologies (Jordan 1968; Hall 1995).

This essay offers, first, a broader discussion of how fairness is racialized in Elizabethan culture, then, a look at the sonnets rooted in a reading of fairness as an emergent ideology of white supremacy. It will end by considering the larger question of why whiteness is such a transferable trope of privilege. My discussion of fairness rests on the assumption that the young man's beauty performs (albeit in a more muted way) as whiteness does in the dialectic described by Morrison in which 'images of blinding whiteness seem to function as both the antidote for and a meditation on the shadow that is the companion to whiteness' (Morrison 1992: 33). I have argued elsewhere that in the later sonnets the poet strives to make darkness 'fair,' thereby demonstrating his poetic prowess (Hall 1995: 66–7). However, the early young man sonnets reveal an equally difficult task – maintaining fairness as a stable and pure linguistic and social quality. This view of fairness does not have to rely on any particular narrative sequence of reading, although it does depend on certain gender assumptions (that there is a triangle featuring the poet, a young man and the dark lady). I am trying here to look merely at the workings of 'fairness,' particularly in the sonnets that urge procreation. These are the poems that, as Bruce Smith terms it, 'argue Elizabethan orthodoxy' (Smith 1991: 251) and it is in such moments that whiteness both lies hidden and produces itself.

I

Looking at white/fairness in other locations might help contextualize the sonnets even as they reveal the problems of fairness. In his 1589 *Arte of English Poesie*, George Puttenham offers as an example of *Antiphrasis* or the 'Broad floute,' the following:

> Or when we deride by plaine and flat contradiction, as he that saw a dwarfe go in the streete said to his companion that walked with him: See yonder gyant: and to a Negro or woman blackemoore, in good sooth ye are a faire one ...
>
> (Puttenham 1589: 201)

In a larger sense the contradiction is obvious – the putative black woman is meant to be the opposite of 'fair'; however, a close look reveals that what Puttenham posits as a 'plaine and flat contradiction' is not so plain after all. Here, the 'Negro or woman blackemoore' is in a way quite concrete. We can locate this instance of an Africanist presence within a range of historical meanings associated with African peoples in England even if we disagree about its specific valences. Rhetorically, 'Negro or woman blackmoore' leaves almost no room for the customary doubt about the blackness of the 'Moores' who inhabit Elizabethan texts. Conversely, the phrase 'ye are a faire one' is frustratingly elusive – it has no 'moorings' – no specific gender or cultural connotations. It presents itself as obvious and in that sense impenetrable. Most certainly, 'faire' here relies on its primary meaning, 'beautiful,' and is meant to mock the black woman as ugly; however, its binary context also makes it a somatic reference. Even if 'complexion' and 'race' do not refer so obviously to a visual regime as they do now, whiteness becomes in such instances a term of what we know as complexion. In addition, as I note elsewhere, 'fair,' another ubiquitous term in praise of female beauty that is closely associated with white, becomes a term referring to skin color (Hall 1994: 178–9).

Puttenham's text is an excellent example of how 'faire' can escape its racial codings in modern readings. Like 'whiteness,' it avoids particularity, and like whiteness, it is represented as 'plain,' obvious and curiously opaque. This example also shows the 'drift' that occurs in representations of whiteness: our attention is almost inevitably drawn to the Africanist presence and away from fairness/literary whiteness which is presented as normative.

Although the language of fairness is key to lyric praise throughout Europe, it becomes highly resonant when thinking more politically about Elizabethan culture. Peter Erickson succinctly reiterates a point made originally by Winthrop Jordan when he reminds us that representations of blacks and blackness in this time 'were played out against a spectacle of whiteness, most prominently figured in the cosmetically enhanced and poetically celebrated version presented by Queen Elizabeth I' (Jordan 1968: 4–11; Erickson 1993a: 517). If, as art historian Roy Strong notes, later paintings of Elizabeth reflect a certain 'imperialist, messianic' cult that presented Elizabeth as an almost magical and divine icon of England, then the fairness that was so reveled in was also a significant part of that imperial fervor (Strong 1987: 133). In the Armada and Ditchley portraits, for example, a dark/light dichotomy plays out in the background which obviously shows Elizabeth/England as key to a larger, cosmic triumph of good over evil (Strong 1986:45). As John Hodge argues, this type of dualist thinking plays a key role in racial oppression (Hodge 1990: 96). With this in mind, what may seem like a simple replay of the good/evil dichotomy is explicitly connected to Elizabeth's queenly physical presence and evocations of nation.

Elizabeth herself is extremely white in these portraits, and if that whiteness reflects her virgin purity and Christian grace, it also, through association of Elizabeth with the kingdom (Strong 1987: 136), represents England as white – as powerful and favored by the forces of good and a Christian God (see Hodge 1990: 94).[8] That whiteness becomes a specific attribute of Englishness becomes more obvious in the Armada portrait, which frames Anglo-Spanish enmity within a cosmic struggle of good over evil in which Elizabeth's enhanced whiteness reigns supreme.

In another context, Richard Dyer notes how lighting works to associate certain film stars with whiteness in a way that identifies them as morally and aesthetically superior. These portraits of Elizabeth likewise make her 'the source of light,' and stress the 'intrinsic transcendent superiority of the colour white' (Dyer 1993:2) while not grafted on to biological accounts of racial difference, this whiteness is melded onto a projection of national solidarity and superiority that portends such future associations. Although I do not have space to go into this here, this representation of fairness as a specific attribute of Elizabeth's Englishness takes place in other ways as well, most notably in the literal denigration of other 'European' cultures, such as the Irish and the Spanish, as 'black.'[9]

The examples of Puttenham and Elizabeth demonstrate how fairness and whiteness become racialized in connection with ideologies of nationhood and physical beauty. On the surface, physical beauty is the focus of the earlier sonnets. Sonnet 1 opens:

> From fairest creatures we desire increase,
> That thereby beauty's rose shall never die,
> But as the riper should by time decease
> His tender heir might bear his memory:

The young man is – at least initially – what we recognize as the 'good, the pure, the beautiful in Western aesthetics' (Mercer 1991: 188). In her perceptive reading of the sonnets, Eve Sedgwick notes that fairness is the young man's principal attribute: 'The male who is paired with/against this female, has, at the most, one trait (if fair means beautiful here and not just coloured) and no energy' (Sedgwick 1985:32). While looking at the juxtaposition of black and white that occurs with the introduction of the dark lady can help us think about the ways in which whiteness acquires racial overtones, we can also assess the value of fairness and its potentially racialized meanings by looking at possible threats to whiteness.

At first, the procreation sonnets easily allow a modern reader to equate fairness merely with an abstracted ideal of beauty since its primary threats are old age and death, as indicated by lines such as 'That thereby beauty's rose shall never die' (1.2) or 'O carve not with thy hours my love's fair brow' (19.9).[10] However, in the later sonnets, female painting becomes a significant threat. The poet's solutions to these possible threats – reproduction and poetry itself – in different ways evoke issues of 'race' in multiple senses of the term.

If the cult of Elizabeth made a virtue of necessity by turning anxieties over the Queen's non-reproductive state into a celebration and revaluing of virgin purity and whiteness, then the opening exhortation of the sonnets: 'From fairest creatures we desire increase' (1.1) reverses that dynamic – revealing fairness as a social quality so valuable that it demands reproduction (de Grazia 1993: 44–5). The young man, like Elizabeth in the paintings I discussed earlier, is placed within a dualist framework in which he is associated with the moral force of the good. As Sedgwick notes, 'the sonnets' poetic goes to almost any length to treat the youth as a moral monolith; while the very definition of the lady seems to be doubleness and deceit' (Sedgwick 1985: 41; see also Fineman 1986: 175–7). This is most obvious in Sonnet 144:

> Two loves I have of comfort and despair,
> Which like two spirits do suggest me still;
> The better angel is a man right fair,
> The worser spirit is a woman coloured ill.

The exhortation to 'increase' in the sonnets is consonant with other Shakespearean texts that more explicitly use whiteness as a prime characteristic for identifying desirable reproductive pairings. Erickson identifies in the comedies a regime of color which uses blackness to place women outside of the social world of the plays – and hence as outside of the marital/reproductive imperatives of the genre (Erickson 1993: 516–19). For example, in *Much Ado About Nothing*, Claudio, in recompense for his wrongs, promises to marry Leontes' niece. His promise, 'I'll hold my mind were she an Ethiope' (V. iv. 38), uses the sense that black women are outside of reproductive/social boundaries to suggest his resoluteness. So, too, the Nurse in *Titus Andronicus* inextricably links fair complexion with reproduction when she brings in Aaron's son, proclaiming: 'Here is the babe, as loathsome as a toad / Amongst the fair-fac'd breeders of our clime' (IV. ii. 66–7). Within this circulation of meanings, the conjunction of fairness with breeding in the sonnets seems more credibly racialized. In a recent essay, Margreta de Grazia likewise notes the critical avoidance of 'the ideological force' (de Grazia 1993: 44) of the sonnet's opening lines and reminds us that '*fair* is the distinguishing attribute of the dominant class' (ibid.: 45) in a way that nicely shows how class intersects with race within the troping of fairness.

Véronique Nahoum-Grappe argues that beauty becomes 'a gift, an identifying characteristic as objective as wealth or education' (Nahoum-Grappe 1993: 86). The young man's beauty has just such material force. It is a kind of currency which the poet encourages the young man to spend wisely in Sonnet 4:

> Unthrifty loveliness, why dost thou spend
> Upon thyself thy beauty's legacy?
> Nature's bequest gives nothing but doth lend,
> And being frank she lends to those are free.
> Then beauteous niggard why dost thou abuse
> The bounteous lárgesse given thee to give?
> Profitless usurer, why dost thou use
> So great a sum of sums yet canst thou not live?
> For having traffic with thyself alone,
> Thou of thyself thy sweet self dost deceive.
> Then how when nature calls thee to be gone,
> What ácceptable audit canst thou leave?
> > Thy unused beauty must be tombed with thee,
> > Which usèd lives th'executor to be.

Paradoxically, the young man is both 'unthrifty loveliness' (1) and 'beauteous niggard' (5), a liberal spender and a miser. The poem's series of repeated pairs ('Upon *thy*self   *thy* beauty's legacy?' [2]; 'bounteous lárgesse *given* thee to *give*' [6]; emphasis mine) mimics the young man's self-absorption. The repetition also reinforces a paradoxical sense that, linguistically, one can both spend freely (with endless repetition) and withhold (the repetition means that no new words are being used). The opening lines, '… why dost thou spend / Upon thyself thy beauty's legacy?' introduce a metaphor of inheritance which makes beauty part of a very specific economy. Despite the use of 'Profitless usurer' (7) and 'ácceptable audit' (12), this is not the economy of the marketplace, but a more insular economy of inheritance based on bloodlines.

That these concerns are specific to the land-owning classes is reinforced by the many references to and images of inheritance and housekeeping in the poems (de Grazia 1993: 44–6).[11] As early as Sonnet 2, the poet introduces the argument for reproduction:

> How much more praise deserved thy beauty's use,
> If thou couldst answer, 'This fair child of mine
> Shall sum my count and make my old excuse'
> Proving his beauty by succession thine.
>
> (10–12)

Again, this reproductive argument is linked to the young man's 'thrift' which may interrupt an orderly pattern of inheritance. Maintaining an estate that demonstrates one's class status and producing a male heir who does likewise are of particular concern to the gentry for whom 'the individual is seen as standing at the apex of a double helix intertwining land and blood' (Heal and Holmes 1994: 22; see also Stone and Stone 1984).[12] Sonnet 3 gives us an inkling of this, as well as some insight into gender concerns when the poet proclaims, 'For where is she so fair whose uneared womb / Disdains the tillage of thy husbandry?' (5–6). Thomas Greene notes that in this line

> an ad hoc meaning 'marriage' joins the traditional meanings of 'thrift' and 'estate management' in the word 'husband' and again when the word is picked up in Sonnet 13, 'Who lets so fair a house fall to decay / Which husbandry in honor might uphold
>
> (Greene 1985: 22)

In both of these poems, the accusation 'of a dereliction of those responsibilities incumbent on the landowning class', is accomplished with the joining of 'fair' with management/marriage. Thus 'fair house' refers both to the young man's body and to his family line which must be perpetuated in a kind of masculine perfection (Greene 1985: 232; de Grazia 1993: 45).[13]

Greene's astute analysis also leaves room to question the relationship between early modern definitions of the word 'race,' and a color politics which might resemble more modern racial attitudes rooted in presumably inherited physical and 'cultural' characteristics. In articulating the dominant class's interest in property and inheritance, the earlier poems link the young man to 'race' in its more dominant usage in the period. As Tessie Liu notes, 'The *OED* makes clear that ideas about descent, blood ties, or common substance are basic to the notion of "race." It is striking that "house," "family," and "kindred" are synonyms for race' (Liu 1995: 565; see also Hendricks 1992: 183–5). This period of obsessive concern over the legitimacy and continuation of elite status (Stone and Stone 1984: 7) combined with the poem's insistence that physical appearance, termed as beauty or fairness, significantly marks that status, suggests that this older usage of race has a visual component as well.

Whiteness and tropings of color may be in fact what links these two equally virulent forms of 'race.' Sara Matthews Grieco notes that the white aesthetic was class-based as well as gendered:

> White was the color associated with purity, chastity, and femininity. It was the color of the 'female' heavenly body, the moon, as distinct from the more vibrant hues of the 'masculine' sun. A white complexion was also the privilege of the leisured city dweller as distinct from the sunburnt skin of the peasant.
>
> (Grieco 1993: 62)

Just as the idea of 'sunburnt skin' comes to have racial overtones during English colonization (see Hall 1995: 92–106), 'color' itself is 'one of the most semantically weighted categories in European writing about the New World' (Greene 1995:148) and whiteness acquires such resonance when non-aristocratic European men begin defining themselves as 'white' against those they perceive as tawny or black. In doing so, they borrow a semantic distinction that already invests them with entitlement. What began as a visible sign of class – particularly of leisure and ownership of property – is a crucial precondition for whiteness as a mark of racial privilege when it later in America becomes a compensatory measure that designated and linked property-owners with those 'free' men who could not be made property (Dubois 1977: 700–1; Roediger 1991b: 55–60; Allen 1994: 21).

Jonathan Goldberg points out the necessary masculinity of the young man's beauty: 'the young man who seems to have a patent on beauty that the sonneteer cannot imagine located anywhere but in him and a progeny of young men who will duplicate and keep forever in circulation his unmatchable beauty' (Goldberg 1994: 224). It is an interesting observation given Grieco's argument that whiteness is usually marked on the bodies of aristocratic women: she suggests that in Renaissance paintings men were consistently given a 'darker, more "virile" complexion': 'White was more feminine, more delicate, more beautiful. Dark was more robust, more masculine, more tenebrous' (Grieco 1993: 62). If Grieco is correct, then the reversal of that dynamic in the sonnets – the marking of fairness on the male body – is worth further attention as it contributes to a certain gender ambiguity that I will comment upon later. Male fairness may also be consistent with the need for the aristocracy to reproduce itself; the idea of the young man's self-reproduction evokes the scientifically outmoded but still ideologically useful Aristotelian trope of reproduction in which men transmit the most important heritable characteristics (here including 'fairness'/skin color) and women's 'uneared womb[s]' (3:5) are merely vessels for male seed. In the sonnets, this dynamic comes close to what Lynda Boose has described as the 'patriarchal fantasy of male parthenogenesis'(Boose 1993: 45). Such a view of procreation requires a 'fair' male and suggests that fairness in the sonnets is a desirable and transmissible characteristic.[14]

II

> A woman's face, with nature's own hand painted,
> Hast thou, the master mistress of my passion –
> A woman's gentle heart, but not acquainted
> With shifting change, as is false women's fashion;
>
> (20: 1–4)

The young man's beauty is also striking in that it is very specifically gendered. Not just fairness, but male fairness is praised throughout. Female fairness is merely an abstraction since the only woman in the sequence is deliberately made, not fair, but black. Women, in fact, become a threat to 'true' fairness. The threat of women and the gendering of fairness become quite obvious in Sonnets 20 and 21, poems whose gender instability has occasioned reams of comment.[15] If the early poems all insist on the uniqueness of the young man's fairness, these sonnets create his singularity by insisting on its difference from (and superiority to) the fairness of women. Moreover, by 'othering' female fairness, Sonnet 20 manages to make the young man's fairness both extraordinary and natural. The conceit of Nature as artist in its first line, 'A woman's face, with nature's own hand painted,' suggests that the fairness of the man is noteworthy, in distinct contrast with women who are commonly 'painted' in a more debased way – through cosmetics.

Sonnet 20, with its extreme ambiguity and complex gender slippages, is a definite turning point in the sequence; it is here that the poet gives up the argument for physical reproduction and concentrates on the powers of poetry. An attention to color imagery in the poem reveals that the gender ambiguity is undergirded by a less transgressive politics of color. Gregory Bredbeck argues that the cognate pun 'own/owne' acts as a structural trope which connects this sonnet to 127 ('In the old age black was not counted fair') and thus works to recirculate and unfix homo- and hetero-erotic desire in the sequence: 'the resurfacing of the hands of nature collapses the linearity of the cycle and draws us back to the "master mistris" even as it pushes us ahead to the mistress' (Bredbeck 1991: 178–9). However, that intertexual connection and recirculation of erotic energy does not destabilize the politics of color in the sequence; in fact, it brings into play the dark/fair binarism and reiterates the bias against female fairness. In his praise of blackness in 127, the poet argues that black has become 'beauty's successive heir' (3) precisely because fairness is debased by cosmetics:

> For since each hand hath put on nature's pow'r,
> Fairing the foul with art's false borrowed face,
> Sweet beauty hath no name, no holy bow'r,
> But is profaned, if not lives in disgrace.
>
> (5–8)

In both cases, the association with cosmetics reinforces an understanding of fairness as white complexion[16] and reiterates the undesirability of female fairness and poems that would praise it.

The instability of fairness becomes in Sonnet 20 linked to the duplicity of femininity, a duplicity which is the cornerstone of the dark lady sonnets. The sexual pun in the lines: 'A woman's gentle heart, but not acquainted – / With shifting change, as is false women's fashion' (4) further joins traditional fears of women's uncontrolled sexual appetites with anticosmetic and misogynist discourses: 'false women's fashion.' In contrast with the chaos suggested by women, the young man evokes mastery: he is 'A man in hue all hues in his controlling' (20). The doubled use of 'hue' suggests an homology of form and color. The line would seem to imply that men – or at least this particular man – has a power over both forms/bodies and color; it gives his fairness a stability and power specifically not accorded it in other arenas (a power, I might add, that women seem to be able to achieve only with cosmetics).[17]

Tellingly, Stephen Booth suggests that one meaning of the line is that the young man has power over other complexions in that he causes people to flush or grow pale' (Booth 1977: 164, n.7). Both blushing and turning pale often come to be seen as the property of whiteness. As late as *Oroonoko* (1688), Aphra Behn feels compelled to repudiate this:

> 'tis a very great error in those who laugh when one says, A Negro can change colour, for I have seen 'em as frequently blush and look pale, and that as visibly as ever I saw in the most beautiful white.

> (Behn 1994 [1688]: 17)

Sonnet 20 suggests that the young man has a superior control over emotions; in this case the lines might then be read as an interesting obverse of Aaron's mocking and proverbial condemnation of white/fairness in *Titus Andronicus*: 'Fie treacherous hue, that will betray with blushing / The close enacts and counsels of thy heart!' (IV. ii. 116–17) and his praise of blackness which 'is better than another hue, / In that it scorns to bear another hue' (IV. ii. 99–100). All of these examples have at their heart concerns over bodily control and suggest the primacy of reason and rationality.

If Sonnet 20 brings to the fore an homoerotic love of the poet for the young man, then Sonnet 21 complements that gesture by suggesting that the more common heteroerotic tradition of epideictic praise, which is generally a praise of female beauty, is inadequate because it cannot create a fairness that transcends material notions of value. This sonnet also announces a link to the 'dark lady' poems, this time through anti-Petrarchism. It duplicates the equation of female beauty with 'painting' and, more specifically, worries how one can find a language of praise suitable for the young man when popular praise has become devalued by its focus on possibly adulterate female beauty: 'So it is not with me as with that muse / Stirred by a painted beauty to his verse' (21: 1).

The competition between these types of fairness is rhetorically suggested by the repetition of 'fair' in line 4: 'and every fair with his fair doth rehearse' which also ironically points out the poet's dilemma. In even making this gesture of rejection he himself 'rehearses' fairness, stubbornly holding on to it six lines later: 'And then believe me, my love is as fair / As any mother's child' (10–11). Throughout the poem, he replaces the allegedly strained couplings of the beloved with objects in epideictic praise with his own punning and repetitive couplings which self-referentially connect the beloved to the intangible or the sanctified. This simile in particular ('as fair as any mother's child'), replaces the earlier urgings to procreate in Sonnet 2 'this fair child of mine / Shall sum my account and make my old excuse' (10–11) with his own creation of the young man as a 'fair' child. However, as Bredbeck notes, the completion of that thought, 'though not so bright / As those gold candles fixed in heaven's air' (21: 11–12), even as it mocks the gestures of otherworldliness in lyric, suggests that there is an absolute source of truth, the transcendent light of heaven's heir.[18] The pun on air/heir suggests that the poet finds refuge (as whiteness) often does, in religious allegory and notions of transcendence. This transcendence is placed within a black /white schema when the poet in Sonnet 70 proclaims, 'The ornament of beauty is suspéct, / A crow that flies in heaven's sweetest air' (3–4).

Sonnet 21's desire 'O let me be true in love but truly write' (9), complements this belief in a transcendent 'fairness' with a need for a pure language which I have argued elsewhere is a driving force behind paradoxical praise. To 'truly write' and to be truly 'right' argue a need for a language that transparently represents the young man's pure beauty without somehow marring it. This sonnet thus seems to initiate what becomes a recurring anxiety – that the young man's fairness is such that the poet's words can never convey it. This theme is also linked to what I have argued is an overwhelming drive/desire for a language that can represent without marring or blotting. Sonnet 83 is an excellent example of this dynamic: unlike the rival poet who damages as he praises, our poet prefers silence: 'For I impair not beauty, being mute, / When others would give life and bring a tomb' (11–12).

So too, Sonnet 68's nostalgic decrying of 'bastard signs of fair' articulates the fear of a deadening, overused language of praise:

> Thus is his cheek the map of days outworn,
> When beauty lived and died as flow'rs do now,
> Before these bastard signs of fair were borne,
> Or durst inhabit on a living brow –
> Before the golden tresses of the dead,
> The right of sepulchers, were shorn away,
> To live a second life on second head –
>
> (1–7)

The imitation of the dominant aesthetic – evoked here by the image of the blond wig made from the hair of the dead – makes preserving the validity and purity of the young man's fairness a central project. In a larger sense, however, the 'bastard signs' that are linked to the 'bastard' beauty in Sonnet 127 connect this anti-cosmetic sentiment to rampant anxieties over birth and legitimacy at the same time as it reiterates poetic fears about language. Bastardy also connotes patriarchal fears over bloodlines, usually in the context of inheritance. The image of the young man as map, repeated twice in Sonnet 68 ('And him as for a map doth nature store / To show false art what beauty was of yore' (13–14)) and nowhere else in the sequence, reinforces the sense of property interests and establishes a connection between fair skin and the land in a way that is reminiscent of the Ditchley portrait. That his body is somehow a map of the past ('his cheek the map of days outworn') may evoke the new interest in maps that are key ground for articulations of Elizabethan colonialism and nationhood accompanied by an interest in English antiquity (see Helgerson 1992 108–24).

Although the poet in the procreation sonnets has asserted a certain value for the young man's fairness in economic terms, he now wishes to withhold the young man's fairness from the devalued marketplace: 'I will not praise that purpose not to sell' (21: 12).[19] This replicates an interesting dynamic in the earlier poems. 'Fair beauty' is established as the highest quality across a number of explicitly social registers. The economic, the juridical and the religious all come into play. This happens as early as Sonnet 2:

> How much more praise deserved thy beauty's use,
> If thou could answer, 'This fair child of mine
> Shall sum my count and make my old excuse' –
> Proving his beauty by succession thine.
>
> (9–11)

However, this 'economic' imperative to reproduce is both a hedge against nature which causes decay and is made to seem completely 'natural' through the use of pastoral metaphor. This movement between the social and the natural suggests that the poems attempt both to circulate a valuable fairness within culture and to insist that it has a value beyond culture. Like the paintings of Elizabeth I, the young man sonnets struggle to produce the 'intrinsic transcendent superiority of the colour white' (Dyer 1993: 2). Heterosexual social order is literally re/produced in a context that responds to new social pressures that force fairness/whiteness into visibility. The poems strive for transcendence even as they reveal fairness as constructed, and not inherently valuable. The dual movement suggests to me that fairness is in fact not hegemonic, that its signification and value have been contested, possibly by increased social mobility, anxiety over gender roles, and colonial encounters.

III

The seemingly abstract descriptions of beauty are a key quality of the sonnets and are one of the factors that would immediately forestall one from thinking about race in the sequence. His beauty is described in terms of Christian transcendence: it has no 'holy bower.' It can be 'profaned.' He is a 'better angel' and 'a saint' (Sonnet 144) who is seemingly beyond the physicality that is a crucial part of more modern racial categories. How can we say that they are racially coded when we are not even sure what the young man looks like, other than that he is generically beautiful?

For my answer, I turn again to Toni Morrison. I was thinking about this issue of transcendence and race while teaching *The Bluest Eye*. This novel is in part an extended meditation on the force of the Western beauty aesthetic and I was particularly struck by her description of a certain class of aspiring bourgeois black women:

> They go to land grant colleges, normal schools, and learn how to do the white man's work with refinement: home economics to prepare his food; teacher education to instruct black children in obedience; music to soothe the weary master and entertain his blunted soul. Here they learn the rest of the lesson begun in those soft houses with porch swings and pots of bleeding heart: how to behave. The careful development of thrift, patience, high morals and good manners. In short how to get rid of the funkiness. The dreadful funkiness of passion, the funkiness of nature, the funkiness of the wide range of human emotions.
>
> Wherever it erupts, this Funk, they wipe it away; where it crusts, they dissolve it; wherever it drips, flowers or clings, they find it and fight it until it dies. They fight this battle all the way to the grave. The laugh that is a little too loud; the enunciation a little too round; the gesture a little too generous. They hold their

behind in fear of a sway too free; when they wear lipstick, they never cover the entire mouth for fear of lips too thick, and they worry, worry, worry about the edges of their hair.

(Morrison 1972: 6)

Morrison describes here the result of a particular form of mental colonization – the exaltation of the mind, spirit and reason at the expense of the body and its passions. She demonstrates how this mind/body split is inflected through gender, class and race. The passage also allows us to see another facet of literary blackness. Black women have more reason to fear 'funk' because blackness and femaleness are so connected to devalued discourses of the body. In early modern England, blackness becomes the mark of bodies – be they female, African, Welsh, Jewish, Irish or lower class – that escape, deny or just cannot be contained by certain cultural boundaries. Eruptions of 'Funk' disrupt the surveillance and discipline of the idealized classical body which is created in lyric by the eruptions of whiteness with which I began this essay.

Such praise of the beautiful white body also implies a certain transcendence of the body and its 'funk' in that it draws attention to certain disciplinary codes of cleanliness and sweetness (Grieco 1993: 47–52). While it may have originated in class differentiation, the very real social, political and emotional effects that Morrison demonstrates in *The Bluest Eye* make it impossible to see transcendent fairness as anything but a contributing factor to white supremacy. The accompanying emphasis on property, wealth and lineage that is so pronounced in the sonnets is also linked to 'race' in its earliest usage and runs throughout discourses of beauty in the period. Moreover, the ideology of white beauty is a 'racial formation,' in that it helps construct a visual regime that uses human bodies and their signification to determine access to political, social and economic power (Omi and Winant 1994: 55–6). The eruptions of whiteness with which I began this essay are part of an aesthetic system that identifies certain bodies as desirable – as entitled to wealth, land and power – and others as dangerous to that entitlement. Certainly in this way they must be seen as a form of colonization as potent as economic imperialism. When we insist on attempting to protect Shakespeare and his works by reading Shakespeare's poems (and Shakespeare himself) as 'universal' and merely as praise of an abstract 'beauty' (male or female) rather than as specific cultural productions that manage fairness, modern teachers and critics produce the invisibility that fuels white hegemony.

Notes

1 Peter Erickson's series of essays on whiteness is a notable exception to this (1993a; 1993b; 1996), as is Barbara Bowen's work on Aemilia Lanier (1998).

2 For more specific discussions on the varied meanings of the term 'race' and the instability of the concept of race, see the essays in *Women, 'Race,' and Writing in the Early Modern Period* (Hendricks and Parker 1994). Lynda E. Boose's essay in that same anthology begins by querying the differences between early modern and contemporary notions of race (Boose 1993: 35–7).

3 All references to Shakespeare's plays are from *The Riverside Shakespeare*, ed. G. Blakemore Evans (1974).

4 My use of 'Africanist' is drawn from Toni Morrison, who uses 'Africanism' 'as a term for the denotative and connotative blackness African peoples have come to signify, as well as the entire range of views, assumptions, readings, and misreadings that accompany Eurocentric learning about these people' (Morrison 1992: 7).

5 For an astute analysis of the problem of 'race,' see Erickson (1993a: 500–3). See also bell hooks's critique of how the use of the term 'ethnicity' can be used to efface political action (hooks 1990: 52).

6 For an overview (albeit dismissive) of how the question of race and the dark lady was addressed (or not) by leading critics from the nineteenth and early twentieth centuries, see Edward Hollins. Appendix IX of Shakespeare (1944), ed. Ryder.

7 The poems individually may have acquired this valence. If, as Patricia Fumerton (1991), has argued, sonnets and jewels circulated in the same rhetorical/social system, we might similarly see these sonnets being read amidst an Africanist presence in visual culture. Thus, a poem celebrating the young man's fairness might be held in the same cabinet as one of the popular cameos featuring an African face.

8 My reading of the Ditchley portrait slightly adjusts Richard Helgerson's sense that the portrait, in sublimating the map to the monarch, resists the developing meaning of maps, which 'strengthened the sense of both local and national identity at the expense of an identity based on dynastic loyalty' (Helgerson 1992: 114). Whiteness as a characteristic is not purely dynastic, but is in portraits a quality ceded to a powerful elite. The joining of land and ruler then allows for a different configuration.

9 We can also see this operating in tandem with both narrative and political exclusions of blacks and blackness from the nation. Citing

the welfare of her own 'natural' subjects, Elizabeth expels 'Negars and Blackamoores' from England in 1596 and 1601; as I noted in *Things of Darkness*, George Best's now-infamous description of a marriage between an 'Ethiopian blacke as a cole' and 'a faire English woman' works to make blackness and Englishness mutually exclusive (Hall 1995: 11–12).

10 All references to the sonnets are from *Shakespeare's Sonnets*, ed. Stephen Booth (Shakespeare 1977).

11 For example, the extended perfuming conceit in Sonnet 5 ('Then were not summer's distillation left / liquid pris'ner pent in walls of glass / Beauty's effect with beauty were bereft,' (9–11)); the use of scents on the clothes and body was a sign of wealth and the manufacture of those scents was characteristic mainly of aristocratic households.

12 They continue: 'Lineage also creates a web both of privileges and of duties. The latter are to friends, neighbours, tenants, servants – but pre-eminently to lineage itself' (Heal and Holmes 1994: 22). See in the writings of Sir John Oglander: 'Oglander insists that the key responsibility is to the continuation of the lineage, or "house" as he calls it, of which the current holder of the estate is representative and beneficiary' (ibid.: 22).

13 Wendy Wall's (1996) discussion of 'national husbandry' is illuminating on this point and suggestive of the way in which the concerns of husbandry are being disrupted by class as well as national agendas. Unlike Markham, Shakespeare seems to be tying husbandry to a particular class in ways that may have nationalist implications. This difference may also be related to the difference of print technology, which Wall sees as key to Markham's publication of a national husbandry.

14 As de Grazia notes, this orderly fantasy is disrupted by the obsession with the dark lady's reproductive body.

15 For discussion of this, see de Grazia (1993); and on Sonnet 20 specifically, see Stallybrass (1993: esp. pp. 94–6).

16 Characteristically, Sonnet 127, with its monetary language ('beauty's successive heir') raises the specter of reproduction seen in the earlier sonnets ('Proving his beauty by succession thine' (2: 12)).

17 I disagree here with Margreta de Grazia's claim that the young man 'is described as a paragon of both masculine and feminine beauty' (de Grazia 1993: 41) as well as with her tendency to reduplicate the binary grid of fair/man, dark/woman. There is an important degree of gender play within the category fair and less absolute hegemony than her reading indicates.

18 Although I absolutely agree with Bredbeck's deconstructive point that 'the continually irreducible punningness of the poem makes poetry itself an other to fixed meaning' (Bredbeck 1991: 170), I take the desire for transcendence at face value. Fineman helpfully sees such

images, 'of an idealizing, clarifying light, transparent even in its burnishing luminosity' (Fineman 1986: 68) as highly visual and referring to both the thing seen and the way of seeing.

19 This line is in some ways extremely typical as the poet attempts to remove the fair beloved from the marketplace of praise.

5

''Tis not the fashion to confess'
'Shakespeare–Post-coloniality–Johannesburg, 1996'
MARGO HENDRICKS

> For truths to become the basis of national policy and, more widely, of national life, they must be believed, and whether or not whatever new truths we take from the West *will* depend in large measure on how we are able to manage the relations between our conceptual heritage and the ideas that rush at us from worlds elsewhere.
>
> (Appiah 1992: 5)

Post-colonial confessions

Following four days of papers, conversations, debates and performances, 'Shakespeare–Post-coloniality–Johannesburg, 1996' concluded with an open forum. Participants were invited to offer their thoughts, critiques and ideas on the issues that had preoccupied the international gathering of cultural critics (many of whom were, in one way or another, involved in Shakespearean studies). The moment soon became what one participant termed 'the confessional' as people spoke eloquently, whether in praise or criticism, about the conference which was in the final stages of conclusion. Tensions had hovered, wraith-like, throughout much of the conference and, in the final hours of the conference, made their presence fully known as the varying cultural, political and ethnic points of reference surfaced; on a fundamental level, although not for the first time, the theory and praxis of 'post-coloniality' itself was subject to interrogation. Was it not indicative of the continued legacy and hegemony of colonialism that many of the speakers at this post-apartheid Shakespeare

conference in South Africa were not South Africans? Can expa-
triates from former colonies, now living in the metropolis or its
surrogate (England or the United States) speak for those who
remain in the former colonized spaces that marked the boundaries of the British Empire? Is it appropriate for black Americans
to express kinship with the black South African? Should there
even have been a conference on Shakespeare and post-coloniality,
given the uses to which Shakespeare's writings have been put
throughout the history of English/British imperialism? That these
issues came at the end of the conference is neither surprising
nor, importantly, problematic. In fact, it would have been deeply
troubling had the conference not ended on this note. What was
noteworthy was the role 'confession' or, more properly, 'testimony' played in the process, simultaneously heightening and
disrupting theoretical and cultural differences.

The 'confession,' as Michel Foucault reminds us, is 'one of the
main rituals [Western societies] rely on for the production of truth.
[In effect, confession] came to signify someone's acknowledgment
of his own actions and thoughts'(Foucault 1980a: 58). What this
acknowledgment entails, however, differs according to the political,
cultural, gender and ethnic dictates of subjectivity. Yet, as Foucault
understood, confession

> frees, but power reduces one to silence; truth does not belong to
> the order of power, but shares an original affinity with freedom:
> traditional themes in philosophy, which a 'political history of
> truth' would have to overturn by showing that truth is not by
> nature free – nor error servile – but that its production is thor-
> oughly imbued with relations of power. The confession is an
> example of this.
>
> (Ibid.: 60)

That my own contribution/confessional narrative to 'Shakespeare–Post-coloniality–Johannesburg, 1996', was figured as a reading of William Shakespeare's *Rape of Lucrece* and the significance of
Lucrece's 'confession' as a complex interpellation of racialization
is not without irony – a point to which I will return later in this
discussion. For now, however, I want to explore the argument that,
upon reflection, like the 'drive'/desire compelling Lucrece to 'pol-
iticize' Tarquin's rape of her body through confession (which leads
to suicide), any attempt to theorize and or come to terms with the
ideological assumptions compelling post-colonial theorization must

also comprehend the significance of confession as a 'ritual' deeply implicated in the identity politics which often constitutes the impulses of post-colonial theorizing.

The contention of this essay is that the confession functions simultaneously as a counter-hegemonic strategy for racial liberation and as a dangerous problematic in Shakespeare's *Rape of Lucrece*. My aim is twofold: first, as part of long-term attempt to destabilize traditional assumptions about 'race' in early modern English culture, I propose to read *The Rape of Lucrece* as a text constitutively implicated in the emergence of the modern notion of race. Race, as I have argued elsewhere, was neither stable nor transcendental in its signification; rather, the word and concept was quite variable in its semantics and semiotics (Hendricks 1992; 1996). Consequently, instead of beginning with the assumption that 'race' exists as an unchanging, transcendental category of social identity, one ought to begin with the supposition that, in each historical and cultural context, race is a newly minted coin whose terminus ad quem is always yet to be codified. Second, and largely in response to a recurring theme during the Johannesburg conference, I hope to illustrate the continuing necessity for post-colonial studies in relation to Shakespeare's canon: in particular, to call attention to those works that are not readily identifiable as works bearing colonialist ideologies. Ultimately, this essay seeks to advocate a recognition of the necessity of not only interrogation but also confession as theoretical strategies important to post-colonial theoretical interventions.

Lucrece's rape/race

In an informative study of the varied cultural (re)presentations of Lucretia's rape, Ian Donaldson traces the long history of artistic and literary treatments of the rape of Lucretia. Of particular note is his discussion of Titian's painting, which represents this most interesting icon of Western culture. In his 'reading' of Titian's work, Donaldson remarks that,

> despite the high color of her face, Lucrece is pale beside Tarquin's darker skin – a tonal contrast which possibly hints at the racial, as well as purely sexual, oppositions of the story: Lucrece is a Roman, Tarquin an Etruscan.

(Donaldson 1982: 13)

For Donaldson, this politicized commentary is intended to provide not only a semiotic register for comprehending Titian's painting but also a specifically modern ideological framework for understanding the significance of Lucrece's rape. Yet, having made this rather provocative statement, Donaldson immediately abandons it. In part, because he is dealing with painting, Donaldson can only draw attention to what is evident in Titian's painting. However, by invoking a specific 'historicity' to Lucrece's rape – the different ethnic backgrounds of Lucrece and Tarquin – Donaldson suggestively reminds his readers that there is, significantly, a dual cultural/historical context to the image before us: the colonized Roman and the colonizing Etruscan.

On one level, Donaldson's notation of the contrasting lightness and darkness of the two figures in Titian's painting evokes the tropic association of light and dark with good and evil and it is not difficult read Donaldson's observations as simply reiterating the type of fetishistic moralizing of color employed in so much early modern discourse concerned with gender relations, sexuality and Christianity. Add to this ideological mix the political idealization of Lucrece's rape as the genesis of Rome's rise to republicanism (and eventually imperial and colonial power), and Donaldson's analysis of Titian's painting bespeaks a familiar post-Enlightenment notion about 'race' based on skin color. Beyond this, Donaldson's remark on the color difference between Lucrece and Tarquin seems almost gratuitous (though his comments do have broader implications for inquiry into Donaldson's 'reading' Titian's reading of the Lucrece/Tarquin narrative). We might well ask: were there actual color differences between Romans and Etruscans? If so, did these color distinctions come into play in the political struggle between the ruling Tarquins and their subjects and, thus, were indelibly etched in the narratives recounting the struggle? Or, is the 'racial opposition' that Donaldson 'sees' an anachronistic reading of Titian's painting – an illusion brought on by the aging of paint pigmentation, for example, or Donaldson's own twentieth-century subjectivity seeking to substantiate color differences where there may have been none? Accustomed as we are to looking for 'familiar markers' (skin color, physical features, code words and so on), it is easy to arrive at the same conclusions as Donaldson.

What discoveries would Donaldson have made had he framed his inquiry with slightly different assumptions about what signified race in Renaissance and early modern visual representations and literary discourses? That is, if he had turned his gaze from one perspectival position to another, would the racial inscriptions be as readily (or as easily) 'readable'? Furthermore, may it not be argued that, when one turns from painting to literary works, the art of representing the racial identities of Lucrece and Tarquin may have a radically different complexity; a complexity not easily reducible to shades of coloring, i.e., 'paleness' and 'darkness'; that race is much more ambiguously rendered because it has not yet stabilized into one dominant signification? It is this mode of inquiry, I would contend, that must be brought to bear on readings of literary and visual 'encounters' with the narrative history of the rape of Lucretia.

William Shakespeare's literary 'encounter' with the narrative account of Tarquin's rape of Lucretia provides a useful exemplum for the complicated figuration of race that I am suggesting. Drawing upon the two major Roman texts recounting the story of Lucretia's rape (Livy's *History of Rome* and Ovid's *Fasti*), Shakespeare's narrative poem shows itself to be part of that process which Stephanie Jed describes when she remarks:

> every encounter with a representation of the rape of Lucretia is an encounter with a literary topos of Western civilization. And, as a *topos*, the meaning of this rape is constructed as universal, transcending historical conditions: in every age and place, Lucretia had to be raped so that Rome would be liberated from tyranny.

> (Jed 1989: 51)

What I would add, or state more categorically, is that Shakespeare's *The Rape of Lucrece* also reveals that every encounter is also an encounter with an ideology of race. What distinguishes Shakespeare's telling of the narrative from the texts that interest Jed is that republicanism is (I would argue) of less concern than the ideology of racial identity. Without ever once using the term 'race,' Shakespeare manages to invest his narrative rendering of Lucretia's rape with all of the semiotic traces of early modern anxiety about defining a concept of race.

It is my contention that Shakespeare's *The Rape of Lucrece* is an attempt to mediate the tensions (and contradictions) generated by competing discourses of race: race as defined by genealogy or lineage and race as defined by ethnicity. In this imprecision, as an expression of fundamental distinctions, race's meaning varied depending upon whether a writer wanted to specify difference born of a class-based concept of genealogy, a psychological (and essentialized) nature, or group typology. None the less, in all these variations, race is envisioned as something fundamental, something immutable, knowable and recognizable, yet we only 'see' it when its boundaries are violated. It is this 'seeing' that Shakespeare's narrative engenders in its rendering of Lucrece's confessional discourse.

In the aftermath of Tarquin's rape, Lucrece engages in an extraordinary lamentation for her lost virtue. Nicholas Abercrombie, Stephen Hill and Bryan S. Turner have argued that

> the insistence on chastity and virtue for wives as a condition for the economic strength of the feudal family was also closely connected with the ideology of chivalry. Since noble birth was a crucial feature of knighthood, only true-born sons would be brave and worthy of their families. ... Confusion of blood produced unreliable men.
>
> (Abercrombie, Hill and Turner 1980: 90)

Shifting between rage, self-pity, shame and despair, Lucrece simultaneously resists and acknowledges the interiority associated with guilt: ''O unseen shame, invisible disgrace! / O unfelt sore, crest-wounding private scar! / Reproach is stamped in Collatinus' face' (827–9). Unable completely to absolve herself of some degree of complicity, 'yet I am guilty of thy honour's wrack; / Yet for thy honour did I entertain him' (841–2), she embraces the role of both judge and executioner to expiate her 'crime' – even though she must rely on her husband, father and kin to punish Tarquin for his actions.

What is central to Lucrece's logic here is her awareness that unlawful sexuality, despite its initial invisibility, inevitably surfaces. What is noteworthy, however, is that when this surfacing occurs, it is described as marking both the body of Lucrece and that of her husband. This 'sign,' ideologically figured as the loss of honor, is linked to a fear not of the act itself but what the act threatens to produce – the illegitimate child. Where this inscription becomes visible, of course, is in the semiotics of genealogy, and more specifically, as Shakespeare depicts it, in the discourse of heraldry. For both Lucrece and Tarquin, heraldry is the place where a nobleman's lineage is figured; the images and shapes to be publicly noted (his shield) provide the metonymic site for revealing the effects of Tarquin's desire. In other words, Shakespeare uses heraldic language to mark the graduated shift from one form of racial thinking to another.

Tarquin's complicated self-reflexivity just prior to his rape of Lucrece marks the first half of this narrative strategy, exemplifying the logic of racial identity as a matter of genealogy. In a tense private moment, Tarquin confronts the 'public' dimension of his 'private' act: ''O shame to knighthood and to shining arms! / O foul dishonour to my household's grave!' (197–8). Tarquin is fully aware that should he carry out the rape, and should he die, the 'scandal will survive' as 'some loathsome dash the herald will contrive / To cipher me how fondly I did dote' (204–6). This concern for family honor will surface once more when Tarquin reflects on the fact that 'he [Collatinus] is my kinsman, my dear friend, / The shame and fault finds no excuse nor end' (237–8). Kinship or family should have been sufficient to prevent Tarquin from carrying out his rape, yet, as both his disputation and subsequently his words to Lucrece demonstrate, lust recognizes no lines of kinship.

Lucrece, in her disputation, also recognizes the significance of her rape as a matter of familial ties. As the reproductive site for the continuation of Collatine's line (race), Lucrece completely understands the immediate and future import of Tarquin's action (miscegenation and possibly a child). Her initial reaction is to vow that Collatine 'shalt not know the stained taste of violated troth'; that, in a noble gesture, she 'will not wrong [his] true affection so, / To flatter thee with an infringed oath' (1058–60). Of course, what Lucrece is alluding to is the threat of pregnancy that may ensue as a result of Tarquin's rape. Promising that Tarquin's 'bastard graff shall never come to growth,' that he 'shall not boast who did thy stock pollute / That thou are doting father of his fruit,' Lucrece concludes her 'disputation,' resolved to commit suicide. For Lucrece, suicide will not only serve to expiate the immediate shame created by Tarquin's rape but also will extirpate any potential offspring.

Though similarly employing the rhetoric of heraldry in confronting the full implications of Tarquin's crime; Lucrece, in her moment of confession, conjoins the two significations of race. However, I want to suggest that not until she 'interpellates' herself as a racial subject can Lucrece resolve the ideological dilemma created by Tarquin's rape. Louis Althusser offers the following explanation of interpellation:

> ideology 'acts' or 'functions' in such a way that it 'recruits' subjects among the individuals (it recruits them all), or 'transforms' the individuals into subjects (it transforms them all) by that very precise operation which I have called *interpellation* or hailing, and

which can be imagined along the lines of the most commonplace everyday police (or other) hailing: 'Hey, you there!'
(Althusser 1971: 174)

When the individual turns around, 'he becomes a *subject*. Why?
Because he has recognized that the hail was "really" addressed to
him, and that "it was *really him* who was hailed" (and not someone
else)' (ibid.).

The disputational mode deployed by Shakespeare in his narrative poem positions, intriguingly, Tarquin and Lucrece as subjects
capable of 'hailing' not only each other but themselves. For Lucrece,
'interpellation' occurs when she declares, "Let my good name, that
senseless reputation, / Collatine's dear love be kept unspotted' (820).
It is her name which enables her to act to expiate the 'unseen shame,'
the 'invisible disgrace,' that marks both her body and Collatine's as
a result of Tarquin's violation of racial lines. Lucrece's 'hailing,'
however, not only interpellates her, but also interpellates the readers of Shakespeare's narrative, effectively making them 'agents in
the reproduction of a violated body, a prod to prurience in a humanistic peep show,' from which the 'narrative of liberation' (Jed
1989: 49) and an ideology of race become simultaneously (re)inscribed
in history and, literally, on Lucrece's body, once 'white' now marked
by Tarquin's racializing 'stain.' It is against this 'stain' that the ekphrasis
on the destruction of Troy must be read. Searching for the face
where 'all distress is stelled' (1444), Lucrece finds solace in the painter's
'anatomized' depiction of Hecuba: 'In her the painter had anatomized / Time's ruin, beauty's wreck, and grim care's reign' (1450–1).
Hecuba's plight is the catalyst, the analogue, for Lucrece's own grief.
Furthermore, her identification with the women of Troy, I would
argue, also reminds the narrative's readers of another link between
Rome and Troy: the commonplace mythography that the descendants of the Trojan Aeneas found the city of Rome.

The ekphrasis serves to illuminate not so much a cultural
historiography but rather Lucrece's movement from one form of
racial consciousness (and thus subjectivity) to another. Thus, while
Lucrece condemns the presumed agent of Troy's fall, Helen – 'Show
me the strumpet that began this stir / That with my nails I may
tear'(1471–2) – Lucrece's condemnation is really directed at the
perpetrator of the heinous crime which directly concerns her, viz.
Tarquin. It is, I would argue, Tarquin that Lucrece has in mind
when she utters the words, 'for trespass of thine eye, / The sire, the

son, the dame, and daughter die' (1476–7). Yet none of this is evident when she asks

> Why should the private pleasure of some one
> Become the public plague of many moe?
> Let sin, alone committed, light alone
> Upon his head that hath transgressed so
>
> (1479–81)

Lucrece's words eventually will prove prophetic when, as a result of her suicide, Rome is plunged into civil war.

Though Lucrece has committed no sin, in her despair and shame she finds in the image of the chaos that is the fallen Troy the subjectivity she will need to castigate the racial possibility of Tarquin's 'bastard graff.' Drawing upon the emotions stirred by the painting of the fallen Troy, Lucrece moves from silence to speech: 'And now this pale swan in her wat'ry nest / Begins the sad dirge of her certain ending' (1611–12). In the presence of her husband and her kin, she performs her own eulogy, 'confessing' the narrative of Tarquin's rape, binding her husband and kin to redressing the wrong against her honor, 'castigating' the pollution created by Tarquin's desire. Like the ekphrasis on the destruction of Troy, Lucrece's 'confession' renders visible the invisible stain of her dishonor. Though assured that she is blameless, Lucrece refuses absolution, saying ' "No, no … no dame hereafter living / By my excuse shall claim excuse's giving" ' (1714–15). From a feminist perspective, Lucrece's words are deeply troubling; in effect, one hears the rape victim blaming herself for the rape.

This image is further instantiated when Lucrece sheaths 'in her harmless breast / A harmful knife, that thence her soul unsheathed' (1723–4). In her attempt to exorcize Tarquin's violation of her body, Lucrece takes her own life. Yet the use of the word 'sheath,' with its obvious erotic signification, subtly undermines the high tragedy of this suicide, shadowed by the image of Tarquin's 'gaze' which also rendered her breast a site of erotic desires. Lucrece's body, therefore, suffers penetration not once but twice. Once more involving the reader in a prurient gaze, Lucrece's self-inflicted wound is intended to purify, to 'tear' away, the flesh that bears not only disgrace but also the very real possibility that Tarquin's 'momentary joy' might breed 'months of pain' (690). Surrounded by her husband, father and kin, Lucrece elicits from these men a vow to revenge her violated body. What Lucrece's demand entails is more than familial revenge, however; the vow the men make binds them as a 'gens' or 'ethnos' against Tarquin. Her confession heard and her shame absolved by the men who stand before her, Lucrece's body becomes the site where the meaning of race and racial identity shifts.

The poem's audience would have been quite familiar with the ethnic mythology signified in the ekphrasis and linked to the final image of the narrative where Lucrece's body is 'paraded' through Rome as a testament to the tyranny of Tarquin. Rome's heritage (genealogy) was understood to have its very genesis in the fallen city of Troy; Aeneas, escaping the destruction of Troy, made his way to Italy where his descendants and those of other Trojans eventually found the city of Rome. Furthermore, though recognized as historically inaccurate even among early modern English historiographers, the mythography of Aeneas' descendant Brutus as progenitor of England's people proved a useful trope for the legitimization of incipient imperialist and colonialist endeavors. In essence, Shakespeare's narrative reproduction and (re)presentation of the Lucretia myth gives life to a new ideology of race; an ideology which defines itself not only in terms of lineage but also in terms of ethnicity. This sixteenth-century encounter with the political and ideological semiotics associated with the rape of Lucrece denotes, in a striking and persistent articulation, the necessary engendering of one's ethnicity through violence against the colonized (and generally female) body. What emerges in the aftermath of Lucrece's suicide is the embodiment of the Roman Republic and unified ethnos, and ultimately the Roman Empire, even as that suicide enacts the deracination of Tarquin's own lineage; what emerges in Shakespeare's retelling of the rape and suicide of Lucrece is the continued necessity to retell the rape to maintain the boundaries of that racial ideology. English imperialism required such a narrative.

Lucrece's rape revisited, 1997

For nearly a thousand years, the Roman Republic has provided the foundational ideology for Western political institutions; and, as Jed's study (Jed 1989) illuminates, the rape of Lucrece sits at the apex of this ideology, even though the politics of republicanism has rendered this presence virtually invisible. What Jed sought to do in her engagement with the narrative was to shift the perspectival position of readers/viewers of Lucrece's rape, so that Lucrece's violated and mutilated body no longer lies on the margins of republican idealism but is the territory upon which that idealism (and Tarquin's rape) is inscribed and continuously rehearsed every time the narrative is retold. Shakespeare's narrative participates in this rehearsal even as it works, I would argue, to conjoin the mythography of Lucrece's rape to a newly emerging ethnos. In subtle ways, the myth comes to serve a didactic purpose in the formation of English nationalism and, markedly, imperialism. Along with the other texts of Shakespeare's canon, *The Rape of Lucrece* performs in both theory and in practice the colonialist impulses that continue to haunt those spaces, cultures and peoples once subject to British rule.

As Jed so astutely demonstrates in her study, every reading, rewriting, and scholarly or critical engagement with the narrative of Lucretia's rape continues the transmission of ideologies central to the development of modern social institutions, and, I would add, modern imperialism as part of the topos of constituting 'civilized man.' Shakespeare's *The Rape of Lucrece*, like the other texts that form his 'canon,' though not necessarily one of the more celebrated works, circulates as part of the cultural hegemony extant in nineteenth-century English imperialism and remains, even today, one of the most pervasive artifacts left in the wake of English colonialism. We might well ponder whether the narrative informed the social consciousness of indigenous women (and men) in their struggles for liberation: did acculturated women see Lucrece's suicide as an exemplary model of resistance to English hegemony? Was the female body literally or figuratively (i.e., as the idealized mother country or female territory) raped and/or sacrificed as part of the struggle for liberation? How did indigenous, Western-educated ('subaltern') women 'read' Lucrece's rape? Did Lucrece's rape and 'confession' become unsettled in the modern colonialist project? Are there post-colonial rewritings of this master narrative of female chastity and sacrifice that challenge not only the humanistic ideology that has kept it in circulation but also the imperialist ideology that requires its continual circulation? Does the distinction between private and public blur the fact that Lucrece's body is a confessional political body?

From the margins

Shakespeare's *The Rape of Lucrece* implicitly links the Roman Lucretia to early modern England's conceptualization of its participation in the humanist project, which in turn becomes a central tenet of modern imperialism and colonialism. Recognition of this, and the syncretic ways this tenet continues to require interrogation, must become part of post-colonial theorizing. The icon of Lucretia serves not just as a strategy of acculturation and assimilation; it equally functions to create a false relationship between self-sacrifice and femininity, politics and ethnicity, rape and progress. Interrogating this and other Shakespearean texts not on Western terms but on those of indigenous cultures' resistance to British hegemony, using these texts as sites of 'cultural intercourse' (Lionnet 1995: 115), using the text to 'write back' to the 'margins,' may be one of the possible and potentially radical strategies available to post-colonialist critics.

Perhaps similar to Lucrece's presence before the males of her family, my presence in South Africa was both a personal and public expression of historical kinship with black South Africans. Yet at the same time, I realize, ironically, that any invocation of the idea of kinship is at best symbolic, in as much as the material and cultural conditions of existence of the black Americans present at the conference were, in all likelihood, fundamentally different. Such are the dialectics of post-coloniality.

In what might be loosely termed 'border theorizing,' post-colonial critics and theorists have isolated a conceptual space where, as Françoise Lionnet argues,

> all of our academic preconceptions about cultural, linguistic, or stylistic norms are constantly being put to the test by creative practices that make visible and set off the processes of adaptation, appropriation, and contestation that govern the construction of identity in colonial and postcolonial contexts.
>
> (Lionnet 1995: 111)

Lionnet's observation, while made in reference to Francophone women writers, has a bearing on the issues that concern this essay. Asked to explore the role of post-colonial theories in the 'business' of Shakespearean studies, the participants of 'Shakespeare–Post-coloniality–Johannesburg, 1996' found themselves 'tested' by not only their perceptions of Shakespeare's creative practices but also by the dilemma of continuing the valorization of Shakespeare. At the center of the discussions, debates and testing was the very real understanding of the uses to which Shakespeare and his writings have been put in colonized spaces. For some, Shakespeare became just another 'white' space, a point of reference on the continuum of producing the civilized native. The confessional moment which marked the final day of the conference, then, not only brought to the surface the narrative of the cultural struggles taking shape in South Africa, it also highlighted that the discourses and politics of post-coloniality have forever altered the ways in which Shakespeare's writings can be engaged.

By way of closure, I want to (re)present one last encounter. In an odd way, the moment was replete with the materiality of post-colonialism: a dozen or so individuals who had journeyed to Johannesburg, South Africa, for a conference on Shakespeare and post-coloniality and who either lived or were born in nation-states designated as 'post-colonial' spaces (India, New Zealand, Canada) or in the metropolis which engendered these spaces, packed in a Toyota van, hurtling away from Johannesburg and towards the black township known as Soweto. Only the driver and the student guide were native to South Africa. As the van moved inexorably toward the icon that had come to symbolize the protracted struggle of black South Africans and their white allies to dismantle the institutions of apartheid, a strange sense of familiarity floated fleetingly to my consciousness, not quite *déjà vu* yet not entirely foreign. The sensation passed as quickly as it came and, like the others in the van, I studied the arid, desert-like landscape between the two cities.

A few months after my return to the United States, I visited my birthplace of Riverside, California: a city of nearly 300,000 people located on the periphery of the largest desert in the United States and approximately 45 minutes from Los Angeles. As the car I drove reached the crest of a small hill and began its descent, images of the topography which divided Johannesburg and Soweto played in my mind, bringing with them memories of the conversations and debates that framed 'Shakespeare–Post-coloniality–Johannesburg, 1996.' The most interesting conversation occured between Wonderboy Peters and myself not long after I had delivered my paper, when he spoke about his curiosity as to the term *mestizaje*; a concept I used in reference to a discussion of Shakespeare's comedy *A Midsummer Night's Dream*. I explained that *mestizaje*, according to the *Diccionario de Uso del Español*, is defined as the '*cruzamiento de razas*,' (literally, cross-breeding of races) or the '*conjunto de mestizos*' (group of mestizos) and related to the verb *mestizar*, which is defined as '*adulterar la puerza de una raza por el cruce con otras*' (adulterating the purity of one race by mixing with others) (Molner 1984). Intrigued by my deployment of the notion of the Spanish term *mestizaje* as a post-colonial critique of early modern discourses of race, Wonderboy spoke of his own *mestizaje*, his status as a colored in South Africa (he is the son of a white father and a black mother) and the politics that inform such subjectivity in both the old and new South Africa. Neither white nor black yet both, Wonderboy considered the idea of thinking through the concept of race in terms of an idea of *mestizaje* as an epistemological, political and theoretical framework, one tied neither to a specific nation-state nor to a linguistic community, a useful theoretical tool. The irony of observing this appropriation of a Spanish word, initially used to frame a critical reading of two Shakespearean texts, one of which was the retelling of an ancient Roman narrative, to come to terms with one's subjectivity in post-apartheid Johannesburg, was not lost on me. On the contrary, if asked to locate an 'appropriate' site for such a deployment, I could not have chosen better. This essay, then, is dedicated to him and the other students who occupied both the center and the margins of 'Shakespeare–Post-coloniality–Johannesburg, 1996.'

6

Nation and place in Shakespeare
The case of Jerusalem as a national desire in early modern English drama

AVRAHAM OZ

Among Shakespearean spokespersons the Chorus of *Henry V* is the shrewd theatrical geographer *par excellence*, ever alert to the inevitable elasticity whereby our wooden O clings to a spatial dimension, from its very own cockpit through immediate London, pouring out her citizens, and on to the farthest fields of France. Yet even he refers exclusively to the real territories to which the narrative frameworks of Shakespeare's histories (a project he is almost in a position to sum up) may stretch the imagination of their audience. He never mentions the loci reached through metaphor or free association, let alone alluding (as Cassius and Brutus are to do after their own fashion) to the measure between the represented presence of 'Pompey's basis' and the virtual one of states unborn. It is that virtual dimension, hovering between geography and ideology, that provides an ideological foundation for the manipulative use of the concept of 'nation' in early modern drama.

A 1996 production of *The Comedy of Errors* in Tel Aviv, representing Shakespearean Ephesus in the shape of a Beirut-like harbor city, turns the geographic location into an ideological comment: in the political/ethnic/religious whirlpool which has got out of hand, nobody figures any more who fights whom. Thus the focus on a charged location informing the consciousness of a specific target-audience turns the conventional game of errors, however mildly, into a political statement resolving in a message of political, rather than solely domestic, peace. An imaginary line drawing on geographic location thus connects the Shakespearean 'basis,' containing the eastern Mediterranean locus, to a state already born, whose delineation in geopolitical terms provides a fresh ideological reading of the text. There exists, however, a more solid point of intersection between two given national narratives – more solid, since it involves material existence (or sometimes absence, for that matter) rooted in place and time, which affects cultural transformations and collective memories both on the 'basis' level and in the target cultural framework. This latter point of attachment manifests itself when one bears in mind that the immediate locus of the later of the two analogous national projects appropriates an ideological space indirectly shared with the collective memory of the earlier one. The obvious products may be the complex meaning affecting the reading of an *Othello* watched by a black community, or the reading of *The Merchant of Venice* as experienced by a Jewish community. But there are subtler cases too, like the one alluded to by Henry IV's call on his subjects to commence 'new broils … in stronds afar remote' (*1 Henry IV*, V. i. 5).[1] It is a juncture sanctified by a narrative well rooted in both 'basis' and target national discourses, in which various degrees of materially geographic presences conveniently intervene with symbolic meaning.

I

In Arnold Wesker's words, I am talking about Jerusalem. Benedict Anderson's distinction between the emergence of Zionism and the birth of Israel in that 'the former marks the reimagining of an ancient religious community as a nation … while the latter charts an alchemic change from wandering devotee to local patriot' (Anderson 1991: 149) embodies two inaccuracies: first, faithful to his contention that nationalism is exclusively a modern phenomenon, he fails to recognize national features in the pre-Zionist Jewish community; and second, he fails to stress the strong element of local patriotism inherent in the very idea of Zionism. A major feature that the Zionist project appropriated from earlier Messianic movements in Jewish history is the centrality of its territorial claim on the biblical locus informing the Jewish national myth. All those forerunning movements were doomed to failure partly because they were historically premature, but partly because of their lack of a pragmatically material appropriation of the mythical locus in which their dreamed reality was planted to counterbalance their Utopian mysticism.

From its inception, the historical narrative inherent in Zionism constituted the collective memory in regarding three phases in the romance-like national biography of the Jewish people: *the ancient period*, stretching from the biblical version of its myth of origin and emigration into its sacred territory to the abortive rebellions against the Romans ending with the fall of Jerusalem; *the long exile period* in which the Jewish people retain their national identity even in the Diaspora; and, finally, *the return to Zion*, a dream of centuries materializing since the late nineteenth century. Territory plays a dominant role in that conception of nationhood, as an answer to assaults on Jewish nationality both by foreign enemies (e.g. aggressive anti-semitism) and internal factors (the yearning for assimilation, conceived as self-denial as a separate nation). The secularization of Zion (i.e. Jerusalem) conceded to Zionist thinking from its very inception by the late nineteenth-century Enlightenment and by the modern European idea of nationalism, brings evenly together myth and history, and national ideology and political pragmatism. Naming the entire nationalist movement of the Jewish people after one particular locus, albeit embued with that highly symbolic value it had always held, inevitably exposed the abstract potency inherent in the symbol to ongoing processes of social and political dynamics.

On some levels, the biblical sacredness of Jerusalem which informed the Christian collective memory, provided political ideology in the Middle Ages with a comparable ideological tool, whereby material distantiation could paradoxically disalienate a local national narrative, rendering to a convenient extent the heavenly Jerusalem of the New Testament (e.g. Revelation 21: 2, 10) real. The destruction of the earthly city in AD 70 was regarded by Christianity as the fulfillment of Jesus's prophecy predicting the destruction of the Temple. In this the Christian view read probably correctly the Roman intention in destroying the major shrines of Jewish culture: the territorial locus of faith thus loses its validity. 'Thus saith the Lord, the heaven is my throne, and the earth is my footstool'; Isaiah is cited in the letter attributed to Barnabas from the second century: 'Where is the house that ye build unto me? and where is the place of my rest?' The bishops of Nicea accorded the city of Jerusalem, a provincial town within the Roman political system, a special spiritual stature, which was given a political emphasis by the convenor of Nicea, the converter of the

Roman Empire to Christianity, Emperor Constantine, who marked the site of Jesus's sepulcher by building above it the *Anastasis* ('Resurrection') shrine: 'So on the monument of salvation itself was the new Jerusalem built,' says Eusebius (*Life of Constantine*, III, 33; see Peters 1985: 136).

Christian pilgrims in the fourth century regarded Jerusalem as Christian in spirit, and conceived the failure of the anti-Christian Emperor Julian's project of restoring the Temple mount a divine intervention designed to prevent the falsification of Christ's prophecies. The proclamation in 451 of the Bishop of Rome, Leo I, as the successor of Peter, established the papacy in Rome in imitation of the high priesthood of the Temple in Jerusalem, a migration read allegorically into Virgil's *Aeneid*, where the travel of Aeneas (suggesting St Peter) from Troy to Rome portended the transfer of the Holy City from Jerusalem to the seat of the papacy.

After the Muslim conquest of Jerusalem in 638, special attention was paid to constituting the city, especially the Temple mount, as a religious center, with the al-Aqsa mosque and the Dome of the Rock erected as the major shrines of worship. Christianity regarded the fall of Jerusalem as a chastisement for falling short of the Christian ideal. Architecturally, however, the Muslim shrines begin to affect Christian ones: what starts with the influence of the Dome of the Rock on the shape of the Church of the Ascension on the Mount of Olives, will later affect church building in Europe, when the Crusaders will mingle the view of the earthly city with the allegorical images of the heavenly Jerusalem. The interest of European Christianity in Jerusalem gains significant momentum with Charlemagne and his son, Louis the Pious, who prescribed an annual tax for the maintenance of the Christian holy places in Jerusalem. The ninth-century Muslim writer AlJahit testifies that the Muslim society appreciated the Christians more than the Jews and the Persians, since the former were supposed to be the subjects of an emperor reigning outside the borders of the Muslim kingdom: national government was a God-given gift to what otherwise would have been considered merely a religious group.

This kind of attachment of the Christian contingency in Jerusalem to the West is typical of the basic conception leading in the late eleventh century to the Crusades, emanating from ideological developments in medieval Europe. Indeed, there is much evidence regarding the persecution of Christians in Muslim Jerusalem: news was spread about pilgrims having been robbed and arrested, and the Church of the Holy Sepulcher was razed ninety years before the First Crusade reached the city. And yet the proclamation of the First Crusade had to do with European religious and secular politics rather than being a mere rescue operation. The convenient conditions developing in the Middle East were matched by the polarization of social discrepancies in feudal Western Europe: the Crusades, proclaimed ideologically as religious enterprises, concealed economic and social motives. Above all, perhaps, the sacred image of Jerusalem served the Church as a tool to exert ideological unity on its European flock, otherwise scattered and divided between conflicting national, economic and class identities.

Though left aside by the initial wave of the crusading zeal, a similar motivation may have applied to the policies of the English throne, which had attempted since the Norman Conquest to foster a national identity in order to separate territorial feudalism from the political sphere. For the inhabitants of that sea-walled garden, detached in many ways from direct Mediterranean interests, Jerusalem could hardly incite the common imagination as a target point of territorial expansion. Thus any involvement of England in the actual crusading project was indirect and sporadic: as in William Rufus's financing, as a settlement of feudal conflict, of the crusading enterprise of his brother the Duke of Normandy; or as in the short participation in the First Crusade of Stephen of Blois, who was to regard England as a piece of territorial inheritance; or as in the individualistic undertaking of Richard Coeur-de-Lion to join the Third Crusade.

With the years, especially since the crusaders' loss of the Holy Land, material Jerusalem stopped playing a significant role in the crusading enterprise. As a shelter for Christian malefactors who had to run away from England or the rest of Europe to save their skins (as Burchard of Mount Sion describes it in 1280), it stood no chance of attracting further large-scale collective undertakings on behalf of later English rulers. The crusading activity might then be seen to dissociate itself from material Jerusalem and confine itself to Europe (see, for example, Housley 1992). Whereas Christopher Columbus may have still urged his sovereigns (as he writes in his diary at the end of 1492) to spend all the profits of his enterprise 'on the conquest of Jerusalem,' the laughter of his sovereigns at his suggestion, saying 'that it would please them and that even without this profit they had that desire,' hardly betrays a serious undertaking. Rather, Stephen Greenblatt tells us in the name of Alain Milhou and other historians:

while the references in Columbus to the rebuilding of the 'arx Sion' and the restoration of the 'Casa Santa' may be meant literally, this literal sense, in the context of Columbus's Joachite Messianism, may serve as a metonymic reference to Christian holy places far from Jerusalem.

(Greenblatt 1991: 165)

From the fourteenth to the sixteenth centuries, Milhou observes, 'millenarian movements frequently translated the struggle to retake Jerusalem into a national campaign against the enemies of the people: the crusading rhetoric was adapted for very different social ends' (ibid.: 158). This new attitude toward the crusading activity made the enterprise more accessible for the English kings, who wished to wage 'holy' wars against the opponents of the Angevin dynasty. Backed by their papal ally, those champions of Plantagenet rule 'sought to sanctify their respective causes and came to harness the sentiment, vocabulary, and symbols of crusade.' Moreover, contemporary observers have noted 'that the royal cause was indeed sublimated as a crusade,' using (in Powicke's words) the 'prestige' of a crusade, with those having taken the crusader's vow for the Fifth Crusade being absolved from the duty of fulfillment as long as they fought for Henry (Lloyd 1985: 113). A similar case applies to the ventures of the historic Henry Bolingbroke, the Earl of Derby, whose two expeditions of 1390–1 and 1392 took him up to Prussia, with Danzig and Vilnius substituting Jerusalem as an ideological goal. It is doubtful what part devotion played in such enterprises. The national churches in both England and France characterized battles waged largely for national supremacy (such as the Anglo-French war) in terms not incompatible with those used earlier for the crusading enterprise.

When reflected in Shakespeare's histories, then, such particular ventures into geography have come a long way since Stephen of Blois participated in the conquest of Jerusalem, or even since the time of Richard I, who never actually saw Jerusalem, but gained pilgrimage rights to it at the negotiation table in Jaffa. Earthly Jerusalem, now under Mamluk rule and inhabited by a small minority of Roman Catholics, was irrelevant to any Christian military enterprise, but continued to be visited sporadically by a few Latin pilgrims. A report by an anonymous English traveler to Jerusalem in the mid-fourteenth century regarded the Muslim domination as a constant situation and betrayed no hope for an imminent crusading project (Hoade 1948: 65–70). Related in Shakespeare to Bolingbroke, now Henry IV, the crusade experience, still officially proclaimed under the pretext of liberating Jerusalem and the Holy Sepulcher, is appropriated into manipulative use by English hegemonic ideology, having much to do with the growing interest in the concept of nation in its particular English mold, for the promotion of which even the obsolete battle for Jerusalem was revived and ideologically recruited.

II

The myth of the nation, in general, is based on continuity: in preserving the constancy of a human collective, it shuns new beginnings, for innovation calls for Utopianism or eccentricity (see Said 1975: 32) rather than that kind of self-assurance depending on widely accepted norms, well-trodden paths of common experience, and lasting patterns of ritual and collective behavior. 'Going to Jerusalem' as both material act and symbolic gesture combined, and involving temporary travel or constant migration, serves Jewish, Christian and Islamic 'imagined communities' (Benedict Anderson's telling phrase stresses the inherent vagueness of the shared attributes implied by any concept of 'nation') as an integrative ritual supported by pragmatic consequence. Whereas literary moves of communal migration typical of pastoral literature are exclusively Utopian, the tangible sense of personal commitment informing communal myths such as the Jewish 'return to Zion,' the Christian Crusade, or the Islamic Jihad, consolidate ritual constancy by involving locus with action and enunciating that '*locality* of culture' which, for Homi Bhabha, 'is more *around* temporality than *about* historicity' (Bhabha 1990: 292). Its inevitable dependence on travel and migration serves, under any circumstance of nationness, to break with an alienating sense of exile (whether from or in the sanctified territorial center informing the particular myth of the 'nation') and to celebrate a material and symbolic sense of naturalization. The complementary presence of both material and symbolic levels is crucial here: the myth of nation is about material ownership no less than about self-transformation and communal cohesion.

European invasions of the Holy Land from the eleventh to the thirteenth centuries, which on the level of material commodity gained the Italian city-states Mediterranean maritime routes, later adorned the titulature of the House of Habsburg, which assigned a special significance to the King of Austria's being 'King of Jerusalem,' or the old Duke Reiner of Anjou, Queen Margaret's father, 'writyng hymself,' as Hall reminds us, 'kyng of Naples, Scicile, and Jerusalem' (Hall 1548: 194), or, closer to Shakespeare's time, Queen Mary, who, jointly with King Philip of Spain, styled themselves 'by the grace of God kyng and quene of England, Franse, Napuls, Jerusalem,' etc. (see Machyn 1848: 34). Toward the end of *1 Henry VI*, Suffolk brings up Margaret's father's title as 'The King of Naples and Jerusalem' as a crucial argument in favor of her becoming Queen of England (V. v. 40; and cf. *2 Henry VI*, I. i. 48), a 'type' clearly devoid of any material substance, as the tortured York will not forget to mention derogatorily when spiting his tormentress:

> Thy father bears the type of King of Naples,
> Of both the Sicils, and Jerusalem,
> Yet not so wealthy as an English yeoman.
>
> > (*3 Henry VI*, I. iv. 121–23)[1]

For Margaret herself, however, that part of her father's title is far from an object of derision, nor is it an empty signifier. Charging the type with its inherent symbolic significance, she conjures at her final defeat 'the holy city, new Jerusalem, coming down from God out of heaven, prepared as a bride adorned for her husband' (Revelation, 21: 2), thus commanding her inherited title to appropriate a transcendent resort to which she, more than the rest of Christianity, is privileged both by divine and secular right:

> So part we sadly in this troublous world,
> To meet with joy in sweet Jerusalem.
>
> > (*3 Henry VI*, V. v. 7–8)

Bereft of all her worldly powers and wealth, Margaret may still cling to the one asset left of her initial dowry: the symbolic standing she claims on a heavenly city through an earthly title.

The identification with scriptural models in the English Renaissance informs not only dramatic texts, from early humanist ones, still affected by the tradition of the Corpus Christi plays to Jacobean plays such as Elizabeth Cary's *The Tragedy of Mariam*, but also many contemporary voyage narratives. It is the sense of material travel such texts exert which appropriates signifiers from the realm of rhetoric to the ideological context of collective rituals. The actual sensation of touching a myth, such as seeing the spots of the Virgin's milk upon the stones of Bethlehem or the step of Jesus's left foot on the Mount of Olives, as John Mandeville testifies to have done, or merely the feeling which tourists in Israel today often vouch for when encountering place-names like Jerusalem, Cesarea or Nazareth on roadsigns, may provide for national cohesion in any 'imagined community' partaking in that myth. This will occur when such a symbolic touch is replaced by a sense of material possession, when owning a myth is translated into a collective property and added to some collective repository of both material and cultural treasure, supported by an appropriate narrative. The possibility for such a move to partake in the constitution of a national myth was enhanced in the sixteenth century, when the discovery of non-European cultures was accommodated within the European experience in Utopian writing. On another level of collective consciousness, a complex sense of nationality may be constructed on multiple narratives complementing one another not solely on the symbolic level but also on material grounds. Such a multiplicity of narratives constitutive of one, more or less integrated national myth may be found in both early modern England and modern Israel.

It is in such a vein that the notion of a holy land (as symbolically represented by The Holy Land) figures as a notable presence behind the dynastic procedures and the national consolidation accounted for in Shakespeare's history plays, written in an era in which 'England's past became an issue in England's present to a degree unknown elsewhere in early modern Christendom' (Cressy 1994: 61). It may be significant that the ascent of the Tudor dynasty to the English throne almost exactly coincides with the printing of the first realistic map of Jerusalem (by Bernard von Breydenbach, Maintz, 1486). This a departure from that Jerusalem which for Sir John Mandeville had been 'the center of a symmetrically distributed set of continents, a center whose perfect mid-point are the sacred rocks' (Greenblatt 1991: 42), and which until then had commonly been conceived as placed by the Lord 'in the midst of the peoples and the circuit of her lands.' Henry VII, who professed at his ascent to lead a crusade, did not manage to collect at court more than eleven guineas for that noble cause, but the symbolic value of such a venerable gesture must still have been considered viable.

Shakespeare, careful not to embarrass his queen with awkward details from the reign of the first Tudor monarch, nevertheless made use of an analogous royal gesture in writing about an earlier English king: besides the various occasional allusions connecting English history to biblical themes, such a notion is manifestly deployed when

1 Henry IV opens with a royal ceremony in which an act of the Crown's interest is presented as a national issue allegedly comprising religious and national concerns – in this case serving the typical Lancastrian policy of aggressive nationalism (more commonly directed against neighboring France). Urged, as later he admits by internal pressures caused by the 'giddy minds' of his aristocratic peers, King Henry proclaims his pious intention to sacrifice lately and precariously achieved peace at home to wage a sacred war 'in stronds afar remote.' His chosen strand, however, is not fortuitous. When Sidney 'urges national renewal through poetry' in quest for military enterprise, Edward Berry reminds us, his desire 'is less an expression of disinterested nationalism than of class solidarity,' pertaining to 'the crisis of the aristocracy' (Newey and Thompson 1991: 2). For such an exclusively aristocratic, elitist brand of nationalism (inspired by the international pressures on England in the political atmosphere of the 1580s) any war anywhere will do. But for Henry to gather his vassals of all ranks under the banner of a common cause at a time of no immediate danger to the Crown, such a project can hardly fall short of launching a spectacular crusade in the Holy Land, an illustrious pageant whereby a universal Christian cause will turn into national enterprise:

> A power of English shall we levy,
> Whose arms were moulded in their mothers' womb
> To chase these pagans in those holy fields
> Over whose acres walk'd those blessed feet
> Which fourteen hundred years ago were nail'd
> For our advantage on the bitter cross.
>
> (*1 Henry IV*, I. i. 20–7)

Contrary to the assumption by Anderson and others, who argue that unifying forms of collective identification in the early modern era originated in narrower (civic) or larger (religious) communities, Henry's stress on 'a power of English' here suggests a manipulative use of a Christian cause to strengthen national cohesion. Obviously, pertaining to a great extent to what for Anderson is 'dynastic identity,' and for Anthony Smith a 'possessive state,' this creation of a combined Christian and national discourse (containing what in Mandeville's accounts is 'a blend of estrangement and familiarity') betrays Henry's shaky claim to the Crown, and hence to the 'pure' prerogative of symbolic representation of national interests. Such a claim requires reinforced validity by an ideologically sound, harmonious image of cohesion, a heroically transcendental narrative whereby the English powers are devoutly ordained to remedy the predicament suffered by the Christian universe at the hands of the heretic other. This trope, combining universal and local concerns, forms a speech-act exemplifying national myth in the making. Henry's invocation of a supreme mission in which his subjects may join him as an integrated nation is primarily designed to initiate a new national entity; and it is done in the biblical spirit of the Genesis prophecy, as later transported by Cranmer to account for the sacred vocation of the English Crown to 'make new nations.'

Thus nation in the making in early modern drama often turns out to be a product of a manipulative gesture, a 'calculated use of national memory' (Cressy 1994: 61), initiated by a hegemonic party whose political or cultural interests such an act is designed to protect. This propagated ideological unity is presented as a social ritual which (as Mary Douglas tells us) creates a reality which would be nothing without its symbolic constituents. Henry's Holy Land is an ideological construct cleverly disguised as a symbolically charged locus. When his intentions are frustrated by the sudden intervention of a genuine, unforged external reality in the shape of acute news from Wales and the north, Henry 'must neglect [his] holy purpose to Jerusalem.' Ironically, the destiny he prophetically wished to forge for his nation as a whole in the shape of a social ritual is eventually to play a personal trick on him in his death by way of the age-old 'Jerusalem chamber' prophecy, itself adopted from a general Christian source to serve as an English national myth.

That little personal ritual set by the king for his own death retains the symbolic meaning of Jerusalem for Shakespeare's audience, ranging from an accessible locus to a transcendental concept. A universally revered symbol, Jerusalem may equally stand pejoratively for London, when William Proctor preaches against the latter's iniquity, or positively for Virginia, when William Crashaw sets it as an ideal model for the builders of that New World colony; or, better still, as in Donne, it may be at once sanctified and the bosom sister of Sodome since Babylon, 'that Church of Confusion' may nevertheless be our sister too. Seeing themselves as the heirs of ancient Israel, English Protestant preachers of early modern England adopted Jerusalem as their symbolic capital. Shakespeare's Henry hits, then, a palpable point in the English collective memory. As has often been noted, Henry's announcement of his intended crusade echoes and challenges John of Gaunt's prophecy of despair in *Richard II*, in which he expresses his loss of faith in the English power's ability to redeem any longer both Christianity and chivalry, and where Jerusalem and the Holy Land figure as the very images of its national impotence:

> This royal throne of kings, this scepter'd isle,
> This earth of majesty, this seat of Mars,
> This other Eden, demi-paradise,
> This fortress built by Nature for herself
> Against infection and the hand of war,
> This happy breed of men, this little world,
> This precious stone set in the silver sea,
> Which serves it in the office of a wall,
> Or as a moat defensive to a house,
> Against the envy of less happier lands,
> This blessed plot, this earth, this realm, this England,
> This nurse, this teeming womb of royal kings,
> Fear'd by their breed and famous by their birth,
> Renowned for their deeds as far from home,
> For Christian service and true chivalry,
> As is the sepulchre in stubborn Jewry,
> Of the world's ransom, blessed Mary's Son,
> This land of such dear souls, this dear dear land,
> Dear for her reputation through the world,
> Is now leased out, I die pronouncing it,
> *(Richard II*, II. i. 40–59)

The multiple reference to England as a throne, an Earth, a seat of gods, a demi-paradise, a breed, a little world, a blessed plot, a realm or a womb, deliberately mixes locus with concept, a device 'built by Nature' with a 'breed of men.' Yet the dizzy dance of the signifier between that host of signified meanings in Gaunt's speech never departs from viewing England as 'built by nature.' The many facets of that harmony, the loss of which the speech laments, are solidly rooted in some nostalgic normative order. There exists in the passage, however, one exception to that order, that stands out verbally as well as geographically and ideologically. The sepulcher of Christ is placed 'in stubborn Jewry' – an awkward phrase, for 'Jewry' suddenly accrues an irregularly added meaning of communality on top of its inherent sense of locality suggested by the syntactic logic of the sentence. It is primarily to this added meaning that stubbornness is imported as a qualifying attribute.

This community of 'stubborn Jewry' is far from being 'a breed of men' constituted by Nature. It represents a deliberately chosen moral orientation, devised and shared by a collective of people whose unifying parameters as a group are at best complex: religion seems to be the obvious suggestion, but then the sentence directs the mind to a territorial attribute, another concept often associated with national identity. But what reality figures beyond that territory? Is it that obscure 'country' which, according to Jessica, rather enigmatically unites Shylock with Tubal and Chus? Presumably not (Chus, here cited as a person's name, is the biblical Hebrew word for the land of Ethiopia): no territorial definition of nationality would possibly apply here. As opposed to Marx's reference to the 'chimerical nationality' of Judaism as 'the nationality of the merchant, of man of money in general,' which may be read as a sociological or theological one, the reference to a Jew as a 'countryman' is purely symbolic, implying absence rather than identity. Since Jews reached Europe through expulsion and through a process of gradual dispersion rather than through conquest, colonization or mass migration, they could possess no economic positions that depended on hegemonic power or expropriation of lands:

> I must confess we come not to be kings:
> That's not our fault: alas, our number's few,
> And crowns come either by succession,
> Or urg'd by force.
>
> (*The Jew of Malta*, I. i. 127–30)

Even where the Jews could be in possession of lands, such as in Barabas's island, whose circumstances Marlowe appears to have studied carefully, they often preferred to deal in landed property as a method of making money, to avoid the taint of plain usury (Wettinger 1985: 40). With the continuing practice of the expulsion of Jews, widespread in Western Europe throughout the fifteenth century, such a prospect becomes a considerable factor in the Jewish investment policy. The lack of lasting property meant a temporary status of citizenship and a perpetual state of alienation. Othello the Moor is theoretically free to join his fellow countrymen in the realm of the Prince of Morocco; Portia's suitors are identified by their countries; there is a clear division, at the outset, between the Venetians and the residents of Belmont; Launcelot Gobbo defines himself as an Italian, and his father, who owns a horse and brings a dish of doves as a present, must own a plot of land in the country. Even 'a poor Turk of tenpence' such as Ithamore would season his fantasy of marrying the courtesan with the vision of settling in 'a country,' namely Greece. Whereas all the others may thus be referred to by local habitation or country of origin, the Jew may cite a list of places he visited for a purpose, or at best be related to his latest country of temporary residence, where, like in Venice, he was residing in 'hell.' Not even the ancient locus of Jewish desire will do: 'creep[ing] to Jerusalem' is brought up by Barabas as a mode of penance only when he shams a wish to become a Christian. Calling fellow Jews 'countrymen' betrays aliens' conspiracy rather than citizens' local pride or patriotism.

Territorial nationality is thus certainly dubious when it comes to Jews, which may partly account for the unpleasant silence in which Jessica's volunteered evidence is received. But it is also ambiguous in relation to Shakespeare's compatriots. Geographic conditions alone, Norbert Elias tells us, are far from accounting in full for established national traits. Further narratives, pertaining to historical development, are inevitable: lack of monopoly on physical power by King and Church contribute to a national character. Shylock is closer in this respect to being a parable for indigenous Europeans than their binary opposite. His otherness thrust upon him no less than insisted upon by himself, he regularly refers to members of his community in the play as a tribe, a term of ethnicity, or a nation: a term the significance of which for early modern consciousness lay mainly in its diffusion.

III

The manipulative social rituals of Renaissance hegemony would not have been so effective, had they not fallen on fertile ground in post-medieval consciousness. The dream of a nation was one of the strongest and most suggestive constituents of the powerful web of the Renaissance desire for self-fashioning. The yearning for a collective identity had become more and more acute with the loss of medieval forms of communal belonging to the newly acquired, relative independence of early modern individuality. Whereas the inclusion of humanity in the religious universe is God-given, national affiliation is constituted by man. This gendered phrase is hardly fortuitous: man rather, not woman, whose participation in this constitutive process of procreation is considered passive as ever. England, as we have seen, is conceived by John of

Gaunt as a 'happy breed of men,' and the best ideological refuge
offered to Parolles by his peers, upon suffering an irrevocable shame
in the world of men, is to 'find out a country where but women
were that had received so much shame,' so that he 'might begin
an impudent nation.' The use of the exact term is crucial here:
Parolles is not to begin a new race, nor an ethnic tribe, for these
are considered natural phenomena. As a cultural, self-fashioned
entity, Nation is negotiable and exclusively human. The woman,
who at man's will is married to the barbarous King of Tunis (Claribel
in *The Tempest*) or the suspicious King of France (Cordelia in *King
Lear*), or co-opted to the English Crown property (Katharine in
Henry V), serves as a living token of that negotiability inherent in
the concept of nationhood. The new 'impudent nation' to be bred
by Parolles will be governed, no doubt, by patriarchal authority;
otherwise it will have to be crushed and tamed, like Hippolyta's
nation of Amazons, whose very existence calls for an intervention
on behalf of male hegemony, unless they could be almost grotesquely transformed into male warriors and recruited at a time
of emergency to serve the interests of united patriarchy in de-
fending chivalrously 'Dear mother England':

> For your own ladies and pale-visag'd maids
> Like Amazons come tripping after drums,
> Their thimbles into armed gauntlets change,
> Their needl's to lances, and their gentle hearts
> To fierce and bloody inclination.
>
> (*King John*, V. ii. 154–8)

The Elizabethan theater, Robert Weimann asserts, flowered in
an era of national awakening; yet it represented this new sense of
nationalism supporting widely divergent viewpoints. Whereas the
economic and political processes the English nation in the making is undergoing at the time are theoretically traceable by
hindsight, the cultural representation of its progress toward civil-
ity is far less tangible. If in the general history of nationalism in
Western culture, 'the Renaissance merely outlined the possibilities of future developments,' and even those were confined to
kings and some elite groups, while 'the people themselves remained
entirely outside the reach of nationalism' (Kohn 1951: 120, 124),
the case of English nationalism in particular hardly reveals any
solid notion of common national identity. There is evidence
in Tudor England of pride of being English and hatred of

foreigners; but such sentiments, which imposed severe restraints on, and eventually defeated, the prospects of Queen Elizabeth's marriage to the Duke of Anjou, hardly amount to any sense of nationalism proper. Orlando Patterson, complaining of the confused use of the term 'nationalism' which has come to label any expression of group solidarity, admits that the Middle English usage of the term 'nation' 'referred simply to a collection of people from a special locality or simply an aggregation of human or animal individuals.' Unlike the usage of the word on the continent, 'the English, with respect to their own political order, have never found the term nation useful, because they have never developed the entity' (Patterson 1977: 67–8). Indeed, such frivolous use of the term 'nation' by Dromio of Syracuse: – 'methinks they are such a gentle nation that, but for the mountain of mad flesh that claims marriage of me, could find in my heart to stay here still and turn witch' (*The Comedy of Errors*, IV. iv. 151–4) – hardly manifests a serious attitude. Given the ethnic history and social conditions of early modern England, the English throne never attempted to base its absolutist project on any consolidated cultural or ethnic traits. Rather it seems that the leaders of the crowd often attempt to foster national pride by insisting on forged parameters of cohesion. Though themselves aware that 'There is a law in each well-order'd nation / To curb those raging appetites that are / Most disobedient and refractory' (*Troilus and Cressida*, II. ii. 181–3) none will refrain from stirring the mutinous emotions of the crowd to manipulate their national feelings as they see fit. In this there is no difference between the arguments of the tribunes of Caesar's Rome, who, opposing Caesar, urge the common citizens of Rome to consider their freedom as a token of their national identity, and Mark Antony, who, mourning his beloved Caesar, would proclaim their nationality as heirs to Caesar's material possessions. As Patterson points out,

> To the English king, the modern state was a political creation concerned strictly with … the lands, the laws, a well-stocked treasury, a strong loyal army, and dependable allies … it was in no way related to the idea of a common nationality … a distinct tribal or cultural heritage.
>
> (Patterson 1977: 74)

Shakespeare's major political concerns, Patterson goes on to argue, are well tuned with those of his Tudor audience:

it was not the celebration of British cultural distinctiveness which was of central concern to Shakespeare but the nature and problems of power, the loneliness and deep unease of authority, the integrity of the state, and the legitimacy of the crown.

(Ibid: 75)

Indeed, much of the narrative which builds a sense of a nation in the history plays depends on the invocation of Saint George who, coupled with a kingly leader, is implored to 'prosper our colours in [some] dangerous fight.' And yet the very image of colors, a common token of national identity, is double-edged. That same image of solidarity that groups the English under a national flag also bears the very mark of individuality in solitary death: 'These eyes, that see thee now well coloured, / Shall see thee wither'd, bloody, pale and dead. (*1 Henry VI,* IV. ii. 37–8). Or, more clearly, in the very act of differentiating the other, be it a social malcontent marked by his 'nighted colour,' an ethnic outsider, rival to all 'the wealthy curled darlings of our nation' (*Othello,* I. ii. 68), 'A gentle riddance. Draw the curtains, go. / Let all of his complexion choose me so' (*The Merchant of Venice,* II. vii. 78–9); or a cowardly buffoon –

Falstaff: Sir, I will be as good as my word. This that you heard was but a colour.
Shallow: A colour that I fear you will die in, Sir John.
Falstaff: Fear no colours;

(*2 Henry IV,* V. v. 85–8)

or a woman 'your own ladies and pale-visag'd maids' (*King John,* V. ii. 154). Moreover, both nation and colour are prone to deception. One is easily believed to be 'misled with a snipt-taffeta fellow … whose villainous saffron would have made all the unbak'd and doughy youth of a nation in his colour' (*All's Well That Ends Well,* IV. v. 1–4).

It is important, then, to note that issues related to the marked complexity of national unity did not go unnoticed in the work of Shakespeare and his contemporaries. 'It is only after one ceases to reduce public affairs to the business of dominion,' says Hannah Arendt, 'that the original data in the realm of human affairs will appear, or, rather, reappear, in their authentic diversity.' And Shakespeare, for all his concern with majesty and authority, never neglects the processes undergone by his individual and common characters. In that area of 'original data,' namely human attitude to its primary individual and social identity, with Henry VII's dubious ethnic descent and his granddaughter's problematic class origin, the Tudor dynasty could hardly set a model for a pure and unified brand of nationalism, based on ethnic or class solidarity. However, the very absence of customary national traits gave rise to a creative and intriguing tension between various potential notions of national distinctions, which find their way to the very core and tissue of dramatic conflict. The loss of both communal affiliation within the feudal unit and the comforting subordination to a medieval theocentric system, imposed on early modern individual consciousness in England a desire for some substitute sense of collective belonging, and the concept of nation was vague enough to satisfy this need without obliging one to an over-specific commitment to what Andrew Hadfield, following Habermas, would call 'a national public sphere.'

And yet the term does not readily avail itself as an obvious part of the popular emotional vocabulary in early modern England. Even after the Church of England was established, much of the popular sense of 'nation' was still not in full accord with the clerical discourse. In texts of sermons delivered by the official clergy, the term is regularly avoided or supplanted by safer terms. Unlike the literary invocation of 'England as of a new Israel, His chosen and peculiar people,' of which Shylock's 'sacred' nation would be considered an unjust and blasphemous parody, official preachers of the Church barely refer to the concept of nation. Their references to forms of communality range from the distinctly royal 'realm' (which is not a far cry from Lyly's own concept of the term 'people'), as in Rev. William Barlow's apology for the execution of Essex: 'Himself a surfet to the realme, to be spewed out justly,' to the more generally divine 'Commonwealth,' as in the Rev. Henry Smith's harangue on poverty: 'every Commonwealth that letteth any member in it to perish for hunger, is an unnaturall and an uncharitable Commonwealth.' For the Rev. Bernard Gilpin 'England' is the location where 'some terrible examples of God's wrath' have occured (Chandos 1971: 119, 87, 33). In the theater of the author of *Julius Caesar*, in which the citizens of Rome are driven to perform national functions without the actual term being mentioned even once, it still takes mainly manipulative social rituals and the forging of tendentious political myths on the part of some hegemonic elite to foster an action based on emotionally accepted national narratives.

Note

1 All Shakespearean quotations are from the New Arden editions. All Marlowe quotations are from *Complete Plays and Poems*, ed. Eric D. Pendry. London, Dent, 1976.

7
Bryn Glas
TERENCE HAWKES

A French connection?

Colonization has its imperatives and it has been rightly observed that, halfway down the cat's throat, any self-respecting mouse ought at least to consider beginning to talk about 'us cats'. For similar reasons, perhaps an essay entitled 'Bryn Glas' ought at least to consider beginning to talk about Jacques Derrida's work called *Glas*. That dismaying celebration of the relationship between texts confronts the reader with two parallel columns of print. On the left hand side, the philosopher Hegel engages in a rational analysis of the concept of the family, the law and the state. Meanwhile, on the right, the text cites and discusses the writings of a notorious thief, homosexual and transvestite – Jean Genet – along with passages about matters such as proper names, signatures, onomatopoeia and the process of signification at large. The mode of negotiation between the columns becomes, of course, a crucial factor.

Texts, Derrida's strategy implies, speak with no single, privileged voice but with one that owes due homage to the work of other texts always covertly juxtaposed with, inserted into, or grafted upon them. In *Glas*, one kind of rationality – Hegel's – literally confronts, even glares at, its opposite, that of Genet: yet, curiously, the one also seems to be shaped by, and finally almost dependent upon the other.

What first appears as a radical disjunction between the two columns turns gradually into a kind of fruitful connection, something that plunges the very notion of 'text' into a revealing crisis, exposing and bringing into question the process of 'smoothing over the joins' in which our production of meaning has such a massive investment. My focus is on that process, and thus on a boundary, a frontier, a 'join' which needs to be smoothed over or dissolved before the texts on either side of it can inherit the coherence to which both lay claim. With the upholders of reason and law on the one side, and with thieves and subversives on the other, that text – to this day – is called 'Great Britain'.

Blue remembered hills

In fact, the title 'Bryn Glas' draws on one of the languages of Britain. The words are Welsh, and if English is the vehicle of reason and the law then, as Welsh, they belong very much in the opposite column. The English rhyme 'Taffy was a Welshman, Taffy was a thief' makes no bones about that: English perceptions traditionally propose for the outlandish Celtic hordes a brisk exclusion from civilization as we know it. The very word 'Welsh' derives from the Old English *wælisc*, meaning, brutally and dismissively, 'foreign'.

Bryn Glas is the name of a place in Wales. 'Bryn' means hill. 'Glas' means blue. The Blue Hill. However, there is a slight complication, which perhaps reinforces some English suspicions about the Welsh capacity for undermining reason and logic, for 'Glas' can mean 'green' as well as 'blue'. What English presents as a clear distinction, Welsh refuses, and, dividing the spectrum slightly differently, confirms its foreignness by challenging a whole view of the world. Nevertheless, in translation, both sorts of hill, blue or green, seem happily to incline towards the other column on the page, where a kind of quintessential Englishness awaits them. 'There is a Green Hill far away' begins a famous nineteenth-century hymn about a carefully Anglicized Jerusalem, its chords evocative, in males of my generation, of nothing more challenging than school uniforms, morning assembly and a gossamer guilt gently yoking football field and bicycle shed. Perhaps more poignant is A. E. Housman's secular hymn to an irrecoverable past, recorded in *A Shropshire Lad*:

Into my heart an air that kills
From yon far country blows.
What are those blue remembered hills,
What spires, what farms are those?

That is the land of lost content,
I see it shining plain,
The happy highways where I went
And cannot come again.

(*A Shropshire Lad*: xl)

Border country

Nevertheless, Bryn Glas remains an actual place concretely and, in view of the ambiguity of its hue, appropriately located in Wales. It lies just inside the Welsh border, a few miles below Knighton, to the west of a small settlement called Pilleth. In fact, Housman's English vision turns out to be rather acute. Bryn Glas, the Blue Hill, lies only a few miles from Ludlow, the setting of *A Shropshire Lad*.

Whether this signals Wales as that 'land of lost content' must remain a moot point. At first sight, in historical terms, 'content' seems the last prospect that such a country might offer to English eyes. The issue is precisely one of colonization. As England's next-door neighbour, indeed as holder of the dubious distinction of being England's first colony, Wales inherits a history of constant and often violent penetration of its borders. The result: a duality of experience and commitment which to this day makes it virtually ungraspable as a single, unified entity. At least two distinct 'readings' of the Principality are always available, one Welsh and one English. The texts they generate are co-terminous, they occupy the same page, so that, shadowing the picture drawn and framed by laws administered from its anglicized towns and cities, another Wales of poets, minstrels and prophets 'apprenticed in ancient lore' has always beckoned, well beyond the English ken.[1]

That clash between 'law' and 'lore' appears invariably to characterize the experience of colonist and colonized in Wales. At the heart of a culture obsessed by genealogy, blood-descent and complex, carefully nurtured family relations, the serpentine character of Welsh kinship structures seem destined – if not designed – to undermine linear English certainties, both legal and constitutional. The major political upheaval of the fourteenth century had, not inappropriately, climaxed in Wales. In the summer of 1399, the deposition of Richard II, the ultimate *de jure* monarch of the old medieval order, removed the last king of Britain to rule by undisputed hereditary right. No doubt the spectacle of Richard's scrambling *de facto* successors helped fan opportunistic flames of revolt in the Principality. An inherited fondness for grandiose titular claims (mocked even in our own century by Dylan Thomas's sobriquet 'The Rimbaud of Cwmdonkin Drive') probably helped.

When insurrection came, it certainly involved an eruption of that 'other', non-English Wales: a rising against law, in the name of lore, and to the clamant flourishing of a title. The revolt of Owain Glyn Dŵr, self-proclaimed Prince of Wales, effectively lasted, with fluctuations of intensity, from his assumption of the title on 6 September 1400, until the degeneration of his campaign into guerrilla warfare, and his decline into a desperate and hunted man by 1409. At its height, an 'awesome Welsh army' was mustered in support of what might be termed a classic anti-colonialist project designed, in Glyn Dŵr's own words, to release Wales from 'the madness of the English barbarians'. Sustained by the prophecies of Merlin and Taliesin, it encouraged those Welsh who had felt exiles in their own land since the victories of Edward I to pursue claims made as the original 'Britons'. Glyn Dŵr had little trouble linking himself with a long line of Welsh 'Messiahs' or 'redeemers', including the fabled King Arthur, who offered to regain for their compatriots control of the whole island.[2]

The Battle of Britain

The climax came on 22 June 1402 and it came at Bryn Glas. There, at the head of his troops, Glyn Dŵr won his only major victory: over an English force led by Edmund Mortimer, uncle of the heir of the Earl of March. The bloodiness of the battle, in which the English were decimated and Mortimer captured, made it immediately memorable. The subsequent alleged mutilation of the bodies of the English dead by Welsh women brought legendary status. Later, in what amounted to a major public relations coup, the captured Mortimer defected and married Glyn Dŵr's daughter Catherine.

Most students of English have already encountered Bryn Glas, perhaps without realizing it, through Shakespeare's version of the events at the beginning of *1 Henry IV*. The King's project for an expedition to the Holy Land has to be postponed owing to the sudden arrival of a 'post from Wales loaden with heavy news',

> Whose worst was that the noble Mortimer,
> Leading the men of Herefordshire to fight
> Against the irregular and wild Glendower,
> Was by the rude hands of that Welshman taken,
> A thousand of his people butchered,
> Upon whose dead corpse there was such misuse,
> Such beastly shameless transformation,
> By those Welshwomen done, as may not be
> Without much shame retold or spoken of.
>
> (I. i. 34–46)

The source of the information is clearly Holinshed:

> Owen Glendouer, according to his accustomed manner, robbing and spoiling within the English borders, caused all the forces of the shire of Hereford to assemble togither against them, vnder the conduct of Edmund Mortimer earle of March. But coming to try the matter by battell, whether by treason or otherwise, so it fortuned, that the English power was discomfited, the earle taken prisoner, and aboue a thousand of his people slaine in the place. The shamefull villanie vsed by the Welshwomen towards the dead carcasses, was such, as honest eares would be ashamed to heare, and continent toongs to speake thereof.[3]

Glendower's 'irregular and wild' function clearly derives from this. But where does Shakespeare's more precise 'beastly shameless trans-formation' come from? Its source is also Holinshed, where the cru-elty of the Scythian Queen Tomyzis and of Fulvia, wife of Mark Antony, is sternly denounced. Yet in neither case, he says, is their cruelty

> comparable to this of the Welshwomen; which is worthie to be recorded to the shame of a sex pretending the title of weake vessels, and yet raging with such force of fiercenesse and barbarisme. For the dead bodies of the Englishmen, being above a thousand lieng upon the ground imbrued in theire owne blood, was a sight (a man would think) greevous to looke upon, and so farre from exciting and stirring up affections of crueltie; that it should rather have moued the beholders to commiseration and mercie: yet did the women of Wales cut off their priuities and

put one part thereof into the mouths of euerie dead man, in such sort that the cullions hoong downe to their chins; and not so contented, they did cut off their noses and thrust them into their tailes as they laie on the ground mangled and defaced. This was a verie ignominious deed, and a woorsse not committed among the barbarous: which though it make the reader to read it, and the hearer to heare it, ashamed: yet bicause it was a thing doone in open sight, and left testified in historie; I see little reason whie it should not be imparted in our mother toong to the knowledge of our owne countrimen, as well as unto strangers in a language unknowne.[4]

Certain features of this passage are worth noting:

1   The stress on female duplicity ('a sex pretending the title of weake vessels, and yet raging with such force of fiercenesse and barbarisme') and its presentation as a central characteristic of an outlandish and destructive savagery plainly directed at – indeed hacking off – the fundamental indicator of native manhood.

2   The stress on the specific location of this unnatural force. It resides in 'Welshwomen', 'women of Wales', etc.

3   The stress on language. Despite the earlier judgement of the event's shamefully unspeakable nature, we now find it spoken of in meticulous detail, with a particularly pious commitment to English: 'I see little reason whie it should not be imparted in our mother toong to the knowledge of our owne countrimen, as well as unto strangers in a language unknowne.' Clearly, the Welsh tongue – here the very badge of deceit and barbarism – must not be allowed to perform its savage, emasculating operations on English.

It's surely also clear that we are not here dealing with transparent factual reporting, but with something that, by the time Holinshed chronicled the issues, was bearing complex cultural freight. Even if the mutilation of the bodies had been actual, some careful symbolic structuring is clearly at work in the narrative. A methodical routine of 'reversal' operates, whereby orifices are systematically stuffed with members from opposite regions. The upper region, the head, receives the penis; the lower region, the 'taile' receives the nose. In this process, men find themselves turned upside-down and inside-out by agents of a fundamental disorder, women, just as

England is subverted by its foreign 'other', Wales. This, surely, is the wholesale inversion hinted at by Shakespeare's 'beastly ... transformation'. If we wanted a *locus classicus* we would need to look no further than Ovid's *Metamorphoses*, or the story of the enchantress Circe.

The play goes some way towards confirming this reading in its subsequent portrayal of the power and implications of a traditional, magical and shape-shifting Welshness. Owain Glyn Dŵr is a far more complex figure than the mere blowhard that English tradition, and Hotspur's well-known gibes, seek to endorse. The sparring between them probably tells us as much about Hotspur as about his adversary:

Glendower. I can call spirits from the vasty deep.
Hotspur: Why, so can I, or so can any man;
But will they come when you do call for them?
(III. i. 51–3)

In fact, enough Welsh princely blood ran in Glyn Dŵr's veins to lend a certain legitimacy to his title and to the revolt mounted in its name. He claimed descent, after all, from Llewellyn, the last native-born Prince of Wales. In his assumption of precisely that title, Glyn Dŵr ranks as a credible alternative to another, rather less authentic-sounding incumbent who was also in the field: Henry of Monmouth, Shakespeare's Hal, invested by his father as Prince of Wales just twelve months before. Shakespeare's version of Hotspur's encounter with the 'great magician, damn'd Glendower' (I. iii. 82) obviously locks on to traditional oppositions that aim to caricature both the Celtic sensibility and the Anglo-Saxon. The one, dealing in mythology, magic, prophecy and lore, duly rants, boasts and carries on in the face of the other's hard-headed commitment to reason, common sense and law. But, not unlike Derrida's *Glas*, the play goes on to blur the edges of exactly those distinctions.

Perhaps most important are the implications at work in the depiction of 'down-trod' Mortimer (I. iii. 133): for here an English hero-figure, a serious pretender to the English throne, 'proclaim'd / By Richard that dead is, the next of blood' (I. iii. 143–4), is seen to be kept wholly in thrall by the charms of a Welsh woman. Holinshed's sparse reference to her, 'daughter of the said Owen', is expanded in the play to create a far more disturbing figure who, Circe-like, seems easily able to subvert Mortimer's English manhood – certainly as measured by the standards of the absurdly leaping Hotspur. Her powers are clearly located in a language that Shakespeare never attempts to transliterate, but presumably hands over to the invention of Welsh-speaking actors working within the company. It is amply displayed. The stage directions indicate a completed interchange with her father '*Glendower speaks to her in Welsh, and she answers him in the same*' followed by three full speeches in which '*The lady speaks in Welsh*' (III. i. 192–206), culminating in her singing of a '*Welsh song*' (line 238).

The strongly suasive powers of the language manifest themselves in Mortimer's response to this. Glendower's daughter seems transformed almost into an embodiment of what she speaks: even her tears become 'that pretty Welsh / Which thou pourest down from these swelling heavens' (III. i. 194–5). But the essential feature of the language appears in a more telling dimension, as a highly wrought 'effeminate' or 'feminizing' capacity. An uncomprehending Mortimer comments,

> … thy tongue
> Makes Welsh as sweet as ditties highly penn'd,
> Sung by a fair queen in a summer's bow'r
> With ravishing division to her lute.
>
> (III. i. 201–4)

– or in her father's translation,

> She bids you on the wanton rushes lay you down,
> And rest your gentle head upon her lap,
> And she will sing the song that pleaseth you,
> And on your eyelids crown the god of sleep,
> Charming your blood with pleasing heaviness,
> Making such difference 'twixt wake and sleep
> As is the difference betwixt day and night,
> The hour before the heavenly-harness'd team
> Begins his golden progress in the east.
>
> (III. i. 207–15)

To stress as 'feminine' the narcotic aspect of Welsh, its capacity to create a 'bower of bliss' whose modes dissolve and transcend the male, order-giving boundaries of an English-speaking world, is to draw attention to the culture's larger, subversive, and in a complex sense 'effeminate' role in early modern Britain. Hotspur's 'manly' rejection of such charms – 'I had rather hear Lady my brach howl in Irish' (III. i. 230) – not only reinforces the contrast, it neatly reminds the audience of that larger Celtic world which its own commitment to English and Englishness had long been trying to suppress.

Of course, that world had – and has – never altogether gone away. In fact, after the battle of Bosworth, Merlin's prophecies about the return of the Welsh hero-king to rule over the whole island of Britain almost seemed about to come true. Henry VII was certainly a Welshman. He packed his court with his countrymen, named his eldest son Arthur, and observed St David's day. As the Tudor dynasty unfolded, Welsh-speakers 'poured in' to London.[5] However, when it came to the construction of a new entity called 'Britain', that massive ideological project which obsessed both the Tudors and Stuarts and on which the history plays focus with consuming intensity, Wales's fate would ultimately prove to be more a matter of incorporation than confederacy. As Gwyn A. Williams observes,

> A nation-state in formation was faced with the little local difficulty that there were actually two nations in it. One would have to be made invisible. So between 1536 and 1543, the English crown put through a series of measures which have gone down in Welsh history as the Act of Union.[6]

The price of such a 'union' was high. As a 'junior partner' in what was to be virtually a new state, Wales had literally to be redefined. Firm borders and boundaries were imposed in the English mode. One result was that the city and county of Monmouth, unable to yield easily to such procedures, turned almost overnight into an anomaly; neither Welsh nor English, its newly invented indeterminacy persisted into the twentieth century. English became the only official language in Wales. The 'sinister usages and customs' of the Welsh people – which included the language – were to be suppressed. Denied status as an authorized tongue, Welsh retreated to the hearth, the kitchen and the street.

To a considerable extent, the new self-confident and London-based Welsh were prepared to accede to such measures, in pursuit of what they saw as the greater prize – or the better pickings – offered by a coherent 'British' nation, and the sense of a complete, English-speaking 'world', separated from the rest of the globe, which it implied.[7] As Gwyn A. Williams puts it 'An integrated Britain becomes visible first in a major migration of the Welsh to the centre of power.' London attracted 'all the exports, human and material, of the novel merchant capitalism' and the Welsh moved into 'every conceivable avenue of advancement', the process reaching its climax in the reign of Elizabeth I.[8] One direct result was the rise to prominence of Welsh families such as that of Dafydd Seisyllt, whose grandson became William Cecil, Elizabeth's key statesman, or indeed that of Morgan Williams, which three generations later produced Oliver Cromwell.[9]

Under Elizabeth, denounced by A. L. Rowse as 'that red-headed Welsh harridan', the 'remote and distinguished past' of the Welsh effectively made available – at least in influential intellectual terms – some sort of underpinning for the new national identity. Their very presence satisfactorily bore out claims for the ancient existence of that complete 'world', that independent Britishness, of which the Arthurian legends spoke. Geoffrey of Monmouth's *British History* swiftly became semi-official doctrine and Welsh scholars responded enthusiastically.[10] A London Welshman, John Dee, is even said to have coined the term 'British Empire'. Certainly, in addressing Elizabeth he styled himself 'hyr Brytish philosopher' and Dee's proposal of the Welshman Madoc as the discoverer of America, 300 years before Columbus, was seized on by a whole generation as a cultural and quasi-legal weapon against Spain.[11]

It may well be that an acquaintance with Welsh people in London accounts for Shakespeare's portrayal of Glyn Dŵr as more sympathetic than his sources would encourage.[12] Obviously, his company contained at least two Welsh-speaking actors. This native Prince of Wales is certainly no babbling Caliban. He can, he tells us, speak English as well as Hotspur, having been 'train'd up in the English court' (III, i, 116–17).[13] Nevertheless, his native Welsh must have inherited a disturbing role in an emerging British state whose interests lay in being monolingual. In the streets of London it would have stalked the English language like an importunate ghost. To most of those familiar with the major European tongues, Welsh would have seemed – as it still does – entirely exotic. In its written form, the apparent senseless conjunction of consonants generates blankness, if not bewilderment. In its spoken form, its requirement of unachievable phonemes, such as /ll/, mark it as impossibly alien, utterly estranging. As opaque to English ears as any African or Indian tongue – not that most Londoners would ever have encountered such exotic rarities – it appeared to lack even the bare referentiality that Elizabethan popular culture was prepared to grant to the Romance languages or to Latin. The status of Welsh in Tudor London was completely different. Its apparent lack of even rudimentary transparency effectively marks it as totally outlandish. For English speakers, to hear Welsh is fundamentally disconcerting. In a sense it is to experience the phenomenon of 'language' itself, as an unmediated, inexplicable system of signs. It is to come face to face with an almost unacceptable 'given': the alarming and inextricable involvement of human beings in the sounds which they make with their mouths. It is to run full tilt into a material human world which seems wholly other. Shockingly, it is one that claims rights to the same island.

This collision is embodied in the battle at Bryn Glas and it offers some insight into Holinshed's anxiety over whether details of what happened should be made available through the medium of English. The importance of the events derives not only from the fact that they involved a decisive and brutal battle in which a large number of English were slaughtered by the Welsh. Shakespeare's play presents it as central to what might be called a genuine Battle of Britain. For in *1 Henry IV*, Bryn Glas and its consequences release that most disturbing of spectres: a militant feminine and feminizing force, with a bloody knife in its hand, an incomprehensible tongue in its head, and with English manhood, the English language, and (on both counts) English reality in its sights. When Welsh erupts onto the stage in that play, its evident complicity with an occluded but horribly violent reading of the past, present and future is what ensures its capacity to sap the claim of English to be the transparent, fully referential transmitter of a new-minted Britishness.[14]

Spirits from the vasty deep

The captive Mortimer's situation, unmanned – at least according to Hotspur – by a Welsh woman, undoubtedly echoes that of his hapless English comrades at Bryn Glas. However, the most potent wearer of that Circean mantle is perhaps located elsewhere. Falstaff is, of course, the play's most resourceful agent of 'beastly shameless transformation'. He has from the beginning nothing to do with the rational, daylight world with its distinctions and calibrations appropriate to truth, to law and to time (I, ii, 1–12). His bluster (II, iv, 164ff.) chimes easily with Glendower's

> ... at my birth
> The front of heaven was full of fiery shapes,
> The goats ran from the mountains ...
>   (III, i. 34ff.)

– and meets the same hard-nosed response from Hal as Glendower's does from Hotspur. Indeed, Hal's and Hotspur's debunking 'English' rejection serves structurally to identify the reverberations of a submerged 'Welshness' which, perhaps surprisingly, turns out to link Falstaff and Glendower. Of course, they are already firmly yoked in other ways. Both have well-established connections with the Devil. Hal warns himself, in the guise of his father, that 'there is a devil haunts thee in the likeness of a fat old man … Falstaff, that old white-bearded Satan' (II. iv. 441–57) and Falstaff himself speaks of 'that devil Glendower' (II. iv. 365). In fact, Glendower's command of 'spirits from the vasty deep' (III. i. 50) presents itself as part of a Welsh repertoire which, as he proposes to Hotspur, 'can teach you, cousin to command the devil' (53). Such 'skimble-skamble stuff' includes, to Hotspur's disgust, 'reckoning up the several devils' names / That were his lackeys' (III. i. 151–2) so that his conclusion that 'the devil understands Welsh' (224) comes as no surprise.[15]

It is therefore not altogether unfitting that an element of 'effeminacy' characterizes Falstaff, particularly when that is set against the project of the creation of a 'manly' unity which will form the basis of the emerging British state. Alan Sinfield makes the point explicitly: 'Falstaff represents in part effeminate devotion to women … above all, with his drinking, eating, jesting, and fatness, Falstaff embodies unmasculine *relaxation* – loosening, softening, languishing, letting go.'[16] We can add that a final and betraying dimension of 'Welshness' accrues to Falstaff as a result of his suppressed links with Sir John Oldcastle (c.1378–1417).[17] Falstaff's 'remote original', as the Arden editor calls him, was a High Sheriff of Herefordshire who became Lord Cobham by marriage in 1409. A friend of young Henry, Holinshed calls him a 'valiant captaine and a hardie gentleman', who was 'highly in the king's favour'. However, Henry casts him off when he is charged with Wycliffite heresy (Lollardism) and condemned. Escaping from the Tower, Oldcastle took refuge in Wales, where his presence served to underline the Principality's notorious and continuing potential for upheaval. Owain Glyn Dŵr's revolt may have been petering out, but a continuing Welsh disaffection could always be exploited by enemies of the English crown, and Oldcastle was thought to have been in contact with Glyn Dŵr's son.[18]

As a Welsh Circe, one whose brand of effeminacy is well capable of suborning the role of 'Prince of Wales', even down to mimicking it at one memorable point, Falstaff's banishment from the new united 'manly' Britain is inevitable. It provokes the official Prince of Wales's ruthless and appropriately 'English' rejection. It is one – to probe the effect of Falstaff's 'effeminacy' once more – whose words deliberately invert the performative utterances of marriage by locating them in the context of a momentous divorce: 'I do, I will' (II. iv. 475).

God for Harry

The unappeased spectre of a subverting, transforming and unmanning Wales haunts the rest of the tetralogy. *1 Henry IV* concludes with Henry's commitment to continue 'To fight with Glendower and the Earl of March' (V. v. 40), but the play's second part presents Welshness in a more dangerously diffused mode. Falstaff remains 'in the devil's book' (II. ii. 43–4) along with Poins, and his 'effeminacy' continues, but in a sour, less ebullient vein. He dwindles, in his own depiction of himself and his page, into 'a sow that hath overwhelmed all her litter but one' (I. ii. 10–11), and his prospective rejection acquires nuances that present him precisely in terms of an outlandish, opaque language whose threat to the supremacy of English must be met by domestication:

> The Prince but studies his companions
> Like a strange tongue, wherein, to gain the language,
> 'Tis needful that the most immodest word
> Be look'd upon and learnt.

> (IV. iv. 68–71)

A play apparently promoting the idea of a united 'British' state must obviously try to shoe-horn untidy exoticisms into a mode in which they can be appropriated to suit the central project.[19] *Henry V* begins with a sifting of the problems of the Salic law (which prohibited women from succeeding to the throne in parts of Europe) in pursuit of a firmer grip on the range and disposition of female power. Welshness duly appears in a different key. Falstaff, and the subversive, 'effeminate', emasculating dimension he represents are notably absent: indeed the fat knight has returned to the bosom of one of the great Welsh heroes, Arthur (II. iii. 9–10). The challenge to English has receded: its militant ascendancy can afford to allow that French is sufficiently referential to be joked at and with: even Pistol is able to mangle it sufficiently to produce a knowing humour (II. i. 72). After all, foreign cultures valuably determine our own. We are what we oppose, and a 'fair and lucky war' may not unreasonably be mounted against any country prepared to square up to – and so define – the oncoming multi-cultural British force as simply 'the English' (II. iv. 1). That, to speak broadly, is what the French (and, latterly, foreign cultures at large) are traditionally for.

In fact, Englishness receives its final polishing in this play and enlistment in that crudely engrossing concept is repeatedly urged on and required of the army that Henry leads. Appropriating Scottishness, Irishness and Welshness, its project can be said to present itself, not as a set of distinctive cultural and linguistic features, so much as a kind of fundamental 'reality' which underlies sophisticated notions of difference. It constitutes the basis of that complete and discrete 'world', which the 'British' project set out to create. To be 'English', and a participant in that world, is thus, by this light, simply to be human. So the English spokesman in France sees 'French' possessions as the mere trappings of a massive pretension, and, speaking for the English King, urges his French 'brother'

> That you divest yourself and lay apart
> The borrowed glories that by gift of heaven,
> By law of nature and of nations, longs
> To him and to his heirs ...
>   ... resign
> Your crown and kingdom indirectly held
> From him the native and true challenger.
> (II. iv. 78–95)

This sense of being the final, fundamental reality, 'native and true', then becomes the licence for a broad process of Anglicization which the play duly chronicles: undertaken, not in the spirit of imposing a particular culture on one that pre-exists it, so much as discovering, and laying bare, a substratum that another competing and outlandish way of life has needlessly and mischievously obscured. There isn't much doubt that an Englishman, a 'plain soldier ... a fellow of plain and uncoined constancy' as Henry V styles himself when wooing Katherine (V. ii. 150–5), with his 'poor and starved band' (IV. ii. 15) of 'warriors for the working-day' (III. iii. 109) is going to prove superior to any effete and pretentious enemy.

The notion that a genuine nuts and bolts reality is discoverable beneath an obscuring complex veil which must, in the name of humanity, be plucked from it, gains increasing momentum in the plays. It underlies Hal's claim that his youthful excesses merely cloud a simple honesty that will subsequently appear. His later kingly penchant for disguising his true status and mingling with the soldiers before Agincourt, only triumphantly to reveal himself after the battle, springs from the same source. The construction of 'England' and Englishness as the model of that grounding reality becomes a major concern. Whenever another culture emerges, as French does through the use of its language, its fortifications prove readily piercable by honest English eyes. Either simple sniggering about names for parts of the body will suffice (III. iv) or, as in the case of Pistol and his prisoner (IV. iv), the opacities of the language yield readily to a more knowing humour. English, the language of the 'real' world, is well able to penetrate and control foreignness simply because a palpable, homespun 'English' truth lies beneath everything. This construction of the world as a kind of enormous *Anglia irredenta* allows, even encourages, those claims to unadorned foundational status which, in the last analysis, show through as what we are always tempted to call 'human nature'. If everyone, under the surface, is really like us, that is English, then to claim simply to be English is to present oneself as pristine, unsullied, unwarped and real. Other people have identifiable cultures and distinctive languages; in the 'land of lost content' we simply live, we simply speak, and we do so with immediate and transparent reference to the true, English-speaking world. Like Adam, in this 'other Eden' (*Richard II*, II. i. 42), we simply name.

Big name

However, as Derrida is at pains to point out, in *Glas* and elsewhere, Adam's project must be doomed to failure. A proper name ought indeed to involve pure reference, but since it is part of language, it works like language, and always retains, willy-nilly, the capacity to signify.[20] This principle obviously works even more powerfully as one language crosses the border of another and engages in the process by which, as we put it in English, names come to be 'Anglicized'. Colonization provides innumerable rich examples of this process, each 'Englished' phoneme containing a miniature history of expropriation. In Wales, names traditionally indicated lineage and place of origin. The Act of Union imposed the English concept of 'surname' on the Welsh, partly out of irritation, and partly as a symbol and symptom of incorporation.[21]

The name 'Owen Glendower', as Shakespeare gives it, offers a poignant example. Over and above its claim to refer to a distinct, placeless individual, its Anglicized form – which systematically elides links of blood and soil – signifies incursion, defeat and expropriation exactly to the degree that it is not Owain Glyn Dŵr. That name, with its Welsh luggage of signs invoking kinship, terrain, political commitment and history, lacks any of the transparency that English may mistakenly try to attribute to, or indeed, in characteristic gesture, to uncover in, 'Owen Glendower'. But the nature of Owain Glyn Dŵr's revolutionary project made his lineage and his connection with Welsh soil indispensable to him. It constituted 'the validating charter of his identity and of his claim'.[22] This kind of blood-and-soil link underwrites his claim to be the true Prince of Wales. The other Prince of Wales's roots – those of Hal – lie much less securely and indeed most significantly in Monmouth: to this day, as has been said, still thought of as border country.

Many names in these plays seem in fact to point to borders. Some of them do so directly because they have evidently crossed the border between one culture and another. Others hint at political borders whose crossing has provoked change. We have already noticed that the play contains vestigial reminders that Falstaff was originally named Oldcastle. A canny deployment of diminutives also operates, dragging a name across the border between formal and informal, often in a political cause. The French Princess Katherine rapidly dwindles to 'Kate' as part of the domesticating, Anglicizing process already noted. Indeed, at a telling moment, after chugging through a ludicrous array of French formal titles

> Up, princes, and with spirit of honour edged
> More sharper than your swords hie to the field.
> Charles Delabreth, High Constable of France,
> You Dukes of Orleans, Bourbon and of Berry,
> Alencon, Brabant, Bar and Burgundy,
> Jacques Chatillon, Rambures, Vaudemont,
> Beaumont, Grandpré, Roussi and Fauconbridge,
> Foix, Lestrelles, Boucicault and Charolais ...

the French King finds himself urging these worthies against the mere, but significantly named, 'Harry England' (III. v. 38–48).

Pig time

None the less, a degree of insecurity hovers around this enterprise, and the playtext records its inescapable and worrying presence. An important location of the attendant stresses is the Welshman who enters right in the middle of *Henry V* (III. ii.). To English eyes, Fluellen could not be more Welsh. Yet he could also not be more acceptable or engaging. Anglicization could wish for no better advertisement. Although, as Gwyn A. Williams has said, his father would probably have supported Owain Glyn Dŵr, Fluellen's commitment to the English, or rather British project seems, at first sight, absolute.[23] His comic pride in his nationality seems even to be fulfilled by that. Indeed, he delights in confirming King Henry's own twice pro-claimed, but still shady, Welshness (IV, i, 52; IV, vii, 104). And although his loquaciousness carries more than an echo of Glendower's, his ebullience and wholehearted loyalty prove redemptive and reassur-ing. Praised for his 'care and valour' (IV. i. 85), he can never be imagined mutilating the body of an enemy. His commitment to those quaint provisions, the 'disciplines' of war, would certainly preclude such an action, and his concern to school his colleagues in the value of such prescriptions, as well as his readiness to berate the foreigners for their ignorance of them, is memorable. He virtually embodies law and order and fully supports the hanging of Bardolph for theft. This is no devil, no monster, but a leek-wearing patriot, vigorous and bustling in the service of his king. As a crowning vir-tue, he speaks no word of Welsh.

Fluellen, in short, appears to be the model Welshman necessary to the project of a united Britain. However, there are complica-tions. The first, since we have spoken of names, arises with Fluellen's. The Folio confirms this as a heavily Anglicized version of 'Llewellyn'. Llewellyn is not, of course, just any Welsh name. All such – as we have seen – trail their own clouds of glory, but this name can claim archetypal status. Llewellyn is the name of the last native Prince of Wales (Llewellyn yr Olaf, Llewellyn the Last). Moreover, fittingly, and notoriously for English ears, it deploys in full fig that distinctive phoneme /ll/ mentioned above, whose accurate pronunciation is a major Welsh shibboleth.[24] Here, immediately recognizable to both Welsh and English ears, is a distinctive sign of Welshness. However, the initial, side-stepping and entirely Anglicized phoneme embod-ied in 'Fluellen' signifies a language – and a highly significant name – crudely enlisted and in the process brutally reduced. Even more clearly than in the case of 'Owen Glendower', in Fluellen's name a maimed linguistic ghost stirs, rattles its English cage, and hints darkly at things that are now literally unspeakable.

Just as Welshness finds itself determinedly Anglicized in Fluellen, the English he speaks is no less heavily inflected, contorted and 'Welshified' to the satisfaction of English ears by the use of stand-ard parodic devices: the repetition of phrases such as 'look you' and confusion over the plurality of nouns ('leeks is good' (V. i. 59) etc.) Comically, endearingly – reassuringly – the phoneme /b/ is con-sistently, to English ears, replaceable by /p/:

> the French is gone off, look you, and there is gallant and most prave passages. Marry, th'athversary was have possession of the pridge, but he is enforced to retire, and the Duke of Exeter is master of the pridge. I can tell your majesty, the Duke is a prave man.

> (III. vi. 90ff.)

Droll, no doubt. But then, momentarily, the process starts to back-fire. Henry's plain, soldierly gallantry, his magnanimity, already showcased at Harflur and to be seen again after the battle of Agincourt, suddenly and inexplicably vanish. Astonishingly, at the height of the fray, they turn into a cold ruthlessness:

> But hark, what new alarum is this same?
> The French have reinforced their scattered men.
> Then every soldier kill his prisoners!
> Give the word through.

> (IV. vi. 35–7)[25]

The opportunity for Fluellen's response to this new turn of events is fully opened by the English captain Gower: 'they have burned and carried away all that was in the King's tent, wherefore the King most worthily hath caused every soldier to cut his prisoner's throat.' To this he adds, with appalling disingenuousness: 'O, 'tis a gallant king!' (IV. vii. 8–10). With Fluellen's reply, the mask of 'good' or 'house' Welshman seems suddenly and decisively to slip as his Welsh 'accent' unexpectedly homes in on and ignites explosive material at the heart of some of the English words: 'Ay, he was porn at Monmouth, Captain Gower. What call you the town's name where Alexander the Pig was born?' (IV. vii. 11–13). The moment is elec-trifying. It remains so however much we stiffen our sinews in an effort to secure the 'proper' reading which the text quickly strains to re-establish. Here, briefly but significantly, the parody itself starts independently to signify. Once more, a name bursts the boundaries of straightforward reference.

Does Fluellen's Welsh accent effectively turn on those who have been laughing at it here? Does it unveil, in 'Alexander the Pig', a glimpse of a potential 'beastly transformation' dormant yet potent at the heart of the new Britain as corrosively as it was at the old? Does a sow-like Falstaff stalk even this field? Is the shining victory of Agincourt to be dimmed by the shadow of the atrocities at Bryn Glas? Fluellen presses home his comparison: Alexander killed his friend Clytus, just as 'Harry Monmouth' turned away Falstaff (IV. vii. 44ff.) 'I'll tell you, there is good men porn at Monmouth' (IV. vii. 51) he continues. As boys are now slaughtered, further throats cut (IV. vii. 62), the ironies gather. Must 'big' or 'great' structures – Alexander the Great, or even Great Britain – inevitably harbour the same repressed beastliness of the sort which Welshness, breaching the boundaries even of the English language, seems always to announce? The Act of Union in 1536 had offered to make Wales and England one nation. Yet whatever Welsh misgivings might have been, a fear amongst the English must have whispered that such a Union could sap, dilute – nay, mutilate – their manhood. Perhaps, as Gower advises Pistol, Fluellen should be listened to: 'You thought because he could not speak English in the native garb he could not therefore handle an English cudgel. You'll find it otherwise' (V. i. 75ff.). We do. We will.

Onlie beget

To attempt to conquer and to pacify an alien culture by force of arms is one thing. To 'unify' one's own culture with a different one and to pronounce them equal in law in pursuit of the same end, is quite another. The Act of Union – the name, given in the nineteenth century, retains remorseless sexual implications – was always a somewhat forced conjunction and the anxiety that grows through the *Henry IV–V* cycle surely reflects that. For any proposal of 'equality' presupposes a likeness, beneath the trappings of language and way of life, whose establishment and maintenance is a vastly tricky project. In this case, its purpose dictates that Englishness, the whole cloth from which Britishness will be cut, be perceived as the defining feature of an unchanging 'human nature' and that it be presented as at least discernible and occasionally verifiable – however much that requires the triumph of faith over experience – in Wales and the Welsh.

Major obstacles to this perception must have been the battle of Bryn Glas and its aftermath, the emergence and rise of a triumphant Owain Glyn Dŵr and the fears of a barbaric Welsh expansion. Passing – like many Welsh events – quickly into the sphere of myth and legend, these became, by the time of Shakespeare's plays, the focus of an ideological contradiction whose complexities had – in the name of the new Britain – to be resolved. With the cementing of the Tudor claim to power, Welshness needed, at whatever cost, to be brought within the English pale, and the stresses and strains of the adjustments required by that programme are surely evident in these texts. As one Welsh Prince of Wales – Glyn Dŵr – sinks, another English one – Hal – dramatically rises to replace him. As, concomitantly, the threatening figure of a Llewellyn seems about to rise, so the wholesome caricature of a Fluellen brings it down to earth.

The volatile, unstable text that is Shakespeare's 'Britain' shares a number of features with the text displayed in *Glas*. Examined historically, it is clear that the column called 'England' has always already been engaged with the column called 'Wales' across whatever borders may be proposed between them. There never was a static, unified and clearly defined England, absolutely distinct and separable from a static, unified and clearly defined Wales. And neither the English language nor the Welsh language has ever been uniformly current throughout each respective culture. All such texts, that is to say, as well as all the texts – in this case plays – which derive from and are addressed to them, covertly partake in the condition which *Glas* makes overt: fractured, dependent, jigsawed into place, their unified 'meaning' turns out to be generated more by our hopes, expectations and readings than by anything in their own material nature.

For many reasons, it has seemed appropriate in recent years to present the Irish dimension of the early modern 'Great Britain' project as its most revealing feature and to stress the unease with which the history plays engage it.[26] My purpose is certainly not to question the existence of this aspect of the plays, or its relevance for us in Britain, so much as to suggest a re-ordering of the priorities which have pushed it into prominence. For what must surely now be sensed is that Welshness and its concerns throb with a no less powerful, if occluded pulse in the vasty deep of these plays. And periodically, its muffled beat invades and disrupts the step by which they march.

Perhaps the greatest irony lies in the extent to which, since the nineteenth century, the very unease about an integrated 'Britain' which the plays embody has been occluded in the name of a British culture which they are systematically used to reinforce. The ideological processes which can in wartime present *Henry V* as a clarion call to British unity are undoubtedly complex ones. The very idea of Great Britain as a single entity clearly depends upon, and is validated by, economic success. The absence of that is bound to generate – as we more recently see – nationalism of a different kind, currently identifiable with Irishness, Scottishness and Welshness. Continued difficulties may of course finally wake the most feared spectre of all: an English nationalism anxious once more to impose itself on those cultures with whom interaction is the price of self-identity.

The first response to that may well be the funereal tolling of Derrida's *Glas* (the word means knell) if not its bloody equivalent, the appalling sound of blades being whetted on the stones of Bryn Glas. Meanwhile, the association of Wales with a feared, emasculating 'effeminacy' and the covert presence of that in the plays casts its own ironic shadow on a British colonial machine which, from the nineteenth century on, promoted Shakespeare in a context of institutionalized homosexuality in same-sex public schools, precisely because both the plays and that context were felt to be efficacious in the establishment and reinforcement of the kind of 'manliness' appropriate to Englishness and Empire.

Perhaps it would be misleading to offer this as an aspect of Housman's response to those 'blue remembered hills'. But it's worth acknowledging that it once again gives us occasion to applaud the perspicacity of two notoriously uncolonizable Irish critics. For it was W. B. Yeats who proposed that, in effect, Shakespeare's history plays dramatized the clash between Celtic and Saxon views of the world, with the continuing battle between claimants for the crown a version of the momentous struggle for the British soul between an imaginative Celtic sensitivity on the one hand, and a calculating Saxon rationality on the other. This analysis led Yeats to admire the 'vessel of porcelain, Richard II', to despise 'the vessel of clay, Henry V', and ultimately, as Philip Edwards comments, to present Shakespeare as an honorary Celt.[27] No less pointedly, it was Oscar Wilde who suggested that the mysterious object of the Bard's private admiration was none other than an irresistible boy actor 'of great beauty', born and bred in Wales. Unlike the demeaning confection 'Fluellen', his name, Wilde claims, was the entirely credible and wholly acceptable 'Willy Hughes'. It remains a thought of special piquancy that the most memorable of the unquiet spirits unleashed by the events at Bryn Glas might finally turn out to be 'Mr. W. H.' And however unlikely, such a prospect would mean that a story which began with willies could also, at the very least, be said to end with one.

Notes

An earlier version of this essay appeared in *The European Journal of English Studies*, 1997, 1(3): 269–90.

   1 A recent historian has presented the two versions of Wales in terms of two different modes of entry into, or readings of, the Principality, which chart its culture from two opposed points of view: on the one hand that of an English official, reliant on the stepping-stones of towns and castles, but otherwise alienated and at risk in a remote and unintelligibly foreign country, and on the other that of a native Welsh-speaking poet, whose 'bardic' role involves precisely the weaving – using legend, myth and genealogy – of a coherent vision of national identity. See Davies 1995: 5–34.
   2 Henken 1996 gives an authoritative account of the role in folklore of the Glyn Dŵr figure, both as redeemer and trickster, throughout Welsh history. For an incisive discussion of the role of Wales in Tudor Britain which deals compellingly with a number of the issues developed in the present essay, see Howard and Rackin 1997: 168–74.
   3 Holinshed 1587: 520.
   4 Ibid.: 528.
   5 See Williams 1985: 117.
   6 Ibid.: 119.
   7 The idea of Britain as a separate but coherent 'world the world without' is discussed in Edwards 1979: 87–8 and in Wind 1967: 224–30.
   8 See Williams 1985: 121–3.
   9 Ibid.: 121.
  10 Ibid.: 123–4.
  11 Ibid.: 124–6.
  12 See Shakespeare 1960: xxvi.
  13 In view of Hotspur's notoriously 'thick' speech, this may be less of an achievement than Glendower supposes.
  14 See the authoritative account of the battle in Davies 1995: 107–8. The 'beastly' Circean transformation wrought by the Welsh on the English was evidently a fundamental one, its implications powerful

enough to initiate a theme of metamorphosis which Shakespeare's whole tetralogy extrapolates. In these plays, ordinary humans such as Bolingbroke can be transformed into kings and it seems almost reasonable for the king to hope that some 'night-tripping fairy' might turn out to have transformed his son (I. i. 85–8). Human beings can be transformed into animals (III. i. 142–55), the course of rivers can be transformed by dams, the whole island of Britain can be transformed by the plans of the rebels, and as the climax of the process, the madcap Hal is ultimately transformed into Henry V.

15 Glendower's Welshness of course needs no demonstration. His standing as native 'Prince of Wales' is variously emphasized, as, for instance, when immediately after his exit at the end of the plotting scene (III. i.), the king enters, with Hal, saying 'Lords, give us leave; The Prince of Wales and I/Must have some private conference' (III. ii. 1–2). Clearly the title 'Prince of Wales' is a disputable one and Glendower's claims to it raise the issue. Not insignificantly, Falstaff's most eloquent plea for his own preservation comes when he too is playing the part of 'Prince of Wales' (II. iv. 469–74). Glendower's entry, moments after Falstaff has been discovered behind the arras asleep, and at his most grotesquely dilapidated, even suggests the possibility of doubling these two roles, to underline, silently but effectively, their connection.

16 Sinfield 1992: 131. See also Traub 1992.

17 See Shakespeare 1960: xii–xiii; xvi–xviii; xxxix and lxviff. Oldcastle's situation is described in Holinshed 1587: 544, 560. Conflicting versions of his story paint him either as scoundrel or 'valiant martyr', depending on the religious viewpoint at stake (an indeterminacy which the play perhaps encourages). However, Oldcastle's name was changed because Sir Henry Brooke, Lord Cobham, or his father Sir William Brooke – both descendants of the historical Oldcastle – objected, early in 1597, to the depiction of their ancestor as a reprobate. The character was then given the name of Sir John Fastolf (1378–1459), one of Henry V's leaders, who fought well at Agincourt. However, at the battle of Patay, he deserted Talbot, who was captured as a result. The *Sir John Oldcastle* play admits that its hero had been travestied.

18 See Davies 1995: 300–1.

19 See Edwards 1979: 74–86. Edwards' account of the play's 'conviction ... of the dominance of England' (ibid.: 74) perhaps underestimates the doubts and insecurities the project of 'Great Britain' was capable of engendering amongst all parties involved.

20 Cf. 'Sense contaminates this non-sense that is supposed to be kept aside; the name is not supposed to signify anything, yet it does begin to signify' (Derrida 1983: 192; see also 193).

21 See Williams 1985: 119.

22 Davies 1995: 129. Glyn Dŵr's full Welsh name was Owain ap

Gruffudd, or Owain Glyn Dŵr, Owain of Glyndyfrdwy. His cognomen derives from his connection with the manor of Glyndyfrdwy (Glendowerdy) in the Dee valley in Wales. See Williams 1985: 106 and Davies 1995: 1.
23 Williams 1985: 114.
24 T.W. Craik offers the strange comment that 'Fluellen' is 'an anglicized spelling of Llewelyn [*sic*] that prevents incorrect pronunciation' (Shakespeare 1995: 205). See also p. 111.
25 I take the view that the killing is not mitigated by being a response to the French attack on the boys: the command is issued before that event. This matter and the larger issue of Henry's 'coldbloodedness' is discussed by Gary Taylor in Shakespeare 1984: 32–3.
26 See Edwards 1979: 74ff. Also, e.g., Murphy 1996 and Baldo 1996.
27 See Edwards 1979: 205–11.

Part 2

8

'Local-manufacture made-in-India Othello fellows'
Issues of race, hybridity and location in post-colonial Shakespeares[1]

ANIA LOOMBA

For some people, when you say 'Timbuktu' it is like the end of the world, but that is not true. I am from Timbuktu, and I can tell you we are right at the heart of the world.
Ali Farka Toure, 'Talking Timbuktu'

I who am poisoned with the blood of both
  Where shall I turn, divided to the vein?
  ... how choose
  Between this Africa and the English tongue I love?
Derek Walcott, 'A Far Cry from Africa'

I

If colonial regimes and ideologies sought to create rigid boundaries between races and cultures, 'hybridity' has become the rallying cry for many post-colonial theorists and writers, especially in the wake of Fanon's *Black Skin, White Masks* (1967). Colonial and post-colonial subjectivities are now widely understood as hybrid conditions; conversely, it has become a kind of common-sense that hybridity is a necessary marker of the post-colonial condition. These equations have also been sharply contested, so that hybridity has become a key issue in ongoing debates about post-colonial studies, their post-structuralist genesis and Western location, their reconfiguration of colonial history and the contemporary globe, and their under-standing of power as well as subversion. In this essay, I shall trace some of these debates, and then discuss how hybridity is now used in some current discussions of race and colonialism in Shakespeare. In the second section, I will consider Salman Rushdie's novel, *The Moor's Last Sigh* (1995) and a 1996 Indian production of *Othello* in the Kathakali style of dance-drama, in order to suggest that any meaningful discussion of colonial or post-colonial hybridities de-mands close attention to the specificities of location as well as a conceptual re-orientation which requires taking on board non-Eu-ropean histories and modes of representation.

Although the term 'hybridization' technically refers to the bo-tanical notion of inter-species grafting and evokes the 'vocabulary of the Victorian extreme right' (Young 1995: 10), in post-colonial theory it is widely used to gesture towards those discursive and be-havioural ways in which this vocabulary was challenged and undermined. One of the contradictions that most defines colonialist regimes is the fact that despite their need to 'civilize' their 'others', and to fix them into perpetual 'otherness', they catalyse and gener-ate crossovers. In Fanon's view, the colonized subject is hybridized most powerfully by his attempt to mimic dominant culture (the male pronoun is used to indicate Fanon's bias). For Fanon (1967), this is a fatal mimicry which leads to a terrible schism between black skin and white masks, to the black subject's disavowal of his roots and to his tragic attempt to fashion a European self. In recent post-colonial theory, Fanon has been appropriated, most notably by Homi K. Bhabha, as 'a premature poststructuralist' (Parry 1987: 31). The divide between black skin and white mask is not, Bhabha contends, 'a neat division' but

> a doubling, dissembling image of being in at least two places at once. … It is not the Colonialist Self or the Colonised Other, but the disturbing distance in between that constitutes the figure of colonial otherness – the White man's artifice inscribed on the Black man's body. It is in relation to this impossible object that emerges the liminal problem of colonial identity and its vicissitudes.
>
> (Bhabha 1994b: 117)

For Bhabha, colonial identities are always hybrid and oscillating, never perfectly achieved, and colonial authority is rendered am-bivalent in the very process of being enforced.

This highly influential model of colonial relations derives from and contributes towards a post-structuralist and psychoanalytically inflected conception of split subjectivity. It transfers a Foucaultian understanding of interpenetration and interdependence of the powerful and the marginalized to the colonial encounter, thus challenging not just the binary oppositions between races and cultures produced both by Orientalist and other imperialist discourses, but also those anti-colonial discourses that merely inverted these binaries and suggest an absolute separation of colonizers and the colonized. Bhabha refracts Fanon through a psychoanalytic-linguistic-post-structuralist lens to suggest also the *radical* potential of in-between states. The ambivalence of colonial discourses indicates a failure of authority smoothly to impose itself upon those it seeks to govern. Conversely, the mimicry of colonized subjects is not a tragic failure, as another reading of Fanon might argue, but a subversion of authority. Bhabha's reading has been extremely influential and in much post-colonial criticism, intercultural and interracial crossovers, in-between-ness, creolization and ambivalence are all interpreted as challenging cultural or ideological fixity, often in ways that remain rather vague and unspecified.

Such an appropriation of Fanon has also been vigorously challenged: Benita Parry argues that Fanon and his comrades were hardly agonized individuals caught in a perpetual oscillation but

> authors of liberation theories ... [who] affirmed the intervention of an insurgent, unified black self, acknowledged the revolutionary energies released by valorising the cultures denigrated by colonialism and, rather than construing the colonialist relationship in terms of negotiations with the structures of imperialism, privileged coercion over hegemony to project it as a struggle between implacably opposed forces.
>
> (Parry 1994: 179)

Colonial ambivalence, according to Abdul JanMohamed, is a strategy of 'imperial duplicity' which actually reinforces a Manichean dichotomy between colonizer and colonized (JanMohamed 1985: 60). Nationalist struggles as well as pan-nationalist anti-colonial movements passionately appropriated the notion of such a dichotomy; liberation, for them, hinged upon the discovery or rehabilitation of their cultural identity which European colonialism had disparaged and wrecked. The dynamics of such anti-colonial nationalisms, it has been suggested, cannot be understood within the parameters of current theories of hybridity.

As a matter of fact, influential accounts of nationalism have interpreted it as a species of hybridity. According to Benedict Anderson, the native intelligentsia in the colonies played such a crucial role in forging nationalist consciousness because they were bilingual and had access 'to modern Western culture in the broadest sense, and in particular, to the models of nationalism, nation-ness, and nation-state produced elsewhere' (Anderson 1991: 116). Anti-colonial nationalism, in other words, is a 'derivative discourse', a Calibanistic model of revolt which is dependent upon the colonizer's gift of language/ideas. Anderson's argument here converges with the standard colonialist writings on nationalism, which went so far as to suggest that Indians learnt their ideas of freedom and self-determination from the plays of Shakespeare! The phrase 'derivative discourse' is the subtitle of Partha Chatterjee's book *Nationalist Thought and the Colonial World* (1986) which challenges Anderson's model, suggesting that the relationship between anti-colonial and metropolitan nationalisms is structured by an intricate relationship of both borrowing and difference. As he puts it elsewhere:

> If nationalisms in the rest of the world have to choose their imagined community from certain 'modular' forms already made available to them by Europe and the Americas, what do they have left to imagine? History, it would seem, has decreed that we in the postcolonial world shall only be perpetual consumers of modernity. Europe and the Americas, the only true subjects of history, have thought out on our behalf not only the script of colonial enlightenment and exploitation, but also that of our anticolonial resistance and postcolonial misery. Even our imaginations must remain forever colonised.
>
> (Chatterjee 1993: 5)

Chatterjee attempts to break away from such a debilitating paradigm by locating the processes of ideological and political exchange in the creation of Indian nationalism – of identifying what he calls 'the ideological sieve' through which nationalists filtered European ideas.

I want to suggest that such 'ideological sieves' have not been sufficiently considered either by post-colonial theorists of hybridity or by Shakespeareans who discuss the contact between cultures in early modern or our own times. At a very obvious level, every culture can be said to be hybrid – in fact even 'authentic' identities are the result of ongoing processes of selection, cutting and mixing of cultural vocabularies. In practice, hybridity and authenticity are rarely either/or positions. Moreover, as Neil ten Kortenaar sensibly reminds us,

> *neither* authenticity nor creolization has ontological validity, but both are valid as metaphors that permit collective self-fashioning. ... Like authenticity, hybridization is a metaphor that does not define a particular political program. Hybridization is most often invoked by advocates of pluralism and tolerance, but it can also underwrite imperialism (as in the case of French nationalist Jules Michelet). ... Authenticity and creolization are best regarded as valuable rhetorical tools that can be made to serve liberation.
> (ten Kortenaar, 1995: 40–1)

The problem with the invocations of hybridity in much postcolonial theory, then, is not merely that they downgrade the radical potential of notions of authenticity, but that they fail to account for the *different* ways in which colonial and post-colonial subjects can be understood as hybrid.

In a related argument, Arif Dirlik complains that 'postcolonial criticism has focused on the postcolonial subject to the exclusion of an account of the world outside of the subject' (Dirlik 1994: 336). This is a somewhat unhelpful formulation, because though in practice it *has* been notoriously difficult for contemporary cultural theorists to pay equally nuanced attention to both socio-political and psycho-sexual aspects of human existence, 'the subject' and the 'world outside the subject' cannot be polarized. Those who ignore 'the world outside the subject' also fail to grasp the nuances of the inner lives of colonial or post-colonial subjects. 'The colonial subject' projected by theorists of hybridity is in fact curiously homogeneous – undifferentiated by class, location or gender and split or hybrid according to a pattern that remains uniform over time and space. Fanon's split subject is in fact not so dislocated, but he cannot be expanded to become the paradigmatic colonized subject both because he is resolutely male and because the kind of psychic dislocations Fanon discusses are more likely to be felt by native elites or those colonized individuals who were educated within, or invited to think of themselves as mobile within, the colonial system than by those who existed on its margins. The colonialist presence was felt differently by various subjects of the empire – some never even saw Europeans in all their lives, and for them authority still wore a native face. For others, but even for some of the elites (as Chatterjee discusses) the foreign presence was daily visible, but physical as well as cultural space was still divided into 'their' sphere and 'ours'. In other parts of the world colonialism had penetrated much deeper into the everyday existence of natives of all classes. These patterns also shifted over time. Thus the resonances of both 'hybridity' and mimicry are enormously variable and we need to peg the psychic splits engendered by colonial rule to specific histories and locations.

This issue was brought home to me while watching a video recording of Janet Suzman's production of Shakespeare's *Othello* designed for the Market Theatre in Johannesburg. Both in terms of the play's own history, which has downplayed its racial politics, and in terms of the South African context, where interracial marriages were legislated against, this was a radical production. And certainly to place Othello in one of the cultures of 'his' origin is to allow us to rethink the entire history of the play. And yet, the play is not just about race in general but about a black man isolated from other black people. His loneliness is an integral feature of the play's racial politics. Shakespeare's *Othello* is about the African in Europe and not the African in Africa. Their histories are connected, then as now, and yet we cannot simply elide the marginalization that arises out of geographic displacement with another in which black people and cultures are devalued but not literally isolated from each other. My point is not that Suzman should have respected the original play, but that in our analyses of hybridity, we need to discriminate between 'forced assimilation, internalized self-rejection, political co-optation, social conformism, cultural mimicry, and creative transcendence' (Shohat 1993: 110).

Most accounts of colonial and post-colonial hybridities in fact effect a reverse collapse from that which we see in Suzman's play, by telescoping diverse post-colonial histories and subjects into the figure of the migrant. Given the enormous shifts of people and ideas engendered by colonial encounters, it would be foolish to deny the radical potential of uncertain location. The problem is not so much *which* location to emphasize but that the *specificities* of each must be respected. Second, accounts of ambivalence and hybridity generally concentrate on colonial culture. Hybridity is read largely by calibrating what happens to dominant culture as it is muddied by foreign influences, or locating to what extent diverse native subjects become Europeanized. Rarely does a theory of hybridity consider with equal attention the other half without which the very term hybridity can mean nothing. We cannot appreciate the specificities of different hybrid forms if we do not attend to the nuances of *each* of the cultures that go into their making, or identify the 'ideological sieve' through which ideas are filtered in each direction.

Both these issues are also important for Shakespearean criticism, as it tries to unravel the racial and colonial dimensions of Shakespearean drama in its own time, in our contemporary world, and in the encounter of the 'then' with the 'now'. As I have discussed elsewhere, even otherwise brilliant and pioneering scholarship on Shakespeare and early modern culture has interpreted representations of non-Europeans according to fashionable models of hybridity, so that all native voices are understood as either being silenced by European domination or to be part of a 'derivative discourse'. Different colonial histories and subjects are therefore collapsed into one another and Caliban and Othello emerge as startlingly similar figures (Loomba 1996). In a recent essay, Emily Bartels (1997) also pleads for a greater attention to diverse histories of early modern contact, and holds 'postcolonial critiques' responsible for over-emphasizing the power of colonialism, with the result that Europeans always come out 'on top'. Bartels, however, seems unaware of the well-established debates on the relationship between colonial domination and subaltern agency, so that she not only collapses the differences between widely divergent positions and critics, but also ends up suggesting that *Othello* is not a play about racial domination at all, but represents a harmoniously integrated subject!

Bartels correctly points out that English colonization of Africa was not an early modern phenomenon. But from this she arrives at the startling conclusion that Africans and blackness carried no negative connotations in early modern England. Arguing that prejudice against blackness in *Othello* is limited to Iago and other characters whom the play denounces, Bartels suggests that Iago's bias is 'deeply personal ... motiveless and malignant as he is' (Bartels 1997: 62). Renaissance travelogues and plays do not use the term 'Moor' only for Africans. It is also important to remember that well before the actual enslavement and colonial plunder of Africans began, racist stereotypes which were obsessed with colour and nakedness were well in place.[2] In fact in several colonial situations these stereotypes provided an ideological *justification* for different kinds of exploitation. Therefore the relationship between racial ideologies and exploitation is better understood as dialectical, with racial assumptions both arising out of and structuring economic exploitation (Miles 1989: 27). And even if only the baddies in the play are racist, their attitudes are surely testimony to some contemporary tensions. In so deliberately resurrecting Coleridge's description of Iago, Bartels reverts to an understanding of 'the personal' and the 'psychic' as untouched by political and social structures, as welling out of some ahistorical inner essence.

Significantly, Bartels begins this essay by lamenting that her students always want to read *Othello* in terms of the blackness of its central figure. In persuading them otherwise, the key concept for Bartels is that of hybridity: for her Othello is not a victim of racial prejudice because 'Shakespeare ... denotes Othello flexibly, particularly along ethnic lines, *as a Moor who is simultaneously of Venice*'. Othello is a figure whose 'ethnicity occupies one slot, professional interests another, *compatibly*' (ibid.: 61; both emphases added). This is clearly a different play from the one I read, in which Othello's painful split between his Moorishness and his status in Venice is graphically enacted on stage in his suicide. The very incompatibility of these two aspects of his position in Venice are the motor of the entire action. Not just Iago and Brabantio, but Othello himself makes many references to his blackness and status as outsider. In recent years critics have abundantly traced how Othello's military competence, his rhetorical flamboyance, and his self-assurance in fact catalyse his downfall – one does not have to erase these in order to trace the work of racism in the play. I cite this essay at some length because, in the name of historical accuracy, it invokes Othello's hybridity to deny our urgent contemporary need to discuss racism. Perhaps Bartels' students are concerned with race because it matters in their own lives. As Ben Okri put it so pithily, even if *Othello* was originally not a play about race, its history has made it one. Historicizing Shakespeare and 'race' cannot be a scholarly project that denies us our own histories and politics.

In an essay that asks similar questions about what blackness means in Shakespeare's play, Carol Neely also suggests that Othello should be read not as a black at all but as a 'mestizo' – a hybrid (1995: 305). Both Bartels and Neely posit Othello's 'hybridity' as a way of stressing his relative agency and power. For both though, hybridity is *counterposed* to blackness and agency to the force of European domination, and these terms become the critical means of underplaying the force of racial difference in the play – both in its own context and now. 'Hybridity', as we have discussed earlier in this essay, does not *automatically* indicate resistance or agency. As this concept is fuzzily imported from a certain kind of post-structuralist post-colonial studies, detached even from the debates that surround it there, it serves only to flatten and decontextualize the Shakespearean text.

Early modern histories of 'contact' cannot be read solely from European representations of others; we also need to set these plays and narratives against those produced in Turkey, Africa, India, the Americas and elsewhere. The need to move beyond European representations becomes even more urgent when we study the Shakespearean encounters with non-English players and intellectuals, encounters that do not always result in the latter mimicking English identities and accents. Sometimes Shakespeare becomes a junior partner, a means for 'other' people to negotiate their own past and contemporary contexts. In early 1996, I taught a course on 'Shakespearean appropriations'. We were lucky to be able to include a spectacular adaptation of *Othello* into Kathakali, a dance-drama form from Kerala, a state on the south-western coast of India. In thinking about this particular staging of Shakespeare's play, I realized that at first I only asked what it was doing to Shakespeare. Slowly, I was compelled to invert that question, and try and understand what the production was doing to Kathakali. By setting this production against Rushdie's *The Moor's Last Sigh*, I hope to indicate the variable dynamics of two Shakespeare-induced hybrid representations.

II

The Kathakali *Othello* is over two hours long. Produced by the International Centre for Kathakali in New Delhi, it includes only five scenes: Roderigo and Iago's initial meeting, the Senate scene, Othello and Desdemona's meeting in Cyprus, a long scene that amalgamates Cassio's meeting with Desdemona, her pleading with Othello on Cassio's behalf, Iago snatching the handkerchief from Emilia and planting seeds of suspicion in Othello's mind, and finally, the bedchamber scene. If the original play were played in full, the production would go on for twelve hours or more, as in fact Kathakali performances often do.

Like Noh and Kabuki, Kathakali is a highly formal style of theatre which evolved at about the same time as Shakespearean drama. This 'story-play' is a hybrid form that drew upon various earlier arts. Its dramatic principles are based upon Bharata's *Natyashastra*, the encyclopaedia of Indian dramaturgy and theatrical techniques which dates between 200 BC and AD 200. Its elaborate and heavy

Plate 1 Iago and Othello (courtesy Arjun Raina)

costumes, mask-like make-up and a complex gestural code or *mudras*, in which over 500 facial, eye or hand gestures are used to 'speak' to the audience, are drawn from an earlier form of theatre, *Kutiyattam*. From the religious theatre *Taiyyam*, Kathakali takes its repeated theme of battles between good and demonic figures. In the *Othello* production, Iago and Othello become such archetypes. The famous martial art form of Kerala, *Kalarippayat*, contributes to Kathakali's choreography and rigorous methods of training. Under colonial rule, Kathakali's patronage by the landed aristocracy or rich households began to crumble and collapsed further with the breakdown of princely estates. Today's 'patrons' are either just those audiences who have grown up with the form, or else state-sponsored schools or institutions such as the International Centre for Kathakali (see Zarrilli 1984).

During the time we were studying this production, I also began reading Salman Rushdie's latest novel, *The Moor's Last Sigh* (1995), which traces its central character's origins to the same Malabar coast to which Kathakali belongs. However, these two rewritings of Shakespeare's Moor are born of two very different kinds of 'post-colonial' dynamics. *The Moor's Last Sigh* is the product of a sophisticated English-speaking intellectual hankering for a remembered home. The Kathakali *Othello* is crafted within a centuries-old form that has only recently begun to become internationally visible. Rushdie, the high priest of diasporic post-coloniality, and master of the hybrid tongue, is at pains to delineate the long and intricate history of cultural and racial intermingling in this region: today's population is almost evenly divided between Christians (mainly Roman Catholics and Syrian Orthodox), Muslims and Hindus. But at the same time, Rushdie's 'hybrid' Kerala is described in terms that are remarkably similar to his 'hybrid' Bombay, with whom he seems more comfortable (both the Bombay of this novel and the one described in *Midnight's Children*). Rushdie's vocabulary and images remain fairly similar for these two fairly dissimilar terrains and cultures because the crucial point for him is that each is 'impure'. The Kathakali production, on the other hand, skirts all questions and histories of difference in its powerful appropriation of this story about difference. It is anxious to craft a vocabulary that will allow it to experiment with plays like *Othello* without violating its own specific codes of signification.

For at least two hundred years, Othello's origins and Moorishness have been the focus of critical debate: what shade of black was he? Where did he come from? What exactly does his blackness mean? Rushdie expands these questions to embrace both the history of racial conflict in early modern Europe and communal and religious strife in contemporary India. His Moor's mother, Aurora, belongs to the Catholic da Gama family of Cochin, pepper traders by profession. She marries the Jewish Abraham Zogoiby, whose mother attempts to forbid this match 'because it was unheard of for a Cochin Jew to marry outside the community' (Rushdie 1995: 70). For Abraham's mother, Moors are the real threat, and she accuses Aurora's family of not being pure 'Christy's' but having Moorish blood in them. Her anger against Aurora erupts as 'A curse on all Moors. ... Who destroyed the Cranganore synagogue? Moors, who else. Local-manufacture made-in-India Othello fellows. A plague on their houses and spouses' (ibid.: 72). Abraham then reveals that he knows of the Moorish blood in his own lineage. As a young boy he had discovered, in a trunk in the synagogue, the crown of the last Moorish Sultan of Granada. In one dramatic sentence, Rushdie brings together the European drive to overseas expansion with the will to cleanse its interior of non-white peoples:

> Thus Abraham learned that, in January 1492, while Christopher Columbus watched in wonderment and contempt, the Sultan Boabdil of Granada had surrendered the keys to the fortress-palace of the Alhambra, last and greatest of all the Moors' fortifications, to the all-conquering Catholic Kings Fernando and Isabella. ... He departed into exile with his mother and retainers, bringing to a close centuries of Moorish Spain.
>
> (Ibid.: 79–80)

Both Jews and Moors fled South, and Boabdil took on a Jewish lover who stole his crown and moved to India. Abraham asks, 'Mother, who is worse? My Aurora who does not hide the Vasco connection, but takes delight; or myself, born of the fat old Moor of Granada's last sighs in the arms of his thieving mistress – Boabdil's bastard Jew?' (ibid.: 82–3).

Rushdie plays on the images of both *Othello* and *The Merchant of Venice* as he weaves the histories of Jews and Muslims. Aurora and Abraham's fourth child is the Moor, whose hybrid genes and abnormal rate of growth become a metaphor for the fecundity of metropolitan India. Against this chaotic history, the novel charts the growth of fundamentalist communal identities in Bombay, evoking the rise of the right-wing militant organization the Shiv Sena, and the violence that followed the destruction of the Babri mosque in Ayodhya in December 1992. His Moor flees back to Spain where he dies, looking at the 'Alhambra, Europe's red fort, sister to Delhi's and Agra's' and hoping to awake in better times (ibid.: 433). His hero's expulsion from Bombay also mirrors Rushdie's own distance from India. But where Othello's last sigh testifies to the agonizing split between Moorish past and Christian present, black skin and white mask, the recurring motif of the Moor's last sigh in Rushdie's novel indicates not psychic but historical and geographic schisms: the hybridity of the post-colonial polity rather than of the individual subject.

The Kathakali *Othello* inflects the Moor's agonies in a different direction and erases the schisms central both to Shakespeare's play and Rushdie's novel. It flamboyantly reshapes Othello's tragedy in the language of a four hundred year-old form first devised to perform stories from the Hindu epic *Ramayana*. Its Othello is neither a black man nor a Moor, but takes the form of a Hindu warrior. Historical arrivals on the Malabar coast do not inflect his story; nor do the contemporary ideologies of belonging and exclusion in India colour his identity. Thus, while one post-colonial revision restlessly searches the globe for histories and motifs which foreground the question of difference, the other uses centuries of stagecraft to reach out and mould difference in its own image. As part of a post-colonial appropriation of Shakespeare, these silences disappoint us. But they speak eloquently about the dynamics of the post-colonial evolution of Kathakali.

The International Centre of Kathakali was founded in 1960, with the aim of addressing the specific problems 'involved in adapting Kathakali to the modern stage' (Zarrilli 1984: 305). It has produced several plays outside of the traditional Kathakali corpus such as *Mary Magdalene, David and Goliath*, and *Salome*. The Kathakali Centre thus marks the attempt to forge traditional, regional traditions into a national (and perhaps nationalist) conception of the Indian Arts. It is one of many similar institutions conceived within the Nehruvian ideal of a multicultural yet united India, evoked lyrically and nostagically in *The Moor's Last Sigh* as the

> dawning of a new world … a free country, above religion because secular, above class because socialist, above caste because enlightened, above hatred because loving, above vengeance because forgiving, above tribe because unifying, above language because many-tongued, above colour because multi-coloured,

Plate 2 Othello and Desdemona

Plate 3 Brabantio, Desdemona and Othello in the senate scene

Plate 4 The murder

above poverty because victorious over it, above ignorance because literate, above stupidity because brilliant.

(Rushdie 1995: 51)

In the face of an aggressive and escalating communalism, the
need to affirm a secular nationalism seems enormous. And yet so
many of the ethnic, linguistic and class tensions of contemporary
India are precisely the product of the exclusions engendered by the
post-colonial nationalist state, as Bengali writer Mahasweta Devi's
short story 'Shishu' (Children) so gut-wrenchingly illustrates. In this,
a well-meaning government officer, Mr Singh, learns that the re-
lief supplies he has come to distribute to a drought-ridden region
are regularly stolen by mysterious children. Many years earlier,
tribals called the Agarias had opposed government attempts to mine
the region for iron and coal. Their myths forbade the attempt to
carve the belly of the earth. But national 'development' has little
space for such local 'fairy stories' and the rebellious Agarias were
driven into the forests and into starvation. Singh's own attitudes
towards the tribals replicates colonialist views of non-Western peoples – they are mysterious, superstitious, uncivilized, backward. At
the chilling climax of the tale, Singh is brought face to face with
these 'children' who thrust their starved bodies towards him:

They cackled with savage and revengeful glee. Cackling, they
ran around him. They rubbed their organs against him and told
him they were adult citizens of India. ...
Singh's shadow covered their bodies. And the shadow brought
the realization home to him.
They hated his height of five feet and nine inches.
They hated the normal growth of his body.
His normalcy was a crime they could not forgive.
Singh's cerebral cells tried to register the logical explanation
but he failed to utter a single word. Why, why this revenge? He
was just an ordinary Indian. He didn't have the stature of a
healthy Russian, Canadian or American. He did not eat food
that supplied enough calories for a human body. The World
Health Organization said that it was a crime to deny the human
body of the right number of calories.

(Mahasweta Devi 1993: 248–50)

Even as it is careful to demarcate what is available to citizens of
different nations, 'Shishu' reminds us that anti-colonial national-

ism has rarely represented the interests of all the peoples of a colonized country. I place this story against Rushdie's evocation of the nationalist ideal to indicate some of the tensions between the local, the national and the international, and between tradition and modernity, all of which are part of Kathakali's contemporary contexts.

What can Kathakali negotiate, and what must it still be silent about? The introduction of women actors may be the most radical change in Kathakali, which until recently was, like Shakespeare's plays in their original context, enacted solely by men. In the *Othello* production, a woman actor only occasionally played Desdemona. Female roles require special training, and according to Sadanam Srinathan, the man whom I saw play Desdemona, real women do not have the 'energy' to enact true femininity. Some of my students, who saw both Srinathan and a woman actor as Desdemona, preferred him for exactly these reasons. The elaborate non-realistic, exaggerated style of Kathakali privileges obvious impersonation rather than any form of naturalistic identification – its mask-like make-up, intensive massages administered to dancers through their training, heavy costumes and formalized gestural codes literally remould the stage body, privilege cross-dressing and establish a theatrical code where impersonation is flaunted.

The appropriate context for the Kathakali adaptation of Shakespeare is thus within indigenous performative and intellectual histories rather than in simply the colonial heritage of English literary texts in India. Of course, the centrality of Shakespeare to colonial and post-colonial Indian education cannot be entirely irrelevant to this production of *Othello*, since Kerala's education system is no exception to the rest of the country, and entirely canonical ideas about Shakespeare's greatness permeate the larger culture. But although some of Kathakali's high-born patrons, learned about its forms and traditions, might also have been schooled in, or familiar with, Shakespeare, Kathakali itself features patterns of training and teaching and the aesthetic philosophies that remained relatively isolated from English education. Within an indigenous high cultural sphere, certain theatrical or musical practices were protected by the elite as embodying an essential spiritual Indianness. Here the Fanonian model of agonistic hybridity is modified by a dualism in which one aesthetic code does not necessarily displace the other.[3]

For Sadanam Balakrishnan, the writer, director and chief actor of *Othello*, the production is an ongoing experiment, which will take at least another year to reach maturity. Scenes have been added each time the play has been performed, and over the next year he hopes a satisfying and creative meeting of the English play and the Indian form will take place. For him, the challenge lies in working within the rigid conventions of Kathakali, and flexing them to tell an alien story. For example, he told me that it would be virtually impossible to play *King Lear* as Kathakali forbids a king to appear without his headgear, and how else could one show a disordered Lear? For him, the daring and innovation lay in playing upon the rules of Kathakali, rather than in producing a new version of *Othello*. Balakrishnan was referring to a 1989 production of *Lear* in Kathakali, jointly mounted by The Kerala State Arts Academy and Keli, a Paris-based theatre group formed by Australian director David McRuvie and French actress Annette Leday, in which Lear did appear without his crown and aroused much criticism in Kerala (see Zarrilli 1992). Balakrishnan's response, like the earlier critiques, can be read both as a conservatism about Kathakali's class-based conventions and a genuine scepticism about a superficial grafting of forms.

For me and my class, the most disturbing element about this production was its almost total erasure of Othello's difference, whether we understand that as a difference of colour or religion. In the context in which it was being performed, what does it mean to recall that Othello was not just a black man but a Moor? Although in early modern England 'Moor' became almost an umbrella term for non-Europeanness, it originally simply meant 'Muslim'. For Kathakali to adopt a Muslim protagonist would be as radical as it was for Shakespeare to stage a black hero. Although Kathakali is necessarily shaped by cultural borrowings (the female headdress is supposed to have derived from the headcoverings of Egyptian women, for example), and although its own social context would have provided it with a rich and complex basis for adapting the racial conflict that lies at the heart of Shakespeare's play, the Kathakali *Othello* repeats its own brand of insularity and virtually erases any notion of Othello's difference. Othello's hands are painted black, it is true, and the narration which accompanies the dancing identifies him as 'malechh', a term that means outcaste, polluted or dirty. His soldier's epaulets add a nice touch of modernity, or Westernization. But on the whole there is little attempt to place Othello socially. Othello's green make-up identifies him as a *pacca* figure, which in Kathakali includes divine figures, kings and heroic characters who are upright and moral and possess 'calm inner poise' (Zarrilli 1984:

170). His blue dress extends such connotations as blue signifies the colour of Lord Krishna's dark skin, and hence empties darkness of social prejudice. Iago, on the other hand, is resplendent in black clothes and is placed within the group of 'black beard' characters who are vile schemers. Thus the binaries of good and evil that Kathakali inherits from religious theatre are mapped on to Shakespeare's play in a fashion that ironically reinforces those readings of the play according to which Iago represents 'motiveless malignity' and Othello is actually a white man!

How could the question of race be inflected for us in India? Should Iago be a Brahmin, outraged by a lower-caste Othello? I was in fact disturbed by the opulence of Iago's costume – class differences, at least to my untrained eye, were totally erased by this production. Should Othello be a tribal? Or a Muslim? Would not these readings simply reinforce existing prejudices about violent Muslims and tribals? My students and I pondered further over this production's erasure of all social difference except that of gender. Was this simply a conceptual lack on the part of Sadanand Balakrishnan, or did it derive from Kathakali's aesthetic codes and modes of representation? Kathakali make-up is not only highly codified but also takes 2–4 hours to put on. As with many stylized forms of theatre, the outside and inside of each character are thus rendered inseparable. This also means that characters cannot fundamentally change in the course of theatrical action (although Kathakali's facial make-up is not quite a mask and permits, indeed facilitates, changes in expression and extremely nuanced muscle movements). In the case of *Othello* this poses a major problem, for Shakespeare's play charts a movement whereby Othello the noble and calm general becomes agonized and disordered; the loving husband becomes the murderer of his wife: the victim of racial prejudice mouths misogynist platitudes as he smothers the white woman he loves.

The murder poses a problem for feminist critics who point out that any reading of Othello as victim must also take note of his power over Desdemona. But within the Kathakali tradition, Desdemona's murder poses an altogether different problem: good women are never killed on stage and '*nari-hathya*' or female murder is not allowed. The *Othello* production flouts tradition in this regard, but its transgression works only to reinforce a misogynist interpretation of the play. If Othello is uncritically depicted as the prototype of a good man, his jealousy cannot be understood as something that is generated in and through his racial position. It becomes a 'universal' (and therefore 'understandable') male response to real or imagined female trans-gressions. To erase the racial politics of *Othello* is therefore to flatten it into a disturbingly misogynist text. Of course it is true that the audience knows that Desdemona is chaste. As one of my students pointed out, Desdemona's make-up and costume place her as a *Minukku* character which in Kathakali signifies benign femininity bordering on divinity. Thus if Othello as a *Pacca* can do no evil, Desdemona as *Minukku* in no way merits her death. This student pointed out too that in a traditional Kathakali battle between good and evil, the two circle each other, but the killing takes place centre stage or right. But in this case, Othello is forced to leave the 'clean' right half and move over to Desdemona's space and the performance closes with Othello, grief stricken, in a faint on her side: 'The convention's "double-coding" system thus allows one register to subvert another'.[4]

My class kept returning to the question of whether or not the strict gestural code of Kathakali could profitably interact with Shakespearean drama, and indeed with its modern Western stage conventions. Gen-der stereotyping is also compromised by the miming central to Kathakali stagecraft. Othello resolves that Desdemona 'must die, else she'll betray more men' (V. ii. 6). In the Kathakali production, Othello 'speaks' these lines by miming Desdemona the seductress who will charm other men. On the eve of the murder, he thus becomes the wife as well as the husband, the victim and the murderer. Even though Othello's split as Christian and Infidel, Turk and Venetian, European and Outsider is erased, we briefly glimpse another sort of doubleness that reso-nates with Kathakali's flamboyant enactment of gender difference. But of course, as on Shakespeare's stage, this is a male tradition of enacting women. Even though it flourished in a matrilineal society, Kathakali is notoriously masculine, not just by virtue of employing only male actors but in its aesthetic codes and its themes. Still, we noted that its Desdemona was not particularly passive, she answers back and is vigorous in her own defence. Sadanam Balakrishnan attributes this to the need for constant movement in Kathakali. Un-like on a conventional stage, Desdemona cannot be still. Thus Kathakali's various conventions and histories interact with, subvert or simply bypass those of Shakespeare's play.

The Kathakali *Othello* does not, then, offer a significant new in-terpretation of the play. It is not anti-colonial. It does not play upon or transgress colonial histories of the play, or of colonial Shake-speare in India, except at the very level of its existence. It does not even engage overtly with contemporary discourses about community and identity, although in its very silences we can read contemporary fissures of gender, caste, religion and ethnicity. Why then does the International Centre for Kathakali play with Shakespeare? I have tried to suggest that it is actually not interested in Shakespeare at all, except as a suitably weighty means through which it can negotiate its own future, shake off its own cramps, revise its own traditions, and expand its own performative styles. Only the Shakespeareans in the audience are concerned with its transgressions, or cognizant of those moments in which it either improves upon the original or fails to do justice to it. And even as 'Shakespeare' remains central for my own analysis of this production, the Kathakali *Othello* obliges me to mark the ways in which it 'provincializes' Shakespeare.[5]

Notes

1 I would like to thank Suvir Kaul, Arjun Raina and Kewal Arora for their generous and valuable inputs into this project. Earlier versions of this essay were presented at the 'Recontextualizing Indian Theatre' Seminar held at Hindu College, University of Delhi in November 1996 and the 'Shakespeare and Ireland' Conference held at Trinity College, Dublin in March 1997, and I would also like to thank various participants for their comments.

2 'Moors' are said to exist also in Turkey, India, the Moluccas and elsewhere and the term primarily connotes a religion (Islam) rather than a colour; see also Burton's essay in this volume. For contemporary ideologies of blackness see Miles 1989; Fryer 1984; Hall 1995.

3 I should qualify that I am not suggesting that this dually schooled audience is not caught in the colonial trauma in other ways.

4 I would like to thank Bhavana Krishnamoorthy for these insights.

5 Dipesh Chakrabarty (1992) asks historians of India to try and 'provincialize Europe' by shedding Eurocentric historical categories and methods.

9

Post-colonial Shakespeare? Writing away from the centre

MICHAEL NEILL

'Shakespeare–Post-coloniality–Johannesburg, 1996' – by the very syntactical abruptness of their title, the organizers of the Witwatersrand conference appeared to register a certain scepticism about its improbably yoked terms. Was there, or could there ever be such a thing as 'post-colonial Shakespeare'? The history of colonial Shakespeare is by now well documented; and the work of Ania Loomba (1989; 1997), Martin Orkin (1987), Jyotsna Singh (1989; 1996), Gauri Viswanathan (1987; 1990) and others has begun to illuminate its neo-colonial afterlife. But it is by no means clear at what point that afterlife can be said to have ended. The high period of neo-colonial Shakespeare was perfectly represented by the coronation-year tour of Australasia mounted by the Shakespeare Memorial Theatre under the direction of Anthony Quayle. The play given most prominence in this mission to the furthest outposts of British influence was, appropriately enough *Othello*; and in a programme note that sought to physic postwar disillusion with a mixture of Cold-War rhetoric and visionary neo-imperialism, Quayle summoned the white dominions to a New Elizabethan cause. He was disarmingly frank about the key role assigned to Shakespeare in the cultural hegemony that (under the benign presidency of the British Council) was to take the place of Empire:

The most remarkable characteristic of the Elizabethan age was its surging and expansive vitality. The inhabitants of a small island in the North Sea became suddenly and proudly aware of their nationhood and of their destiny, and with the energy born of that awareness they flung themselves into every possible adventure, mental, physical and aesthetic; they fought, they built, they governed, they wrote, they explored. ...

We, who live three and a half centuries later, are the inheritors of a greatly expanded, but at the same time much more cramping world. We belong to a weary and cynical age in which exploration of any kind is the privilege of the specialist, and enterprise of any kind is increasingly shackled. ... The old Elizabethan zest is almost gone, but the old Elizabethan dangers remain, looming greater and with more deadly import than Philip's Armada. Our heads today are so bowed with the stubborn effort to maintain our individual and national way of life that we can hardly raise them to glimpse ... our place in History.

Yet History has challenged us. This very year a young and gallant Queen will be crowned in Westminster. ... Inevitably we are the New Elizabethans, and inevitably the two epochs will one day be weighed one against the other. May ours not be the less glorious.

But what are we to do, we twentieth-century Elizabethans? Can we only look back regretfully to those twenty fabulous years of 1580–1600, when our nation was in the very May-day of its youth and vigour, when every horizon was unbounded? ... The impulse which drove the old Elizabethans to expand outwards was one of intense nationalism: the impulse we new Elizabethans must achieve is of practical internationalism; ours must not only be an outward voyaging, but a drawing and binding together of what is already so far-flung. ... In this adventure of unification, the theatre has a great part to play, and especially the theatre of William Shakespeare – a man whose words and whose characters have become a very part of our subconscious lives, a man whose writing is so potent that it would be hard to say whether he interpreted more than moulded the English character. ... While the English tongue is spoken on this earth his works will stand, a mysterious and ennobling human document. ... And I find it fitting that our theatre's contribution to Her Majesty's coronation should be this visit to her farthest Dominions. ... [I hope] that you, our audience, may have some idea of the ... ardent hope which we all share that this visit and these plays may make their contribution to the flowering of the New Elizabethan Age.

(Shakespeare Memorial Theatre Tour Programme, 1953)

In 1997 Quayle's successors in the shape of Adrian Noble's Royal Shakespeare Company are mounting another antipodean tour. Now, however, the images of imperial authority are confined to the courtly fantasies of *A Midsummer Night's Dream*. The programme includes a full-page colour portrait of the RSC's own Faery King, in the person of the Prince of Wales, whose accompanying epistle urges the enchantments of an 'elegant and witty production, which I and my children have much enjoyed'. In addition to this moving assertion of Royal Family Values, a message from the British High Commissioner lauds the tour as 'part of a year-long programme of events co-ordinated by the British Council and the British High Commission' to promote what is euphemistically described as 'the modern and evolving relationship between Britain and New Zealand'. But in the wider publicity for the *Dream*, these relics of the imperial order have been much less conspicuous than the sponsorship of commercial backers such as the multinational Allied Domecq, and its local co-sponsors, Optus Communications and the (recently privatized) commercial radio-station, Newstalk ZB. The tour is managed by a company best known for its outdoor opera spectaculars, and the RSC is sold as 'the world's best known theatre company' in publicity that pays as much attention to their season on Broadway and their success in the Tony Awards as to their Stratford and London work. Noble's programme note, which concentrates on the commercial prowess of the RSC ('selling in excess of 1.25 million tickets for more than 2,000 performances annually') identifies Australia and New Zealand as no more than stopping points in an 'international touring programme'.

In so far as it marks a partial displacement of the old centre, this is post-imperial Shakespeare of a sort, I suppose; but it can hardly be said to disturb the structures of cultural dependency for which Shakespeare has for so long been both signifier and instrument. Indeed, the sponsorship of Allied Domecq is a reminder of the missionary zeal of an earlier advocate of the spiritualizing alliance between Shakespeare and the market, Henry Clay Folger, President of Standard Oil and founder of the Folger Shakespeare Library in Washington DC. In Folger's funeral sermon, the Revd S. Parkes Cadman conjured up an extraordinary vision of Shakespeare and

Folger as angelic heralds of a new imperium erected on the twin foundations of capital and culture:

> Perhaps you may think I am presumptuous if I should tell what I have imagined ... [that] Will Shakespeare took Henry Clay Folger by the hand, and led him up to the blessed Christ. ... If Shakespeare is not there, who is there, after the blessed Apostles themselves? ... [Henry Folger's] dust will repose in the marble temple that will rise in Washington. His spiritual presence will overshadow it as the years come and go. The golden gates of another Renaissance will open. A new America will come, just as providential in the order of succession as that of Washington or Lincoln; an America which shall do on a wholesale scale what he did individually, which shall take the gifts of the market place and lay them without regard to cost or labour upon the altar of a more spiritualized existence for men and for nations.
>
> (Cadman *et al.* 1931: 18–19)

It is worth keeping Cadman's prophecy in mind, I think, when contemplating what the advertisement for one of the conference seminars described, in a blandly inclusive phrase, as 'our post-colonial condition'. Anyone practising Shakespeare now is, one might argue, a denizen of the world that Folger helped to build – one that is only dubiously 'post-colonial', and scarcely 'post-imperial' at all. For those of us who dwell on the margins of the new imperial order it is, I think, important to resist the totalizing implications of any claim to a common post-coloniality. Indeed, it is apparent that (as subaltern voices have increasingly insisted) there is not one 'post-colonial condition' but many: that of former colonizers differs in significant ways from that of the formerly colonized; that of Third-World societies from that of 'Fourth World' indigenes who have become minorities in their own countries; that of diasporic peoples from that of the metropolitans with whom they uneasily cohabit; and within these broad divisions there are innumerable differences determined by local combinations of class, gender and culture.

This essay necessarily comes out of my own highly particular experience as a *pakeha* ('European') teacher of both Shakespeare and post-colonial literature in that equivocally post-colonial space known as New Zealand/Aotearoa. In it I want to argue for the importance of the local in critical practice, while at the same time suggesting that those of us who (as the Americans say) 'do Shakespeare' at the margins of Folger's world have a common interest in interrogating the designs of metropolitan criticism. 'Not wishin' to say anything derogatory', as Fluther Good remarks in Sean O'Casey's dramatized meditation on the meanings of nation, history, and 'home', 'I think *it's all a question of location*'(O'Casey 1957: 138).

If current theory has made us familiar with the idea that *reading* is always done *from somewhere*, it is, I think equally important to recognize that *writing* is always addressed *to someone*; and that whom you address conditions what you can say. This is, I think, what lies behind Martin Orkin's insistence that *Shakespeare Against Apartheid* was aimed specifically at 'South African students' encountering Shakespeare for the first time (Orkin 1987: 9) – just as it underlies Ania Loomba's identification of female Indian undergraduates as the primary audience for a book that consciously seeks to identify ways in which the texts can intersect with the students' 'own reality' (Loomba 1989: 11, 23, 34, 38). Yet the key chapter of Orkin's book appeared first in *Shakespeare Quarterly*, whilst *Gender, Race, Renaissance Drama* was published by Manchester University Press as part of the Dollimore/Sinfield *Cultural Politics* series – facts that highlight the ambiguous predicament of writing from the margin in a globalized academic market. The discomfort created by the question of audience is nicely registered in the Afterword to David Johnson's recent *Shakespeare and South Africa*, where he records his awareness of 'at least four distinct audiences' for a book whose arguments were addressed 'in the first instance' to a metropolitan audience like that at which its Oxford publishers clearly aim, but whose most important 'imagined' constituency was always the South African students, 'many of whom were Xhosa speaking', who he ruefully admits are 'unlikely' ever to buy or read it (Johnson 1996: 213–14).

Where the auspices of Loomba's book proclaim an affiliation with British cultural materialism, and Orkin cites both cultural materialists and new historicists in the list of metropolitan critics whose work has helped to map 'the future of Shakespeare studies in South Africa' (Orkin 1987: 11), Johnson's local allegiances make him properly sceptical of easy assumptions about the translatability of metropolitan theory to post-colonial contexts. Not that he, or anyone else, would underestimate the liberating effect of recent historicist work for Shakespeareans on the margin. It has helped us to understand the complex ways in which Shakespeare's writing was entangled from the beginning with the projects of nation-building, Empire and colonization; and by its uncovering of the processes through which Shakespeare was simultaneously invented as the

'National Bard' and promoted as a repository of 'universal' human values, it has shown how the canon became an instrument of imperial authority as important and powerful in its way as the Bible and the gun. In this way, it announced the possibility of a Renaissance that we could fashion to our own purposes, instead of being passively fashioned by it – a Renaissance in which the work of Shakespeare and his contemporaries could be significantly relocated.

In the excitement generated by the sense of participating in a common project to re-plant Shakespeare in a historical narrative that can help to define our own sense of place, it is easy to forget, however, that the origins of the project lie elsewhere, and that its British and American practitioners address historical needs that are distinct from (though connected to) our own. Thus the British cultural materialist project was inseparable from the New Left attempt to think its way out from under the shadow of Empire in its final Thatcherian decadence. Greenblattian new historicism, by contrast, has partly to be understood as the latest stage in a takeover bid, designed to institutionalize that shift in the centre of cultural authority from Britain to the United States, whose advent was announced in Cadman's sermon. Because the primary 'market' for which Shakespeareans on the margins must produce lies elsewhere, success can seem to depend on our speaking in an accent that is familiar to metropolitan consumers; and while it is certainly impossible (even supposing such provincialism were desirable) to insulate ourselves from this pressure, we need to be alert to the dangers of ventriloquizing the voice of metropolitan orthodoxies whose ambitions are arguably no less hegemonic than those they seek to replace.

Of course, anxieties about location can sometimes produce grotesque exhibitions of self-consciousness: in a recent issue of the Australian journal *Southern Review*, for example, the author of a piece rather bafflingly entitled 'The Anti-Imperialist Approaches to Chaucer (Are There Those?)', devotes more space to analysing the semiotic implications of a photograph of herself in her Anglo-Indian grandmother's sari than to her nominal subject, strategies for reading Chaucer in what she circumspectly calls 'the changing reality that is the context of "Australia" ':

> The dispersal of this narrative [of miscegenation] across my own body, made emphatic by a dark-coloured sari, draped across my own white skin, makes feminist (that is, political and conflictual)

agency out of the sexualised, racialised, embodied self I am constructing here.

(Mead 1994: 413)

Deconstruction in this instance, oddly echoing the breathless tone of fashion-writing, becomes a mode of narcissism. But the questions out of which such apologetics arise are not in themselves foolish. I should like to approach them through some reflections on Shakespeare in the South Pacific.

In 1992 the Summer Shakespeare at Auckland University provoked a small storm of controversy. Co-directed by a young Samoan director and playwright, Justine Simei-Barton, and a well-known *palagi* poet and avant-garde theatre practitioner, Alan Brunton, it was a production of *Romeo and Juliet* transposed to nineteenth-century Samoa ('In fair Apia where we lay our scene') during the period of Civil War between rival branches of the ruling Malietoa family. Hostility to the production came less from conservative Shakespeareans in the university, than (surprisingly enough) from certain sections of the Samoan community, among them the chief Leifi Maua Puti Faleauto, editor of the *Samoa Sun*, who read the production as 'suggesting incest' in the family of the Head of State of Western Samoa: 'It's so horrible, you know that people can die for things like this'. Simei-Barton defended the production as an assertion of immigrant confidence, even of cultural sovereignty over the totems of *palagi* superiority: 'They should be really proud that we are venturing the last bastion of Western society ... we're breaking that barrier.' But for Leifi, Shakespeare could only figure as an intrusive outsider, an extravagant and wheeling stranger who could have no honest business in the Pacific, let alone in a place whose name translates as 'the Sacred Centre':

> look at what it says in the Bible as a example: it says you must not add anything or take anything away ... by taking away anything it will take away all your honour, so by adding things, personally I feel that it would be wrong, because the younger generation they feel this could be their history.
>
> ('Holmes' programme, NZ TV1, 13 Feb. 1992)

The argument raises in a conveniently crude form a number of familiar questions regarding the place of Shakespeare in the so-called 'post-colonial' world. For Simei-Barton, Shakespeare's play offered a vantage-point for critiquing the values of her own society;

for the Elder, the application of this alien fable could only result in the falsification of sacred truths – telling lies about the gods and heroes. For Simei-Barton, as her programme note made clear, Shakespeare was infinitely translatable because he dealt in universals – versions of the *Romeo and Juliet* story existed 'in all cultures'. For the Elder, such translation could only lead to the bastardization of 'true' Samoan culture – though it is eloquent of the complex and deeply ironized cultural history we share that he should have used Hebrew scripture to prove his point; and, as Alan Brunton's programme note insisted (citing shipboard performances on whalers and merchantmen), Shakespeare had been part of Pacific history since the early nineteenth century at least – for as long as that other Book whose authority was invoked to expel him.

Indeed, so far as the Anglophone Pacific is concerned, Shakespeare was there at the very beginning: included in the small library of mainly scientific and technical books that competed with other essential gear for accommodation in the cramped spaces of Captain Cook's *Endeavour* was a copy of the collected works of William Shakespeare (Salmond 1991: 102). Beyond this tantalizing detail, historians have nothing to tell us: exactly who insisted on including this text and why, who read it and when, how they read it and where, and in what ways their reading was inflected by the locations in which it occurred, we can only conjecture. But it reveals a great deal, of course, about the prestige that had accrued to Shakespeare's writing since Ben Jonson had somewhat optimistically presented him, in verses attached to the 1623 Folio, as the harbinger of a new literary *imperium* to whom not merely 'insolent Greece' and 'Haughty Rome', but 'all ... Europe' would defer. It also serves as a reminder of the way in which Jonson's hyperbolic imperial metaphors had, by the second half of the eighteenth century, begun to assume the appearance of fact.

As it happens, Shakespeare had begun to move out along the arteries of Empire even in his own lifetime: the first production of *Hamlet* of which we have any record took place on the deck of an East India Co. ship anchored off what is now Sierra Leone in 1607–8. But between Captain Keeling's *Hamlet*, performed for the entertainment of some foreign merchants, and the stocking of the *Endeavour* library, Shakespeare had undergone a significant transformation. In 1607/8 *Hamlet* was still so much a work of popular theatre that the records do not even bother to specify the name of the dramatist: it was simply the sort of thing which the captain thought would serve 'to keep my men from idleness or sleep' in the glaring mid-day sun – at most a means of performing Englishness in a disturbingly alien place, like the weirdly displaced Accession Day pageant with which the beleaguered agents of that same company had chosen to display their sense of national difference in Bantam three years before (Neill 1995). By the time of Cook's first voyage, 160 years later, Shakespeare's writing enjoyed a very different status: it had become literature, and travelled now (probably in the authoritative new edition by Dr Samuel Johnson) not merely as a prestigious written text, but as essential equipment, part of an educated man's apparatus for understanding the world, and an important talisman of the superior English culture of which he was the emissary. It seems entirely appropriate, therefore, that Cook's departure should have coincided with another key moment in the history of imperial consciousness: he set sail on the virtual eve of the David Garrick's Shakespeare Jubilee – the great patriotic pageant which formally initiated the cult of Shakespeare as the National Bard, thereby ensuring that his birthday would thenceforth be celebrated on the feastday of England's patron, St George.

By a strange chance, then, the foundation of 'Shakespeare' as an imperial institution exactly coincides with what is sometimes thought of as the foundational moment in the history of 'New Zealand' (as opposed to the obscure piece of coastline to which Abel Tasman gave a very similar Dutch name, or the islands which the Maori came to call 'Aotearoa'). And that coincidence can serve as a useful metaphor for the way in which, for better or for worse, Shakespeare has been not merely part of our history, but (no less than for those voyagers on the *Endeavour*) part of the cultural apparatus by which we have learned to know that history and our place in it – for the colonizers an essential beacon of location; for the colonized, arguably, an instrument of displacement and dispossession.

In the late 1960s, when I began my teaching career in Auckland, the place of Shakespeare in our syllabus appeared quite unproblematic. M. K. Joseph had recently published his *A Pound of Saffron*, a campus novel whose plot turns on the tragic exploitation of racial casting in a production of *Antony and Cleopatra* by a machiavellian British academic; but New Zealand readers seemed more interested in reading this as a *roman à clef* satirizing members of the Auckland English Department, than as a comment on the cultural politics of South Pacific Shakespeare. Despite the strenuous efforts of other writer-academics like Bill Pearson and C. K. Stead to bring about a historical and geographical reorientation of 'English' to a specifically New Zealand context, the Department's official position was effectively defined by what would nowadays be called a 'mission statement', undertaking to introduce students to the whole sweep of English literature from *Beowulf* to the present day, 'with Shakespeare as its centre'. That no-one would now be able to use such a phrase without embarrassment is a measure of the displacement of old verities that has occurred, not merely as result of widespread changes in the discipline itself, but also as part of the local process of national self-definition that has transformed the cultural landscape of New Zealand.

Yet the question of Shakespeare's local significance was not really brought home to me until the early 1980s, when (at the same time as I was helping to introduce post-colonial literature to the Auckland curriculum) I found myself having to offer a course of lectures on *Othello* for the first time. With that play I inherited a text that caused me serious problems: this was M. R. Ridley's (now notorious) Arden edition, whose bizarre discriminations of colour and 'contour' appeared to make it quite unsuited for classroom use – except, as Martin Orkin would later demonstrate, in apartheid South Africa. In 1982, however, the British literary establishment appeared strangely unembarrassed by Ridley's effusions. When, after an unsatisfactory correspondence with the unrepentant publishers, I wrote to the *Times Literary Supplement* calling for an academic boycott of the edition, that journal refused even to acknowledge my letters. The Arden general editor, meanwhile, honestly perplexed by the strength of my feelings, enquired whether I could not simply explain away Ridley's racist solecisms as 'an historical curiosity'; he insisted that Ridley's introduction had never caused *him* any difficulties at London University, but generously conceded that: 'teaching where you do, you are no doubt more sensitive to these matters than I should be'. For a long time I was baffled by the anachronistic confusion of this response: what sort of *London* did this man inhabit? It certainly couldn't be anything like Salman Rushdie's Ellowendeeowen, 'proper London, yaar!' I slowly came to recognize, however, that (for all its very English condescension) a significant truth was reflected in that 'teaching where you do', one that involved not simply our very different estimates of the relative importance of two paragraphs in a rather lengthy essay, but also (by implication) very different ways of reading the play itself – different ways, that is to say, of discriminating between the 'central' and the marginal, ways that were themselves inflected by our own positions on a particular cultural map. To read Othello in New Zealand – especially in the wake of the 1981 Springbok tour which had brought the country to the brink of civil war over the 'historical curiosity' of apartheid and its vexed relation to our own colonial history – was to read a subtly different text.

The issues of location highlighted by the Arden editor's incomprehension were raised again in a more systematic fashion by Ngũgĩ wa Thiong'o's 1984 Robb Lectures on 'The Politics of Language in African Literature' – the remarkable series that would later be published as *Decolonising the Mind*. There Ngũgĩ traced the history of his own revolt against the supposed 'centrality and universality of the English tradition', beginning with his struggle to transform the Nairobi English Department into an Afrocentric Department of Literature. Shakespeare, inevitably, was at the heart of this struggle; and Ngũgĩ recalled how as a student he had spent innumerable seminars 'detecting ... [the] moral significance in every paragraph, in every word, even in Shakespeare's commas and fullstops'. Ngũgĩ argued that the effect of presenting such writers as 'mindless geniuses whose only consistent quality was a sense of compassion' was not merely to pass off the local as the universal, but precisely to obscure their real interest and significance as artists immersed in the historical particularities of their own societies:

> These writers, who had the sharpest and most penetrating observations on the European bourgeois culture, were often taught as if their only concern was with the universal themes of love, fear, birth and death. Sometimes their greatness was presented as one more English gift to the world alongside the bible and the needle. William Shakespeare and Jesus Christ had brought light to darkest Africa. There was a teacher in our school who used to say that Shakespeare and Jesus Christ used very simple English, until someone pointed out that Jesus spoke Hebrew.
>
> (Ngũgĩ 1986: 91)

The issues raised by Ngũgĩ and his colleagues when they struggled to displace the ideological centrality of the European canon, have since been debated in all those former territories of Empire where the old cultural mappings have become increasingly discredited: John Higgins' questions in a recent issue of *The Southern African Review of Books* about the desirability of 'replac[ing] the

Anglo- or Eurocentric canon with an Afrocentric one' (Higgins 1996: 17), echo Ania Loomba's reflections on the paradox of her own writing about texts 'whose very presence in [Indian] classrooms is questionable' (Loomba 1989: 7), which in turn resonate with the current cultural studies debate in the Australian Academy. But Ngũgĩ did not propose discarding the Western canon – his own fiction, after all, has reworked material from Shakespeare and Conrad – but changing the terms on which it was read in a way that would acknowledge both the historical and geographical particularities of its production and its entanglement in local, African history.

Similar claims were implicit in a play that came out of Makerere University at the same time as Ngũgĩ was fighting the canon-war at Nairobi. Murray Carlin's *Not Now Sweet, Desdemona* (1969), which imagines a production of *Othello* with a black West Indian and a white South African woman in the lead roles, grew out of a quarrel with criticism's systematic occlusion of the racial dimension in Shakespeare's tragedy. Through his own 'Othello' character, Carlin urges the need for an Afrocentric reading of the Moor – one that explicitly locates the play's moment of writing in relation to the building of Fort Jesus in Mombasa and the establishment of European empire in East Africa; this, he insists, is 'the first play of the Age of Imperialism' – one that 'is about colour and nothing but colour'. Yet, for all its historicizing gestures, Carlin's work falls short of 'decolonizing' Shakespeare in terms that Ngũgĩ would accept, since it accepts the premise of a mysteriously 'universal' Shakespeare, who (as Carlin's introduction claims) 'knew everything': 'William Shakespeare – genius that he was – understood and foresaw all the problems of [the Imperial] Age' (Carlin 1969: 1, 32).

A barely less explicit universalism provided the rationale for the intensely local reading that underpinned Janet Suzman's celebrated production of *Othello* at Johannesburg's Market Theatre in 1987. For Suzman (who would hardly dispute Dr Johnson's view of Shakespeare's characters as 'the genuine progeny of common humanity, such as the world will always supply, and observation will always find' (Johnson 1968:62)), the play 'shows us a cross-section of most societies', and in the process 'addresses the notion of apartheid 400 years before the epithet was coined'.[1] Suzman's enthusiasm is easily mocked, but it is possible, I think, to detect a certain uneasy congruence between it and the position adopted by Martin Orkin in *Shakespeare Against Apartheid* when he insists (in spite of his own professed historicism) that *Othello* 'as it always has done, continues to oppose racism' (Orkin 1987:188).

There were excellent tactical reasons, of course, why Orkin should have wanted to challenge the appropriative readings of Shakespearean texts imposed by a racist education system; and the equivocal cultural niche occupied by Shakespeare in the apartheid state is illustrated by Nadine Gordimer's novel *My Son's Story*. At the centre of its narrative is the activist schoolteacher, Sonny, for whom Shakespeare is a 'source of transcendence' (Gordimer 1990: 17) and a privileged location of meaning outside the imprisoning definitions of the state. Believing as he does that 'with an understanding of Shakespeare there comes a release from the gullibility that makes you prey to the great shopkeeper who runs the world, and would sell you to cheap illusion' (ibid.: 11), Sonny treasures the Bard both as a high-cultural bulwark against the bourgeois aspirations of the coloured community from which he comes, and as a humane corrective to the 'crudely reductive' sloganizing of the activist world: ' "Equality"; he went to Shakespeare for a definition with more authority than those given on makeshift platforms in the veld' (ibid.: 48, 23). Through Shakespeare he can offer his son (whom he has named 'Will' in homage to his liberator) 'the freedom, at least, of great art' (ibid.: 99).

For Will, however, who serves as Gordimer's narrator, Shakespeare, aligned as he is with the authority of the father, represents not freedom but constraint. The Bard's patriarchal role in the symbolic topography of their home is carefully delineated: '*Our house is where we are, our* furniture, *our* things, *his* complete Shakespeare' (ibid.: 85; emphasis added); and the given name that stamps Will with his writer's destiny feels 'like a curse'. 'I'm supposed to take it as my fate', he tells his mother, 'I'm to be something you and he don't really want to give up? Not even for the revolution?' (ibid.: 254–5). Will signals his resistance to this inheritance by organizing his narrative around an elaborate pattern of Shakespearean quotations and allusions. Culled from Sonny's battered copy of the Complete Works, these serve partly as ironic reflections of Shakespeare's totemic role in the father's house. But, in decorating Sonny's life with superficially apposite quotations from *Othello, Lear* and *As You Like It*, Will also takes a malicious pleasure in exploiting the uncomfortable gap between these reminders of his father's 'old habit of pedantry' and the experiences to which they are applied. Faced with the loss of his favourite daughter, for example, Sonny becomes an absurdly diminished Lear:

Best thou had'st not been born, than not t'have pleased me better ... Oh
schoolmaster taunted by the tags of passion he didn't understand when he read them in the little son-of-sorrow house ...
Beat at this gate that let thy folly in

(ibid.: 252)

Even more suggestively in the novel's South African context, Sonny's affair with a white woman is made into a parodic replay of
Othello: 'The cause was the lover, the lover the cause,' Will writes,
'*Oh thou weed: who art so lovely faire, and smell'st so sweet that the senses ache
at thee, Would thou had'st never been born*' (ibid.: 223–4).

Beyond Will's conscious manipulations, however, it's possible to
discern an underlying pattern in which Shakespeare continues to
serve as an unchallenged master text. For *My Son's Story*, like Gordimer's
earlier novel of Oedipal fixation, *Burger's Daughter*, to which it is in
some sense a pendant – is itself constructed as a partial reworking
of *Hamlet*. This larger structural irony is hardly surprising, since
Gordimer, whose own criticism has consistently sought to negotiate
a space for high culture within the imperatives of social and political 'responsibility', is hardly about to jettison Shakespeare as an
imprisoning relic of empire, or an instrument of colonized false
consciousness. The real centre of *My Son's Story* lies in the metanarrative
that traces Will's own emergence as a writer, and in the process
reconciles him to his roles as both biological and literary 'son'.

My Son's Story ends in a conflagration – the burning of the home
whose claim upon him Will has defiantly acknowledged to the
white mob ('*This is my father's house*'), though he is 'glad to see it
go'; and as he visits the fire-bombed shell with Sonny, he records
'Flocks of papery cinders ... drifting, floating about us – beds,
clothing – his books?' Yet the burning of these books does not
signify any absolute destruction, only a phoenix-like metamorphosis (ibid.: 272–4). For it is precisely at this point that Will breaks
off his narrative to announce himself as the maker of his own
book; and even though, as he wryly admits, 'It's not Shakespeare',
he nevertheless claims his vocation with a last Shakespearean flourish:
'*I have that within that passeth show*'. This assertion (as the recent
fortunes of *Hamlet* in Romania or Mizoram might suggest) has a
politics to it: what Will claims to have within him is nothing less
than history, the suppressed, hidden history of a rotten state, whose
story (like Horatio now, rather than Hamlet) he will remain to tell:
'I'm going to be the one to record, someday, what ... it really was

to live a life determined by the struggle to be free ... I am a writer and this is my first book' (ibid.: 276).

On this level then, *My Son's Story*, both is and is not Shakespeare: a pastiche of *Hamlet/Lear/Othello* and something much closer to home:

> It's an old story – ours. My father's and mine. Love, love/hate are the most common and universal of experiences. But no two are alike, each is a fingerprint of life. That's the miracle that makes literature and links it with creation itself in the biological sense.
>
> (Ibid.: 275)

What Shakespeare has come to stand for is what Gordimer has called the writer's 'essential gesture' – the integrity Chekhov demanded: 'to describe a situation so truthfully ... that the reader can no longer avoid it' (Gordimer 1988: 299).

Nevertheless *My Son's Story* is certainly aware of the constricting power of culturally dominant narratives, and the ability of the Shakespeare who 'knew everything' to give us a present that seems always already known – illustrated, for example, in the routine deployment of Othello as an explanatory template for the O. J. Simpson case.[2] In Tayeb Salih's Sudanese fable, *Season of Migration to the North*, a novel from the early phase of African decolonization, *Othello* appears to function solely as an instrument of destructive cultural conditioning, part of the baggage of Empire in the protagonist's secret library – that 'mausoleum' of European culture which the narrator, in another symbolic book-burning, plans to incinerate towards the end of the novel: 'At the break of dawn tongues of fire will devour these lies' (Salih 1991: 154). In what he mistakenly construes as an act of counter-appropriation, the expatriate Mustapha Sa'eed had assumed the role of Othello, exploiting its exoticism ('I am like Othello – Arab-African') in a strategy of racial revenge upon white women (ibid.: 38). But the choice, we have been made to see, was never really his own: on trial for the murder of his English wife, Mustapha finds himself the prisoner of a script he is unable to discard, for all the desperate insistence of his protests: 'I am no Othello. Othello was a lie!' (ibid.: 95). Ironically enough, Mustapha Sa'eed's escape from this narrative prison will come only in the form of an apparent suicide – an action that obliquely asks to be read (like Othello's own) as a final concession to the imperial fiction that has shaped him.

Yet Tayeb Salih's delicately poised novel is hardly unconscious of the irony that makes a knowledge of *Othello* an essential instrument for its own understanding. Its narrator looks forward to a time when the colonizers leave, when

> the railways, ships hospital, factories and schools will be ours and we'll speak their language without either a sense of guilt or a sense of gratitude. Once again we shall be as we were – ordinary people – and if we are lies we shall be lies of our own making.
>
> (Ibid.: 49–50)

But the novel exposes the naïvety of this notion of return to a pristine world, uncontaminated by the fictions of others. Mustapha Sa'eed's books are not in the end burnt: 'Another fire would not have done any good' (ibid.: 166).

The elaborate Arab-African-English palimpsest of Katarzyna Klein's cover-illustration for the paperback edition of *Season* neatly emblematizes the irredeemably hybrid condition of the world that Tayeb Salih contemplates. In this it bears an interesting resemblance to the jacket design for a more recent novel whose reinscriptions of Shakespearean narrative exemplify a very different take on post-imperial hybridity – Salman Rushdie's *The Moor's Last Sigh* (1995). 'Christians, Portuguese, and Jews; Chinese tiles promoting godless views; pushy ladies, skirts-not-saris, Spanish shenanigans, Moorish crowns', sighs the eponymous narrator-protagonist contemplating the mingle-mangle of his own story, 'Can this really be India? *Bhararat-mata, Hindustan-hamara*, is this the place?' Yes, he insists, 'this too is an Indian yarn ... *everything in its place*'(Rushdie 1995: 87). To say Indian yarn, for Rushdie, is to say tangled skein, and to invoke the proprieties of place is only to acknowledge the necessary dislocations of the imaginary homeland which the narrator's mother calls 'Palimpstine', described as a 'Place where worlds collide, flow in and out of one another, and washofy away' (ibid.: 226).[3] Palimpstine, as these shamelessly mixed metaphors suggest, is born from a metamorphic 'sea of stories' – fictions that help to shape this hybrid world but are themselves dissolved and reshaped within it; and among the more prominent fictions that flow into the autobiographical narrative of Moraes Zogoiby (known as 'Moor'), are a number of Shakespeare plays, *Hamlet, The Merchant of Venice, Macbeth*, and once again, of course, that ur-narrative of Moorish otherness, *Othello*.

Moraes's overbearing and manipulative mother takes advantage of his nickname in a series of paintings that include a self-portrait entitled '*To Die upon a Kiss*', where she appears as 'murdered Desdemona flung across her bed', while Moraes recognizes himself in the 'stabbed Othello, falling towards her in suicided remorse as I breathed my last' (ibid.: 224–5). In the echo of this expiring sigh, Shakespeare's tragedy once again threatens to become a narrative template, determining Moor's destiny, much as it shaped the fate of Mustapha Sa'eed. Moraes's story, however, though it moves towards a form of narrative suicide in the annunciation of his own death, actually escapes this predestined closure by anticipating a future of miraculous translations and recuperations, as it assimilates Moor's history to a whole series of well-travelled myths of return – King Arthur, Barbarossa, Finn MacCool and Rip Van Winkle. If Shakespeare's Moor has any lingering presence at the end of this expatriate fiction, it is as that briefly triumphant figure of hybridity, the 'extravagant and wheeling stranger' whose travellers' tales worked their entrancing spell upon his metropolitan audience.

Moraes's loyalist great-grandmother, Epifania, had seen her world as the passive artefact of Empire: 'What are we but Empire's children? British have given us everything? – Civilisation, law, order, too much' (ibid.: 18); and Rushdie is slyly aware of the role assigned to Shakespeare in the cultural programming of imperial education. Moraes acknowledges his own vulnerability to that project when he repudiates the accusation that he and his kind belong to the very comprador intelligentsia envisaged by the pioneer of Indian education, Macaulay, as '*interpreters between us and the millions whom we govern*' (ibid.: 376). But for Rushdie, apostle of the hybrid, the mongrel and the liminal magic of 'translated people', the role of go-between is more devious and more ambiguous than Macaulay could ever have imagined: and something, he insists, is gained in the translation (1984: 29; 1991: 17).

'How stories travel,' reflects Rushdie's Moor as he starts to spin his Indian yarn, 'what mouths they end up in' (1995: 3); and for Rushdie, Shakespeare's stories, whatever the motive for bringing them to India, have become (he could cite Bengali popular theatre) Indian fables. But there are reasons to be cautious about such glad hybridity. In Derek Walcott's *A Branch of the Blue Nile*, where a group of West Indians rehearse *Antony and Cleopatra*, a disillusioned actor voices a profound ambivalence about what it means for Shakespeare to 'end up' in her West Indian mouth: 'I wanted to please Shakespeare as much as Jesus', she says, having given up the part of Cleopatra

But they were right, the stage isn't my place …
I stepped from it down to the congregation …
that's where an ambitious black woman belongs
either grinning and dancing and screaming how she has
soul, or clapping and preaching and going gaga for Jesus …
… not up there contending with the great queens
Cause the Caroni isn't a branch of the river Nile
and Trinidad isn't Egypt, except at Carnival
so the world sniggers when I speak her lines …
What do you think? You think that I don't miss her,
the way a jug needs water? That my tongue feels parched
sometimes, just to repeat her lines? How do you think
it feels to carry her corpse inside my body
the way a woman can carry a stillborn child
inside her and still know it …
My body was invaded by that queen
Her gaze made everywhere a desert.
When I got up in the morning, when I walked to work,
I found myself walking in pentameter. …
… I heard my blood
Whispering like the Nile, its branches,
instead of traffic. … Egypt was my death.

(Walcott 1986: 284–5)

A similar ambivalence can be detected, I think, in a fascinating
but curiously fractured play performed by Auckland's Theatre at
Large in 1994: *Manawa Taua/Savage Hearts* employed a pastiche
of idioms and conventions, including music hall routines, melo-
drama, Victorian Shakespeare, and Maori performance arts
(*waiata*, *whikorero*, *haka*, and *karakia*) within a framework of French-
influenced improvisational theatre, to create a fantastical version
of Shakespeare's translation to colonial New Zealand. Stunning
as *Manawa Taua* was in performance, its surviving texts reveal a
great deal about the contradictions in the cultural politics of
Shakespearean appropriation. As its double title suggested, the
play was conceived by Christian Penny, co-director of the company, as a self-consciously bicultural project: Penny, himself
part-Maori, but fundamentally *pakeha* in his cultural affiliations,
had envisaged 'a cross-cultural nineteenth-century love-story',
using *Othello* as a kind of template, whose effect would be to challenge what he saw as the dangerously separatist rhetoric of

contemporary racial politics. For this he commissioned the dramatist David Geary, whose bulky script was workshopped and
extensively cut before being rewritten by the Maori playwright
Willie Davis, whose job was 'to get the Maori side right'. Davis's
draft was then itself completely transformed in rehearsal – through
improvisational sessions with bicultural cast under the direction
of Penny and his co-director, Anna Marbrook. In the course of
this process bitter divisions opened up which left the two play-
wrights at odds with the directors and with each other, and the
cast itself divided along broadly ethnic lines. In the end these
divisions seem to have been resolved only by an extraordinary
agreement to suppress the play at the end of its highly successful
run, so that it would neither be published nor made available for
further performance. At the heart of the dispute lay a deep disagreement about the kinds of stories it was appropriate to tell about
our history – a disagreement in which Shakespeare's ur-narrative
of miscegenation was profoundly implicated.

Manawa Taua is plotted around the brilliantly theatrical fable of
a nineteenth-century Maori chief who, on visiting Queen Victoria
to seek redress for land grievances, is promised help provided he
agrees to return to New Zealand with a troupe of Shakespearean
actors who are planning a tour of the colonies (starting with Scotland). More than royal caprice is involved: the play they are to perform
is *Othello*, and Tupou, the *rangatira*, is to be cast as the Moor. 'It
would seem most apt,' says the Queen, 'in that Othello deals with
the savage heart. No offence …' Her promise, she insists 'will mean
absolutely nothing, have no weight whatsoever until you perform
Othello in New Zealand'.[4] As a result of this casting, Tupou finds
himself progressively drawn into an affair with his Desdemona,
Lottie Folly, wife of the company's actor-manager (and usual Othello),
Roy Folly. What ensues is a curiously refracted replay of Shakespeare's story, leading to a predictable catastrophe in which life and
performance become entirely confused: goaded by the jealous husband, who has adopted the role of Iago, Tupou strangles his lover
whilst speaking Othello's words. But no sooner has he performed
this ventriloquized murder, than the play abruptly repudiates Lottie's
'romantic tragic Shakespearean death' in favour of an alternative
comic ending. Lottie revives, and the three principals unite to punish a renegade member of their company who has busily been
appropriating Maori land. In this triumph of bicultural goodwill,
love, along with their production of Shakespeare's play, reigns

victorious. By choosing our histories, the play appears to suggest, we can choose our present. But as the ironic wit of Tupou's exchange with Victoria suggests, there are elements in *Manawa Taua* that sit rather uneasily with this soft-focus post-modernism – and they turn out to involve rather different notions of Shakespeare's place in our history.

Having sworn upon the Bible to give her protection to the Maori, Victoria secures Tupou's compliance with what she calls their 'verbal treaty' by making him swear on another 'book of great power' – more powerful, she suggests, than holy scripture itself: it is, of course, a copy of the *Complete Works of Shakespeare*. By linking Shakespeare's text with two other hermeneutically contentious documents – the Bible and the Treaty of Waitangi, which established imperial sovereignty by simultaneously affirming the contradictory principles of British governorship (*kawanatanga*) and Maori chieftainship (*rangatiratanga*) – *Manawa Taua* associates it with a politics of reading that is first articulated by Tupou when he converses with Victoria about the teachings of Jesus:

> I like your Bible. It has good stories. Some of them are very like our own … But you English all read it differently. Wesleyans … one way. Anglicans another. Methodists. Catholics. So many meanings all from one book. … Just like your Treaty.

Implicit in Tupou's puzzlement is the same notion of meaning as single, essential and given, rather than multiple and constructed, which informs his shipboard argument with a member of the crew who argues that Polynesians must have arrived in New Zealand by accident (a *cause célèbre* in recent anthropology): 'Even if we weren't able to navigate', he replies, 'we would've been guided by our *kaitiaki* [guardian]. By our *wairua* [spirit].'

– What kind of compass is that?
– The one that's in our heart.
– How do you read that? How do you plot it?
– You don't read it, you listen to it. You don't plot it, you trust it.

No wonder that Tupou should find himself repeating, as a kind of chant, Othello's essentialist assertion of identity 'I am found. / My parts, my title, and my perfect soul / Shall manifest me rightly.' On this level *Manawa Taua* is a play about the power of words, and about conflicting ideas of the sources of that power: one sacramental, the other instrumental. At one point in the action, shortly after her 'murder', Tupou and Lottie actually engage in a ferocious but indecisive flyting-match, hurling chunks of Shakespearean text and *karakia* [chants] at one another. Significantly, however, this element in the play (with all that it might rather uncomfortably imply about the role of Shakespearean translations) was substantially purged from the version staged at the Watershed.

I have concentrated on reworkings of Shakespeare in this somewhat disparate group of texts because they help to explain why it is that, even in more consciously 'post-colonial' academies, the decentring of Shakespeare has generally been more rhetorical than real. This seeming paradox can be attributed partly, of course, to factors that are structural to the profession and to the globalized intellectual market in which it operates. But, as the texts I have been discussing all illustrate, the long and complicated history of Shakespeare's entanglement with Empire has ensured that (for better or worse) his work has become deeply constitutive of all of us for whom the world is (to a greater or lesser degree) shaped by the English language – or, in the wicked revealing phrase that adorns Saleem Sinai's tin globe in *Midnight's Children*, 'made as England'. Through four hundred years of imperializing history our Anglophone cultures have become so saturated with Shakespeare that our ways of thinking about such basic issues as nationality, gender and racial difference are inescapably inflected by his writing. A recent issue of *The Guardian Weekly* made easy fun out of the fact that Shakespeare was still being taught at the University of Cape Town. But I would argue that the rehistoricization of Shakespeare that has taken place over the last two decades ought to make the study of his work in an antipodean context a more rather than less urgent priority. To cut oneself off from Shakespeare in the name of a decolonizing politics is not to liberate oneself from the tyranny of the past, but to pretend that the past does not exist. The question that needs to be resolved is not *whether* but *how* he should be taught.

Notes

1 I am quoting from Suzman's spoken introduction to the televized version *Othello in Johannesburg*.
2 'Hey OJ, at least Othello felt sorry for what he did', reads a piece of graffiti on the walls of the public lavatory outside the Folger Shakespeare Theatre; 'yeah', someone has scrawled underneath, 'and he

killed himself too'. Ugly, but instructive, this exchange demonstrates not just a widely dispersed misreading of the play (it is about the tragic inability of an essentially savage black man to maintain his veneer of civilization under conditions of emotional stress), but also the way in which that reading conditions popular understandings of 'race' ('all black men are like that'). Newspaper accounts of the Simpson affair, in New Zealand as in the United States, have repeatedly exploited the *Othello* template, seemingly unembarrassed by the absence of a Iago-figure, even as they continue to replicate a metaphoric reading of blackness that Iago fully articulated for the first time. Because *Othello* is a tragedy about 'race' written before the terminology of 'race' was even invented, we cannot (as some recent critics have attempted to do) read it as either 'racist' or 'anti-racist'; instead it is an essential document of the process by which we learned to think about such ideas at all – something that we need to come to terms with as part of the slow and painful process of thinking our way out of this pervasive and deeply destructive fiction.

3 See also the title essay of Rushdie's *Imaginary Homelands* (1991: 9–21).
4 As its complicated authorship history might suggest, *Manawa Taua* is textually very unstable. The text from which I am quoting is an advanced typescript version held in the archive of Playmarket in Wellington. In the only surviving version of the performance text, an audiotape held by Theatre at Large, much of the material I quote appears to have been cut – evidently as part of the process of reducing the play's political complexities at the expense of a fable of reconciliatory miscegenation. I am informed by Willie Davis, however, that contenious material from earlier versions of the script was imported back into the script by the actors in the course of some performances.

10
Possessing the book and peopling the text
MARTIN ORKIN

The historian Dipesh Chakrabarty, amongst others, has remarked on the extent to which Western theories in historiography and literary studies have embraced the entirety of humanity although 'produced in relative, and sometimes absolute ignorance of the majority of humankind – i.e. those living in non-Western cultures'(Chakrabarty 1992: 2, 3). Asking 'What allowed the modern European sages to develop such clairvoyance with regard to societies of which they were empirically ignorant? Why cannot we, once again, return the gaze?'(ibid.: 3) he advocates the development of what he calls 'symmetrical knowledges' to counter this one-way process which perpetuates, he argues, an 'asymmetrical ignorance'.

At face value it would seem that the mere use of the Shakespeare text would in the literary sense provide for Chakrabarty a case in point, but I would like in this essay to seek out modes of using Shakespeare's plays that might contribute to the development of such symmetrical knowledges, rather than ones that encourage reproduction of the dominance of Europe. To put it another way, in present-day South Africa, I want to ask whether Shakespeare might still be used in ways that are enabling or in a manner that does not merely reproduce and confirm 'metropolitan' epistemologies characterized by 'asymmetrical ignorance'. I am not pretending that we can at this time or perhaps ever escape Western epistemology – a dilemma implicit perhaps in Chakrabarty's use of the phrase 'symmetrical knowledges'. But I am asking whether we can now use the texts in ways that will work for the encouragement of a greater sense of agency within the South African location.

In this essay my concern then is a very limited one. What might Shakespeareans hope to accomplish with the Shakespeare text itself, rather than with appropriations, rewritings or even cannibalizations of it? The latter have provided a much-favoured field of enquiry in writings on 'post-colonial' Shakespeare, particularly in North America. But in South Africa at present I think it a mistake to bypass the Shakespeare text – as well as, of course, from different, but equally important points of view, the instability and plurality of the Shakespeare text and the larger seventeenth-century culture of which it is only a particular part. This is because, although the presence of Shakespeare within South African literary study and education is paradoxical and increasingly in question, one side of the paradox is prompted by the fact that so far it still penetrates the education system quite extensively. Shakespeare has been and remains at the present moment a compulsory set text for all matriculation candidates. In tertiary education Shakespeare's plays are read by undergraduates at most universities throughout South Africa. Such facts demand or require that, at least while Shakespeare is still there, we continue to address the uses to which the text itself may be put. But, as this essay will show, I am also concerned to argue that, in a very different way from their deployment in the past, and only after dislodging their historical primacy within schools and universities, Shakespeare's plays may retain usefulness in the future in providing possible (amongst other) historical perspectives and frames for our own contemporaneity.

Such a project may of course also be set in the context of the claim that it is only after the general election of 1994 that South Africa has been able to embark on a truly 'post-colonial' enterprise. But it is important to stress at the outset that the term 'post-coloniality' is itself problematic. If we are to use it at all, we need to register the fact that it has different meanings depending upon its particular location. Within the United States academy it seems sometimes to suggest a non site-specific, if well-intentioned generalized empathy with struggles for racial and social self-definition. The notion of post-coloniality also has powerful currency, as we know, in diasporic communities, within which are to be found migrant intellectuals predominantly located within Europe or North America. Again, it is used within what some have called the settler communities of Canada, Australia and New Zealand; moreover it may be applied within Africa, Asia and the Caribbean. These different locations cannot be homogenized. Thus Kalpana Seshadri-Crooks offers a useful general description of post-colonial studies when she argues that

> post-colonial studies is concerned more with the analysis of the lived *condition* of unequal power-sharing globally ... it is interested, above all, in the materialist critique of power, and how that power or ideology seeks to interpellate subjects within a discourse as subordinate or without agency.
>
> (Seshadri-Crooks 1995: 67)

But her description is located primarily within a discussion of marginality in migrant communities. In the South African location the majority of the population is now, at least politically, relatively empowered. In such a context, models of marginality, subordination or diaspora will need re-examination. But again, if the use of Shakespeare in South Africa, because of the recent elections, may now qualify it for categorization within a 'post-colonial Shakespeare', this can only be in another tentative and highly suspect sense, for, while the elections have empowered the majority of people in South Africa in the political arena, apartheid remains relatively firmly in place in the economic one.

I

What, then, are the problems that confront present-day South African Shakespeareans? I should like to begin with a particular instance that suggests some of the uncertainties and confusions within the academy at the present time. In 1995 an English Department Committee at one of the largest of the universities in South Africa proposed the following course description as Shakespeare component for a new postgraduate MA by coursework in education. This was designed specifically for English teachers, and has since been instituted by the faculty concerned:

> Many teachers of English are required to teach Renaissance Drama – usually one or more plays by Shakespeare. This area of English literature has been the subject of much debate and critical discussion in recent years, and ways of reading Renais-

sance literature have become a lively area of contestation. This course will encourage critical awareness of diverse approaches to Shakespeare, and, where applicable, to other Renaissance dramatists and will include gender studies (the playwright concerned with sexuality), cultural studies (the playwright and the intellectual and social milieu) and genre studies (the playwright and the history of drama) so as to encourage critical reflection of the relation of teachers themselves to these texts and ideas within the context of the multi-racial, multi-cultural classroom. The questioning of canonicity in relation to these texts and in relation to critical paradigms of reading, within particular societies and at particular times, is part of this endeavour, thus enabling students to engage with different methods of interpreting the texts. The various theoretical perspectives will be applied to selected primary texts.

(University of Witwatersrand, English Dept 1995)

This formulation evidences a desire for change and also proclaims marks of enlightenment: it acknowledges 'the relations of teachers themselves to these texts and ideas within the multi-racial and multi-cultural classroom'; it proposes 'the questioning of canonicity'; it acknowledges that certain ways of reading the texts have become a 'lively area of contestation'. Such acknowledgements indicate an unquestionable advance on the old establishment South African Shakespeare agenda. At the same time, however, the formulation retains an emphasis in its concern with the 'playwright' on the primacy of the author, while manifesting a measure of confusion about gender and cultural studies – the one defined as concerned with 'sexuality', the other with an 'intellectual and social milieu'. More important, however, is its easy collocation of 'gender studies' and 'cultural studies' with what it calls 'genre studies (the playwright and the history of drama)'. While, again, the primacy of the author and 'history of the drama' are neither adequate articulations of any concern with 'genre', it can be argued that historically, within the South African academy, 'the playwright and the history of drama' approach characterized the attention of apartheid Shakespeare. This focused exclusively upon 'Shakespeare's mastery' with plot, character and 'genre' – particularly a caricatured version of the Bradleyan version of tragedy – encouraging, on the one hand, a highly depoliticized, privatized view of the 'moral' subject, gendered inevitably as male, and, on the other, an exclusive focus upon the aesthetics of form. It might, moreover, be argued that the dominance of this approach positively impeded – to an extent still does – the development of cultural and gender studies. If then the above formulation claims to announce a new departure, it is at the same time couched in a disarmingly familiar tone of resolved (Western) rationality. It suggests a seamless academic enquiry in which the study of Shakespeare is purely a matter of hermeneutics. It elides completely the problematic that in South Africa, as all available research has so far confirmed, the Shakespeare text has been and to a significant degree still is used as a telling weapon within fierce and in many ways ongoing pedagogic and hegemonic struggles. The course description avoids completely the question of institutional location, recognition of colonization, segregation, apartheid, neo-colonialism, the struggle towards the possibility of 'post' coloniality. Indeed, none of these imperatives is even mentioned.

Another serious apparent clarification but simultaneous occlusion of key issues occurs in the easy reference to the 'multi-racial' classroom. It is doubtful first, whether, in the near future, classroom populations will be in any extended sense non-racial or multi-racial. In the interim, the old problems remain: foremost amongst them for Shakespeareans is the historical use of Shakespeare in the classroom as ideological weapon of oppression. It is worth recalling here the point that Shakespeare was used in black schools, populated by children whose home language was not English in the early years of their instruction in the English language – a measure designed to impede rather than facilitate acquisition of the language. Nor is the text in consequence a neutral issue – a journalist recently observed in a newspaper article that 'Shakespeare is dust in the townships'. Similarly, the formulation begs the question of whether Shakespeare's plays should be used at all within a genuine if still largely hypothetical multi-cultural situation – it envisages only a shift in the relationship between teacher and, it is assumed, the permanently prescribed Shakespeare text. While this is not a problem that can be easily resolved, as I hope this essay recognizes, it is not in this articulation even admitted.

The formulation provides, then, ample evidence of Vijay Mishra's observation that although attempts at new formations involve 'modes of translation and encoding because erstwhile distinctions cannot, must not suffice' (Mishra 1995: 13–14), at the same time, there is always the possibility that the 'disavowed leaves its traces' – in this instance more than merely traces – 'behind' (ibid.: 14). Its presentation as part of a 'universal' [Western] academic inquiry', of an untroubled, partly modish collocation – gender, cultural studies, genre – within the already soon to be achieved apparently universalized 'multi-racial' and 'multi-cultural' classroom may be set also against Benita Parry's identification of the way in which in another context

> A ... disciplinary mode of occluding the structure of domination in an embattled colonial past and of mystifying the continuing asymmetrical nexus between the hegemonic centres and their peripheries, has been procured by 'commonwealth studies' and its progeny 'commonwealth literature', where the choice of an anodyne name denoting a multi-cultural community existing in perfect harmony, acts to suggest that there exists an association of diverse peoples, joined together in a past of common endeavour and a present of shared purpose.
>
> (Parry 1987: 33)

This is not to argue that the goal of reconciliation in present-day South Africa is not vital, but it is doubtful whether this is attainable by occluding the institutional history within which such impulses towards change occur. As Njabulo Ndebele warned some years ago, institutional transformation is not always designed to deliver what it promises:

> [T]here have been diverse cultural interests to whom the challenge of the future has involved the need to open up cultural and educational centres to all races. Missing in these admirable acts of goodwill is an accompanying need to alter fundamentally the nature of cultural practice itself. It is almost always assumed that, upon being admitted, the oppressed will certainly like what they find ... Where there has previously been absence of freedom, the mere exercise of making facilities available may easily be mistaken for the presence of freedom. That way, a dominant hegemony is left intact as it gains more supporters from the ranks of the oppressed.
>
> (Ndebele 1987: 7–8)

II

If Shakespeareans in South Africa – predominantly if not entirely members of or descendants of settler groups in the country – form on the whole in the context of transition, a reluctant, not to say recidivist community; they face fundamental future change. In November 1995 the South African Department of Education circulated a discussion document suggesting a policy of multilingualism in South African education. It argued for 'the equal treatment and use of eleven official languages', as well as 'measures to promote African languages to ensure redress in the light of historical discrimination'. This proposal downplays English as a lingua franca and promises a radical shift away from the apartheid system's exclusive use for matriculation of Afrikaans or English as learning languages. If the document does not spell out in any detail what the Department understands to be the long-term outcome of such a shift from the present education system to one in which students could conceivably complete their entire secondary education in languages other than English, it is clear that it proposes a far more equitable and benign learning space for different language speakers within South Africa. It should also be noted that this policy of multilingualism which has, as its expressed intention, the encouragement of 'self-affirmation' and 'cognitive development' (South African Dept of Education 1995: 25–6) has implications different from, say, that brand of 'multiculturalism' which, in the United States, has been described as providing, as Seshadri-Crooks has it, 'an epistemology of the other that can only make sense within the Christian liberal tradition' and which, for purposes of study, 'reinscribes the Western cultural relativist as universal subject with the other serving as informant'(Seshadri-Crooks 1995: 51, 52).[1]

Whatever the final detailed outcome of this particular proposal, its direction and tenor help to focus certain crucial imperatives facing anyone using the Shakespeare text within present-day South African education. The establishment South African Shakespearean's predilection for justifying use of the Shakespeare text as bearer and marker of a universal system of knowledge as well as means of affiliation with a European/North American metropolis becomes obviously less than ever operable. But even those Shakespeareans who do not advocate a traditionalist presentation of Shakespeare in South Africa need, within such a climate, to rethink possible uses of the text. How then is the Shakespeare text now to be addressed? Ought it to be used at all? I want to address these questions in full recognition of the fact that present-day research energy within the academy is firmly and rightly lodged within Southern African studies. In what follows I do not intend any displacement of the priority of the study of local oral and literary history, local literatures, local histories. This shift in the academy's attention so far as the study of literature was concerned, began in the late 1960s and occurred initially outside English literature departments. It has since, rightly, become a centre of focus in the academy. But I wish now to argue that our sense of the local should involve as well, those global literatures which, imbricated in multiple ways in South Africa's past and present, help to constitute our current condition.

First, if in order to effect meaningful change, future transition depends upon adequate understanding of our present and past, then research into the reception of the Shakespeare text within South Africa and the process of its institutionalization is one of the prerequisites for future moves in education towards a condition free of the dangers of neo-colonialism. Second, the Shakespeare text, produced at an incipient moment in a process of colonization to which the South African terrain was subsequently subject, itself addresses multiple interactions between peoples and endeavours to engage with cultural difference. This is of intrinsic interest within a South Africa that is currently engaged in the endeavour not only to recognize but also to respect difference: many of the issues evident in Shakespeare are still current today. Third, if South Africa's move to majority rule initiates a new struggle against the dangers of neo-colonialism and towards a putative future that may one day be significantly 'post'-apartheid and 'post'-colonial, a new effort of imagination will be required to negotiate some of the (hegemonic) assumptions – about subjectivity, structurations of gender and sexuality, human interaction, social structures – that have travelled/travel to the South African terrain from other places. Some of these have been transmitted in part via the Shakespeare text. We need to identify not only the similarities but, where possible, the inappropriateness of such assumptions and, where necessary, actively to return the text to its own seventeenth-century European location.

III

If Shakespeare has been crucially imbricated, at least in the nineteenth and twentieth centuries, within colonialist, segregationist and apartheid education, then concern with the historical reception of the text, with the epistemic violence of colonial institutions, with, as John and Jean Comaroff have it, 'the colonization of consciousness and the consciousness of colonization' (Comaroff and Comaroff 1992: 236) is likely to remain an ongoing project within the South

African academy. How we imagine or construct agency in present-day South Africa depends in part upon understanding of how past oppressions remain imbricated in present structures, or the ways in which past productions of knowledge still inform present assumptions or current knowledge systems.

Relatively recently, Peter Mtuze, Shole J. Shole and Laurence Wright have made somewhat bardolatrous forays into the question of Shakespeare as object of knowledge within twentieth-century Africa.[2] By contrast David Johnson (1996) examines the political mission underlying the teaching of Shakespeare in the Cape Colony in the nineteenth century and its part in processes of imperial social and economic control in the twentieth century. At the end of his detailed study, Johnson argues that the use of Shakespeare in South Africa has been 'part of much larger histories of imperial violence in which the Bard plays a central and deeply compromised role' (Johnson 1996: 214). This prompts him to contemplate briefly 'the option, which might arise in a post-apartheid South Africa, of choosing a different set of texts' (ibid.: 120). But his work nevertheless confirms the extent to which the text has historically – in his argument, for the worse – penetrated secondary and tertiary education institutions.

While his scholarship is vital in redressing the balance away from the imperialist and colonialist Shakespeare, and contributive to the project of understanding the nature of 'epistemic violence', it is also important to explore the ways in which the text has been appropriated by South Africans in genuinely enabling and emancipatory ways. In this respect, despite his commitment to contingency, Johnson, ironically, collapses or elides history at times, to suggest that all appropriations of Shakespeare in Africa are testimony to a 'false consciousness'. He presents a formidable array of African intellectuals and activists including Sol Plaatje, Albie Sachs, Herbert Dhlomo, Peter Abrahams, Can Themba, Bloke Modisane, Es'kia Mphahlele, Chris Hani, Mzwakhe Mbuli and John Matshikiza as effective agents of an imperial project in their use of Shakespeare. But if such a varied group of people have drawn on Shakespeare for enlightened or radical ends, the 'false consciousness' notion does not help us to think far enough about the complex and contradictory ways in which texts function within culture. More care is needed in the investigation of the multiple contradictions in the particular historical situation of each of these moderate, progressive or sometimes radical individuals and the ways in which each might appropriate or mobilize Shakespeare (as well as merely replicating or serving an attendant imperial project). It is worth noting by way of analogy that Carolyn Hamilton observes that the disagreements in treatments of the *mfecane* or the population movements and upheavals associated with the reign of Chaka

> over the relative weighting of European and African agency re-
> peat the continual bifurcation of the southern African past into
> black histories and white histories, meeting only in conflict. This
> division continues despite the wealth of evidence which reveals a
> more fluid situation in which European and African actions ...
> are but different ingredients in a well-shaken cocktail ...
>
> (Hamilton 1995: 8)

She argues for greater engagement with 'the full complexity of relations of domination, subordination, resistance and interaction'
(ibid.: 8). Mark Heywood who cites Z. K. Matthews' comment in
his autobiography that he 'discovered Shakespeare had things to
say not only to his England or to the [Westerners] who have read
him since, but also to me, a twentieth-century African' (Heywood
1994: 54), is currently investigating just such a possible impact in
the writing of the early twentieth-century political leader A. C.
Jordan.[3] To offer only one other example here, the extent to which
the South African dramatist Herbert Dhlomo may have had Shakespeare as a model in his endeavour to write plays in the 1930s and
1940s which were not merely attempts at affiliation but which, within
the constrictions and pressures of their own period, anticipated
incipient forms of black consciousness as well as developed an
oppositional stance towards segregation, similarly invites further
research.

IV

To argue that we need to escape the dominance of Europe does not
of course mean that current work in both Europe and North America
that attempts to identify hegemonic workings, the emergence of
structurations of gender and sexuality and the exploration of ways
in which cultural difference and 'race' is negotiated in early modern texts is anything but helpful. On the contrary, such work feeds
into current endeavour in South Africa which struggles, for example in the writing of a democratic Constitution based on a culture
of 'human rights', to free itself from discursive positionings enunciated in those early modern texts, and recycled in the subsequent

widespread and persisting use of them in education and performance. Critical writing such as that of Richmond Barbour, which
situates the problems about the Duke's control in *Measure for Measure*
within the context of the East India Company's lack of control
over its colonial agents, or Kim Hall's argument that

> descriptions of dark and light, rather than being mere indica-
> tions of Elizabethan beauty standards or markers of moral
> categories, became in the early modern period the conduit
> through which the English began to formulate the notions of
> 'self' and 'other' so well known in Anglo-American racial dis-
> courses

(Hall 1995: 2)

or, again, the essays in *Women, 'Race' and Writing in the Early Modern
Period*, edited by Margo Hendricks and Patricia Parker (1994), all
help to locate the Shakespeare text within the incipient moment of
colonization and incipient representations of cultural difference.

One of the few instances of work from within South Africa that
might contribute to such a reading is to be found in Shelley Malka's
study of the representation of the Jew in *The Merchant of Venice* and
in Jewish writings of the seventeenth century. Her examination of
sixteenth- and seventeenth-century Jewish writing, particularly by
Jewish thinkers living in or associated with Venice shows, for example, that Jewish representations of concepts of mercy, justice and
revenge are entirely unrelated to the (mis)representations of them
in *The Merchant of Venice*. Such writing indicates that sixteenth- and
seventeenth-century Jews conceived of their God as powerfully
merciful, this quality being emphasized and recited seventeen times
on their Day of Atonement, as well as informing their daily rituals
of prayer. Jewish thinkers specifically prohibit any literal enactment
of the injunction 'an eye for an eye'. They also expressly disapprove
of the impulse towards revenge. Representations of the Jew in both
Marlowe and Shakespeare draw on older (non-Jewish) European
traditions of hate literature. Malka shows how critics have in turn,
in their representations of the play, taken the text's misreading of
the 'Jew' as authoritative representation of Jewish versions of mercy,
justice and revenge. Both the text itself and critical readings of it
thus establish and institutionalize a form of 'knowledge' which serves
the political and material interests of particular groups and deni-
grates others.

This and other such work offers particular evidence of the process, at one of the originating moments of colonization and empire, whereby, as Seshadri-Crooks has it, 'groups arrogate to themselves the function of granting or denying recognition and respect'(Seshadri-Crooks 1995: 52). As I have argued, within South Africa, such readings enable us to engage with historically incipient representations of interaction between peoples that in turn intersect in a variety of ways with twentieth-century modes of reading place and subjectivity, within our own location. Such tasks remain necessary in South Africa, not simply to chart a process of disempowerment but also because to register ways in which past epistemic violence was engendered, is a means of future empowerment. It provides for the possibility of what Ania Loomba has referred to as the task of 'dismantling not only … imperialist and colonialist versions of history but also their contemporary effects' (Loomba 1993: 306). Even at the level of secondary education, it is possible to conceive of teachers examining some of Shakespeare's texts in clear and controlled ways in terms of constructions of 'race', ethnicity, notions of difference involving sexuality, gender, religion. The use of a play such as *The Tempest* in tandem with a play such as Kani's, Ntshona's and Fugard's *The Island*, might similarly facilitate awareness of basic issues involved in encounters, clashes, continuing relationships between different cultural groups, colonial or settler communities and indigenous populations. Again, the kind of cultural constructions to be found in plays such as *Macbeth* might be profitably juxtaposed against concepts of subjectivity, power and incipient nationhood evident in Dhlomo's presentation of monarchy and government in *Cetshwayo*.

V

The Shakespeare text provides a means of exploring our sense of interaction with Europe and North America not only in terms of the history of its reception, and in its concern to negotiate difference, but also in offering a frame as further means for imagining our South African future. When Lisa Jardine argues that 'to read Shakespeare historically is to undertake a dialogue with those culturally freighted residues of our own past in order more clearly to illuminate the culture we currently inhabit' and when she speaks of 'the particular situation of the interlocutor relative to the historicized Shakespearean text – a situation focused by the bright light of contemporary events and our pressing need to understand them in a larger than parochial context' (Jardine 1996: 148) she refers to a past that for South Africans can only be 'ours' in a general and problematically colonial sense. Moreover, within the South African terrain, we have limited access to the culturally freighted residues of that past, at best infrequent physical access to the European or North American archive. To understand aspects of the cultural history of which the Shakespeare text is part, we are for the most part reliant upon readings or narratives of those archives marketed in this country. Nevertheless – to adapt Jardine's thinking about her relationship to her own (European/British) past – it can be argued that use of such work which travels to us from other places and the global text that comes with it is one route whereby we may come, not only to understand aspects of our own contemporaneity, but also do so 'in a larger than parochial context'. As I remarked earlier, this is not to question the imperative of a central focus, in the South African academy, on local literatures. This should not, however, blind us to some of the dangers that in other locations, certain nativist movements have sometimes entailed. Irene Silverblatt notes, for example how '[n]ativist ideologies' attempting to construe '"Indian" senses of place and possibility' in the Central Andes of seventeenth-century Peru, in the context of Spanish empire building, 'were ultimately bound by colonial terms of living: they did not directly challenge colonial power' (Silverblatt 1995: 292). Awareness of the global text, situated within its own location and moment, may help us to avoid becoming parochial about our own South African present. Moreover, Jardine's foregrounding of the dialogic nature of the act of reading hints at a specific area of potential enablement for the current South African reader of Shakespeare. If, without archives, to historicize the Shakespeare text we depend upon the research that travels to us predominantly from Europe and North America, our situation as interlocutors brings with it other particular possibilities. As I have argued before now, the darkness of apartheid placed and places the South African interlocutor in a relationship with the historicized text that remains worthy of exploration. I would also like briefly to argue that the concept of 'hybridity' as an assumption that might shape our reading of the text is, in the present South African situation, worth re-examining.

As is well known, one current strand in post-colonial studies and perhaps at present the most dominant, is concerned with the question of hybridity in migrant and diasporic communities and how the text itself negotiates the differences of its own world, what Mishra defines as 'the hermeneutics of the liminal, the borders of culture, the unassimilable, the margins ... the critique of the centre through the kinds of hybrid, hyphenated identities occupied by the diasporic'(Mishra 1995: 11). In exploring the ways the text itself negotiates the differences of its world and the ways in which we in turn might negotiate between it and our world, how might the South African experience modify notions of hybridity which come to us primarily from diasporic criticism located in the West? How may this, in turn, help us to approach questions of agency in the Shakespeare text?

Articulations of hybridity have sometimes encountered opposition, as is also well known, most famously perhaps for suggesting that the 'subaltern' is ultimately always subject to dominant colonial discourse. But, as others have argued, it is important to focus on the aspects of resistance within any model of hybridity. Vijay Mishra's discussion of Rushdie's works foregrounds an energetic strand of resistance in their presentation of heterogeneity, one that exemplifies 'the blasting open of agonistic politics in embattled ethnicities within nation-states that can no longer construct their nationalisms through a homogeneous and synchronous imagining of a collective body consensually reading its newspapers or responding to global events as a totality' (ibid.: 10). The 'entry of strange people into so many parts of the globe presents the older inhabitants with precisely the threat of the new, the threat of "ideas" no longer commensurable with pre-existing epistemologies' (ibid.: 12). Again, in terms of a project to restore agency to the subaltern or the oppressed, we may note that South African theatre in the 1970s and 1980s also provides instances of hybridity in which the move to resistance is at least as powerful as any suggestion of divided subjectivity and alienation. In Kani, Ntshona and Fugard's *Sizwe Bansi Is Dead*, Styles's mimicry of Baas Bradley is a means of the reassertion of community and resistance against his oppressive stance. In Maishe Maponya's *The Hungry Earth*, which draws upon black consciousness and tries to construct an authentic pre-colonial origin, the industrialized and hybridized culture of the mineworkers is shown nevertheless to have its own inbuilt modes of resistance that are not determined by the rulers. Both texts, particularly Maponya's, use African languages as one means of resistance and empowerment.

As I suggested earlier, the location of present-day South Africa also presents different conditions from those encountered in migrant communities with at present greater – although so far crucially non-economic – possibilities for empowerment for the (formerly) oppressed populaiton. Recognition of hybridity and heterogeneity is no longer only a means of resisting hegemony from the position of *totalized* 'subaltern' disempowerment. Moreover, as the language discussion document I referred to earlier announces, policy in the present government aspires to provide space for and empowerment of – at least a linguistic – heterogeneity. It further involves a population that is not always perceived as permanently to be 'split' in a 'migrant' condition of hybribidity. It is worth noting here that Seshadri-Crooks remarks of the 'vigorous state of transitional music in the North and South of India', that its practitioners 'not only presuppose the possibility of going home but would probably argue (despite their itinerant life-styles) tha they have never left home in the first place (Seshadri-Crooks 1995: 57). In his recent work on oral literatures in South Africa, David Copland examines Sesotho migrant song/self-praise which 'for well over a century if not longer Basotho male migrants and their women have been composing and recomposing'.[4] While he recognises elements of hybridization in this work, and the extent to which, as Hofmeyr observes (1995: 140), 'this genre cannibalizes popular forms like radio, record and cassette', he asseverates that:

> the practitioners themselves do not subscribe to notions of 'hybridity', and rather see culture as discrete and bounded. For whom is 'culture' unbounded – the anthropologist or the native? Is it in other words for (Western) theory or for the (local) discourse with which theory is endeavouring to engage or inquire upon? … To say a priori that 'cultures' are not 'bounded' therefore is misleading since local discourses do, in fact, establish authoritative traditions, discrete temporal and spatial parameters, in which it is made singularly clear to cultural subjects and their others what is (and who are) to belong within these parameters, and what (and who) not.
>
> (Copland quoted in Hofmeyr 1995: 140)

Again, Ania Loomba has argued that no hybridity can be understood by reading only the colonized culture. In the interaction between colonizer and colonized, the colonized always comes from a culture of her or his own. She maintains that 'only the insistent placing of Shakespeare alongside other texts can help us to think seriously about "cultural difference" even "in" Shakespeare' (Loomba 1996: 165) and cites Mary Louise Pratt's description of a letter written to Philip

III of Spain, a bilingual attempt by a colonized subject to represent himself 'in ways that *engage with* the colonizer's own terms' (Pratt 1992: 7) and that involve only 'partial collaboration with and appropriation of the idioms of the conqueror' (ibid.).

Such or other endeavours may argue a more active attempt, within conditions of colonization, incipient post-coloniality and the dangers of neo-colonialism, to develop notions of hybridity in ways that also acknowledge a clash of cultures – rather than merely the slipperiness of discourse – the importance of resistance and, as well, variations in the possibilities of agency. Moreover, for the South African reader of Shakespeare, how the Shakespeare and other Renaissance texts in turn negotiate cultural difference, their equivalents of subalternity or subordination, or the question of agency may be addressed in terms of such modifications of or developments in the model of hybridity. We may recall here Alan Sinfield's argument that 'stories comprise within themselves the ghosts of the alternative stories they are trying to exclude' (Sinfield 1992: 47). Evidence of the nature and formation of agency taken from local histories may alter the paradigmatic assumptions about non-elite men or women we otherwise take for granted in our readings of the plays. For instance, the South African critic Malvern van wyk Smith has explored the extent to which sixteenth-century European writing about Africa, a mixture of fable and fact, draws on classical, patristic and primitivist traditions as well as on travel writing. Although he is not at all concerned with notions of hybridity, he uses his findings to argue in effect that Othello is interpellated with just such (disabling) traditions. How we locate Othello, who is after all on Cyprus the supreme agent of a colonial power, is complicated. But if we pursue here those aspects of particularly his early narratives that raise the issues of European perceptions of Africa, or in terms of his interactions elsewhere in the play, assumptions regarding relations between proto – at least – colonizers and colonized, it is worth noting John and Jean Comaroff's argument that in Southern Africa

> much of the Tswana response to the mission encounter was an effort to fashion an awareness of, and gain conceptual mastery over a changing world ... to grasp the *bases* of the colonial production of value, and to redirect it to the well-being of the dominated.
>
> (Comaroff and Comaroff 1992: 259, 260)

Belinda Bozzoli argues for an even greater complexity in her study of the Tswana woman Mrs Molefe, who lived in Alexandra township and was during the 1950s a vociferous supporter of the ANC. She stresses the factors of history, structure and experience, involving Mrs Molefe's

> sense of herself as a Mofokeng, as an African, as a Christian, a woman, a migrant, a junior and a potential wife. Each of these strands evolved over time, and their evolution was affected by where she thought she was going ... her 'peaks' of consciousness relate to the rebellions against enormous challenges, by both township life and the apartheid state, to the 'self' which had thus been created.
>
> (Bozzoli 1991: 305)

Such recognitions of the complexity of the formation of consciousness and agency may be suggestive for questions of agency in *Othello* and the way in which we might think him into being in the play. Thus Othello's use, even of those very narratives of his past, that appear to imprison him, as well as his interactions throughout the play, might be investigated in terms of strategic manipulation of the 'master/mistress discourse', as well as modes of self-defence or means to survival and to power – what Bozzoli might refer to as his 'life-strategy'.

In these endeavours we need to probe too the extent to which the Shakespeare text might provide a frame for South African projects of recovery, rather than be used to identify and recycle traces of disabling and neo-colonial paradigms which, in current South African terms, work for disablement. Modifications of the notion of hybridity as postulating dependence may be challenged beyond those plays that overtly negotiate cultural difference. It is possible, for example, to contemplate a project which might identify as a seventeenth-century English 'other' the view of action to be found in *Hamlet* as it is explicated in Nigel Alexander's *Poison, Play and Duel*. To locate this text within a Christian culture is to focus on the problematic and fallen nature of human action, which in its entirety offers a fundamentally flawed and tragic vision of human agency, that has pessimistic and possibly even conservative implications regarding achievement and change. We may locate these implications within the play's own habitus and field, in ways that will confirm primarily the *difference* between such a construction of human agency and that experienced in recent South African history, where, decades of what might be construed as extended and profound processes of hybridization have not ultimately disabled resistance or prevented the attainment of at least a measure of liberation, with the possibility at least of even greater change.

However, again, as is commonly acknowledged, the location of this focus upon action in the play primarily within the male body has powerfully negative implications so far as the female body is concerned. And this, in turn, does not contrast so much as link up with similar tendencies in South African cultural practice both before and during the rule of the Nationalist Government as well as beyond it in certain procedures both in city and township.[5]

We need, then, to examine the Shakespeare text not only to explore its reception and its institutionalization in South Africa or its negotiations with cultural difference, but explicitly to register its own cultural difference from (as well as its similarities to) our condition/location. In this we will be working to establish a South African imaginative 'centre' and we will be also separating ourselves from that in the Shakespeare text which is 'other'. To reformulate slightly Dipesh Chakrabarty's argument that historiography needs to provincialize Europe, the aim must partly be, to provincialize the text, to return it to Europe. And, at this moment in the commencement of a journey towards a future convincingly post-apartheid community, the question of action and agency needs particular foregrounding in ways that will not disable projects involving reconciliation, reconstruction and a more equitable sharing of the wealth of the country. The 'otherness' of the Shakespeare text may have a small part to play in helping us to bring such projects more clearly into focus, too.

Acknowledgements

I should like to thank Barbara Bowen, Neville Hoad and Denis Salter for reading earlier drafts of this essay, for their invaluable criticisms, and for their generous advice.

Notes

An earlier version of this essay appeared in *Études Théâtrales / Essays in Theatre* (Nov. 1996), 15 (1); 45–57.
  1 Albie Sachs, a judge of the Consitutional Court of South Africa, writes: 'The right to equality, in fact, protects the right to be different.

Difference becomes harmful when it is associated with subordination – what has to be tackled is the subordination, not the difference. Pluralism becomes safe and beneficial when it is detached from political hegemony. The right to be the same in terms of political rights is the foundation of the right to be different in respect of language and culture. As has been pointed out, common citizenship protects language diversity, and language diversity gives texture to common citizenship' (Sachs 1994: 124).

2 See Mtuze (1990/1), Shole (1990/1), and Wright (1990/1).
3 I am grateful to Mark Heywood for discussing this with me, for making his current ongoing research available to me, and for giving me permission to mention it here.
4 Copland, cited in Hofmeyr (1995: 134).
5 The absence of women in South African theatre until the late 1980s, for example, is not entirely explained away by the real practical physical dangers facing participants in dissident theatre, which precluded attendance at regular rehearsals and performance.

11
Shakespeare and Hanekom, *King Lear* and land
A South African perspective
NICHOLAS VISSER

For the benefit of non-South African readers, who might be won-
dering if my title refers to some obscure Renaissance figure who
bears a relation to *King Lear* even more subtle, far-reaching and
unlikely than Samuel Harsnett, I should immediately state that Derek
Hanekom is South Africa's Minister of Agriculture and Land Affairs.[1] What he is doing in the company of Shakespeare will, I hope,
become clear as I go along. In any event, I want to begin by situating my remarks on *King Lear* in Hanekom's present-day South Africa
rather than in Shakespeare's early modern England.

Most visitors to South Africa sooner or later make their way to
Cape Town. While there, they are likely to visit one of its favourite
tourist attractions, the Kirstenbosch National Botanical Garden,
with its magnificent setting on the slopes of Table Mountain. Along
the Garden's footpaths are occasional signs pointing the way to
something called Van Riebeeck's Hedge. Anyone taking the trouble to follow the signs is likely to be disappointed; the hedge is one
of the Garden's less impressive sights. To add a final bit of Cape
Town geography, a lovely stream that rises in Kirstenbosch is, within
a few kilometres, channelled into a narrow concrete ditch, barely
noticeable to those who cross the bridges over it, as it passes through
nearby suburbs. This is the Liesbeck River.

On 21 February 1657, Jan Van Riebeeck, commander of the
Dutch East India Company's recently established revictualling station

at the Cape, announced the first freehold grants of land to nine Dutch burghers. These were in all likelihood the earliest freehold properties on the continent of Africa. Six of the holdings were to be on the east bank of what the Company, in good colonial fashion, had named the Amstel River, later renamed the Liesbeck. After stating a few conditions, Van Riebeeck declared, taking for granted his authority to declare, that the land would 'remain their property forever to do with as they like, that is, they may sell, lease or otherwise alienate it' (quoted in Davenport and Hunt 1974: 2). Three years later, in 1660, following a war against the Khoikhoi inhabitants of the Cape (who may be more familiar to readers by the no longer acceptable name, 'Hottentots'), Van Riebeeck used slave labour to plant a thick hedge of bramble and indigenous bitter almond, interspersed with fortified posts, to separate land forcibly occupied by the Company from the now excluded and dispossessed Khoikhoi. Thus, within five years of the establishment of European settlement at the Cape, and within a few decades of the performance of *King Lear* before James I at Christmastide in 1606, South Africa experienced its first colonial division of the kingdom.[2]

Among the many things *King Lear* may be said to be 'about', the issue of land – of its control, its ownership, its forms of inhabitation and settlement, its relations to fundamental human needs, its relation crucially to power as well as to powerlessness and poverty – is central. Even beyond Lear's division of the kingdom, land is a preoccupation of the play. Martin Orkin, in his pioneering work *Shakespeare Against Apartheid* (1987), was the first to connect the play's concern with land to the history of dispossession in South Africa. In his chapter on 'Cruelty, *King Lear* and the South African Land Act of 1913', he is careful to insist on the manifest differences between early modern England and present-day South Africa, yet at the same time he enables the play to find a new context within which to resonate, the context of South Africa in the late 1980s, in the darkest period of the State of Emergency, when political repression in South Africa reached its greatest intensity. Now, some ten years later, and under changed circumstances, I want to revisit Orkin's concern with land in the play and in South Africa.

Part of the changed circumstances to which I refer are the recently passed laws on land reform, ushered through parliamentary consideration by Minister Hanekom, who has been charged with the complex task of undoing much of what followed on that earliest

colonial appropriation of land. The intense debates of the past few
years, and especially during the months preceding the finalizing of
South Africa's new Constitution in October 1996, over land reform
and over the inclusion of a 'property clause' in the Bill of Rights,
provide an obvious occasion for an enquiry into land in *King Lear*.[3]
In taking up that occasion, however, I want to move in a slightly
different direction from Orkin's chapter. At several points I will risk
pressing, somewhat more strongly than he did, connections between
the world of the play and the world in which I am discussing these
things. In any event, his discretion was bootless since it could not
forestall the hostile attacks of those South African critics who are
loath to see Shakespeare connected with politics at all, never mind
with South African politics. But beyond questions of analogies and
other possible resonances for South African readers or audiences
of the play, I want to enquire into the discursive frameworks in
which land is represented and contested both in the play and in
wider social intercourse; enquire, that is, into the conceptions and
assumptions that underpin the way we talk about land.

Declining to contribute to the panegyrics in which her sisters so
readily indulge, Cordelia addresses Lear not as 'Father' but as
'your Majesty', and declares that she loves, 'According to my bond'
(I. 1. 91–2). For some critics of the play, 'bond' stands for far more
than the inflated protestations of Goneril and Regan; it is part of
what became, in the commentaries on imagery and themes that
dominated Shakespeare studies for so long, the 'Great Bonds' of
affect and duty and reciprocity that supposedly bind together families,
courts and whole societies. These bonds are at the centre, for instance, of Derek Traversi's influential essay on the play of the
1930s; he speaks eloquently of the imagery of bonds, seeing them
as 'the central conception of the play' (Traversi 1969: 142). Oddly,
the most sustained study of the imagery of the play from the same
period and in the same critical vein, Robert Bechtold Heilman's
This Great Stage: Image and Structure in 'King Lear', sees Cordelia's
choice of words in a different light. For Heilman, Cordelia, in
speaking of her bond, 'expresses her real feelings in a most mat-
ter-of-fact metaphor from the world of business and law' (Heilman
1948: 163).

Heilman does not identify any further such imagery. He devotes
chapters respectively to images of blindness, clothing, nature and
human nature, age and justice, values, madness, rationalism and
religious attitudes. However much we have left behind the New

Critical focus on imagery, those of us who were raised on such criticism, were we to be asked what are the major patterns or clusters of images in *King Lear*, would almost certainly provide a listing much like Heilman's tabulation. Those were the images identified as central by that critical mode, and hence the ones we recollect from our early study of the play. Since we no longer focus so closely on imagery in the old manner, we are likely to remain unaware of the pervasiveness and centrality of the language of commerce and law (in particular the law of contract) in the play, and the application of that language to land.

That language includes references to dowries, portions, deeds, interest (in the sense of legal right), moiety, revenue, profit, property, inheritance, earnest (in the sense of money), hire, rent, monopoly, unpaid lawyers, cases in law, depositories (legalese for trustees), usurers, debts and so on. The language of commerce and law infiltrates itself into and debases the everyday discourse of the play, such that Lear can express his angry rejection of Cordelia as if she were just so many no-longer valued goods: 'When she was dear to us we did hold her so, / But now her price is fallen' (I. 1. 195–6), where 'dear' slides so easily from its relation to affection to its relation to money.

This language of commerce and law merits further attention in its own right; for immediate purposes, however, emphasis must turn to the application of that language to land. When Lear outlines his plans in the opening scene, he speaks of publishing his daughters' dowries. On reflection, it is an unusual choice of words since 'dowry' ordinarily referred to the land and other forms of wealth which a bride brought to her husband on marriage. With reference to Cordelia, who is about to get married, treating the intended land settlement as a dowry makes sense. In the cases of Goneril and Regan, however, the announcement of dowries at some point after the marriages have taken place makes less sense. In any event, throughout the scene, in the language in which Lear describes the division as well as in the language in which Burgundy and France respond to the question of their willingness to marry Cordelia in the absence of a dowry, land is spoken of as disposable property, something properly considered in contractual dealings and settlements. To us that may seem unremarkable; however, conceiving of land in this way distorts Lear's monarchical relation to the land and to those who act under him as landed vassals.

The division we witness in the play is more than a particular apportionment of land; it marks the beginnings of the splitting off of different, historically significant ways of construing land. At one level, the play displays highly traditional conceptions of land in apparently organic relation to sovereignty and settlement. In such feudal conceptions, the fundamental source and repository of sovereignty is the ruler's relation (whether as monarch or as baronial power) to land, to a particular territory or realm. This relation is foregrounded in the very names by which most of the major male characters are addressed or referred to – Albany, Cornwall, Gloucester, Kent, Burgundy. Curiously, one character not so addressed is Lear himself, who is never called 'Britain', though the King of France carries the name of his realm.

This is one conception of land, and within such a system of feudal conventions it is entirely proper for Cornwall (who in any event would be associated with the south of Britain) and Albany (associated with the north) to have baronial authority as dukes of the realm, and for Lear to confer such power and authority upon them as his highest-ranking vassals. Such arrangements reveal the historical relation of land to sovereignty. Treating land as a matter of dowry, on the other hand, signals the transformation of land into private property.

For all that he talks about the land as property, Lear, in describing the 'portions' to be granted to his daughters' husbands, does not provide anything like a cadastral survey of the land, even in the broad manner of the Domesday Book. Instead of enumerated fields and dwellings and the like, and statements of their value, we hear of 'shadowy forests', 'plenteous rivers' and 'wide-skirted meads' (I. i. 63–4). In short, the land is described in terms that efface all traces of human occupation. What Lear describes is 'empty land', an expression bound to have a fair amount of resonance for any South African audience, since the (in fact spurious) claim of 'empty land' was long used by conservative South African historians to legitimize the appropriation of land by white settlers. (As we shall see, there is actually a long tradition of seeing inhabited land as somehow simultaneously empty.)

The conception of land as property – inheritable, transferable, subject to the workings of law and contract – is most visible in the machinations of Edmund. Where Lear apparently hovers between different conceptions of land, Edmund is, characteristically, clear-sighted about land as a source of social and economic status – as, in short, a form of commodity. Edmund's illegitimacy is, among other things, a matter of strictly legal standing; he may not in law inherit land. In the brutal expression he falsely attributes to Edgar, he is truly an 'unpossessing bastard' (II. i. 66). In the scene of his forged letter and his discussion with his father regarding Edgar's alleged plotting, emphasis falls on 'fortunes', in the sense of inherited wealth (I. ii. 46), and, repeatedly, 'revenue' (I. ii. 51, 54, 71). Personal wealth, not some quaint notion of the duties of vassalage, informs Edmund's understanding of the meaning and value of land: hence his famous lines in Act 1, Scene 2: 'Legitimate Edgar, I must have your land' (I. ii. 16), and 'Let me, if not by birth, have lands by wit' (I. ii. 180). In a little noted ironic twist of the play, while the illegitimate Edmund is ultimately foiled in his efforts to have land, Edgar, who in both law and custom has no legitimate claim whatever to the throne of Britain, who is not even of the highest rank of the nobility, winds up sovereign of all the land.

At the dawn of the modern age, *King Lear* captures the emergence of a development that would be a salient feature of the transition to modernity, the transformation of land into private property, the transformation, to put the point more precisely, of having rights and responsibilities of authority and tenure, which were traditionally embedded in a set of relations of homage and deference, obligation and reciprocity, replaced by Edmund's more purely individual and privatized having land by wit. So thoroughly naturalized has the notion of private property become, that today we find it difficult to imagine any other sort of property relation. During the protracted wrangling over the property clause in the new South African Constitution, it was clear, for instance, that nearly all parties to the negotiations had no conception of property beyond private property, beyond that is, a right of exclusive use of and benefit from ownership that is 'unlimited in amount, unconditional on the performance of social functions, and freely transferable' (Macpherson 1978: 10). Even Minister Hanekom's Land Reform (Labour Tenants) Act of 1996, while it does speak to the problem of greater security of tenure for certain categories of farm labourers, ultimately envisages granting long-term occupants of land a legally enforceable opportunity to acquire freehold title to a parcel of land. In other words, rather than recognize and institute forms of tenure rights in property different from private ownership, the law simply seeks to extend access to private property rights to more people. Left unanswered are questions about how many can afford to exercise such a right, or why people who have occupied land for generations should now have to purchase it. Colin Murray, author of one of the most illuminating studies of the history of land in South Africa, argues the compelling need for the 'development of a framework for the practical recognition of rights to land other than those expressed in the possession of title deeds' (Murray 1992: 287).[4]

It can come as a surprise to discover how historically recent is the collapse of what was once a wide variety of often simultaneous and overlapping property rights in land into the single, uniform and exclusive notion of private property that prevails today. We can date some of the most important early developments in this process to Shakespeare's own period; indeed, his purchases of New Place in Stratford in 1597, 107 acres of arable land and associated rights to adjoining common pasturage in 1602, and a half-share in a lease of 'tithes of corn, grain, blade and hay' in three Warwickshire villages in 1605 point to the variety of property rights in land in operation at the time (Schoenbaum 1977: 246). By the end of the seventeenth century, however, private property had become the norm in England.

South Africa is interesting to examine in relation to this process because its course both runs parallel to England's (with freehold, as we have seen, being instituted as early as the mid-seventeenth century) and departs from it, since in South Africa the process remains incomplete. As the struggles over land legislation and the property clause in the Constitution have shown, the transformation of land into property is still, at some levels, actively contested in South Africa. Given the continued existence on a fairly wide scale of land still held under 'traditional' or 'customary' forms of tenure, coupled with the fact that so many of the often violent impositions of modern capitalist forms of private property are still part of the living memory of those who were dispossessed, it is hardly surprising that the notion of private property has not yet been fully naturalized by the majority of the country's population. Nevertheless, it is clear that in post-apartheid South Africa, private property ownership is becoming increasingly normative in all areas of the emerging legal system, while no one in a position of power is proposing new, alternative forms of property rights in land. Where *King Lear* represents (in more than one sense of the word) a moment near the inception of the split in ways of understanding individual and social relations to land, South Africa furnishes a moment of potentially imminent closure, in which a single notion of property seems destined, sooner rather than later, to displace all others, with all the conflict and tension such closures entail.

Although *King Lear* provides us with a fascinating glimpse of the beginnings of these developments, a process as politically and economically significant as the transformation of land into private property cannot take place without a full theorization of the issues involved. Beginning with Jean Bodin's *Six Books of the Commonwealth* late in the sixteenth century – one of the first works to describe the private property right as an essential part of good government – a succession of philosophers, jurists and social thinkers has attempted to provide moral justification for private property, interestingly, the only form of property right that has required a moral justification. Central in this project was a thinker who bears interesting and manifold relations to the present South African context, John Locke. Locke has several claims on South Africa's attention. Clearly, any fashioning of a modern Constitution of the kind recently promulgated for South Africa, with the inevitable concerns over separation of powers, statements of rights, and the like, takes place in the long shadow of Locke. Efforts at land reform similarly have to come to terms with his legacy, since he was, as C. B. Macpherson has noted, 'the first to make a case for property *of unlimited amount* as a *natural* right of the individual, prior to governments and overriding them' (Macpherson 1978: 15). In other words, he was the first to argue not only that one could privately own land and other forms of wealth, but that one could own as much as Harry Oppenheimer.

A third way in which Locke relates significantly to present-day South Africa involves the warrant he provides for colonial incursion into South Africa and other lands, and the dispossession that accompanied it. Chapter 5 of Locke's *Second Treatise of Government*, entitled 'Of Property', first published in 1689, sets out his justification of private property on the basis of labour; he asserts that 'he [who] hath mixed his *Labour* with [nature], and joyned to it something that is his own ... thereby makes it his *Property*' (Locke in Macpherson 1978: 18). Human labour, then, rather than, say, occupation or a history of use, is the basis of Locke's defence of private property. Although the labour theory of property is plausible enough, and possesses a certain ethical warrant, the history of South Africa shows how dangerous it is, for what it provides is justification not just for unlimited private property but also for colonial dispossession.

The connection between the two becomes clear in key moments of Locke's exposition. In explaining his labour theory, he writes at one point:

[H]e who appropriates land to himself by his labour, does not lessen but increase the common stock of mankind. For the provisions serving to the support of humane life, produced by one acre of inclosed and cultivated land, are … ten times more, than those, which are yielded by an acre of Land, of an equal richnesse, lyeing wast in common.

(Ibid.: 22)

He goes on to suggest that the ratio of ten-to-one understates matters; a hundred-to-one is more like it. By way of demonstration he offers, chillingly, this:

For I aske whether in the wild woods and uncultivated wast of America left to Nature, without any improvement, tillage or husbandry, a thousand acres will yield the needy and wretched inhabitants as many conveniencies of life as ten acres of equally fertile land doe in Devonshire where they are well cultivated.

(Ibid.: 22)

After increasing the ratio of value once again, this time to a thousand-to-one, Locke suggests that while land has become scarce in those countries that have 'the *Use of Money*', which is to say, in Europe,

yet there are still *great Tracts of Ground* to be found [outside Europe], which (the Inhabitants thereof not having joyned with the rest of Mankind, in the consent of the Use of their common Money) *lie waste*, and are more than the People, who dwell on it, do, or can make use of, and so still lie in common.

(Ibid.: 25)

What this ever so blandly says is that land occupied only by such 'wretched inhabitants' as, say, the Khoikhoi at the Cape in the seventeenth century is 'waste', land not really inhabited in any meaningful sense, and accordingly its appropriation by those prepared to 'develop' the land through labour is tacitly justified by their putative thousand-to-one addition to the value of the land's production. Looked at another way, Locke's labour theory of property lays the groundwork for the creation of the colonial stereotype of 'idle natives', who do not deserve the land because they do not intensively cultivate it.

Locke's formula for dealing with the 'uncultivated wast of America' in the seventeenth century, during England's first period of Empire, is taken up by one of the most controversial colonial officials of the second period of Empire in the mid-nineteenth century, George Grey, called admiringly by his first biographer 'Pioneer of Empire in Southern Lands' (Henderson 1907). Writing in 1852, Grey is clearer than Locke about colonial entitlement:

> The waste lands of the vast Colonial possessions of the British Empire are held by the Crown, as trustee for the inhabitants of the Empire at large, and not for the inhabitants of the particular province … in which any such waste land happens to be situate.
> (Quoted in Kerr 1976: 50)

Grey's role as colonial Governor of the Cape in the destruction of the independence of the Xhosa people in 1856–7 helped to add some 300,000 hectares to the 'waste lands' of Britain's Empire, most of which was handed over for white, freehold occupation (see Peires 1989).

It is not, however, solely land in distant, colonizable territories that Locke's justification of private property places in jeopardy. 'Wast' for him lies closer to home. Repeatedly he contrasts 'inclosed and cultivated land' with land held 'in common', which is synonymous with 'waste'; and he makes it clear that the former is by far the more desirable state of affairs. What is being justified here is the long process of land engrossment and enclosure in Britain. Indeed, Devonshire, which Locke cites as a model for how land should be dealt with, was one of the earliest and most completely enclosed districts in England. However much economic historians debate the weighting that should be given to the supposed long-term economic benefits of enclosure on the one hand and the human costs on the other, two things are clear. First, in Marx's words, those who did the enclosing, arrogated 'for themselves the rights of modern private property in estates to which they had only a feudal title' (quoted in Morton 1968: 273). And second, ordinary people at the time regularly pointed to enclosure as a principal cause of the dearth and impoverishment they were increasingly suffering, especially during and after the severe economic troubles of the 1590s.

Simultaneously absent from and central to the play, the impoverished in *King Lear* ('impoverished', not 'poor', since 'poor' implies a state of being, as in 'the poor will always be with us'; while impoverishment is something that happens to or, as likely, is inflicted on people) emerge from the context of the enclosures and improvements later enthusiastically endorsed by Locke and against the background of the Elizabethan Poor Laws that attempted, however clumsily and in some respects even brutally, to address the rapidly growing poverty of the later sixteenth and early seventeenth centuries. When Edgar in disguise describes himself as one 'who is whipp'd from tithing to tithing, and stock-punish'd, and imprison'd' (III. iv. 131–2), he is referring to the penalties prescribed by the Poor Laws to control 'vagabondage', the official and typically pejorative term for the poor and homeless.

The figurative language of the prayer scene in Act 3, Scene 4 is cued by Lear's comment, prompted by the evident discomfort of the fool, on 'houseless poverty' (III. iv. 26). At the beginning of the 'prayer', he continues in this figurative vein by referring to 'houseless heads', and derives from such language a further reference to 'window'd' (III. iv. 30, 31). Here and elsewhere in the play, poverty is associated directly with homelessness, with landlessness. At this juncture in the play, furthermore, we may recall Lear's earlier descriptions of the realm in Act 1, Scene 1. Devoid of people as the described land is, it is nevertheless notably lush, with 'plenteous rivers and wide-skirted meads' and the like (I. i. 64). In these descriptions there is no suggestion of the bleak, marginal land to which the impoverished have increasingly been driven, the blasted heath on which Lear, bereft and derelict, belatedly discovers the existence of those who are, in a quite basic and literal way, 'unaccommodated' (III. iv. 105). These are the people who have been pushed off the land by engrossing and enclosure and related social and economic developments. They are ones who are silently left out of Locke's thousand-to-one equation as 'wast' is converted to production, as land is transformed into commodity.

Today, in South Africa, the great number of people left landless and homeless through what are at bottom the same social and economic forces glimpsed in *King Lear* and endorsed by Locke are our 'outies' and 'bergies', our street children and squatters.[5] Four centuries on they await the more equitable distribution of the social product recognized as essential by both Lear and Gloucester.

I am aware that in making such a blunt assertion I am transgressing the generic conventions that ordinarily govern work in literary studies, since my emphasis lies perhaps rather too much with the world of Hanekom and not quite enough with the text of Shakespeare. At the same time, it is worth remembering, as we grapple with the dilemma of what, if anything, should be the nature and role of Shakespeare studies in a 'post-colonial' South Africa, that

South Africa's colonial legacy has not in fact ended with the installation of a post-apartheid government, no matter how welcome that is. That legacy will find adequate resolution only when we have found ways to redress its more pernicious costs.

In any event I am less concerned with having breached the frame of critical commentary by somewhat crude references to the present than I am with the likelihood that my remarks will be taken to have a moral or even moralistic rather than a political thrust. The ending of *King Lear*, in which the status quo is restored without the slightest indication of redress for the poor, not even a shaking of a bit of superflux, suggests the inadequacy of a moralized politics based on empathy, that ability to feel what others feel. The sentiments expressed by Lear and Gloucester stem from deeply human and humane feelings, but they are transient, and they are politically inconsequential. The political point I would want to derive from the play's exploration of property and poverty can be made in several ways. With C. B. Macpherson, one of the foremost modern historians and philosophers of property, we can note that,

> If ... societies are to be the guarantors of rights essential to the equal possibility of individual members using and developing their human capacities, the individual property right that is needed is not the exclusive right but the right not to be *excluded* from the use or benefit of those things ... which are the achievements of the whole society.
>
> (Macpherson 1978: 184)

Or, with the South African Freedom Charter, now effectively discarded by the African National Congress in its readiness to embrace neo-liberal economic policies, we can reassert the determination that, 'The land shall be shared among those who work it.' Or, finally, with Shakespeare's Gloucester we may insist (with a bit of tactful misquotation) not as moral insight but as political demand, that 'distribution should undo excess, / And each [person] have enough' (IV. i. 69–70).

Notes

An earlier version of this essay appeared in *Textual Practice*, Spring 1997, vol. 11, no. 1, pp. 25–37.

1 The allusion, of course, is to Stephen Greenblatt's essay 'Shakespeare and the Exorcists' (1985).

2 Historians typically single out the discovery of diamonds and gold, the so-called mineral revolution, as the defining moment of South African history. One authority on early Cape history, Richard Elphick, suggests otherwise: 'The formation of a society of free white farmers was probably the most significant event in the history of modern South Africa, and it would one day affect the lives of millions of the region's inhabitants' (Elphick 1985: 110).

3 Those who campaigned most vigorously for a property clause sought to restrict the transfer of land that is currently privately owned, even if it was obtained under apartheid land laws, to voluntary transactions involving 'willing seller and willing buyer'. The effect of such a formulation would have been to preclude any serious efforts at land reform in South Africa. Eventually a somewhat more flexible property clause, Clause 25, was included in the Bill of Rights.

4 Discussions of land dispossession in South Africa typically focus on either colonial dispossession by force or on dispossession inflicted under the various land acts. Left out of account are the deliberate efforts of the South African state over a long period through low-interest loan schemes and other forms of public subsidy to advance white commercial farming and simultaneously undermine the black, landowning and sharecropping peasantry, such that the latter inevitably lost their access to land, albeit through strictly 'legal' means. For analysis of this process see, in addition to Murray (1992), Keegan (1987). As yet, no policy exists to reverse the devastating consequences of this pseudo-legal form of dispossession.

5 'Bergies' (from Afrikaans *berg*, mountain) is used in the Cape to refer to homeless people who live rough along the mountain sides; the word is often used to refer to homeless people, especially homeless men, generally, and has inevitably taken on pejorative connotations.

12
From the colonial to the post-colonial
Shakespeare and education in Africa
DAVID JOHNSON

Introduction

My definitions here of the colonial and post-colonial are historical, rather than in terms of changing fashions in literary criticism. In other words, the colonial Shakespeare I explore is the Shakespeare of the period of colonial rule, and the post-colonial Shakespeare the Shakespeare of the post-colonial period. More precisely, I have chosen the 1930s, the twilight decade of the British Empire, to represent the colonial, and the 1980s, the decade of late capital and globalization, to represent the post-colonial. For both periods, I focus on Shakespeare's journeys to Africa. My versions of the colonial and post-colonial Shakespeares are assembled from representative metropolitan Shakespeare critics, and educational policy-makers for Africa. For the colonial Shakespeare, I accordingly focus on G. Wilson Knight's criticism of *The Tempest*, and British education policy-maker for Africa, A. Victor Murray. My picture of the post-colonial Shakespeare is based on Stephen Greenblatt's criticism of *The Tempest*, and World Bank plans for education in Africa.

In focusing thus on the metropolitan mind, I inevitably present an incomplete picture. A more comprehensive study would provide detailed examination of distinct African contexts and their histories, analysis of English school syllabuses, and Shakespeare performances in the different African settings, and instances of African resistance to and appropriations of Shakespeare.[1] In confining my attention in this way, however, my hope is to convey some sense of the wider contexts in which metropolitan productions of the colonial and the post-colonial Shakespeare resonate.

The colonial Shakespeare

Writing in Oxford during the Great Depression, G. Wilson Knight's influential work *The Imperial Theme* (1931) appeared as part of a larger movement in literary criticism, away from the style of the Victorian gentleman-of-letters, and towards a more modern and professional approach to literature. Despite its title, Knight has little to say directly about histories of imperialism or colonialism. Such matters are irrelevant to the study of Shakespeare; instead, for Knight, the 'correct procedure is to interpret an age in the light of its great books and men of visionary genius, not the men of genius in the light of their age' (Wilson Knight 1951: xii). Accordingly, Shakespeare must be related not to 'minor writers of his day, theological, philosophical, psychological or historical, [but to] his great peers across the centuries; with Aeschylus before, with Byron after' (ibid.: xiii). What follows then is criticism concerned with uncovering the universal truths encoded in symbolic form in Shakespeare by close, exclusive attention to the plays themselves. What Knight discovers by this method is that order and unity should prevail over chaos, in life as in art, and that music and tempests are the organizing oppositions in all Shakespeare's plays. In his next book, *The Shakespearean Tempest* (1932), he repeats similar arguments, adding for the reader a detailed map of Shakespeare's symbolic universe, which includes an Area of Divine Music in the top left-hand corner, a Conflict zone in the middle which balances Human Passions and Political Order, and an Area of Evil Music, Surf and Silence in the bottom right-hand corner. As regards the play *The Tempest*, he argues that tempests connote tragedy, bestiality and loss, and in Caliban '[a]ll Shakespeare's intuition of the untamed beast in man is crystallized' (Wilson Knight 1932: 258). Music, on the other hand, is associated with revival, spirituality and restoration, and Prospero is the benevolent conductor who orchestrates a harmonious climax.

Recent critics have seen Knight as pre-eminently a *modernist* critic: Gary Taylor in *Re-inventing Shakespeare* (1989), Terence Hawkes in *Meaning by Shakespeare* (1992) and, most elaborately, Hugh Grady in

The Modernist Shakespeare (1991) convincingly argue that Knight's preoccupation with symbol, his interest in spatial as opposed to temporal thematics, and his elevation of the work of art above history, place him firmly in the modernist frame. Grady, for example, concludes:

> Knight's hermeneutics of the spatial text is not only the innovation in Shakespeare interpretation that it claims it is; it is also a method closely paralleling and unconsciously modeled on the aesthetic innovations of the poetry and fiction of the Anglo-American avant-garde of the Twenties. Knight is doing for the *reception* of Shakespeare what Joyce had done for the *production* of the novel: both writers re-function a received aesthetic form to downplay its temporality and emphasize a different kind of aesthetic structure that can conveniently be called spatial.
>
> (Grady 1991: 100)

This construction of Knight-as-modernist, however, is complicated by arguments like those of Fredric Jameson and Paul Gilroy, which emphasize connections between modernism and colonialism. In his essay 'Modernism and Imperialism' (1990), Jameson, for example, explores the sublimated place of the Empire in the imaginations of the metropole, arguing in the particular case of modernism that the relation to colonialism is decisive:

> [C]olonialism means that a significant structural segment of the economic system as a whole is now located elsewhere, beyond the metropolis, outside of the daily life and existential experience of the home country, in colonies over the water whose own life experience and life world – very different from that of the imperial power – remain unknown and unimaginable for the subjects of the imperial power. … Such spatial disjunction has as its immediate consequence the inability to grasp the way the system functions as whole. … This new and historically original problem in what is itself a new kind of content, now constitutes the situation and the problem and the dilemma, the formal contradiction, that modernism seeks to solve; or better still, it is only that new kind of art which reflexively perceives this problem and lives this formal dilemma that can be called modernism in the first place.
>
> (Jameson 1990: 51)

The characteristic modernist technique for overcoming this formal dilemma lies in adopting a 'new spatial language, [in which] modernist "style" now becomes the marker and the substitute ... of the unrepresentable totality' (ibid.: 58). Even this cursory summary of Jameson's argument suggests that Knight's modernist Shakespeare owes its form to a sublimated colonial presence. Most obviously, the preoccupation with maps found in the work of key modernists like Joseph Conrad and E. M. Foster and identified by Jameson is repeated in Knight's symbolic map in *The Shakespearean Tempest*. We might conclude then – extending Jameson's terms – that Knight's Shakespearean universe is ordered by an elaborate complex of spatial metaphors which substitutes for the unrepresentable colonial totality.

Although Jameson insists on the need to 'approach the moderns and their historical specificity' (ibid.: 59), he himself pays no attention here to the histories of Africa, or of any of the colonies for that matter. As a tentative approach to the 'historical specificity' of the 1930s modernist/colonial Shakespeare, I offer in the next section the work of the British colonial administrators, who were organizing African education at the same moment as Knight was mapping Shakespeare's universe.

Education policy for the colonies had proceeded up until the 1920s in *laissez-faire* fashion, with missionaries entrusted with the responsibility for African education. However, the increasing demands of the expanding colonial economies, and the perceived failures of the existing education system to meet those demands, led to new initiatives in the form of the Advisory Committee on Native Education in British Tropical Education set up in 1923, and the Phelps-Stokes Commission of 1924.[2] Taking their lead from Lord Lugard's famous policy of 'indirect rule', which claimed to respect African authority structures, and to allow Africans to advance along 'their own lines',[3] the educational policy-makers in the 1920s committed themselves to greater investment in African education in pursuance of the following guiding principles: education should take into account the needs of Africans; vocational and industrial education should be expanded; teaching in vernacular languages should only be superseded at secondary level by English; religious and moral instruction should be at the centre of the curriculum; girls should have the same access to schooling as boys; and finally, a literary education according to the 1935 *Memorandum on Education in the African Communities* should always be available to the minority 'who are required to fill posts in the administrative and technical services as well as those who, as chiefs, will occupy positions of exceptional trust and responsibility' (Watson 1982: 21).[4] In effect, the proposals for African education repeated substantially the nineteenth-century divide in England between utilitarian instruction for the masses, and a literary education for the rulers.

There were, however, a number of colonial educationalists who disagreed with these policies, and the 1930s saw numerous proposals as to what form African education should assume.[5] A. Victor Murray in *The School in the Bush* (1929) argues energetically, in the spirit of *The Newbolt Report* (1921), in favour of a common literary education for *all Africans*. Indeed, in many ways, Murray's arguments are a distinctly radical version of *Newbolt*. First, he opposes attempts to treat native education as a unique case, since for him the terms 'peasant', 'workman' and 'native' are almost interchangeable, and 'it would almost seem as if the race problem is simply one aspect of the class problem' (Murray 1929: xi). Second, he questions Matthew Arnold's definition of culture, seeing 'a great deal of truth in the contention of James Conolly, the Irish leader, that the real inheritors of the culture of a people are its working class rather than its intellectuals' (ibid.: 319). Finally, by detailed juxtaposition of quotations, he argues that the enslavement – and the potential for liberation – of the medieval peasant, the English worker and women in England, precisely parallels the position of the African in the 1920s. These generous declarations notwithstanding, Murray reproduces many of the stock stereotypes of Africa and Africans: Africa has no past because '[t]he native Africans when discovered by Europeans were primitive people with no written language ... They were physically strong, but docile and easily made cheerful' (ibid.: 20); Africa is the child, Europe the adult, as '[t]he defects of the Native are also the defects of the child, and his loyalty is a like a child's also, free, unquestioning, and generous' (ibid.: 378); in terms of art and literature, 'Africans are centuries behind European peoples in literary expression' (ibid.: 152); and further, the treasures of the past are all European – 'for [the African] Beethoven played, Leonardo painted, Shakespeare wrote, Pascal disputed, and James Watt invented. ... There is this universal heritage waiting to be taken up by him' (ibid.: 323). What Murray ultimately seeks is that the best of European culture should be freely accessible to Africans through a modernized education system, or, as he trenchantly puts it: '[i]t seems unreasonable to introduce rotation of crops and to withhold Shakespeare' (ibid.: 326).

Where Murray in 1929 expresses complete confidence in the global benefits of English culture, H. V. Routh in *The Diffusion of English Culture outside England* (1941) starts to express some doubts. Writing as an ex-adviser to the British Council, Routh recognizes that different aspects of English culture are received differently: the social mobility offered by a knowledge of the English language means that 'very few of these hundreds and thousands of learners cared for more than a practical working knowledge of the language' (Routh 1941: 23). After the English language, the next most-prized knowledge among foreigners is scientific or technological knowledge, as '[s]cience has so completely revolutionised both civilisation and culture that the older humanistic influences appear to be superseded' (ibid.: 38). What then of English literature? With the honourable exception of Shakespeare, 'the ever fashionable and inexhaustible subject' (ibid.: 28), English high culture has a minority appeal. Among foreigners, its supporters are confined to 'the middle-aged [who] listen best with their eyes closed' (ibid.: 23), and even in England itself its claims to popular appeal are in decline:

> But any experienced examiner in a faculty of English will tell you what percentage of candidates for the B.A. have any feeling or talent for their chosen subject. There would barely be enough to save Sodom and Gomorrah from destruction.
>
> (Ibid.: 27–8)

Drawing together the discussion of Knight, the arguments about modernism and colonialism, and the prescriptions of colonial administrators from the 1920s to the 1940s, what would then be the defining characteristics of this Shakespeare of the colonial dusk? The following necessarily incomplete list of qualities might be ventured: he is a visionary genius, and a formidable source of discursive power; in plays like *The Tempest*, he demonstrates moral absolutes which transcend history; he celebrates order, hierarchy, and unity; he owes his particular 1930s modernist form to a complex sublimation of colonial anxieties; he transcends effortlessly the national boundaries of his Englishness to achieve universal appeal, even among Africans; he represents a bulwark against industrialism and anarchy, both in England and in the colonies; and even where other forms of English culture lose their lustre, he continues to capture willing audiences.

The post-colonial Shakespeare

Written at Berkeley in the 1980s, Stephen Greenblatt's *Shakespearean Negotiations* (1988) appeared as part of a major modernizing movement in Shakespeare studies, in which new critical and Leavisite orthodoxies were swept away by the theoretical sophistication of new historicism. Greenblatt adopts a different route to Shakespeare and colonialism to Wilson Knight. For Greenblatt, 'Elizabethan and Jacobean visions of hidden unity seemed like anxious rhetorical attempts to conceal cracks, conflict, and disarray' (Greenblatt 1988: 2). Renaissance literature was produced by multiple competing discourses, and power or 'social energy' in Renaissance England did not radiate from a single source or origin; rather, it was circulated/negotiated/acquired/appropriated/subverted/transgressed in complex ways. To take due account of this complexity, Greenblatt proposes 'to look less at the presumed center of the literary domain – Shakespeare – than at its borders, to try to track what can only be glimpsed, as it were, at the margins of the text' (ibid.: 4). An important corollary of giving similar weight to the text and to the context is that the genius Shakespeare is replaced with 'a subtle, elusive set of exchanges, a network of trades and trade-offs, a jostling of competing representations, a negotiation of joint stock companies' (ibid.: 7). Further, over time the meaning of Shakespeare has mutated, since 'the circumstances in which [he] was originally embedded have been continuously, often radically, refigured' (ibid.: 6).

What then happens to the play *The Tempest* on this approach? Greenblatt compares meticulously the rhetorical strategies employed in the sermons of the martyred Protestant minister Hugh Latimer, an unpublished letter about a shipwreck in the Caribbean of colonial entrepreneur William Strachey, and *The Tempest* by William Shakespeare. He then argues that the name Shakespeare has since the Jacobean Age been transformed from being associated with the theatre, to being associated with the institution of literature. None the less, what persists is 'the continued doubleness of Shakespeare in our culture: at once the embodiment of culture, freed from the anxiety of rule, and the instrument of empire' (ibid.: 161). An anecdote told by the explorer H. M. Stanley is used by Greenblatt to conclude his argument about the double nature of Shakespeare in contemporary culture: in the anecdote, Stanley sacrifices his Collected Shakespeare in order to save his travel notes, which subsequent empire-builders would use to exploit the Congo region. Greenblatt concludes: 'What matters is the role Shakespeare plays in it, a role at once central and expendable – and in some obscure way, not just expendable but exchangeable for what really matters: the writing that more directly serves power' (ibid.: 163). In this way, Greenblatt thus attends both to the context in which Shakespeare wrote, and to his subsequent production as Genius.[6]

As with G. Wilson Knight, Greenblatt has recently been categorized in relation to modernism rather than to colonialism, with Hugh Grady in the final chapter of *The Modernist Shakespeare* defining Greenblatt as a leading proponent of a post-modern Shakespeare. Acknowledging that there are important continuities from the modern to the post-modern Shakespeare, Grady identifies two fundamental characteristics of the post-modern Shakespeare, namely (a) 'the abandonment of organic value as an aesthetic value and practice' and (b) 'the overthrow of formerly hierarchical oppositions' (Grady 1991: 207). It is the latter characteristic that underlies the post-modern sympathy for the 'Others of Western rationality and Third World peoples' (ibid.).

Greenblatt's criticism, both in its multidimensional reflections on power and repression, and in its sensitive attention to oppressed Others, would appear to exemplify post-modernist concerns. In his Conclusion, Grady endorses these impulses, arguing with some energy that:

> 'culture' needs to be seen to include the products of the electronic revolution and the collapse of the old distinction between high art and the popular; it needs to be decentred, opened up to the voices of the marginalised and repressed majority who have been excluded and denigrated even in the greatest and most indispensable works of our heritage.
>
> (Ibid.: 245)

In following such a path, Shakespeare studies too will find new audiences and interpretations.

Can my use of Jameson's argument to connect Knight and colonialism be extended to the 1980s, so that Greenblatt's Shakespeare criticism might be seen to sublimate traces of neo-colonialism? Jameson is again helpful in suggesting the connections, but again fails to move much beyond aesthetic considerations. In *Postmodernism, or the Cultural Logic of Late Capitalism* he notes 'a correlation between the transition from the modern to the postmodern, and that economic or systematic transformation of an older monopoly capitalism (the so-called moment of imperialism) into its new multinational and high-tech mutation' (Jameson 1991: 156–7), but when he moves on to analyse new historicism, he accepts with little demur Greenblatt's work on Renaissance theology and imperialism. Placing imperialism again in parentheses, Jameson's concluding assessment of Greenblatt is generous:

> (Imperialism, in Greenblatt, still remains a much more intensely political issue, but in a situation today in which a kind of alternate radicalism, of a Foucauldian and Third World, more exclusively anti-imperialist, type, has opened up alongside the Marxist one.)

(Ibid.: 193)

For Jameson then, the modernism/ colonialism nexus applied to Forster and Joyce – in the updated form of a post-modernism/ neo-colonialism nexus – does not apply to Greenblatt because the latter is so acutely aware of imperialism.[7] None the less, I want to resist Jameson's comforting conclusion by pursuing the affiliations between the post-modern Shakespeare and neo-colonialism along the following two routes: by looking briefly at possible connections between a post-modern and a post-colonial Shakespeare in metropolitan literary theory (other than Jameson's), and second, by outlining the dominant educational policies for Africa of the 1980s, which have framed the African reception of Shakespeare.

Grady's optimistic linking of the post-modern to sympathy for the interests of others – including Third World peoples – is not unusual. Simon During in 'Postmodernism or Post-colonialism Today' describes 'postmodern thought … as thought which refuses to turn the Other into the Same [thus providing] a theoretical space for what postmodernity denies: otherness' (During 1987: 33). Robert Young in *White Mythologies: Writing History and the West* defines postmodernism as 'European culture's awareness that it is no longer the unquestioned and dominant centre of the world' (Young 1990: 19). And Homi Bhabha in *The Location of Culture* (1994a) has an essay entitled 'The Postcolonial and the Postmodern: The Question of Agency', in which he flamboyantly though somewhat enigmatically plots transgressive possibilities open to the post-colonial in a post-modern world.

There have, however, been angry objections to conflating the post-modern and the post-colonial too readily. Arif Dirlik in 'The Post-colonial Aura: Third World Criticism in the Age of Global

Capitalism' (1994), for example, recognizes that post-colonial criticism has been premised on the 'repudiation of post-Enlightenment metanarratives ... enunciated first in post-structuralist thinking and the various post-modernisms that it has informed' (Dirlik 1994: 336). But where Grady *et al.* regard this encounter as helpful, Dirlik regards it as one in which the analytical categories of post-modernism swamp crucial questions about neo-colonialism:

> Postcoloniality ... disguises the power relations that shape a seemingly shapeless world and contributes to a conceptualization of that world that both consolidates and subverts possibilities of resistance. Postcolonial critics have engaged in valid criticism of past forms of ideological hegemony but have little to say about its contemporary figurations. ... They have rendered into problems of subjectivity and epistemology concrete and material problems of the everyday world.
>
> (Ibid.: 355–6)

Aijaz Ahmad in 'The Politics of Literary Postcoloniality' (1995) is similarly hostile towards post-modern appropriations of the post-colonial. Attacking the preoccupation in post-colonial theory with 'globalised, postmodern electronic culture, which is seen at times as a form of global entrapment and at other times as yielding the very pleasures of global hybridity' (Ahmed 1995: 10), Ahmad parodies the way in which the post-colonial and post-modern have come to be connected in the minds of a small elite of intellectuals from the former colonies and living in Europe and the US:

> we live in the postcolonial *period*, hence in a postcolonial *world*, but neither all intellectuals nor all discourses of this *period* and this *world* are *postcolonial* because, in order to be properly *postcolonial discourse*, the discourse must be *postmodern*, mainly of the deconstructive kind, so that only those intellectuals can be truly *postcolonial* who are also *postmodern*.
>
> (Ibid.: 10)

Like Dirlik, Ahmad insists on distinguishing between the post-colonial theories of diaspora intellectuals in the First World, and the lives of the majority of people in the Third World: 'Among the migrants themselves, only the privileged can live a life of constant mobility and surplus pleasure. ... Most migrants tend to be poor and experience displacement not as cultural plenitude but as torment' (ibid.: 16).[8]

How would Greenblatt's post-modern Shakespeare connect with these two very different versions of the post-colonial? On the definitions of Grady, During, Young and Bhabha, the awkward silence mediating modernism and colonialism is replaced with multiple new voices exploring the exciting affinities between the post-modern and the post-colonial. Greenblatt's Shakespeare demonstrates therefore these affinities between the post-modern and post-colonial by excavating the long-buried colonial barbarisms of European modernity. On the basis of Dirlik and Ahmad's post-colonial theories, however, the post-modern Shakespeare indeed echoes the silences of the colonial Shakespeare, at least in so far as discussion of *contemporaneous* connections with neo-colonialism is absent. Despite promising gestures, the post-modern Shakespeare continues to marginalize Africa.

My second concern is to place Shakespeare in the context of education policy for post-colonial Africa. Whereas the British Colonial Office decided education policy for Africa in the 1930s, the World Bank is now the major player, and where 'indirect rule' was the ideology of the 1930s, 'structural adjustment' came to dominate the 1980s. Responding to deepening economic crises in the Third World, structural adjustment was initiated by the World Bank in 1980. It involved Third World governments adopting a range of austerity measures, including combinations of the following: currency devaluation, reduced public expenditure, reduced subsidies to consumers, reduction or elimination of price controls, revised trade policies to encourage exports, increased user charges for public services, and privatization of enterprises and social services.

Structural adjustment has been extremely controversial. Senior World Bank researcher, Elliot Berg, for example, presents structural adjustment as a 'set of general prescriptions ... transformed and adapted when it is applied to individual countries' (Berg 1986: 59), and as such is the only available route for Africa to escape further impoverishment. This stance is repeated in a 1994 editorial in *The Washington Post* surveying the years since structural adjustment:

> The rise of wealth in the late twentieth century has been more sustained and more widespread than ever before in history. ... Economic growth is measured in dollars, but it translates into other and much more important things – better health and longer lives, less harsh physical labour, greater economic security. There are drawbacks, like development's threats to the environment and the dismaying tendency of governments to spend too much

of their new wealth on weapons. But it is hardly Pollyannaish to say that the balance remains strongly in favour of essential human values.

(Leys 1996: 22–3)

There are other commentators, however, who are less enthusiastic. An editorial in *The New Internationalist*, for example, defines structural adjustment as 'neo-colonial rule imposed by international banks on behalf of Western and Japanese corporations' (*New Internationalist* 1993: 13). And economists Andrew Glyn and Bob Sutcliffe summarize the effects on Africa of changes in the world economy since structural adjustment:

The share of Africa, Asia and Latin America in world trade is now substantially lower than before 1913 ... Africa's share [of world exports since 1980] all but disappeared: in 1950 it was 5.2%, in 1980 4.7% and in 1990 only 1.9% ... The picture for foreign investment is rather similar. Between 1950 and 1980 the share of all foreign investment going to the third world held roughly constant at about 25%. But after 1984 the share fell sharply to well under 20% ... [and] very unequally distributed. ... In the second half of the 1980s [the so-called 'least developed countries'] received only 0.1% of all foreign investment. ... Once again Africa and most of Latin America and some Asian countries are failing to participate in the growing globalisation of the rest of the world. ... They are increasingly marginalised within the system of which they form part.

(Leys 1996: 23)[9]

Whatever the long-term effect of structural adjustment, in the short term it had a profound effect on education in Africa in the 1980s. As part of the public sector, state expenditure on education has been cut, with a range of strategies adopted in order to satisfy the conflicting demands for budgetary restraint and a better-educated workforce. These include reduced expenditure on teaching materials, increased pupil–teacher ratios, reduction in the number of students allowed access to educational institutions, and diversification into private-enterprise training schemes.[10] One strategy of particular relevance here is the energetic promotion of vocational or technical education above a general 'literary' education. This policy is widely endorsed, with the World Bank in its most recent publication pledging its commitment to 'higher education

projects increasingly [to] support universities and institutions responsible for advanced scientific training and research' (*The World
Bank* 1995b: 150). What this means is that unlike in the 1930s,
when the colonial education system ensured that Shakespeare was
available at least for those who entered secondary education, the
dramatically increased emphasis now on scientific and vocational
education threatens Shakespeare's survival in post-colonial Africa.[11]

Finally, it is difficult to offer a coherent summary of the post-
colonial Shakespeare on the basis of Greenblatt's criticism, and the
policy documents for African education in the 1980s. Where in the
1930s, Knight and the likes of Murray shared a similar worldview,
which placed great value on Shakespeare, no clear symmetry ob-
tains in the case of Greenblatt and the directors of the World Bank.
On the basis of Greenblatt's reading of *The Tempest*, one form of
post-colonial Shakespeare emerges: 'he' is a text authorized and
constituted by historical processes; 'he' is profoundly implicated in
colonialism, from the sixteenth century to the present; and 'he'
negotiates and is negotiated by complex and contradictory discourses
of power; 'he' is, alternately, a productive space where the post-
modern and the post-colonial coincide, or a sophisticated censor of
Third World material realities. But on the basis of World Bank
education programmes proposed for Africans, Shakespeare is a much
diminished figure: 'he' is reduced from universal genius enjoyed by
all to cultural treasure of the Northern Hemisphere, although both
the English language and the scientific knowledge associated with it
continue to be of global importance. In Raymond Williams's terms,
for the British and US academies, the post-colonial Shakespeare
might be seen as an emergent cultural form, but for Africa, the
post-colonial Shakespeare is certainly a residual presence.

An anti-colonial Shakespeare?

It is important finally to distinguish earlier forms of resistance to
Shakespeare in Africa. In the period of independence from colonial rule, African resistance to the European literary canon led to a
diminution in Shakespeare's stature within English syllabuses at
many African universities. The bold innovations at Makarere College in the late 1960s described by Ngũgĩ wa Thiong'o represent
the most distinctive instance of this tendency (Ngũgĩ 1986:
87–109). Clearly current World Bank efforts to promote scientific
and vocational education for Africa constitute a threat to

Shakespeare from quite a different quarter. Whereas the choice for African university teachers in literature departments in the 1960s might have been between Shakespeare and Soyinka, in the 1990s much smaller literature departments are likely to watch university administrators make choices between Soyinka (with Shakespeare as a possible ally) and applied electronics.

In making these choices, teachers of literature in Africa and their students might of course deviate dramatically from the scripts handed to them by the West. Indeed, the fate of the grand plans of 'indirect rule' in the 1930s suggest that they are likely to do so. But in the meantime, for those involved in the study of post-colonial Shakespeares, the need remains as urgent as ever to attend carefully to the very different contexts in which Shakespeare is deployed. Although at the level of literary criticism, there might appear to have been real progress from the colonial to the post-colonial periods in readings of *The Tempest*, with the conservative Knight happily superseded by the more radical Greenblatt, beyond the world of literary studies, the picture is less hopeful. If we place the many post-colonial Shakespeares in their distinct historical contexts, *including* a variety of African contexts, a more troubled and critical Shakespeare study is likely. This is not an attempt to install the metanarrative of History; it is simply an appeal to remember the post-colonial world beyond the academy, in which 'progress', particularly since 1980, has been celebrated not by the majority of people living in Third World countries, but by the Western powers and their agencies.

Notes

1 In *Shakespeare and South Africa* (Johnson 1996), I try to address these important themes in South Africa's encounter with Shakespeare: the specific histories – economic, political, educational – framing Shakespeare dissemination in South Africa are examined, and appropriations of Shakespeare by South African writers and critics are dealt with in detail (see particularly pp. 74–110). I have chosen to focus on Wilson Knight and Greenblatt here not because they are more interesting than Shakespeare critics from colonial and neo-colonial spaces, but rather because their influence globally is so much greater.

2 For useful summaries of educational policies for Africa in this period, see H. S. Scott (1937: 411–38), Keith Watson (1982: 18–22), Clive Whitehead (1982: 47–60), and Anthula Natsoulos and Theodore Natsoulos (1993: 116–19).

3   The rationale of 'indirect rule' is set out by Lord Lugard himself in detail (Lugard 1929: 174–229). 'Indirect rule' is analysed generously by Margery Perham (1960: 138–54), and critically by Bill Freund (1984: 138–40), R. F. Betts (1985: 317–20), Mahmood Mamdani (1996: 65–71, 102–8), and Frederick Cooper (1996: 43–50).

4   In his comprehensive study, *An African Survey* (1938), Lord M. H. Hailey provides the educational statistics for British colonial Africa. They reveal the percentages of indigenous students above Standard VI (i.e. those who would have encountered Shakespeare) to be very small:

Country	Enrolment (%)
Cape of Good Hope (1935)	0.4
Natal (1935)	1.1
Transvaal (1935)	0.1
Orange Free State (1935)	0.8
Bechuanaland (1934)	0.0
Southern Rhodesia (1935)	0.1
Nyasaland (1936)	0.1
Uganda (1936)	0.1
Kenya (1936)	0.2
Nigeria (1935)	1.1
Sierra Leone (1935)	5.4

Add to these statistics the fact that large numbers of Africans were at this stage still not attending formal Western schooling, and the size of the educated African class shrinks further.

5   In the 1920s and 1930s, there was much discussion of colonial education policy. For a sense of the scale of intellectual effort in this direction, the bibliography in the back pages of *The Journal of the Royal African Society* during these decades is illuminating. The two I consider – Murray and Routh – are the ones that dwell in most detail on the relation between European high culture, epitomized by Shakespeare, and African students.

6   Greenblatt's rhetorical flourish gesturing to Shakespeare's subsequent global dissemination is not matched either in this work or elsewhere with any sustained engagement with the histories and forms of contemporary neo-colonialism. His attitude to the new world order appears to drift between complacent resignation and guarded optimism: in revealing anecdotes about his holiday in Bali, for example, he suggests that 'the Balinese adaptation of the latest Western and Japanese modes of representation seemed so culturally idiosyncratic

and resilient that it was unclear who was assimilating whom'
(Greenblatt 1991: 4). Greenblatt's contributions to two recent South
African publications – *Shakespeare in Southern Africa* (1995) and Pippa
Skotnes's collection on the Bushmen, *Miscast* (1996) – reinforce the
impression that his grasp of contemporary politics, including the poli-
tics of publishing, is uncertain when he moves outside the First World.
Both the journal and the collection have been vigorously criticized
from the left in South Africa (see Martin Orkin (1997)on *Shakespeare in
Southern Africa* and Kaitira Kandjii (1997) on the Skotnes collection).

7 For more critical discussion of Greenblatt's work, see Carolyn Porter
(1990: 27–62), Howard Felperin (1990: 140–7), James Holstun (1989:
189–225), and Shane Moran (1996: 128–37).

8 The pessimistic tenor of Dirlik and Ahmad's discussion of Third World
prospects within the global economies of the 1990s coincides with
that of recent left critiques of development theory. The titles of such
critiques convey a sense of defeat and disorientation: Colin Leys, *The
Rise and Fall of Development Theory* (1996); Nigel Harris, *The End of the
Third World* (1986); Frans J. Schuurman (ed.), *Beyond the Impasse: New
Directions in Development Theory* (1993). Though slightly out of date now,
the best overview of recent shifts in development theory remains Jorge
Larrain's *Theories of Development: Capitalism, Colonialism and Dependency*
(1989). Even a cursory acquaintance with this literature places the
up-beat projections about post-modernism of Grady, Young *et al.* in
serious doubt.

9 For more statistics confirming these patterns, see the annual UNDP
publication, *Human Development Report* (1996). It should of course be
added that certain African countries confound the general trends, and
also that the World Bank itself contains within its ranks competing
tendencies, with some more committed to neo-liberalism and structural adjustment than others. Catherine Caulfield's recent *Masters of
Illusion: The World Bank and the Poverty of Nations* (1997) emphasizes how
the Bank's policies have responded and changed over time, and particularly in the last ten years, to different pressures. In the particular
context of the Bank's influence on education policy in Southern Africa, Bobby Soobrayan (1995: 5–32) stresses the strategic need to go
beyond treating the Bank as a monolith.

10 Two recent studies emphasizing the harsh effects of structural adjustment in Africa are Michael Barratt Brown and Pauline Tiffens's *Short
Changed: Africa and World Trade* (1992) and David Simon (ed.) *Structurally Adjusted Africa: Poverty, Debt and Basic Needs* (1995). Barratt Brown
and Tiffen, for example, observe that 'contrary to World Bank wisdom, the economies of sub-Saharan African countries which have
pursued structural adjustment most strongly have declined in the period 1980–7. By contrast weak adjusters and non-adjusters experienced
economic growth' (Barratt Brown and Tiffen 1992: 138). And Anders

Narman in the Simon collection surveys a range of social indicators and concludes that 'structural adjustment will perpetuate the glaring inequalities, whether expressed in gender relations or between regions, ethnic groups or classes (Simon 1995: 51). For an alternative and more optimistic view of the prospects for education in sub-Saharan Africa, see Clive Harber's *Education, Democracy and Political Development in Africa* (1997). Harber pays very little attention to economic and social indicators, and his optimism rests on the growth of multi-party political activity in Africa since the end of the Cold War. Also more sanguine is literary critic Laurence Wright (1990/91: 31–50), who ignores both economic and political changes in 1980s Africa in his anecdotal reflections on Shakespeare in post-colonial Africa.

11 For more detailed discussion of how the opposition between vocational and general education has evolved in the 1980s, see Joel Samoff (1994: 18–20), Martin Carnoy (1990: 77–81), Bikas C. Sanyal (1987: 40–2), and Shane J. Blackman (1992: 203–25). It should be added though that as in the 1930s, so in the 1980s, the number of African pupils enrolled in secondary schools (and therefore with access to a literary education) is very small. The statistics (for the same countries as those surveyed by Lord Hailey) are as follows:

Country	Enrolment (%) (1980)	(1990)
South Africa	(statistics unavailable)	
Zimbabwe	8	50
Malawi	3	4
Uganda	5	–
Kenya	20	29
Nigeria	19	20
Sierra Leone	14	16

Source: The World Bank 1995b: 353

A vast majority of Africans in the former colonies therefore continue to remain outside Shakespeare's universe.

13
Shakespeare, psychoanalysis and the colonial encounter
The case of Wulf Sachs's *Black Hamlet*
ANDREAS BERTOLDI

I

In a rather remarkable little essay, 'Notes on *Hamlet*', C. L. R. James writes, rather aptly, that 'Shakespearean criticism is a jungle, a wilderness and a forest; and the wildest part is the jungle of modern criticism on *Hamlet*' (James 1992 [1953]: 243). For C. L. R. James, *Hamlet* is above all a political drama, 'in which two ideas of society are directly confronted', and more importantly for our present concerns, 'the two societies confront one another within the mind of a single person' (ibid.: 243). What James asserts, in a manner reminiscent of Freud, is that *Hamlet* is 'the central drama of modern literature', and further:

> What gave Shakespeare the power to send it expanding through the centuries was that in *Hamlet* he had isolated and pinned down the psychological streak which characterised the communal change from the medieval world to the world of free individualisation.
>
> This was nothing less than the freedom of the individual mind. … This colossal change in the organisation of social function was the very basis of individual personality. But from the start it was inseparable from a tension between individual freedom and social responsibility. To the extent that any modern man thought at all, he was subject to this tension.
>
> (Ibid.: 244)

James suggests the path that Sigmund Freud, Ernest Jones and lastly Wulf Sachs (in 1930s Johannesburg) took when they argued for the universal presence of Oedipus and Hamlet. Importantly, James's 'Notes on *Hamlet*' (1992 [1953]) provokes a number of questions in relation to the issue of *Hamlet* and psychoanalysis in the colonial and post-colonial world. These questions concern the transition/imposition of modernity and the modern, psychological form of power in the colonial space. Further questions concern the role that the material drawn from Shakespeare, in this case *Hamlet*, plays in psychoanalytic argumentation – how does the 'central drama of modern literature' relate to the colonial question? Another question is the role of psychological explanation in an understanding of social and political configurations. It is in the matrix of these two concerns that a whole host of other issues come to be raised: primarily the relationship between Oedipus, *Hamlet*, and forms of social organization and power in the colonial world.

In recent years there has been a revival of interest in questions about psychology, colonialism and racism, and more specifically the history of psychology and psychiatry and its collusion with the colonial apparatus. But in most investigations into the role of psychology and psychiatry as discourses and practices under colonialism, psychoanalysis has either been subsumed under these categories, or simply ignored. Consequently psychoanalysis has most often been dismissed together with the often overtly racist discourse of ethnopsychiatry and its colonial (institutional) manifestations.[1]

The general suspicion is that psychoanalysis, especially as a practice, is implicated in oppression in the colonial situation and is founded on a Eurocentric, patriarchal and even racist theoretical foundation. Seshadri-Crooks in her recent essay, 'The Primitive as Analyst: Post-colonial Feminism's Access to Psychoanalysis' (1994) has articulated this well, arguing that Freud's 'writings on culture exemplify the tendency within psychoanalysis to pathologize cultural difference', and that, 'Psychoanalysis, in pertaining to non-Western countries, is always imbricated with anthropology (as ethnopsychiatry), which largely precludes the specificity (and thus normativity) of the object of study' (Seshadri-Crooks 1994:177).[2]

These post-colonial criticisms of psychoanalysis and its theoretical presuppositions, can be traced back to Franz Fanon, himself a psychoanalyst, and his famous objection in *Black Skin, White Masks* (1967) that in Africa, 'The Oedipus complex is far from coming into being among the Negroes' (Fanon 1967: 151–2). The figure of Oedipus is challenged as *the* locus of the Euro/ethnocentrism of psychoanalysis and its false claim to universal applicability. The suggestion is that psychoanalysis is both culture- and time-bound, and some would even argue, fundamentally racist. Fanon himself is far from clear on the subject, especially as a psycho-analytic approach is central to his very investigations of the colonial situation. Fanon for instance writes that, 'only a psycho-analytic interpretation of the black problem can lay bare the anomalies of affect that are responsible for the structure of the complex' (ibid.: 10).

Nevertheless Fanon's statement has become the foundation of common claims made in post-colonial criticism, that psychoanalysis and its central claims are nothing but a 'European Phantasy' (Hitchcott 1993: 62) – a fantasy in the service of colonialism. The dominant opinion on this topic is captured well by two recent articles. Diana Fuss writes for instance that,

> Fanon's effort to call into question the universality of the Oedi-pus complex may constitute what is most revolutionary about his theoretical work, a political intervention into classical psy-choanalysis of enormous import for later theorists of race and sexuality. Responding to an allusion by Lacan to the 'abundance' of the Oedipus complex, Fanon shows instead the limitations of Oedipus, or rather the ideological role Oedipus plays as a limit in the enculturating sweep of colonial expansionism. Prone to see Oedipus everywhere they look, Western ethnologists are im-pelled to find their own psychosexual pathologies duplicated in their objects of study. Under colonialism, Oedipus is nothing if not self-reproducing.

> (Fuss 1994: 33)

Another recent review article states the post-colonial opposition, with a clear reference to Deleuze and Guattari (1983), to psycho-analysis in the strongest terms:

> None of the structuring mechanisms of Freud's European Oedi-pus have been found to exist on the African continent. ... 'Oedipus is always colonization pursued by other means' ... Although the Oedipal triangle is a highly seductive formula, we must resist the temptation to contain that which is outside our empirical knowledge. We have a responsibility, as critics, to

recognize our own humility, to resist the trap of universalism and to decolonize ourselves.

(Hitchcott 1993: 65)

This hostile assessment of psychoanalysis in post-colonial criticism can be summarized as follows. First, that Oedipus is a European invention and imposition. Second (which ties in with the first concerning Oedipus), the claim by psychoanalysis to universalism is nothing but a ruse for (psychic) colonisation and obliterates the space of cultural difference. And third, Freud (especially in his cultural/historical writings) visualized historical and cultural development (phylogenesis) as akin to individual, psychic and biological growth (ontogenesis). In effect this 'pathologises non-Western cultures' (Seshadri-Crooks 1994: 192), and establishes as *the* universal norm 'civilised', white, patriarchal, monotheistic, Western culture. As Seshadri-Crooks argues, the upshot of this is that,

> The place and relation of the primitive to the civilized man can be plotted as an equation: the primitive tribe (group) = the civilized child and the modern neurotic (individual):: the primitive man = the modern group. The cultural other is thus always a collectivity and is the pathological proof of 'our' predilections.
>
> (Seshadri-Crooks 1994:193)[3]

Yet within much post-colonial criticism, psychoanalytic theory occupies a crucial place as an explanatory procedure.[4] The role of psychoanalysis in the colonial context is however, as I will seek to show in this essay, more complex and ambiguous than often presented. At the practical or institutional level, McCulloch (1995) reminds us that there were very few trained psychoanalysts in Africa in the 1920s and 1930s, and that most were concentrated in South Africa and Algeria. Indeed, most ethnopsychiatrists and psychological practitioners were neuropsychiatrists originally trained as physicians.[5] Furthermore, although the figure of the 'primitive' is crucial to Freud's psychoanalytic speculations, especially his phylogenetic accounts, notably 'Totem and Taboo' (1985a [1913]), its usage is far from clear. The argument Freud presents for the similarity between the sexual life of 'savages' (primitives) and neurotics, as well as the need for external control (prohibitions etc.) due to a weak super-ego are well known. Although Freud's writings on 'primitives' to a large extent reflected the views current in his day (especially evolutionist ideas), he does insert some radical viewpoints.

Specifically Freud rejects the idea of the 'primitive' as being characterized by unrestrained libido, and reveals 'primitive' society as complex and highly repressive. For Freud the 'primitive' has nothing to do with race, but rather relates in the final instance to a characterization of mental functioning and ways of viewing the world. Freud himself cautions against pushing the 'analogy of neurotics' and children too far (Freud 1985a [1913]: 224). Ernest Jones has also argued that the equation between primitive and infant has been misconstrued. What is at stake is not the primitive acting like a child, but rather a difference 'between two modes of thinking which are present in both [adult and child]' (quoted in Rose 1996b: 51). All of this of course simply begs the question as to whether or not Africans in the twentieth century under colonialism or apartheid can legitimately be equated with Freud's 'primitive' – I suggest not.

In addition to Freud's own caution and specific views on the 'primitive', there is good evidence to suggest that Freud strongly opposed any racial use of the term. At stake is the extent to which psychoanalysis relies on an explicit or implicit racism. Some of the post-colonial arguments against psychoanalysis have claimed that psychoanalysis contains a racial hierarchy either in spite of, or because of its claims to universalism. But Stewart (1976) has suggested that we should read psychoanalysis, and Freud's pursuits, against the dominant ideas of his time that moral degeneracy was inherent in madness. Specifically Freud comes to reject the dominant view of the organic and hereditary origins of 'nervous disease', and was bolstered by theories of racial and family degeneracy in vogue at the time. As Stewart points out, it was at the time that Freud was in Paris, 1896, that Gustav Le Bon published a paper on the inheritance of psychological racial attributes. Freud's rejection of the idea of the hereditary origins of mental disease can be understood as a reaction to the racial theories prevalent at the time. As Stewart comments,

> Sometimes, one must be reminded that Freud did not conceive of his sexual etiology in a social vacuum. When one considers the environment in which Freud developed his criticism of hereditary disposition, it becomes clear that any concept of organic degeneracy, given its racial undertones, was totally unacceptable to him. ... The rejection of the idea that the neuroses were based primarily on a hereditary disposition was the key to Freud's discovery of sexual etiology. Such sexuality was found to exist within

the family, in particular through the Oedipus complex, and therefore sexual etiology was an alternative, rather than contradictory,
hypothesis to that expressed by the Charcot school. Hence, sexuality still had a parallel organic element however limited.

(Stewart 1976: 221, 227)

Yet despite all of these qualifications within psychoanalysis, it
must be admitted that what post-colonial criticism establishes,
whether or not it has any resort to psychoanalysis, is that there is an
inherent tension that exists between psychoanalysis in its
universalizing mode and any socio-political analysis of a specific
colonial dynamics. Bulhan has for instance argued that the invocation of cultural relativity and difference in post-colonial criticism
can be seen as an attempt at introducing the centrality of 'socio-
historical co-ordinates' that are overlooked in narrow psychological
approaches, and that lie at the heart of the tension between psychoanalysis and post-colonial criticism (Bulhan 1980: 254). If
psychoanalysis as a practice is implicated in colonial oppression,
and as a theory is Eurocentric at best and fundamentally (that is
structurally) racist at worst, then is there any gain to be had by its
application in the analysis of colonial situations, psyches and
pathologies? And can psychoanalysis even provide any adequate
explanation of the colonial situation on its own terms?

Through a reading of Wulf Sachs's *Black Hamlet* (1937), as well
as its source text, William Shakespeare's *Hamlet*, this essay will suggest that the issues are far from clear-cut. Just as post-colonial readings
of the work of William Shakespeare and its relation to the colonial
space have established the necessary recognition of its contradictory nature, so psychoanalysis is revealed as equally contradictory
within the colonial space. Therefore even though we can admit the
difficulties of psychoanalysis and the contradictory readings it offers, as well as the idea that in the colonial situation psychoanalysis
may confront its own limits as an explanatory model, the post-
colonial position of dismissal or the strategy of 'difference' is not
an adequate response to the tension that exists between psychoanalytic critique and political analysis.

Thus, without wishing to gloss over the problems that exist within
Freud's corpus of work, this essay offers a somewhat different reading
of psychoanalysis and the colonial situation. This is a reading suggested by Wulf Sachs's *Black Hamlet* (1937) and its explicit disavowal
of a politics of difference in favour of a universalist mode – a universalism

that seeks its source in psychoanalysis and a reading of Shakespeare's *Hamlet*.

II

It is in the light of current positions within post-colonialism on the relevance and usefulness of psychoanalysis that Wulf Sachs's *Black Hamlet* (1937) presents itself as a remarkable ground for debate. In particular, it is Sachs's explicit universalist mode, erasing any notion of difference altogether, that strikes one as significantly different. But also to be found within his work is a strong tension between the claims for the applicability and explanatory value of psychoanalysis in the colonial context, and its apparent incapacity to offer a reading of the political and social context of a racially articulated colonial society on its (psychoanalysis's) own terms.

Black Hamlet: The Mind of an African Negro Revealed by Psychoanalysis (1937), to give it its full title, was written between 1933 and 1936, following Sachs's 'analysis' through 'free association' of John Chavafambira. It had its origins in the meeting of Sachs, a white, Jewish doctor and psychoanalyst, with John ('Black Hamlet') in a slumyard known as Rooiyard in Johannesburg. The book – whose genre is difficult to define, being part case history, part narrative, part projection, part anthropological research – concerns Sachs's account of the life story of this Manyika (present-day eastern Zimbabwe) *nganga* (healer-diviner) who moves from Rhodesia (now Zimbabwe) to Johannesburg in the early 1920s. In an important essay, Dubow has argued that: 'As an attempt to understand the complex pathology of South African race relations, *Black Hamlet* is greatly in advance of its time. However, it remains a document *of* time. That too is part of its fascination' (Dubow 1993: 520). For Dubow, Sachs's account remains above all a text of its time, and as such must be understood within the context of the anthropological and racial discourse, especially the culture contact theory, prevalent at the time (see Dubow 1984).[6] This was also a period that saw the increasing legislation of racial segregation, rapid industrialization and urbanization, as well as the emergence of organized African resistance (Dubow 1993: 520–2). Sachs's interventions need to be understood in a context where for 'the majority of white South Africans, then as today, black South Africa was scarcely understood outside of the master–servant relations which governed daily interaction' (ibid.: 523).[7] Against this background, Sachs's proposals emerge as radical for the time.

According to Sachs, John was suffering from 'Hamletism', 'a universal phenomenon symbolising indecision and hesitancy when action is required and reasonably expected' (Sachs 1937: 176). Following Freud and Jones, Sachs suggests that this phenomenon be traced back to an unresolved Oedipus complex. Sachs argues further that 'the situation which occurs in *Hamlet* is common to all humanity, and this is the primary reason why Shakespeare's tragedy appeals to men of all races and nations' (ibid.: 177). At one level this argument is the consequence of Sachs's acquaintance with Ernest Jones's book, *Hamlet and Oedipus* (1949 [1923]). However this merely begs the question as to why psychoanalysis (Jones and Freud) resorts to Shakespeare's (Renaissance English) play in the first place. What purpose could it possibly fulfil?

The aim of *Black Hamlet* is, as Dubow observes, to 'show that the structure of the "native mind" is identical to that of whites, and to demonstrate this similarity in terms of the universal applicability of Freudian analysis' (Dubow 1993: 540). Thus Sachs's resort to 'Hamlet' is nothing less than an attempt to write John's story into a universal narrative of humankind – in short, it is I suggest, a radically progressive move in the political/social context of the time.[8] Many disputed such observations at the time, arguing for the fundamentally different nature of the 'native mind', and as Dubow argues, in the 'context of prevailing views about race in the 1930s, the idea of extending the notion of Hamletism to the analysis of a black man would have seemed odd or even perverse' (ibid.: 541). Africans were seen as being at some primitive, arrested or child-like stage of human development – the dominant view was certainly that there were fundamental differences in the mental structures of 'whites' and 'blacks'.[9] But already in 1933 Sachs had suggested that, 'The delusions and hallucinations of the insane native were in structure, in origin, and, partly, in content, similar to those of the European' (Sachs 1933: 710).

The parallels between Hamlet's and John's stories are striking: both are born to a family of power and leadership; the death of both their fathers occurs under mysterious circumstances (John suspects that Charlie his uncle has poisoned his father, in a repetition of Claudius's murder of Hamlet's father); and the uncle marries the mother in both cases. Sachs makes clear that John is infatuated with his mother Nesta, just as Hamlet is unable to separate himself from Gertrude. Like Hamlet, John is unable to form successful relationships with women. Finally, according to Sachs, John's devotion to medicine arises from the desire to usurp the position of his uncle.

The main point is that both John and Hamlet possess a conscious desire to revenge a father's murder, and in both cases the
murderer is the uncle. ... In both Hamlet and John there existed
a conflict between duty to custom and tradition and repressed
inner desires; this unconscious conflict led in both to a loss or
deficiency of will power.

(Sachs 1937: 181)

In lectures presented at the University of the Witwatersrand in 1933
– and published as *Psychoanalysis: Its Meaning and Practical Applications*
(1934) – Sachs elaborated his theory of the universal nature of the
psychic apparatus. For Sachs, as for Freud himself, the universality
of 'Hamletism' cannot be separated from its ground of origin –
the universality of Oedipus, or specifically the psychic conflict engendered by an unresolved Oedipal complex.

The fundamental question for both Freud and Jones is why Hamlet
hesitates and does not act, even though he is obviously capable of
decisive action in certain situations. The answer in short is – because Hamlet does not want to, due to inner conflict – a conflict
that results from ambivalence, a sense of filial duty and repugnance,
that is Oedipus.[10] Hamlet is unable to kill his uncle because he 'recognizes' in himself the Oedipal wish that has been thwarted by his
uncle.

The internal conflict of which Hamlet is the victim, consists in a
struggle of the repressed mental processes to become conscious.
This cannot be permitted. The conscious morality, which is very
strong in Hamlet, makes these inner conflicts still more complicated. Hamlet belongs to the type which, according to Freud's
classification, could be called compulsive and obsessional. These
are people in whom the super-ego, the unconscious morality, is
very strongly developed.

(Sachs 1934: 206–7)

Thus Sachs's reasons for returning to Shakespeare's text are to be
found in its 'universal nature'. *Hamlet* for Sachs, as for Freud, is *the*
drama of modernity, the drama of the over-developed super-ego,
of Oedipus in its modern form. By resorting to the story of Shakespeare's *Hamlet* Sachs can suggest, not only that John is like any
other ('white') South African in psychological terms, but, perhaps
even more interestingly for our present concerns, that he is in fact
fundamentally a 'modern man'. In this regard Sachs's intervention

reminds us of the suggestive remarks made by C. L. R. James, and must also be seen as radical beyond the limitations of a 1930s South African context. Jacqueline Rose in her recent book, *States of Fantasy* (1996) makes the important point that,

> In writing *Black Hamlet*, Sachs saw himself as effecting a dialogue across racial boundaries. Racism, he believed, could be countered by demonstrating that the unconscious of the Western and the African 'native' was fundamentally the same. What might appear at first glance as the ultimate gesture of literary appropriation (Shakespeare goes to slumtown), the clearest case of psychoanalysis in its specious universalizing mode (your unconscious is the same as mine) turns out to be, as well as all of that, part of a claim for the radical destabilizing power of the unconscious. If fantasy moves across the racial front line, it is not only the ego's self-possession that flounders; such mobility also gives the lie to the doctrinal and symptomatic rigidity of racial difference doing its deadly work above ground.
>
> (Rose 1996b: 49)

However what Rose also points out is the paradox that 'the most rigid racial categorizations *and* a belief in a universal family of man can belong equally to the rhetoric of racism' (ibid.: 50). But for Sachs, as Rose agrees, psychoanalysis was a 'discourse of justice' and in the narrative, especially in the 1947 version published as *Black Anger* this 'passes into the service of a revolutionary ideal' (ibid.: 80–1). It is, however, precisely this transition within Sachs's narrative from a 'discourse of justice' to a discourse of revolution, that reflects an important shift in Sachs's thinking, and more importantly indicates a limitation to psychoanalytic intervention in the colonial situation.

The seamless mapping of Shakespeare's *Hamlet* on to the South African case of 'Black Hamlet' is less successful than it at first suggests, and points to important limitations in Sachs's attempt to understand John's situation in terms of psychoanalysis alone. Sachs, in order for his psychoanalytic argument to succeed, must explain John's hesitation and difficulties in term of 'Hamletism' and an unresolved Oedipus. But it seems difficult to reduce John's social and political obstacles to such a psychological configuration alone. This is highlighted in particular by the fact that the 'resolution' of John's problems seems to have less to do with a psychoanalytic resolution, than the very material interventions of Sachs himself – the provision of monetary and other assistance. For instance, the narrative of *Black Hamlet* concludes with John assuming his father's position as district *nganga*, and his committing incest with a girl who was of the same *mutopo* (totem animal, in this case *soko* – or monkey). Following this incident John flees his family home, and en route to Johannesburg with his son Daniel saves the life of a monkey being stoned by passing white motorists, and ostensibly makes amends with his ancestors for his incest. John returns to his wife Maggie, resolves to find work as a waiter to provide an education for Daniel, and the narrative concludes with John's realization that blacks and whites must work together.[11]

What occurs in the narrative is the 'resolution of Oedipus' in actual and not psychic terms – the incestual wish is actually fulfilled and John assumes his father position. In addition, these wish fulfilments in the real are facilitated by Sachs's material involvement in the form of financial assistance and transport to his family *kraal*. It is suggested that this cannot be explained in terms of 'Hamletism', as the resolution and conditions of the resolution of the Oedipus complex are not psychoanalytic. There is no clinical intervention, no proper analysis, and thus no psychological resolution.

The most significant causes of John's problems, as *Black Hamlet* itself will suggest, is the nature of a racist, colonial-type society – that is the political/social situation of South Africa in the 1930s. What is in dispute is the attribution of a classically Oedipal neurosis to John, as his 'cure' is effected by external, that is extra psychic factors, and in the end 'John's Oedipus and its resolution is in actual, rather than psychic history' (Van Zyl and Bowyer 1994: 9).

Sachs is aware of the difficulties with his own presentation, and points to the 'many other factors', the socio-political factors which enter the (psychoanalytic) equation. Sachs writes:

> In Hamlet's case, as shown by Shakespeare, the weakness is localised to the one question of killing the uncle; in John's case it was more generalised, *for there were many other factors*, as we have seen, which were responsible for this inertia and lack of decision.
>
> (Sachs 1937:181; my emphasis)

These 'other factors', as Sachs will make explicit in his revised 1947 edition *of Black Hamlet* published as *Black Anger*, are the socio-political realities of living in a racially segregated capitalist society, built on the exploitation of cheap black labour. What Sachs in fact confronts, but does not deal with, are the very political limits of psychoanalysis in a colonial or apartheid society – limits revealed in the failure of his analysis. The classical Oedipal aetiology is doubtful in the case of 'Black Hamlet', and even though Sachs himself seems to be aware of this, he forces his narrative to comply with the universal Oedipal model in the form of 'Hamletism', and thereby erases all difference and specificity.

The upshot of these concerns with Sachs's interpretation is that it leaves the post-colonial critic, especially the psychoanalytically inclined one, with a major dilemma. If the argument via the universality of Oedipus presents difficulties, then what are the alternatives? Is psychoanalysis nothing but 'colonisation pursued by other means' (Deleuze and Guattari 1983: 170), that is, a Eurocentric culturally specific mode of investigation? These questions become particularly urgent when we note that Sachs, like many of his contemporaries, also sees in John the 'inability to cope with the rational demands of modern western life'. In this regard, as Dubow observes, 'Sachs is less free of the conventional views on "native mentality" current at the time' (Dubow 1993: 542). John, according to Sachs, is unable to reconcile rural and urban life. John was 'forced to live a psychological "double life", caused by the strain of reconciling competing moral codes, religious beliefs and modes of life' (ibid.: 543) – his rural upbringing had not equipped him for a different space in which he was unable to adapt. In the words of Sachs, 'John … had an additional tragedy which shadows the life of almost every African … the clash of his two worlds' (Sachs 1937: 174–5). *Black Hamlet* can thus be 'seen as lending broad support to the general paradigm of "deculturation" or "detribalisation", though he [Sachs] cannot easily be associated with the conservative implications of that framework' (Dubow 1993: 543).[12]

Although I am in agreement with Dubow that Sachs is not entirely free from the ideas of his time, *Black Hamlet* can nevertheless provide an important counter to ethnopsychiatry, especially if we note with Megan Vaughan that,

> The writings of colonial psychiatrists and psychologists provided one language, and perhaps a potent one, in which to describe and define the 'African' in general and not just the 'mad' African. The changing nature of African insanity itself could stand for the more general problems of colonial rule – the social and economic upheavals of industrialization and the problems of

social order. But the languages of psychology and psychiatry ... described these problems largely in terms of cultural and 'racial' difference. 'The African' in the twentieth century, like the European woman in the nineteenth century, was simply not equipped to cope with 'civilization'.

(Vaughan 1991: 107)

Vaughan suggests an interesting alternative way to read the psychological and other writings of this period, including that of Wulf Sachs – an alternative I wish to explore in the next section of this essay in order perhaps to rescue some of the aspects of Sachs's psychoanalytic model of 'Hamletism', in order to accommodate both universality as well as space for difference.

III

Black Hamlet raises important questions as to whether or not the *Hamlet* analogy actually works, and what the place of the social and political is in psychoanalysis. More specifically it suggests the need to re-read the very function of *Hamlet* and its relationship to Oedipus in psychoanalytic theory and history, as well as the relationship of *Hamlet* to the colonial situation. Such as re-reading may well offer the possibility of some resolution of the universalism versus difference debate.

In Freud's own work, Oedipus and *Hamlet* are almost universally linked in their references. As Starobinski has argued:

Shakespeare was on his [Freud's] mind ... in the final stages of uncertainty preceding the discovery of what would later come to be known as the Oedipus complex. No sooner did he give the crucial formulation of his idea, moreover, than he turned to a discussion of the case of Hamlet, which sticks to the Oedipal paradigm like a shadow. The two tragedies are linked throughout Freud's work.

(Starobinski 1989: 151)

It is significant that in Freud's very first formulation of Oedipus, following its discovery in self-analysis, it is mentioned together with Hamlet (Letter 71, 15 October 1897 to Fliess in Freud (1954: 221–5)). For Freud 'the gripping power of *Oedipus Rex*' is a result of the fact that each one of us 'was once a budding Oedipus in phantasy', and he suggests the 'same thing may lie at the root of Hamlet' (ibid.: 224). After this initial observation, Freud returned to the question of Oedipus and Hamlet in *The Interpretation of Dreams* (1900), in which he argued that the universality of the Oedipus complex is

> confirmed by a legend that has come down to us from classical antiquity: a legend whose profound and universal power to move can only be understood if the hypothesis I have put forward in regard to the psychology of children has an equally universal validity.
>
> (Freud 1976 [1900]: 362–3)

For Freud *Oedipus Rex* moves the modern audience no less than the ancient Greek audience, not because of the enduring appeal of the idea of fate, but because of Oedipus, which 'is the fate of all of us' (ibid.: 364). In the same passage Freud continues with an observation whose significance may have escaped even him. Freud writes:

> Another of the great creations of tragic poetry, Shakespeare's *Hamlet*, has its roots in the same soil as *Oedipus Rex*. *But the changed treatment of the same material reveals the whole difference in the mental life of these two widely separated epochs of civilisation: the secular advance of repression in the emotional life of mankind.* In the Oedipus the child's wishful phantasy that underlies it is brought into the open and realised as it would be in a dream. In Hamlet it remains repressed; and – just as in the case of a neurosis – we only learn of its existence from its inhibiting consequences.
>
> (Ibid.: 366; my emphasis)

All humanity has the same potential for neurosis due to this primary psychic structure with its dynamic principle of repression, that is the universality of the ontogenetic path. What Freud will suggest is that Oedipus is precisely a mechanism that is at once universal and particular, in that on the one hand it sets out universally applicable ontogenetic features which reveal the 'unity of humankind', while at the same time accounting for particular social/cultural difference.

This becomes clearer when we understand Oedipus not as some European, Victorian sexual myth, but rather as the fundamental *mechanism* that ensures the transition from nature to culture. In short, Oedipus exists as a result of the opening of the gap between sexuality in its instinctual form and its cultural outcome. To close the nature/culture gap would in essence be to argue against the necessity for Oedipus (and the incest prohibition). However, there is no culture that does this, and in fact all cultures expend a great deal of energy in reproducing themselves both materially and culturally. As Laplanche and Pontalis argue,

> The Oedipus complex is not reducible to an actual situation – its efficacy derives from the fact that it brings into play a proscriptive agency (the prohibition of incest) which bars the way to naturally sought satisfaction and forms an indissoluble link between wish and law … Seen in this light, the criticisms first voiced by Malinowski and later taken up by the 'culturalist' school lose their edge. The objection raised was that no Oedipus complex was to be found in certain civilizations where there is no onus on the father to exercise a repressive function. In its stead, these critics postulated a nuclear complex typifying one or another given social structure. In practice, when confronted with the cultures in question, psycho-analysts have merely tried to ascertain which social roles – or even which institutions – incarnate the proscriptive agency, and which social modes specifically express the triangular structure constituted by the child, the child's natural object and the bearer of the law. Such a structural conception of the Oedipus complex conforms to the thesis put forward by Claude Levi-Strauss who … makes the prohibition against incest the universal law and the minimal condition of the differentiation of a 'culture' from 'nature'.
>
> (Laplanche and Pontalis 1988 [1973]: 286)

There is therefore a universal necessity for *an* Oedipus as a result of the nature/culture distinction. But the question then becomes one of the details or ingredients making up the culturally specific forms of Oedipus. Freud's particular account involves the Oedipus complex located in the nuclear family. He however does not endorse this Oedipus nor does he suggest that this specific form is universal (but no sustained argument to this effect is really present in his work). For Freud the Oedipus complex is fundamental and constitutive of our very subjectivity, in that it explains how the body in nature becomes the body in culture and how sexual instincts are transformed into culturally determined drives. In short, Oedipus for Freud is equivalent to the process of enculturation or 'civilization' (in its non-pejorative usage). Thus, post-colonial criticism's suggestions that Oedipus does not exist fail to take into account the implications of this non-existence of Oedipus in Africa – in effect the supposition (at least in Freudian terms) that Africans are not enculturated and have no super-ego.

Part of this failing is the fact that few writers have taken seriously the idea that Freud presents us with a history of the modern psychic apparatus. Most critics have recoiled from an engagement with Freud's often controversial observations, especially in his phylogenetic accounts. As a result a great deal of Freud has been neglected, in particular the role and the place of the political in the psychoanalytic and vice versa. We must after all recall the passage from *The Interpretation of Dreams*, where Hamlet is equated with 'the secular advance of repression in the emotional life of mankind' (Freud 1976 [1900]: 366).

Steven Marcus in his *Freud and the Culture of Psychoanalysis* (1984) has recognized some of these aspects in Freud. Marcus suggests that once we begin to think about cultural change, political transformation, and the individual in relation to the collective, a number of questions must arise:

> Does the psyche itself have a history? Can we ascribe a significant historical existence to unconscious mental structures, and can we write some parts of that history? Does cultural change affect us in the sense that it is registered by inferable and describable alterations in the institutions of our unconscious minds?
>
> (Marcus 1984: 165)

Marcus argues convincingly that Freud did have a history of the psychic apparatus, both of the individual psyche (ontogenesis), as well as the psyche in human culture, primarily in the history and conception of the super-ego. It is in the 'The Ego and the Id' (1984 [1923]), that Freud postulated the existence of this special psychic agency whose task was to watch over the ego and to measure it in comparison to the ideal. This agency, the super-ego, has the function of 'conscience' – it is the critical faculty and sense of guilt. It is the resolution of the Oedipus complex that is the birth of the super-ego and the source of cultural transmission. As I suggested earlier, Oedipus is the fundamental mechanism that ensures the transition from nature to culture. However, what is immediately striking is that Freud's own views seem to be far from clear, especially when read through the prism of post-colonial criticism.

If the heir to Oedipus is necessarily the super-ego, as Freud would suggest, then like Oedipus, the super-ego must be a universal feature of the psychic apparatus. Yet the suggestive remarks of both

Foucault and Freud point to the idea that the super-ego is a particularly modern phenomenon and is the feature of *Hamlet par excellence*, as C. L. R. James has observed. With the acquisition of a super-ego, we enter the history of modernity, individualism and the modern, psychological form of power.

Freud himself suggests that 'one gets the impression that the simple Oedipus complex is by no means its commonest form, but rather represents a simplification or schematization' (Freud 1984 [1923]: 372) – in other words it has variable forms and thus variable outcomes. But Freud does write:

> The differentiation between ego and id must be attributed not only to primitive man but even to much simpler organisms, for it is the inevitable expression of the influence of the external world. The super-ego, according to our hypothesis, actually originated from the experiences that led to totemism.
>
> (Ibid.: 378)

This suggests that the super-ego is indeed a universal feature of humanity. But what do we then make of the cryptic comments on *Hamlet* in *The Interpretation of Dreams*? – 'the secular advance of repression in the emotional life of mankind' (Freud 1976 [1900]: 366). In one of his last writings, 'The Future of an Illusion', Freud provides a possible response:

> It is not true that the human mind has undergone no development since the earliest times and that, in contrast to the advances of science and technology, it is the same today as it was at the beginning of history. We can point out these mental advances at once. It is in keeping with the course of human development that external coercion gradually becomes internalized; for a special mental agency, man's super-ego, yokes it over and includes it among its commandments. Every child presents this process of transformation to us; only by that means does it become a moral and social being.
>
> (Freud 1985c [1927]: 190)

In yet another text, 'Psychopathic Characters on the Stage', written around 1904, Freud provides an account of the 'evolution' of various forms of tragedy – a history of drama with its concomitant 'psychic types'. Thus we have Greek tragedy as a struggle against divinity, its gradual replaced by the belief in the 'human regulation of affairs', where 'the hero's ... struggle is against human society', the class of 'social tragedies' (Freud 1942 [1905–6]: 124). Then emerge the tragedies of character – defined by 'struggle between individual men', and finally the psychological drama where the struggle is in the hero's mind, which can also be combined with other forms, the 'earlier types' (ibid.: 125). Within this final category we find the psychopathological drama, and *Hamlet*, 'the first of these modern dramas' (ibid.: 126), that concerns itself with repressed unconscious impulses, and whose 'precondition for enjoyment is that the spectator should himself be a neurotic' (ibid.: 125).

Although Freud does not say so explicitly, the upshot of his argument is that there have been changes in the organization of the psychic apparatus. In particular, *Hamlet* is only conceivable in a modern configuration, with a unique psychic apparatus. Perhaps it is significant that Sachs entitled his draft novel manuscript of *Black Hamlet*, 'African Tragedy: The Life of a Native Doctor' (Dubow 1996: 16).

Despite these remarks however, we are still left with conflicting viewpoints as to the universality of both Oedipus and the super-ego. For Freud they are 'universals' that are transhistorical and common to all humanity, together with the primary drives, the consequences of species prematurity, and the incest taboo. Géza Róheim, the psychoanalytic anthropologist, argues that if there are any differences in the 'unity of mankind', these are to be found 'not in our instinctual life, but in our ideals; not in the id, but in the analysis of the super-ego' (Róheim 1934: 388). For Róheim then, the 'process of becoming civilized [perhaps we should read modern] is identical with the extension and intensification of the scope of the super-ego' (ibid.: 403). As Melford Spiro has argued, the Oedipus complex must here be understood to have three important dimensions – structure, intensity and outcome – and can display cross-cultural variability in all three.

> Cross-cultural variability in the outcome of the Oedipus complex is anthropologically important because its outcome has social and cultural consequences. … The latter differences are especially marked when we compare societies in which extinction and repression are the dominant outcomes with those in which incomplete repression is dominant. … Those societies in which incomplete repression is the dominant outcome of the Oedipus complex are societies in which the implementation of the taboos

on mother–son incest and father–son aggression by the enculturation and socialisation techniques ... is not entirely successful in achieving their internalisation. This being the case, rather than relying on the boy's own psychological resources – extinction, repression and reaction formation – to ensure compliance with those taboos, many of those societies achieve compliance by means of social and cultural resources, as well.

(Spiro 1988: 458)

We may therefore very well concede to the universality of Oedipus, but attribute a historically contingent status to the particular form of resolution that a specific culture calls for, and thus the historical variability of the form and structure of the super-ego. Or in the words of Juliet Mitchell:

Freud gave the name of Oedipus complex to the universal law by which men and women learn their place in the world, but the universal law has specific expression in the capitalist family. (Anthropological arguments that make the Oedipus complex general without demarcating its specificity are inadequate; political suggestions that it is only to be found in capitalist societies are incorrect. What Freud was deciphering was our human heritage – but he deciphered it in a particular time and place.)

(Mitchell 1975: 409)

Thus what separates the ancients from Hamlet and the moderns is not the absence or presence of a super-ego, but rather the differential nature of the culturally specific forms of the resolution of Oedipus. In other words what separates various social formations is precisely the 'secular advance of repression', the increasing internalization of the super-ego and the psychologization of power. This is what Shakespeare's *Hamlet* represents, and it is this that Sachs reads into the South African colonial context. What we have in *Black Hamlet* is nothing less than a difference and conflict between a modern form of power and a 'pre-modern' social formation where the super-ego requires external social and cultural resources, such as initiation rituals, 'witchcraft' and 'magic' to ensure compliance.[13]

As Deleuze and Guattari (1983) have suggested, Oedipus only becomes immanent to the functioning of the psychic apparatus (the modern super-ego) with the advent of the modern form of power and capitalism – which is the very possibility of *Hamlet*. This means that every social formation has its form of repression in order to maintain that social formation – repression is a fundamental operation to human culture – but its specific form, inscription on the body, ritual, or internalized super-ego (immanent Oedipus) is entirely historically contingent.

This suggests the need to return to the notion of 'culture conflict' and recoup some of Sachs's insights, but on a radically different terrain – a terrain that rejects essentialist culturalist, tribalist and racist assumptions. Sachs's resort to Shakespeare's *Hamlet* needs to be understood as pointing to the very position of this text in a changing society – *Hamlet* is a 'symptom' of the shift to the modern; and equally *Black Hamlet* is the twentieth-century South African equivalent. Jacqueline Rose, although critical of some of the possible implications of Sachs's approach, nevertheless suggests that *Black Hamlet* may be legitimately used 'to identify a form of personhood bereft once outside its collectively or ancestrally sanctioned domain' (Rose 1996a: 41). What we find in *Black Hamlet* is thus a case study of the confrontation of two different social orders 'within the mind of a single person' (James 1992 [1953]: 243). We find here a conflict between a public, communal, ancestral and collective Oedipus, and a modern internalised super-ego with its immanent Oedipus. *Black Hamlet* read in this way becomes an account of the psychological impact of colonization and modernization and the destruction of the social fabric.

The modern social formation is characterized not so much by a dubious 'civilizational advance', but rather by a conflict between the 'bond' and the 'contract' (Van Zyl 1990). The bond of which the feudal is the prototype, and that is characterized by filial ties, rights, duties and obligations assigned according to age and social rank (fathers, elders, chiefs and kings), becomes confined to the family in the modern. The modern form of power in turn is characterized by the contract – which has as its precondition the resolution of Oedipus in order to ensure an internalized super-ego. In short, modern social formations organize their cultural transmission (and thus ideology and power relations) through the production of individual psychological subjects no longer in need of external control (Foucault 1977: 1982). However, an unjust modern state such as a colonial society or apartheid South Africa, which relies on the preservation of the disjuncture between two different social formations, 'cannot for necessary rather than contingent reasons produce subjects in the position it itself enjoins' (Van Zyl 1990:15).[14] The South Africa of *Black Hamlet* must therefore be understood as a 'psychopathological state', a political configuration 'where the individual (subject) it makes possible is not that which it wants and must have' (ibid.). A colonial-type society cannot produce the modern subjects it requires for structural reasons – reasons to be found in an exploitative regime that seeks to prevent the dissolution of the 'pre-modern'. A radically different reading of *Black Hamlet* is suggested by this – *Black Hamlet* as a document of the complex interaction of psychic structure and social formation in a 'psychopathological' society.

The project that remains is to begin to think the history of modes of power and the forms of the social, and the subjects these require and produce in South Africa. Partha Chatterjee has suggested that we need to analyse the co-presence and continued conflict of communal, feudal and modern modes of power in colonial and post-colonial societies (Chatterjee 1988). Such an analysis would enjoin us to think the simultaneity of the communal, feudal and the modern, where the 'modern' must be understood as that disjunctive space of the co-existence of all three modes of power, and where the feudal and communal are both remnants of, as well as modes of resistance to the expansion of capitalism and the modern mode of power.

Wulf Sachs's *Black Hamlet*, albeit in an indirect manner, raises these concerns about psychoanalytic explanations of the colonial. What remains to be done, however, is to relate the history of the psyche to this history of modes of power and modes of production. For Sachs, then, the reference to Shakespeare's *Hamlet* is not simply an explanatory device, to argue for the universality of psychoanalysis or Oedipus. It is equally a radical ethical gesture, since Sachs will place 'Black Hamlet' (John) not in the 'primitive', but rather in the moment of the modern. This is to suggest that Hamlet is the figure of the modern rupture – an 'advance' that does not proceed, as Freud and Foucault know all too well, without an increase in secular repression, nor in a unilinear fashion that extinguishes 'earlier' cultural forms. The Renaissance space of *Hamlet* and the colonial space of *Black Hamlet*, is that space 'where the reinvention of the self and the remaking of the social are strictly out of joint' (Bhabha 1994a: 244).

Acknowledgements

I wish to thank Ulrike Kistner and Susan van Zyl for their assistance. I also wish to thank Ania Loomba for extensive comments and helpful suggestions in the revision of this paper. Thanks are also due to Martin Orkin for his patience, support and editorial input.

The financial assistance of the Centre for Science Development (HSRC, South Africa) towards this research is hereby acknowledged. Opinions expressed and conclusions arrived at, are those of the author and are not necessarily to be attributed to the Centre for Science Development.

Notes

1   Recent books such as Megan Vaughan's *Curing Their Ills: Colonial Power and African Illness* (1991) and Jock McCulloch's *Colonial Psychiatry and 'The African Mind'* (1995) provide a comprehensive overview of this history.

2   I wish to thank Ania Loomba for the reference to this paper.

3   Seshadri-Crooks's paper (1994) presents an interesting and informative reading of Freud and the Indian colonial situation. Nevertheless it contains a number of problematic assertions which for reasons of space and focus, cannot be addressed here in any detail. Specifically Freud's negative portrayal of 'primitives' is far from clear. Indeed I would argue that it is fundamentally ambivalent when one takes into account his stressing of the strong 'primitive' super-ego and the existence of a high degree of instinctual repression ('as a measure of the level of civilization' (Freud 1985a [1913]: 79). Furthermore Freud's 'Civilization and Its Discontents' (1985d [1930]) reveals an uncertainty in his thought about this so-called 'progress' of civilization. Seshadri-Crooks is herself, I think, aware that Freud's pronouncements in 'Totem and Taboo' (1985a [1913]) reveal significant doubts about the analogy of primitives and neurotics and children – and I would argue, that if nothing else, Freud's essays cannot sustain this analogy, especially if his pronouncements are not taken at face value. Finally I would argue that what is still required is a careful disentangling of various terms in Freud. For instance the notion of culture as used by Freud and post-colonial critics – culture as opposed to nature (a universal claim), and culture as a 'specific, historically defined way of being in the world'. Another would be the notion of civilization as used in Freud and post-colonial criticism – civilization as culture in opposition to nature, and any developmentalist understandings thereof. Finally it would be important to disentangle a current pejorative understanding of the term 'primitive' and Freud's usage thereof, and more specifically to question the rather quick conclusion often made that Freud's 'primitive' is the modern colonial subject. All of this

is not to 'absolve' Freud, but rather a plea for a more nuanced reading, and the avoidance of what I would term a 'retrospective
moralizing'.

4 See for instance the work of Homi K. Bhabha (1994a) among many
others.

5 The South African Psycho-Analytical Society was only founded in
May 1949 by Wulf Sachs: see Gillespie (1992). By contrast the Indian
Psychoanalytical Association had already been founded in 1922, see
Hartnack (1990) and Sinha (1966).

6 See Dubow (1984) and Vaughan (1991) for an account of culture
contact theory.

7 I characterize South Africa in the 1920s and 1930s as a form of colonial society, in agreement with Harold Wolpe's understanding of
segregation and later apartheid, as a 'colonialism of a special type'
(see Wolpe 1972 and 1975).

8 For Sachs 'Freudianism' was universalist and therefore conclusively a
non-racist theory. However, such assumptions have been criticized.
Dubow (1993) and Vaughan (1991) have both pointed out the dangers in such universalist assumptions, and in particular the ease with
which such notions in the hands of more conservative and racist thinkers can be adapted to a theory of evolutionary and racial hierarchy.
However, the relations between universalism, particularism and difference warrant more careful consideration than there is space for
here.

9 See Vaughan (1991: ch. 5) for a good discussion of these views. See
also *Sex, Custom and Psychopathology: A Study of South African Pagan Natives*
(1937) by B. J. F. Laubscher, a psychoanalytically inclined/influenced
state psychiatrist.

10 The much-quoted passage from *Hamlet* comes to mind here:

> To be, or not to be, that is the question:
> Whether 'tis nobler in the mind to suffer
> The slings and arrows of outrageous fortune,
> Or to take arms against a sea of troubles
> And by opposing end them, To die – to sleep,
>
> .   .   .   .   .   .
>
> Thus conscience does make cowards of us all,
> And thus the native hue of resolution
> Is sicklied o'er with the pale cast of thought,
> And enterprises of great pitch and moment
> With this regard their currents turn awry
> And lose the name of action.

(III. i. 56–60, 83–8)

11 See Rose (1996a, 1996b) for an interesting comparison of the 1937
version of *Black Hamlet* and the 1947 version published as *Black Anger*,

as well important insights into the complex intrusion of Sachs's own desires and wishes into his relationship with John.

12 Implications such as racial legislation justified in the name of 'protecting' and 'preserving' cultures – the ideology of 'separate but equal' development. See Dubow (1984).

13 The notion of the modern form of power is derived primarily from the work of Michel Foucault (1977, 1980a, 1980b, 1982). The distinction between the modern and pre-modern as used here *does not* imply any pejorative usage, but is used to suggest different social regimes and organisations.

14 The social formations referred to here are the capitalist and the pre-capitalist as understood in Wolpe's account of the emergence of apartheid and its attempt to preserve rural reserves of cheap labour. See Wolpe (1972 and 1975).

14

Shakespeare and theory
JONATHAN DOLLIMORE

The disputes in literary theory have been many and vicious. Across the last couple of decades some of the most conflicted, most invested disputes have concerned the relationship of politics to literature, and have focused on Shakespeare. They have split academic departments, ended friendships, established implacable enmities, produced interminable correspondence in letter columns, and just occasionally made headline news.

When I wrote the preceding paragraph it was in relation to my own UK context, but in preparation for the conference in Johannesburg from which this collection of essays derives. I knew from the work of those like Martin Orkin and, more recently, David Johnson, that Shakespeare had become, as never before, a figure of contest and conflict in South Africa. Still, I didn't want to address 'theoretical' issues appropriate mainly to my own context. I subsequently discovered that the disputes around theory in South Africa have become no less intense. On the one hand there has been the familiar general conflict between those deploying some kind of theory and those adamantly against it. At the conference itself the more intense disputes seemed to be between different kinds of theory, and they were inflected by an acute sense of the difference made by difference itself, including different cultural, geographical and racial histories.[1] There was, for example, distrust of 'metropolitan' theory, including by myself; a sense that this theory which gestured so much towards difference as a fundamental philosophical premise, disregarded its material realities. But what struck me, as an outsider, as the most hostile divide of all was that between a materialist tradition of criticism and subsequent developments conveniently (though again reductively) lumped together as 'the' post-modern.[2]

With that dispute in mind, in this essay I argue for the importance of intellectual as well as social history for the cultural materialist project as I encounter it now. The disregard of intellectual history in much current post-modern theorizing is one of its greatest limitations. More generally, cultural politics has never been more in need of historical analysis – and historical memory. Mindful also of the South African context as well as my own, I reconsider the place of pessimism within the political project in the spirit of Gramsci's familiar yet never more apposite remark: 'pessimism of the intellect, optimism of the will'.

Politics and literature: some contesting positions

So how much clearer are we now about how politics and literature relate? Here's a sketch of three very different positions. First the 'idealist' argument that confronted us a decade or more ago: the precious thing about art is that it transcends the sordid world of politics, reaching towards a realm of enduring truth and value which politics can at best ignore, at worst contaminate and betray. We countered by saying (among other things) that this separation of art and politics rested on metaphysical ideas of transcendence and essentialist notions of an unchanging human nature which were contradicted by the historical realities of literary production. Did we win this argument? I'm biased of course, but I think so, intellectually at least, and to some extent politically. Whatever, I'm not rehearsing that battle today; I, for one, am bored of encountering oppositional postures in contexts where they are no longer necessary, or, at least, where they are already well known, even if the battles haven't been won.

In retrospect I think the idealist argument just referrred to was certainly significant, especially in English studies, and never more so than around canonical figures like Shakespeare. However, in the larger frame, it was probably not as important as we thought at the time. Besides, beyond Shakespeare studies if not beyond English studies, there was always a more powerful right-wing account of how art and politics connect, one based not upon their ultimate separation, but, on the contrary, their fusion in the form of a radical aestheticizing of the political. Historically this connected with an important aspect of the fascist sensibility – especially what I want to call the aesthetics of energy, most seductively evolved by Nietzsche, and then futurists like Filippo Marinetti, and proving irresistible in strains of modernism especially as embraced by D. H. Lawrence, W. B. Yeats and others.

The influence of futurism on fascism was significant but limited and short-lived.[3] What I'm calling the aesthetics of energy is something both futurism and fascism shared but is not to be exclusively identified with either. It is also a complex and seductive sensibility which shouldn't be simplified. In *The Birth of Tragedy* (1956 [1872]) Nietzsche suggests that existence can only be justified in aesthetic terms and he imagines the creator as 'the supreme artist, amoral, recklessly creating and destroying, realizing himself indifferently in whatever he does or undoes, ridding himself by his acts of the embarrassment of his riches and the strain of his internal contradictions' (Nietzsche 1956: 9). The cost of such violent self-realization is necessarily considerable, and always justified by the beauty, purity and power of its expression. This is D. H. Lawrence, in *The Plumed Serpent* (1968 [1926]) as it were 'humanizing' the idea: 'what do I care if he kills people? His flame is young and clean' (1968: 410). Thus, though only in part, the erotics of Lawrence's notorious blood consciousness. W. B. Yeats's 'Leda and the Swan' (1923) is a poem partly about the supposedly irresistible desire to submit to the coercions of a creature whose beauty is inseparable from its omnipotent, rapacious amorality:

> A sudden blow: the great wings beating still
> Above the staggering girl, her thighs caressed
> By the dark webs …
>
> How can those terrifed vague fingers push
> The feathered glory from her loosening thighs?

It is also a poem about how history begins in an act of sexual violence, of rape, and then becomes an 'heroic' repetition of the 'beautiful' violence of its conception:

> A shudder in the loins engenders there
> The broken wall, the burning roof and tower
> And Agamemnon dead.

In both Yeats and Lawrence the aesthetics of energy are inseparable from an erotics of energy and violence in which the writer
sometimes identifies with mastery and omnipotence, sometimes with
submission to them, and often both. It fantasizes an erotic beauty
whose preconditions include amorality, potency, indifference. If you
like, a kind of highly exalted, seriously straight, rough trade –
although in truth the aesthetics of energy can be heterosexist or
homoerotic or (again) both together. Certainly its gender coordinates are not simple. In Yeats's legendary celebration of Maud
Gonne in 'No Second Troy' (1908) the Nietzschean superman[4]
becomes a woman, to whom a male poet relates abjectly. The subject of this poem is of course Maud Gonne, a woman engaged in a
violent anti-colonial struggle, though you wouldn't know it from
the poem:

> Why should I blame her that she filled my days
> With misery, or that she would of late
> Have taught to ignorant men most violent ways,
> Or hurled the little streets upon the great,
> Had they but courage equal to desire?
> What could have made her peaceful with a mind
> That nobleness made simple as a fire,
> With beauty like a tightened bow, a kind
> That is not natural in an age like this,
> Being high and solitary and most stern?
> Why, what could she have done, being what she is?
> Was there another Troy for her to burn?

The aesthetics of energy also involve this fantasy purification and
erasure of history in a way that tends to feed directly into nationalism and racism. Here, for Yeats, the actual anti-colonial struggles
of Ireland are important as a platform for the same link between
amoral beauty and erotic violence that's there in 'Leda'; the squalid
masses full of ignorance and cowardly desire really only exist for
Helen to burn – except she can't, because one thing these degenerate modern democracies suppress is the heroic impulse to go around
destroying whole cultures and cities just for the hell of it. Of course
Yeats was wrong: you can go around doing exactly that, as the fas-
cists whom he came to admire well knew. And centuries before
them Fortinbras too. At least Hamlet had the decency to be fazed
by all this. Seduced he may have been, but fully signed up? Defi-
nitely not.

So maybe it is time to forget so-called, mis-called, liberal humanism with 'his' genteel universal values and equally genteel
essentialist human subject: it's the aestheticizing of politics, rather
than the aesthetic escape from it, that post-modernism is making
attractive once again, and which may yet be the greatest future
challenge to the last of my three positions, namely the cultural
materialist. How exactly to define this? Provisionally: the attempt
to recover for our understanding of art the conditions of its production and reception, conditions that are invariably marked by
conflicts and contradictions which the art work sometimes addresses, sometimes effaces, but never escapes. As for the literature
of the early modern period, some materialists have gone further,
finding in it a dangerous knowledge: not just an ambivalent revealing expression of political anxieties, but a challenging, insightful,
complicit knowledge of what was making the culture anxious.
And, along with that, an emerging sense of historical complexity
and cultural contradiction.

The culture of pessimism

Three positions then on the relationship of art to politics – the
idealist, the fascist and the materialist. I shrink from the crudeness
of this threefold sketch but it serves a certain purpose, namely to
reveal that, while the extensive differences between them are obvious, they do have something in common: all three tend to be pessimistic,
though in different ways, about the existing political order, and this
pessimism stems directly from a sense of the political failures of the
past and the present.

The idealist wants art to be separate from politics because only
then can it compensate for, and transcend, the failures of the latter
which are regarded as more or less inevitable in a postlapsarian
world. In completely different ways the fascist and the materialist
share an even more acute sense of historical failure, and they also
share one further thing in common which distinguishes them from
the idealist, namely a conviction that radical social change is both
possible and imperative. So if one kind of fascist wants to destroy
the degenerate and decadent forces which, under the banner of
liberalism, have led to the perceived historical failures of (say) nation and race, then one kind of Marxist construes fascism itself as
made possible by the historical failures of liberalism and/or capitalism. And this attribution of failure can run and run, often in

circles: for those like D. H. Lawrence in the 1920s, it was the failure of Italian socialism that resulted in Italian fascism.

What's so striking is that the question of how art and politics relate (or properly disconnect), is usually asked most urgently in the context of the perceived historical failure of one or the other, and usually both. It is also a question which typically occurs in the context of what might be called a culture of pessimism. Is this sense of being beleaguered by historical failure distinctively Western? That's plausible. Might it be most acute in post-colonial European cultures? That's less probable: after all, the sense of historical failure and the culture of pessimism was never more acute than in Shakespeare's time, when the expansionist, imperialist, colonialist and commercial ambitions of England were getting underway. In fact, I want to argue for a significant symbiosis in Western culture between the expansionist enterprise and the culture of pessimism, between quest and quietism.

But does this mean that the culture of pessimism, that sense of historical failure, is at heart always a mystification of something more insidious? (One thinks in passing of how far the culture of pessimism took the Christian radicals in terms of world domination.) Or may it not also be the regrettable, inevitable starting point for a progressive politics that still honestly believes in human potentialities still unrealized, still repressed, still thwarted by existing societies? In other words, is not a degree of pessimism also inevitable in that unstable mix of utopianism, realism and radicalism which inflects the deep wish for social change? One thing seems sure: leftward criticism has no adequate account of pessimism, either as a concept or a cultural experience with a history. And that's a real problem, if only because it's something that the reactionary and the progressive strangely if differently share. This isn't especially surprising; antagonistic positions typically have histories which at significant points strangely converge or disturbingly overlap.

More specifically, leftward critics of early modern culture have never adequately confronted the pessimism endemic to it, which included (though not being confined to), the notorious pessimism of Jacobean literature, most notably its drama. Even, or especially, when it was more secular than Christian, that literature was haunted by a theology of failure. Change was generally change for the worse; hence the recurring idea of mutability, time and change as the grounds of failure, dissolution and defeat. The tragedies are full of it, but here is an instance from Shakespeare's histories. In the second part of *2 Henry IV* the insomniac, beleaguered king laments the way that time's destructive effects somehow trigger an innate tendency to dissolution:

> O God! that one might read the book of fate,
> And see the revolution of the times
> Make mountains level, and the continent,
> Weary of solid firmness, melt itself
> Into the sea!

(III. i. 45–59)

So corrosive is all this that to foresee it would rob even the most ardent youth of the desire to live:

> … how chance's mock,
> And changes fill the cup of alteration
> With divers liquors! O, if this were seen,
> The happiest youth, viewing his progress through,
> What perils past, what crosses to ensue,
> Would shut the book, and sit him down and die.

(III. i. 52–57)

In other words, foresight would reveal the same history of chronic failure that hindsight confirms. In Walter Ralegh – one of the great expansionists of this period, in legend as much as in fact – we find the same sense of time destroying not only living things, but human projects:

> all droopes, all dyes, all troden under dust
> the person, place, and passages forgotten
> the hardest steele eaten with softest ruste
> the firme and sollide tree both rent and rotten

Mutability, transience, loss: the erosion, the dissolution of what is precious; and their corrosive effects reach most devastatingly into human identity, human endeavour, human achievement – as Ralegh also says: 'all is desolvde, our labors cume to nought'.[5]

No self-respecting critic of the left has much truck with this kind of pessimism, and is happy to consign it to the introspective fatalism of a Christian, and soon-to-be bourgeois nihilism – what Herbert Marcuse in a powerful essay written in 1959 called 'the ideology of death'. I think this interpretation contains an element of truth inseparable from a significant disavowal.

It is imperative to search that overlap between realism and pessimism, if only to avoid the fate of those psuedo-radicals whose response to defeat is to flip into reaction – like those intellectuals in the 1930s who, at the first set-back, switched from belief in the possibility of radical social change to belief in original sin – i.e., to that which would explain reassuringly why such change wasn't after all possible, and so relieve one of any further responsibility for it. Without realism radicalism flips into reaction; yet realism runs the risk of the pessimism which, if it becomes defeatist, also permits reaction. This is especially relevant now because, as I'll be arguing shortly, certain recent developments in metropolitan literary and cultural theory are shot through with a pseudo-radicalism which, paradoxically, is marked by what might be called a ludic defeatism. Arguably, as Gramsci and many others have always known, radicalism must be afflicted by genuine doubt.

Tragedy

For some of us, as dealers in Shakespeare, the problem gets worse. As Shakespeareans we have to deal with tragedy, if not in life then at least in literature. Tragedy is conventionally regarded as the most profound of all Western literary genres, and Shakespeare is said to be its greatest ever exponent. And tragedy in the idealist cultural tradition is, of course, not only directly about chronic failure, but also the mystification, the sanctifying, even the enjoyment of it – the seeking of redemption in and through failure – even or especially as the expansionist enterprise proceeds apace. To this extent tragedy has been regarded as the most politically regressive of all aesthetic forms. Certainly, to engage with the aesthetic history of tragedy is to discover something unnerving: if Western culture is driven by a secular fear of failure, it is no less dependent upon a spiritual reassurance that failure is inevitable and even desirable. It's apparent too that this fear of failure, and the reassurance of its inevitability, are insidiously interconnected and never more so than in relation to the expansionist enterprise. It is not simply that those afflicted with quietism and fatalism sit back passively, leaving the way clear for the expansionists to master, exploit, aggrandise or whatever (Yeats's 'The best lack all conviction, while the worst / Are full of passionate intensity'); rather – as the case of Ralegh suggests, and as we'll see shortly in relation to the question of identity – quietism and conquest are related identifications within the one cultural formation.

Bertolt Brecht's entire attempt to rewrite tragedy – literally to rewrite past tragedies and in the process to evolve a new conception of it – can be seen as an attempt to overcome the Western theology of failure. Brecht was realistic about the cost in violence of effective social change, not least because of the ideological effectiveness of existing social and economic regimes. He focused this in the memorable figure of Mother Courage, who had so thoroughly internalized the values of the culture which was also literally her ruin. As Brecht put it: 'The tragedy of mother Courage and of her life … consisted in the fact that here a terrible contradiction existed which destroyed a human being, a contradiction which could be resolved, but only by society itself in long terrible struggles.'[6] This contradiction is tragic because of the brutalisation which it entailed – not just for Mother Courage but for the activist or intellectual recognizing it. Revolutionary failure is agonizing – so much sacrificed for nothing, or worse; but even revolutionary success is haunted by its own failures, by the necessary, inevitable betrayal of its ideals even as they are being fought for. Thirty years ago, in the chapter in *Modern Tragedy* entitled 'Tragedy and Revolution', Williams wrote memorably about just this, the ways in which revolution is unavoidably tragic.[7]

In the race for theory such things were largely ignored, attention being paid instead to Brecht's theory of the alienation effect. Ostensibly this was in opposition to the quietism of a conservative literary criticism, yet arguably fed a new kind of complacency typical of a certain kind of academic theory. After being laboriously reprocessed by (for example) film theory, the alienation effect meant that what in the text or in the cinema didn't seem to work, or wasn't interesting or even comprehensible, really was perfectly radical if only you knew how to look at it, where to sit, and were up on the theory. Here are the origins of something that has become much more prevalent in more recent academic theory, namely wishful theory. I've described this elsewhere[8] but summarize it here for somewhat different purposes.

At its worst this is the kind of theorizing that gestures towards difference yet from a perspective that remains intellectually totalizing and reductive; which is self-empowering in a politically spurious way, and which, despite its ostentatious performance of a high sophistication, tends to erase the psychic, social and historical complexities of the cultural life it addresses. Critical theory originally sought to integrate theory with praxis. But what did that mean,

exactly? For some of the Frankfurt School it entailed a commitment to emancipation inseparable from painful and difficult historical
analysis – praxis as the pursuit of philosophy by other means. Marx
had said, famously, that hitherto philosophers had sought only to
understand the world; now they were to change it too. But, if anything, this effort to change the world itself required an even greater
effort of understanding. To change in the direction of emancipation meant above all that one had to understand the ideological
conditions that prevented change. Whatever we may now think of
the Frankfurt School, its sustained analysis of the historical conditions that prevented change has to be respected. Arguably, those
who now completely reject Marxism have abandoned not only any
serious intention of changing, but also the serious commitment to
understanding. Certainly an aspect of the tradition of cultural critique has been lost: the effort to understand the historical real as we
inherit it – in Marx's words, those historical conditions we don't
choose and which profoundly affect the choices we do make.

Let me be more specific. There is a particular model of social
struggle which has been influential in recent theory. Very briefly, it
concentrates on the instabilities within the dominant, identifying,
for instance, ways in which the marginal is subversive of the dominant, especially at those points where the dominant is already rendered
unstable by contradictions intrinsic to it and which include the fact
(disavowed by the dominant yet apparent within the subordinate)
that the two are connected in complex ways. If this model origi-
nates with Hegel, its modern form has been deeply influenced by,
among other movements, Marxism, psychoanalysis and deconstruction. It's because I've been influenced by this account of social struggle,
and remain persuaded by it, that I can't subscribe to what I regard
as a wishful theoretical deployment of it most pronounced in some
strands of post-modernism. Bits and pieces from all sorts of different theoretical sources are expertly spliced together, often with the
aim of demonstrating a repressive dominant always allegedly on
the edge of its own ruin and about to be precipitated over the edge
by the marginal, the other or the different. The marginal is first
appropriated, then theoretically reworked as radical, subversive, avant-
garde or whatever.

The result of such theoretical reworking is not so much a demonstration of the intrinsic instability of the social order, or its effective
subversion by forces within or adjacent to it, but an abstract, highly
wrought re-presentation of it – a theoretical narrative whose plau-

sibility is often in inverse proportion to the degree to which it makes its proponents feel better. To that extent, wishful theory is also feel-good theory. It is also a theory in which human freedom is emphatically denied, only to be endlessly replayed in intellectual fantasies of subversion. And this same 'sublimation' of freedom is apparent in the way that so much theoretical denial of freedom is strangely written from a masterful, omniscient subject position.

The contrived narratives of wishful theory insulate their adherents from social reality by filtering it, and this in the very act of fantasising its subversion. So much so that in some contemporary theory, the very concept of subversion has become a form of disavowal. Theory is deployed in a way that is usually self-exonerating, hardly at all in a way that is self-questioning. This kind of theory can be so quickly updated because it is so tenuously connected with the real. Drop this bit of theory, splice in that, and the whole thing can be updated to correspond to intellectual fashion. What is disappearing from theory is the intellectual commitment to engage with the cultural real in all its stubborn contingency, surprising complexity and – in Brecht's phrase, terrible contradictions – that which makes change necessary but which also makes it terribly difficult and likely to exact a terribly cost. Nor does scepticism about such theory imply a disregard for that which is so often its subject – the marginal, otherness, difference; on the contrary, I believe that such scepticism is now the precondition for a more thoughtful (but not necessarily uncritical) encounter with them.

And what of instabilities in the dominant? Those who pretend that deconstruction is *only* about the undecidability of texts, or about reducing everything to the status of a text, are just wrong. But in the context of literary criticism, a certain use of it has encouraged a tendency to move too quickly from spotting a tension, an instability or inconsistency in dominant formations to speculating that here the text, and the culture being represented by the text, were in crisis. We discern an instability or a contradiction in gender domination, sexual difference or masculinity – but so what? I mean: what follows, exactly? Especially if we always bear in mind the materialist commonplace that dominant ideologies not only mask contradictions and instabilities but also mobilize them, and that it is when ideology is pushed nearly to incoherence that such instabilities and contradictions may be most brutally and most effectively mobilised. What price then some local disruption within sexual difference – whose *frisson* is this anyway? One of the wishful aspects of some queer theory is the assumption (hope?) that heterosexual masculinity is so riven with contradictions and insecurities it will any day now collapse into itself – or better still, collapse into the homosexuality which is its constitutive repression.

A more thoughtful encounter with both the dominant and the dissident has for some time been an aspect of social history. Some years ago we argued that theory was becoming too self-referential and remained far too contemporary. We argued for a critical practice in which we could use history, especially social history, to read theory, as well as vice versa. Now I feel more than ever that theory, or at least some strands of post-modern theory, needs history. And if social history remains as important as ever, I would now stress the importance of intellectual history as well. Post-modernism desperately needs both kinds of history.

The decentred subject

Consider the subject in crisis which is always discovered in or around the struggles between the dominant and the dissident (and is more often than not focused in terms of gender instabilities). Modern theories of identity have been preoccupied with the alleged, recent disintegration of Western humanism. The argument usually goes like this: once Western culture was underpinned by a confident ideology of subjectivity. The individual experienced himself as unified and (spiritually if not socially) self-determining in virtue of the imagined possession of a pre- or asocial essence from which spiritual (not social) value and freedom derive. It was this conception of subjectivity which fed the predominantly masculinist Western ideologies of individualism, and its universal counterpart 'Man', and influences the idealist criticism mentioned at the outset. But these ideologies were relatively short-lived. Often the full subject was said to have emerged in the Renaissance, become ideologically consolidated in the Enlightenment, experienced its high point in the nineteenth century, before collapsing in our own time, and in a way corresponding to the crisis of the West, of capitalism or Empire. This collapse is not usually regarded with regret; in some post-modern versions of this narrative the modern 'decentered' and mobile subject is also fantasized as the subversion of, or at least the radical alternative to, the ideologies which the individual and Man once served. In some ways this supposed collapse of Man is a secularized rerun of the Fall narrative – itself a founding text for Western subjectivity. More importantly, it is a narrative which, though purporting to herald the ending of 'Man', actually confirms his characteristic existence.

What I mean by this is that the crisis of subjectivity was there at the inception of individualism in early Christianity, and has been as enabling as it has been disturbing (enabling because disturbing). In other words, what we might now call the neurosis, anxiety and alienation of the subject-in-crisis are not so much the consequence of its recent breakdown, but the very stuff of its creation, and of the culture – Western European culture – from which it is inseparable, especially that culture in its most expansionist phases (of which the 'Renaissance' was undoubtedly one). The crisis of the self isn't so much the subjective counterpart of the demise, disintegration or undermining of Western European culture, as what has always energized both the self and that culture.

It is in Augustine's *Confessions* (*c*. 397–401) that we find one of the more influential accounts of how 'modern' subjectivity is founded in that same sense of crisis which imparts the restless expansionist energy which is the making of civilization itself. Augustine suggests how individualism was from the beginning energized by an inner dynamic of loss, conflict, doubt, absence and lack, and in a way that feeds into our culture's obsession with control and expansion. The identity of everything, from self to nation, is under potentially disintegrative pressures which have to be rigorously controlled. Yet this is a kind of control that is necessarily always exceeding and breaking down the very order it restlessly quests for, and is forever re-establishing its own rationale even as it undermines it. The experience of instability is inherited by Augustine and deployed in a religious praxis; the subject in crisis becomes a crucial element in the triumph of Western individualism and all that this has meant. It is this which we have inherited; what we are living through now is not some (post-)modern collapse of Western subjectivity but another mutation in its enduring dynamic.

Appropriating Shakespeare

So where does this critique of wishful theory leave one in relation to the conservative reaction to all theory? Consider a book that has become a rallying point for that reaction, Brian Vickers' *Appropriating Shakespeare*.[9] The most damaging thing about this book is not its reaction against theory, but the way that the 'non-theoretical' tradition it supposedly defends gets silently censored and reduced in the process. Crucial aspects of intellectual history are ignored. And if there is one thing that some anti-theorists share with some post-modernist theorists, it is this ignoring of intellectual history. It is tempting to attack Vickers on what I regard as his weakest ground, and where my own intellectual and political investments are obviously the highest, namely his dismissal of cultural materialism. I propose instead to confront him on his strongest ground, namely his critique of Freud. Strongest in the sense that Vickers is at least right in this: some highly implausible criticism of Shakespeare has proceeded in the name of Freud; that criticism might well be regarded as a precursor of wishful theory. But, in his critique of Freud, Vickers betrays the very scholarship he wants to defend. He demands careful attention to literary texts which he then denies to other kinds of writing, especially Freud's.

In an unremitting rejection of everything Freud argued for, Vickers relies entirely on selective quotations from secondary sources, some of which he misrepresents by suggesting they are hostile when they are not. In his entire account I could find only one direct quotation from Freud – and that too was culled from a footnote in a secondary source which is actually contradicting Vickers' own reductive argument about Freud. Vickers criticizes Freudian critics for being ahistorical and unscholarly. Nothing is more ahistorial and unscholarly than Vickers on Freud. Most of his rejection of Freud is in the service of showing that psychoanalysis is not a science. He assumes that this totally discredits Freud, failing to realize that intellectual interest in Freud today virtually *begins with* with the realization that psychoanalysis is a failed science (the seduction, the danger, and the necessity of concepts like displacement and condensation surely begin here). Like so many anti-theorists, Vickers can't understand that most crucial yet difficult of intellectual activities: being historically and culturally inside something that one is also critically resisting; struggling to escape its errors, even its harmfulness, while recognizing that one has already been changed by it. Such is the history of much dynamic thought. Reading Vickers, one sometimes feels his is a sensibility blunted by *ressentiment*. He also repeatedly displays a kind of *intellectual* reductiveness. Each of these limitations discredits his own claim to a superior scholarship, since the best scholarship, and especially traditional scholarship, requires both intellect and sensibility. To repeat: the greatest limitation of Vickers is not his attack on theory but his speaking for a tradition whose intellectual significance he has censored and reduced in the process.

Cultural materialism/new historicism

Let me finally address cultural materialism not through its critics but its defenders, and note that the defence has included the too-easy assumption that cultural materialism is politically right-on and new historicism is in political bad faith especially around its theory of containment. It's ungracious of me to say so, but this very defence is a bit wishful. It's just not true that Stephen Greenbatt invented containment theory with a little help from Foucault, and that it can be thereby be largely discredited as a product of the quietism of tenured US academics, or the fatalism of French intellectuals post 1968.

Perhaps the most significant, least acknowledged source for containment theory is Herbert Marcuse, and, via him, the Frankfurt School of cultural theory and the sense of failure that has preoccupied Western Marxism from the outset. Marcuse's work of some thirty to forty years ago makes fascinating reading in the 1990s. I'm thinking especially of how the optimistic radicalism of *Eros and Civilisation* (1966 [1955]) came to be replaced by the radical pessimism of *One Dimensional Man* (1964). I've no time to chart this move except to remark that his notion of 'repressive desublimation' is a paradigm instance of containment and that, with the recent 'triumph' of advanced capitalism, *One Dimensional Man* is worth a revisit.

The case of Marcuse reminds us that, as Perry Anderson has written, the major works of the Western Marxist tradition are distingished by 'a common and latent pessimism', a 'diminution of hope and loss of certainty'. And this essentially because 'the hidden hallmark of Western Marxism as a whole is ... that it is the product of *defeat.* ... Its major works were, without exception, produced in situations of political isolation and despair'.[10] Reasons included the defeat of left-wing, working-class movements in Western Europe after the First World War; the degeneration of the Russian revolution into Stalinism; the rise of fascism and Nazism. Anderson than goes on to list some of the major writers for whom this was the case including Lukács, Gramsci, Adorno, Sartre and of course Benjamin, who wrote memorably of history as that storm blowing from paradise. Anderson wants to make a distinction between the pessimism of Western Marxism and the relative optimism of an early phase: what he calls classical Marxism. It's a valid distinction, but we shouldn't forget that political failure, and what we now call the politics of containment, were also formative for Marx. In fact for him they were linked. In the *Eighteenth Brumaire* he famously declares that we make history but not in conditions of our own choosing. Those conditions include 'the tradition of all the dead generations [which] weighs like a nightmare on the brain of the living'. And just at that moment when men seem most capable of 'revolutionising themselves and things', they become trapped in these past traditions. In previous revolutionary situations the past was an inspiration, glorifying the new struggles and '*magnifying the given task in imagination, not of fleeing from its solution in reality*'.

But, continues Marx, in France in 1848, something like the reverse happened: revolutionary fervour was defeated by this relapsing back into the past: 'An entire people, which had imagined that by means of a revolution, it had imparted to itself an accelerated power of motion, suddenly finds itself set back in a defunct epoch.' What had seemed 'long decayed' came back to life. Modern revolution must no longer look to the past but the future: 'It cannot begin with itself before it has stripped of all superstition in regard to the past. … In order to arrive at its own content, the revolution of the nineteenth century must let the dead bury the dead.'[11] Here is the acute challenge for a materialist philosophy of praxis: on the one hand it can only avoid failure by endlessly learning from the past and even finding inspiration in it; on the other it can only avoid failure by killing off the past, before it kills off our potential for revolutionary change in the present.

I've been talking about some of the limitations of recent theory in relation to the complex, difficult and often contradictory social realities which we inherit. I suggested that, far from anticipating the wider crises of Western culture, a conflict-ridden subjectivity has not only been there from the beginning, but has actually energised that culture, especially in its expansionist ambitions. Also, and relatedly, that Western culture is driven by a fear of failure which is compliant with a metaphysical assurance that failure is inevitable. And, correspondingly, that the Western tragic vision teaches us that failure is inevitable, that 'all labour comes to nought', and in so doing strangely endorses rather than checks the expansionist enterprise of the very culture that nurtures that vision. Further, that the radical project for social change has its roots in the same culture of pessimism which such change needs to abolish as a precondition of its own success; that radical thought remains to some extent inside what it struggles to escape; that it must simultaneously learn from the past and escape its influence. Last but not least – it was my point of departure – I've suggested that we have been too preoccupied with the liberal humanist divorce of art and politics when the more enduring challenge may come in the form of their fusion. Tell me by all means that such thinking is Chekhovian – only the product of a tired culture overburdened by its own histories of failure; tell me that even to dwell on it is a sign of cultural privilege. Tell me that in places like South Africa above all such talk is inappropriate. I'll listen but forgive me if I remain unconvinced, especially if, on the conference circuit, the radical alternative comes heralded as the after of the beyond of the post of the most recent brand of wishful theory.

This is not – I repeat not – an argument for the wholesale rejection of theory, nor even of post-modernism. It's rather to insist that we need a theory that embodies a greater effort of historical understanding; a theory adequate to understand, challenge and maybe even change those complex cultural realities that we inherit. An effort of understanding which knows that we always risk misrecognizing the real structure of the 'terrible contradictions' we live, and the struggles they imply, and that going back into the past via intellectual history is one way of reducing that risk. For this purpose the materialist concepts of contradiction and dialectic remain, for me, imperative. Arguably they remain significant too for any cultural politics prepared to confront and not evade the complexities of our cultural histories, and which knows, *contra* post-modernism, the importance of the traditions of intellectual history and even philosophical anthropology; which knows, in short, that there is so much more to be learned from the past than either the current reactionary defenders of tradition, or their post-modern critics, allow. The cultural politics that matters is the kind which strives to understand the contradictions we live and which, after making that effort, does not lack the courage to risk truth claims about the real; a cultural politics that knows the difference between human agency and human essence and that recognizes that the feeble relativism of post-modernism is only viable because it's never tested. For all its cosmopolitan affect, much post-modernism thrives on a new parochialism – that self-absorbed, inward-looking and relatively insulated existence characteristic of intellectual urban life, and which reminds us once again that material conditions profoundly influence not only the direction of our thought but the very structure of what it includes and excludes, of what is thinkable and what is not. A cultural politics, then, that knows we have to believe in what we write but also that we might well be wrong; which is, in a word, and in the broadest sense of that word: ethical.

Notes

1   I have in mind especially David Johnson's essay 'Importing Metropolitan Post-colonials' in *Current Writing* 6(1), 1994, 73–83, and his chapter 'Travelling Theory: To the Present' in his *Shakespeare and South Africa* (1996: 181–211); Kelwyn Sole's article 'Democratising Culture and Literature in a "New South Africa": Organisation and Theory' in *Current Writing: Text and Reception in Southern Africa*, 1994, 6 (2): pp. 1–37, and the responses to that article, in the same issue, from Guy Willoughby, Isabel Hofmeyr, Gareth Cornwall and Lewis Nkosi (pp. 38–59); see also Leon de Kock's review of the conference 'Letter from Wits', in *Southern African Review of Books*, July/August 1996, pp. 19–20, and the letters in response to it in subsequent issues.

2   Criticism of both the metropolitan and the post-modern remain in my own text for this collection, but with hesitation since both are becoming demonised categories. The charge of condemnation instantly attaching to them gains its plausibility precisely because what is included in them remains vague yet all-inclusive.

3   See James Joll, 'F. T. Marinetti: Futurism and Fascism', in *Three Intellectuals in Politics*, New York, Pantheon Books, 1960.

4   On the bow metaphor of line 8, cf. Nietzsche: 'it is precisely through the presence of opposites and the feelings they occasion that the great man, *the bow with the great tension*, develops' (Nietsche 1968: 507).

5   *Ocean to Scinthia*, ll. 253–6, 235 in *The Penguin Book of English Verse 1509–1659*, selected with intro. by David Norbrook, edited by R. Woudhuysen, London, Penguin, 1992, pp. 108–9.

6   Cited in H. M. Block and H. Salingar (eds) *The Creative Vision: Modern European Writers and Their Art*, New York, Grove Press London, Evergreen Books, 1960, pp. 158–61.

7   Raymond Williams, 'Tragedy and Revolution', *Modern Tragedy*, London, Verso, 1979. First published 1966.

8   'Bisexuality and Wishful Theory', in *Textual Practice*, 1996, 10(3), pp. 523–39.

9   Brian Vickers, *Appropriating Shakespeare*: Contemporary Critical Quarrels, New Haven and London, Yale University Press, 1993.

10 Perry Anderson, *Considerations on Western Marxism*, London, Verso, 1979, pp. 42–3, 88–90.

11 Marx and Engels, *Selected Works*, London, Lawrence & Wishart, 1968, pp. 97–9, my emphasis.

References

Abercrombie, Nicholas, Hill, Stephen and Turner, Bryan S. (1980) *The Dominant Ideology Thesis*, London: George Allen & Unwin, 90.

Africanus, John Leo (1969 [1600]) *A Geographical Historie of Africa*, Amsterdam: Da Capo Press, Theatrum Orbis Terrarum Ltd.

Ahmad, Aijaz (1995) 'The Politics of Literary Postcoloniality', *Race and Class* 36(3): 1–20.

Alexander, Nigel (1971) *Poison, Play and Duel*, London: Routledge & Kegan Paul.

Allen, David G. and White, Robert A. (eds) (1992) *The Work of Dissimilitude: Essays from the Sixth Citadel Conference on Medieval and Renaissance Literature*, Newark: University of Delaware Press.

Allen, T. (1994) *The Invention of the White Race, Volume One: Racial Oppression and Social Control*, London and New York: Verso.

Althusser, Louis (1971) 'Ideology and Ideological State Apparatuses (Notes towards an Investigation', *Lenin and Philosophy and Other Essays*, trans. Ben Brewster, New York: Monthly Review Press, 174.

Alva, J. Jorge Klor de (1995) 'The Postcolonization of the (Latin) American Experience, A Reconsideration of "Colonialism", "Postcolonialism" and "Mestizaje" ', in Gyan Prakash (ed.) *After Colonialism, Imperial Histories and Postcolonial Displacements*, Princeton, NJ: Princeton University Press, 241–75.

Anderson, Benedict (1991) *Imagined Communities, Reflections on the Origin and Spread of Nationalism*, London and New York: Verso.

Anderson, Perry (1979) *Considerations on Western Marxism*, London: Verso, 42–3, 88–90.

Andrews, K. (1984) *Trade, Plunder and Settlement: Maritime Enterprise and the Genesis of the British Maritime Empire*, Cambridge: University of Cambridge Press.

Appiah, Kwame Anthony (1990) 'Race' in Frank Lentricchia and Thomas McLaughlin (eds) *Critical Terms for Literary Study*, Chicago: University of Chicago Press, 274–87.

—— (1991) 'Is the Post- in Postmodernism the Post in Postcolonial?', *Critical Inquiry* 17: 336–57.

—— (1992) *In My Father's House: Africa in the Philosophy of Culture*, New York and Oxford: Oxford University Press.

Archer, John (1997) 'Toward the Old World'. Paper presented at the Annual Meeting of the Shakespeare Association of America, Washington, DC.

Arendt, Hannah (1970) *On Violence*, New York: Harcourt, Brace & World.

Arnold, Sir Thomas (ed.) (1931) *The Legacy of Islam*, Oxford: Clarendon Press.

Baldo, Jonathan (1996) 'Wars of Memory in *Henry V*', *Shakespeare Quarterly* 47(2): 132–59.

Barbour, Richmond (1996) '"There is Our Commission": Deputized Authority in *Measure for Measure* and The London East India Company'. Paper presented at the World Shakespeare Congress, Los Angeles.

Barker, F. and Hulme, P. (1985) '"Nymphs and Reapers Heavily Vanish": The Discursive Con-texts of *The Tempest*', in John Drakakis (ed.) *Alternative Shakespeares*, London: Methuen, 191–205.

Barker, F. *et al.* (eds) (1984) *Europe and Its Others*, Colchester: Essex University Press.

Barratt Brown, Michael and Tiffens, Pauline (1992) *Short Changed: Africa and World Trade*, London: Pluto.

Bartels, Emily (1990) 'Making More of the Moor: Aaron, Othello, and Renaissance Refashionings of Race', *Shakespeare Quarterly* 41(4): 433–54.

—— (1997) 'Othello and Africa: Postcolonialism Reconsidered', *The William and Mary Quarterly*, 3rd Series, 54(1): 45–64.

Behn, A. (1994 [1688]) *Oroonoko, and Other Writings*, (ed.) Paul Salzman, New York: Oxford University Press.

Berg, Elliott (1986) 'The World Bank's Strategy', in John Ravenhill (ed.) *Africa in Economic Crisis*, London: Macmillan.

Berry, Edward (1989) 'The Poet as Warrior in Sidney's *Defence of Poetry*', *Studies in English Literature*, 29: 22–34.

—— (1991) 'Sidney's Poor Painter: Nationalism and Social Class' in Vincent Newey and Ann Thompson (eds) *Literature and Nationalism*, Savage, MD: Barnes & Noble.

Betts, R. F. (1985) 'Methods and Institutions of European Domination', in A. Abu Boahan (ed.) *General History of Africa. VII. Africa under Colonial Domination 1880–1935*, London: Heinemann.

Bhabha, Homi K. (1990) *Nation and Narration*, New York: Routledge.

—— (1994a) *The Location of Culture*, London and New York: Routledge.

—— (1994b) 'Remembering Fanon, Self, Psyche and the Colonial Condition' in Patrick Williams and Laura Chrisman (eds) *Colonial Discourse and Postcolonial Theory*, New York: Columbia, 112–23.

Black, Jeremy (1996) *The Cambridge Illustrated Atlas: Warfare, Renaissance to Revolution 1492–1792*, Cambridge: Cambridge University Press.

Blackman, Shane J. (1992) 'Beyond Vocationalism', in Phillip Brown and Hugh Lauder (eds) *Education for Economic Survival. From Fordism to Post-fordism?*, London: Routledge.

Block, H. M. and Salingar, H. (eds) (1960) *The Creative Vision: Modern European Writers and Their Art*, New York: Grove Press and London: Evergreen Books, 158–61.

Boose, Lynda (1993) '"The Getting of a Lawful Race": Racial Discourse in Early Modern England and the Unrepresentable Black Woman' in M. Hendricks and B. Parker (eds) *Women, 'Race', and Writing in the Early Modern Period*, London: Routledge, 35–54.

Booth, Stephen (ed.) (1977) *Shakespeare's Sonnets*, New Haven: Yale University Press.

Bowen, B. (1998) 'Amelia Lanyer and the Invention of White Woman-hood', in Susan Frye and Karen Robertson (eds) *Maids and Mistresses, Cousins and Queens: Women's Alliances in Early Modern England*, New York: Oxford University Press.

Boyajian, J. (1993) *Portuguese Trade in Asia under the Hapsburgs, 1580–1640*, Baltimore: Johns Hopkins University Press.

Bozzoli, Belinda (1991) 'Explaining Social Consciousness: The Case of Mrs Molefe', *Cahiers d'Etudes africaines*, 123: XXI–3.

Braudel, F. (1995) *The Mediterranean and the Mediterranean World in the Age of Phillip II*, abr. Richard Ollard, London: HarperCollins.

Bredbeck, G. W. (1991) *Sodomy and Interpretation: Marlowe to Milton*, Ithaca, NY: Cornell University Press.

Brenner, R. (1993) *Merchants and Revolution: Commercial Change, Political Conflict, and London's Overseas Traders, 1550–1653*, Princeton, NJ: University of Princeton Press.

Brotton, J. (1997) *Trading Territories: Mapping the Early Modern World*, London: Reaktion Books.

Brown, P. (1985) '"This Thing of Darkness I Acknowledge Mine": *The Tempest* and the Discourse of Colonialism', in J. Dollimore and A. Sinfield (eds) *Political Shakespeare: New Essays in Cultural Materialism*, Manchester: Manchester University Press, 48–71.

Brown, R. (ed.) (1871) *Calender of State Papers, Venetian, 1603–7*, London: Longmans.

Brummet, P. (1994) *Ottoman Seapower and Levantine Diplomacy in the Age of Discovery*, New York: State University of New York Press.

Bulhan, Hussein Abdilahi (1980) 'Frantz Fanon: The Revolutionary Psychiatrist', *Race and Class*, 21(3): 251–71.

Burchard of Mount Sion (1971 [1896]) trans. from the Latin by A. Stewart, Palestine Pilgrims Text Society, 12, New York: AMS Press.

Cadman, Revd S. Parkes *et al.* (1931) *Henry C. Folger*, New Haven, privately printed.

Carlin, Murray (1969) *Not Now, Sweet Desdemona*, Nairobi: Oxford University Press.

Carnoy, Martin (1990) 'Education and the Transition State', in Martin Carnoy and Joel Samoff (eds), *Education and Social Transition in the Third World*, Princeton, NJ: Princeton University Press.

Cartelli, T. (1987) 'Prospero in Africa: *The Tempest* as Colonial Text and Pretext', in J. Howard and M. O'Connor (eds) *Shakespeare Reproduced: The Text in History and Ideology*, London: Routledge, 99–115.

Carusi, Annamaria (1989) 'Post, Post and Post: Or Where is South African Literature in All This?' *Ariel*, 20(4): 79–85.

Caulfield, Catherine (1997) *Masters of Illusion: The World Bank and the Poverty of Nations*, London: Macmillan.

Césaire, A. (1969) *Une Tempête*, Paris: Seuil.

Chakrabarty, Dipesh (1992) 'Postcoloniality and the Artifice of History: Who Speaks for "Indian" Pasts?' *Representations*, (Winter) 37: 1–24.

Chandos, John (ed.) (1971) *In God's Name: Examples of Preaching in England 1534–1662*, London: Hutchinson.

Chatterjee, Partha (1986) *Nationalist Thought and the Colonial World: A Derivative Discourse?*, London: Zed Books.

—— (1988) 'More on Modes of Power and the Peasantry', in Ranajit Guha and Gayatri Chakravorty Spivak (eds) *Selected Subaltern Studies*, New York and Oxford: Oxford University Press, 351–90.

—— (1993) *The Nations and Its Fragments, Colonial and Postcolonial Histories*, Princeton, NJ: Princeton University Press.

Chew, Samuel (1937) *The Crescent and the Rose: Islam and England during the Renaissance*, New York: Oxford University Press.

Cohen, Walter (1985) *Drama of a Nation: Public Theatre in Renaissance England and Spain*, Ithaca and London: Cornell University Press.

Columbus, Christopher (1989) *The 'Diario' of Christopher Columbus's First Voyage to America, 1492–1493*. Transcribed and translated by Oliver Dunn and James E. Kelley, Jr. Norman: University of Oklahoma Press.

Comaroff, John and Comaroff, Jean (1992) *Ethnography and the Historical Imagination*, Boulder, Col.: Westview Press.

Cooper, Frederick (1996) *Decolonization and African Society: The Labour Question in French and British Africa*, Cambridge: Cambridge University Press.

Cressy, David (1994) 'National Memory in Early Modern England', in John R. Gillies (ed.) *Commemorations: The Politics of National Identity*, Princeton, NJ: Princeton University Press.

D'Amico, Jack (1991) *The Moor in English Renaissance Drama*, Tampa: University of South Florida Press.

Daniel, Norman (1960) *Islam and the West*, Edinburgh: Edinburgh University Press.

Davenport, T. R. H. and Hunt, K. S. (1974) (eds) *The Right to the Land*, Cape Town: David Philip.

Davidson, B. (1990) 'The *Navigatione d'Enea* Tapestries Designed by Perino del Vaga for Andrea Doria', *The Art Bulletin*, 72(1): 35–50.

Davies, R. R. (1995) *The Revolt of Owain Glyn Dŵr*, Oxford: Oxford University Press.

De Grazia, M. (1993) 'The Scandal of Shakespeare's Sonnets', *Shakespeare Survey* 41: 35–50.

Deleuze, Gilles and Guattari, Felix (1983) *Anti-Oedipus: Capitalism and Schizophrenia*, Robert Hurley, Mark Seem and Helen R. Lane (trans.), Minneapolis: University of Minnesota Press.

Derrida, Jacques (1976) *Of Grammatology*, trans. Guyatri Chakravorty Spivak, Baltimore: Johns Hopkins University Press.

—— (1983) 'Signeponge' Part 1, in *Francis Ponge: Colloque de Cerisy*, Paris: Union Générale d'Editions, 146. Cit. Jonathan Culler, *On Deconstruction*, London: Routledge.

Dirks, Nicholas (1992) 'Introduction, Colonialism and Culture', in Nicholas Dirks (ed.) *Colonialism and Culture*, Ann Arbor: University of Michigan Press.

Dirlik, Arif (1994) 'The Post-colonial Aura: Third World Criticism in the Age of Global Capitalism', *Critical Inquiry* 20: 328–56.

Dollimore, Jonathan (1996) 'Bisexuality and Wishful Theory', *Textual Practice*, 10(3): 523–39.

Donaldson, Ian (1982) *The Rapes of Lucrece*, Oxford: Clarendon Press, 13.

Donne, John (1958) *The Sermons of John Donne*, ed. Evelyn M. Simpson and George R. Potter, Berkeley, University of California, 9.

Douglas, Mary (1979 [1966]) *Purity and Danger: An Analysis of the Concepts of Pollution and Taboo*, London: Routledge & Kegan Paul.

Dubois, W. E. B. (1977 [1935]) *Black Reconstruction in the United States, 1860–1880*, New York: Kraus-Thomson.

Dubow, Saul (1984) '"Understanding the Native Mind": Anthropology, Cultural Adaptation, and the Elaboration of a Segregationist Discourse in South Africa, c.1920–36', *Africa Seminar Paper*, Centre for African Studies, Cape Town: University of Cape Town.

—— (1993) 'Wulf Sachs's Black Hamlet: A Case of "Psychic Vivisection"?', *African Affairs*, 92: 519–56.

—— (1995) *Scientific Racism in Modern South Africa*, Cambridge: Cambridge University Press.

—— (1996) 'Introduction – Part One', in Wulf Sachs *Black Hamlet*, Johannesburg: Witwatersrand University Press, 1–37.

During, Simon (1987) 'Postmodernism or Post-colonialism Today', *Textual Practice* 1, (1): 33.

Dyer, R. (1989) 'White', *Screen*, 29: 44–64.

—— (1993) 'The Colour of Virtue: Lillian Gish, Whiteness and Femininity', in Pam Cook and Philip Dodd (eds) *Women in Film: A Sight and Sound Reader*, Philadelphia: Temple University Press, 1–9.

Edbury, Peter W. (ed.) (1985) *Crusade and Settlement*, Cardiff: Cardiff University College Press.

Eden, Richard (1971) *The Decades of the New World* in *The First Three English Books on America*, ed. Edward Arber, New York: Kraus Reprint Co.

Edwards, Philip (1979) *Threshold of a Nation: A Study in English and Irish Drama*, Cambridge: Cambridge University Press.

Elias, Norbert (1994) *The Civilising Process*, trans. Edmund Jephcott, Oxford (UK) and Cambridge, MA.: Blackwell.

Elphick, Richard (1985) *Kraal and Cattle: Khoikhoi and the Founding of White South Africa*, Johannesburg: Ravan Press.

Epko, Denis (1995) 'Towards a Post-Africanism', *Textual Practice* 9 (1): 121–35.

Erickson, P. (1993a) 'Representations of Blacks and Blackness in the Renaissance', *Criticism* 35: 499–528.

—— (1993b) 'Profiles in Whiteness', *Stanford Humanities Review* 3: 98–111.

—— (1996) 'Seeing White', *Transition* 67: 166–85.

Fanon, Frantz (1967) *Black Skin, White Masks*, trans. Charles Lam Markmann, New York: Grove Press.

Felperin, Howard (1990) *The Uses of the Canon: Elizabethan Literature and Contemporary Theory*, Oxford: Clarendon Press.

Fiedler, L. (1972) *The Stranger in Shakespeare*, New York: Stern & Day.

Fineman, J. (1986) *Shakespeare's Perjured Eye: The Invention of Poetic Subjectivity in the Sonnets*, Berkeley: University of California Press.

Foucault, Michel (1977) *Discipline and Punish: The Birth of the Prison*, trans. Alan Sheridan, Harmondsworth: Penguin.

—— (1980a) *The History of Sexuality*, vol. 1, trans. Robert Hurley, New York: Vintage Books, 58.

—— (1980b) 'Two Lectures' and 'Truth and Power', in *Power/Knowledge*, (ed.) C. Gordon, New York: Pantheon Books, 78–108, 109–33.

—— (1982) 'The Subject and Power', *Michel Foucault: Beyond Structuralism and Hermeneutics*, (ed.) H. L. Dreyfus and P. Rabinow, Chicago: University of Chicago Press.

Freud, Sigmund (1942 [1905–6]) 'Psychopathic Characters on the Stage', *The Penguin Freud Library Vol.14: Art and Literature*, trans. James Strachey, London: Penguin 119–27.

—— (1954) (ed.) *The Origins of Psychoanalysis: Letters to Wilhelm Fliess, Drafts and Notes 1887–1902*, ed. by Marie Bonaparte, Anna Freud and Ernst Kris and trans by Eric Mosbacher and James Strachey, London: Imago.

—— (1976 [1900]) *The Interpretation of Dreams, The Penguin Freud Library Vol. 4*, trans. James Strachey, London: Penguin.

—— (1984 [1923]) 'The Ego and the Id', *The Penguin Freud Library Vol. 11: On Metapsychology*, trans. James Strachey, London: Penguin, 341–407.

—— (1985a [1913]) 'Totem and Taboo', *The Penguin Freud Library Vol. 13: The Origins of Religion*, trans. James Strachey, London: Penguin, 43–224.

—— (1985b [1921]) 'Group Psychology and the Analysis of the Ego', *The Penguin Freud Library Vol. 12: Civilization, Society and Religion*, trans. James Strachey, London: Penguin, 91–178.

—— (1985c [1927]) 'The Future of an Illusion', *The Penguin Freud Library Vol. 12: Civilization, Society and Religion*, trans. James Strachey, London: Penguin, 179–241.

—— (1985d [1930]) 'Civilization and Its Discontents', *The Penguin Freud Library Vol. 12: Civilization, Society and Religion*, trans. James Strachey, London: Penguin, 243–340.

—— (1986 [1913]) 'The Claims of Psychoanalysis to Scientific Interest',

The Penguin Freud Library Vol.15: Historical and Expository Works on Psychoanalysis, trans. James Strachey, London: Penguin, 27–56.

Freund, Bill (1984) *The Making of Contemporary Africa*, London: Macmillan.

Fryer, Peter (1984) *Staying Power: The History of Black People in Britain*, London: Pluto Press.

Fuchs, B. (1997) 'Conquering Islands: Contextualising *The Tempest*', *Shakespeare Quarterly*, 48(1): 45–62.

Fugard, Athol (1978) *Sizwe Bansi is Dead* in A. Fugard, *Statements: Three Plays*, Oxford: Oxford University Press.

Fumerton, P. (1991) *Cultural Aesthetics: Renaissance Literature and the Practice of Social Ornament*, Chicago: University of Chicago Press.

Fuss, Diana (1994) 'Interior Colonies: Frantz Fanon and the Politics of Identification', *Diacritics*, 24(2): 20–42.

Gillespie, Sadie (1992) 'Historical Notes on the First South African Psycho-analytic Society', *Psycho-Analytic Psychotherapy in South Africa*, 1, Spring: 1–6.

Gillies, John (1994) *Shakespeare and the Geography of Difference*, Cambridge: Cambridge University Press.

Goldberg, J. (1994) '*Romeo and Juliet*'s Open Rs' in Jonathan Goldberg (ed.) *Queering the Renaissance*, Durham, NC: Duke University Press, 218–35.

Gordimer, Nadine (1988) *The Essential Gesture*, (ed.) Stephen Clingman, London: Jonathan Cape.

—— (1990) *My Son's Story*, London: Jonathan Cape.

Grady, Hugh (1991) *The Modernist Shakespeare*, Oxford: Clarendon.

Grafton, A. and Jardine, L. (1990) '"Studied for Action": How Gabriel Harvey Read his Livy', *Past and Present*, 129: 30–78.

Greenblatt, Stephen (1985) 'Shakespeare and the Exorcists', in Patricia Parker and Geoffrey Hartman (eds), *Shakespeare and the Question of Theory*, London: Methuen, 163–87.

—— (1988) *Shakespearean Negotiations. The Circulation of Social Energy in Renaissance England*, Oxford: Clarendon.

—— (1991) *Marvelous Possessions: The Wonder of the New World*, Chicago: University of Chicago Press.

—— (1995) 'Remnants of the Sacred in Early Modern England', *Shakespeare in Southern Africa* 8: 23–9.

—— (1996) 'Mutilation and Meaning', in Pippa Skotnes (ed.) *Miscast. Negotiating the Presence of the Bushmen*, Cape Town: University of Cape Town Press.

Greene, R. (1995) 'Petrarchism among the Discourses of Imperialism', in Karen Ordahl Kupperman (ed.) *America in European Consciousness*

1493–1750, Chapel Hill: University of North Carolina Press, 130–65.

Greene, T. M. (1985) 'Pitiful Thrivers: Failed Husbandry in the Sonnets', in P. Parker and G. Hartman (eds), *Shakespeare and the Question of Theory*, London: Methuen, 230–44.

Grieco, S. F. (1993) 'The Body, Appearance and Sexuality', in Natalie Zemon Davis and Arlette Farge (eds) *A History of Women in the West: Renaissance and Enlightenment Paradoxes*, Cambridge, MA and London: Harvard University Press, 46–84.

Hadfield, Andrew (1994) *Literature, Politics and National Identity: Reformation to Renaissance*, Cambridge: Cambridge University Press.

Hailey, Lord M. H. (1938) *An African Survey*, Oxford: Oxford University Press.

Hall, Edward (1548) *Chronicle: The Union of Two Noble and Illustre Families of Lancastre & Yorke*, London.

Hall, K. F. (1994) '"I rather would wish to be a blackamoor": Race, Rank and Beauty in Lady Mary Wroth's *Urania*', in M. Hendricks and P. Parker (eds) *Women, 'Race' and Writing*, London: Routledge, 178–94.

—— (1995) *Things of Darkness: Economies of Race and Gender in Early Modern England*, New York and London: Cornell University Press.

Hallett, Robin (1965) *The Penetration of Africa: European Enterprise and Exploration Principally in Northern and Western Africa up to 1830*, London: Routledge & Kegan Paul.

Hamilton, Carolyn (ed.) (1995) 'Introduction', *The Mfecane Aftermath*, Johannesburg: Witwatersrand University Press.

Harber, Clive (1997) *Education, Democracy and Political Development in Africa*, Brighton: Sussex Academic Press.

Harris, Nigel (1986) *The End of the Third World: Newly Industrialising Countries and the Decline of Ideology*, London: Touris.

Hartnack, Christiane (1990) 'Vishnu on Freud's Desk: Psychoanalysis in Colonial India', *Social Research*, 57(4): 921–49.

Hartsock, Nancy (1987) 'Rethinking Modernism: Majority versus Minority Theories', *Cultural Critique* 7: 187–206, 160.

Hawkes, Terence (1985) 'Swisser-Swatter: Making a Man of English Letters', in John Drakakis (ed.) *Alternative Shakespeares*, London: Methuen, 26–46.

—— (1992) *Meaning by Shakespeare*, London: Routledge.

Haynes, Douglas and Prakash, Gyan (eds) (1991) *Contesting Power*, Delhi: Oxford University Press.

Heal, F. and Holmes, C. (1994) *The Gentry in England and Wales, 1500–1700*, Stanford: Stanford University Press.

Heilman, Robert Bechtold (1948) *This Great Stage: Image and Structure in 'King Lear'*, Baton Rouge: Louisiana State University Press.

Helgerson, R. (1992) *Forms of Nationhood: The Elizabethan Writing of England*, Chicago: University of Chicago Press.

Helms, M. (1988) *Ulysses' Sail: An Ethnographic Odyssey of Power, Knowledge, and Geographical Distance*, Princeton, NJ: Princeton University Press.

Henderson, George C. (1907) *Sir George Grey: Pioneer of Empire in Southern Lands*, London: J. M. Dent.

Hendricks, Margo (1992) 'Managing the Barbarian: *The Tragedy of Dido, Queen of Carthage*', *Renaissance Drama* 23: 165–88.

—— (1996) 'Obscured by Dreams: Race, Empire and *A Midsummer Night's Dream*', *Shakespeare Quarterly* (Spring): 37–60.

Hendricks, Margo and Parker, Patricia (eds) (1994) *Women, 'Race' and Writing in the Early Modern Period*, London: Routledge.

Henken, Elissa R. (1996) *National Redeemer, Owain Glyndwr in Welsh Tradition*, Cardiff: University of Wales Press.

Herrick, R. (1965) *Poems*, ed. L. C. Martin, New York: Oxford University Press.

Hess, A. (1972) 'The Battle of Lepanto and Its Place in Mediterranean History', *Past and Present*, 57: 53–73.

—— (1978) *The Forgotten Frontier: A History of the Sixteenth-Century Ibero-African Frontier*, Chicago: University of Chicago Press.

Heywood, Mark James (1994) '"Books made the white man's success," they said, and it shall make ours: Lovedale, Literature and Cultural Contestation 1840–1940'. Unpublished MA dissertation, University of the Witwatersrand, Johannesburg.

Higgins, John (1996) 'Critical Literacy in Action', *Southern African Review of Books*, 41: 16–17.

Hitchcott, Nicki (1993) 'African Oedipus?', *Paragraph*, 16(1): 59–66.

Hoade, E. (1948) *Western Pilgrims*, Jerusalem: Franciscan Printing Press.

Hodge, J. (1990) 'Equality: Beyond Dualism and Oppression' in David Theo Goldberg (ed.) *Anatomy of Racism*, Minneapolis: University of Minnesota Press, 89–107.

Hofmeyr, Isabel (1995) 'Making Symmetrical Knowledge Possible: Recent Trends in the Field of Southern African Oral Performance Studies', *Current Writing* 7: 2.

Holinshed, Raphael (1587) *The Chronicles of England, Scotland and Ireland*, 3 vols, London.

Holstun, James (1989) 'Ranting at the New Historicism', *English Literary Renaissance*, 19: 189–225.

hooks, bell (1990) *Yearning: Race, Gender and Cultural Politics*, Boston: South End Press.

Horn, H. (1989) *Jan Cornelisz Vermeyen*, 2 vols, Netherlands: Davaco.

Housley, Norman (1992) *The Later Crusades: From Lyons to Alcazar 1274–1580*, Oxford: Oxford University Press.

Howard, Jean E. and Rackin, Phyllis (1997) *Endangering a Nation*, London and New York: Routledge.

Hulme, Peter (1986) *Colonial Encounters: Europe and the Native Caribbean 1492–1797*, New York: Methuen.

Hunter, G. K. (1978) *Dramatic Identities and Cultural Tradition: Studies on Shakespeare and His Contemporaries*, New York: Harper.

James, C. L. R. (1992 [1953]) 'Notes on *Hamlet*', in Anna Grimshaw (ed.) *The C. L. R. James Reader*, Oxford: Blackwell, 243–6.

Jameson, Fredric (1990) 'Imperialism and Modernism', in Seamus Deane (ed.) *Nationalism, Colonialism, and Literature*, Minneapolis: University of Minnesota Press.

—— (1991) *Post-modernism, Or, The Cultural Logic of Late Capitalism*, London: Verso.

JanMohamed, Abdul R. (1985) 'The Economy of Manichean Allegory: The Function of Racial Difference in Colonialist Literature', *Critical Inquiry* 12: 59–87.

Jardine, Lisa (1996) *Reading Shakespeare Historically*, London: Routledge.

Jed, Stephanie (1989) *Chaste Thinking: The Rape of Lucretia and The Birth of Humanism*, Bloomington: Indiana University Press.

Johnson, David (1996) *Shakespeare and South Africa*, Oxford: Clarendon.

Johnson, Rosalind (1986) 'Parallels between Othello and the Historical Leo Africanus', *Bim* 18 (70): 9–34.

Johnson, Samuel (1968) *Johnson on Shakespeare*, (ed.) Arthur Sherbo, The Yale Edition of the Works of Samuel Johnson, vol.7, New Haven: Yale University Press.

Joll, James (1960) 'F. T. Marinetti: Futurism and Fascism', in *Three Intellectuals in Politics*, New York: Pantheon Books.

Jones, Anne Rosalind (1991) 'Italians and Others: *The White Devil* 1612' in *Staging the Renaissance*, London: Routledge, 251–62.

Jones, Eldred (1965) *Othello's Countrymen*, London: Oxford University Press.

—— (1971) *The Elizabethan Image of Africa*, Charlottesville: University of Virginia Press.

Jones, Ernest (1949 [1923]) *Hamlet and Oedipus*, London: Victor Gollancz.

Jordan, W. (1968) *White over Black: American Attitudes toward the Negro, 1550–1812*, Chapel Hill: University of North Carolina Press.

Kandjii, Kaitira (1997) 'Pippa Skotnes's *Miscast*', *Current Writing*, 9(1): 110–13.

Keegan, Tim (1987) *Rural Transformations in Industrializing South Africa: The Southern Highveld to 1914*, Johannesburg: Ravan Press.

Kegle, Rosemary (1994) *The Rhetoric of Concealment: Figuring Gender and Class in Renaissance Literature*, Ithaca: Cornell University Press.

Kennedy, Dennis (1993) 'Introduction: Shakespeare without his Language' in Dennis Kennedy (ed.) *Foreign Shakespeare*, Cambridge: Cambridge University Press.

Kennedy, Paul (1997) *The Rise and Fall of the Great Powers: Economic and Military Conflict from 1500 to 2000*, New York: Random House.

Kerr, A. J. (1976) *The Customary Law of Immovable Property and of Succession*, Grahamstown: Faculty of Law, Rhodes University.

Knapp, J. (1992) *An Empire Nowhere: England, America and Literature from 'Utopia' to 'The Tempest'*, Berkeley: University of California Press.

Kock, Leon de (1996) 'Letter from Wits', *Southern African Review of Books*, July/August, 19–20.

Kohn, Hans (1940) 'The Genesis and Character of English Nationalism', *Journal of the History of Ideas*, 1: 69–94.

—— (1951) *The Idea of Nationalism: A Study in Its Origins and Background*, New York: Macmillan.

Kortenaar, Neil ten (1995) 'Beyond Authenticity and Creolization: Reading Achebe Writing Culture', *PMLA* 110(1): 30–42.

Kott, J. (1976) '*The Aeneid* and *The Tempest*', *Arion*, 3(4): 424–51.

Lamming, George (1960) *The Pleasures of Exile*, London: Allison & Busby.

Laplanche, J. and Pontalis, J. B. (1988 [1973]) *The Language of Psychoanalysis*, trans. Donald Nicholson-Smith, London: Karnac Books and the Institute of Psychoanalysis.

Larrain, Jorge (1989) *Theories of Development: Capitalism, Colonialism and Dependency*, Oxford: Polity.

Laubscher, B. J. F. (1937) *Sex, Custom and Psychopathology: A Study of South African Pagan Natives*, London: Routledge & Kegan Paul.

Lawrence, D. H. (1968 [1926]) *The Plumed Serpent*, Harmondsworth: Penguin.

Leys, Colin (1996) *The Rise and Fall of Development Theory*, London: James Currey.

Lionnet, Françoise (1995) '"Logiques metisses": Cultural Appropriation and Postcolonial Representations', in Kostas Myrsiades and Jerry McGuire (eds) *Order and Partialities: Theory, Pedagogy, and The 'Postcolonial,'* New York: State University of New York Press, 111–36.

Liu, T. (1991) 'Teaching the Differences among Women from an Historical Perspective', *Women's Studies International Forum*, 14(4): 265–76.

—— (1995) 'Race,' in R. Wrightman Fox and J. T. Klopprnberg (eds) *A Companion to American Thought*, Oxford: Blackwell, 564–7.

Lloyd, Simon (1985) ' "Political Crusades" in England, *c.* 1215–17 ad. *c.* 1263–5', in W. Edbury, *Crusade and Settlement*, Cardiff: Cardiff University College Press, 113–20.

Locke, John (1978) 'On Property', in C. B. Macpherson (ed.) *Property: Mainstream and Critical Positions*, Oxford: Blackwell, 17–27.

Loomba, Ania (1989) *Gender, Race, Renaissance Drama*, New York: St Martin's Press.

—— (1993) 'Overworlding the "Third World" ', in Patrick Williams and Laura Chrisman (eds) *Colonial Discourse and Post-Colonial Theory*, Hemel Hempstead: Harvester.

—— (1996) 'Shakespeare and Cultural Difference', in Terence Hawkes (ed.) *Alternative Shakespeares Vol. 2*, New York: Routledge, 164–91.

—— (1997) 'Shakespearean Transformations', in John Joughin (ed.) *Shakespeare and National Culture*, Manchester: Manchester University Press, 109–41.

Lugard, Lord F. D. (1929) *The Dual Mandate in British Tropical Africa*, 4th edn, London: Blackwood.

Lupton, J. (1997) '*Othello* Circumcised: Shakespeare and the Pauline Discourse of Nations', *Representations*, 57: 73–89.

Lyly, John (1902) *The Complete Works*, ed. R. Warwick Bond, Oxford: Clarendon Press.

McClintock, Anne (1992) 'The Angel of Progress, Pitfalls of the Term "Post-colonialism"', *Social Text* 31/32: 84–98.

—— (1995) *Imperial Leather: Race, Gender and Sexuality in the Colonial Contest*, New York: Routledge.

McCulloch, Jock (1995) *Colonial Psychiatry and 'The African Mind'*, Cambridge: Cambridge University Press.

Machyn, Henry (1848) *The Diary of Henry Machyn, Citizen and Merchant-Taylor of London, from A.D. 1550 to A.D. 1563*, ed. John Gough Nichols, London: Camden Society.

Macpherson, C. B. (ed.) (1978) *Property: Mainstream and Critical Positions*, Oxford: Basil Blackwell.

Mandeville, Sir John (1900) *The Travels of John Mandeville: The Version of the Cotton Manuscript in Modern Spelling*, London: Macmillan.

Mahasweta Devi (1993) 'Shishu', in Susie Tharu and K. Lalita (eds) *Women Writing in India*, vol. II, New York: The Feminist Press, 236–50.

Malka, Shelley (1996) 'The Representation of "the Jew" in selected sixteenth and seventeenth century writings, in *The Merchant of Venice* and in its criticism'. Unpublished PhD thesis, University of the Witwatersrand, Johannesburg.

Mamdani, Mahmood (1996) *Citizen and Subject: Contemporary Africa and the Legacy of Late Colonialism*, Princeton, NJ: Princeton University Press.

Mannoni, O. (1956) *Prospero and Caliban: The Psychology of Colonisation*, trans. P. Powesland, London: Methuen.

—— (1964) *Prospero and Caliban: The Psychology of Colonization*, New York: Praeger.

Maponya, Maisha (1984) *The Hungry Earth*, in Temple Hauptfleisch and Ian Steadman (eds) *South African Theatre: Four Plays and an Introduction*, Pretoria: Haum.

Marcus, Steven (1984) *Freud and the Culture of Psychoanalysis: Studies in the Transition from Victorian Humanism to Modernity*, Boston, London and Sydney: George Allen & Unwin.

Marcuse, Herbert (1959) 'The Ideology of Death' in H. Feifel (ed.) *The Meaning of Death* New York: McGraw-Hill, 64–76.

—— (1964) *One Dimensional Man*, Boston: Beacon Press.

—— (1966 [1955]) *Eros and Civilisation: A Philosophical Enquiry into Freud*, Boston: Beacon Press.

Marienstras, Richard (1985) 'Elizabethan Travel Literature and Shakespeare's *The Tempest*', in *New Perspectives on the Shakespearean World*, Cambridge: University of Cambridge Press.

Marinetti, Filippo (1972) *Marinetti: Selected Writings*, ed. and intro R.W. Flint trans. R. W. Flint and A. A. Coppotelli, London: Secker & Warburg.

Marx, Karl (1975) 'On the Jewish Question' in *Early Writings*, trans. Rodney Livingstone and Gregory Benton, Harmondsworth: Penguin.

Marx, Karl and Engels, Friedrich (1968) *Selected Works*, London: Lawrence & Wishart.

Matar, Nabil I. (1994) ' "Turning Turk": Conversion to Islam in English Renaissance Thought', *Durham U. Journal* 86: 33–41.

Matthews, Z. K (1979) *Freedom for My People: The Autobiography of Z. K. Matthews: Southern Africa 1901–1968*, Cape Town: David Philip.

Mead, Jenna (1994) 'The Anti-Imperialist Approaches to Chaucer (Are There Those?): An Essay in Identifying Strategies', *Southern Review* 27: 403–17.

Mercer, K. (1991) 'Skin Head Sex Thing: Racial Difference and the Homoerotic Imaginary', in *How Do I Look: Queer Film and Video*, ed. Bad Object-Choices, Seattle: Bay Press, 211–22.

Miles, Robert (1989) *Racism*, London: Routledge.

Mishra, Vijay (1995) 'Post-colonial Differend: Diasporic Narratives of Salman Rushdie', *Ariel*, 26: 3.

Mitchell, Juliet (1975) *Psychoanalysis and Feminism*, Harmondsworth: Penguin.

Molíner, Maria (ed.) (1967) *Diccionario de Uso del Español*, Madrid: Editorial Gredos.

Moran, Shane (1996) 'Always Historicise! Neoconservatism, Postmodernism and New Historicism', *Current Writing*, 8(2): 128–37.

Moretti, Franco (1982) '"A Huge Eclipse": Tragic Form and the Deconsecration of Sovereignty', in Stephen Greenblatt (ed.) *The Power of Forms in the English Renaissance*, Norman, Okla.: Pilgrim Books, 7–40.

Morrison, T. (1972) *The Bluest Eye*, New York: Washington Square Press.

—— (1992) *Playing in the Dark: Whiteness and the Literary Imagination*, Cambridge, Mass.: Harvard University Press.

Morton, A. L. (1968) *A People's History of England*, New York: International Publishers.

Mtuze, Peter (1990/1) 'Mdledel's Xhosa Translation of *Julius Caesar*', *Shakespeare in Southern Africa*, 4: 65.

Murphy, Andrew (1996) 'Shakespeare's Irish History', in *Literature and History*, 3rd Series, 5 (1): 38–59.

Murray, A. Victor (1929) *The School in the Bush*, London: Longman.

Murray, Colin (1992) *Black Mountain: Land, Class and Power in the Eastern Orange Free State 1880s–1980s*, Johannesburg: Witwatersrand University Press.

Nahoum-Grappe, V. (1993) 'The Beautiful Woman', trans. Arthur Goldhammer, in Natalie Zemon and Arlette Farge (eds), *A History of Women in the West: Renaissance and Enlightenment Paradoxes*, Cambridge, MA and London: Harvard University Press, 85–100.

Natsoulos, Anthula and Natsoulos, Theodore (1993) 'Racism, the School and African Education in Colonial Kenya', in J. A. Mangan (ed.) *The Imperial Curriculum*, London: Routledge.

Ndebele, Njabulo (1987) 'The English Language and Social Change in South Africa', *The English Academy Review*, 4.

Neely, Carol (1995) 'Circumscriptions and Unhousedness; *Othello* in the Borderlands', in Deborah Barker and Ivo Kamps (eds) *Shakespeare and Gender: A History*, London and New York: Verso, 305.

Neill, Michael (1995) 'Putting History to the Question: An Episode of Torture at Bantam in Java, 1604', *ELR* 25: 45–75.

New Internationalist (1993) 'Editorial', August 246: 13.

The Newbolt Report. The Teaching of English in England (1921), London: Board of Education – HMSO.

Newey, Vincent and Thompson, Ann (eds) (1991) *Literature and Nationalism*, Savage, MD: Barnes and Noble.

Ngũgĩ wa Thiong'o (1986) *Decolonising the Mind: The Politics of Language in African Literature*, London: James Currey.

Nietsche, Friedrich (1956 [1872]) *The Birth of Tragedy* and *The Genealogy of Morals*, trans. Francis Golffing, New York: Doubleday.

—— (1968) *The Will to Power*, trans. Walter Kaufmann and R. J. Hollingdale, ed. Kaufmann, New York: Random House.

Nixon, Rob (1987) 'Caribbean and African Appropriations of *The Tempest*', *Critical Inquiry*, 13: 557–78.

Norbrook, D. (1992) '"What Cares These Roarers for the Name of King?"': Language and Utopia in *The Tempest*', in G. McMullan and J. Hope (eds) *The Politics of Tragicomedy*, London: Routledge, 21–54.

O'Casey, Sean (1957) *The Plough and the Stars*, in *Three Plays*, London: Macmillan.

Ogle, M. B. (1965) 'The Classical Origin and Tradition of Literary Conceits', *American Journal of Philology*, 34 (2): 125–52.

Omi, M., and Winant, H. (1994) *Racial Formation in the United States: From the 1960s to the 1990s*, New York: Routledge.

Orkin, Martin (1987) *Shakespeare Against Apartheid*, Johannesburg: Ad. Donker.

—— (1997) 'Whose Things of Darkness? Reading/Representing *The Tempest* in South Africa after April 1994', in John Joughin (ed.) *Shakespeare and National Culture*, Manchester: Manchester University Press.

Ortelius, A. (1968) *The Theatre of the Whole World*, Amsterdam: Theatrum Orbis Terrarum.

Ortiz, A. (ed.) (1991) *Resplendence of the Spanish Monarchy: Renaissance Tapestries and Armor from the Patrimonio Nacional*, New York: Metropolitan Museum of Art.

Pagden, A. (1993) *European Encounters with the New World: From Renaissance to Romanticism*, New Haven: Yale University Press.

Parry, Benita (1987) 'Problems in Current Theories of Colonial Discourse', *The Oxford Literary Review*, 9: 1–2, 27–58.

—— (1994) 'Resistance Theory/Theorising Resistance or Two Cheers for Nativism', in Francis Barker *et al.* (eds) *Colonial Discourse/Postcolonial theory*, Manchester: Manchester University Press, 172–96.

Patterson, Orlando (1977) *Ethnic Chauvinism: The Reactionary Impulse*, New York: Stein & Day.

Peires, J. B. (1989) *The Dead Will Arise: Nongqawuse and the Great Xhosa Cattle-Killing of 1856–7*, Johannesburg: Ravan Press.

Perham, Margery (1960) *Lugard. The Years of Authority*, London: Collins.

Peters, F. E. (1985) *Jerusalem*, Princeton, NJ: Princeton University Press.

Phaer, T. (1573) *The Whole XII Bookes of the Aeneidos of Virgill*, London.

Pitcher, J. (1984) 'A Theatre of the Future: *The Aeneid* and *The Tempest*', *Essays in Criticism*, 24 (3): 193–215.

Porter, Carolyn (1990) 'Are We Being Historical Yet?', in David Carroll (ed.) *The States of 'Theory': History, Art and Critical Discourse*, New York: Columbia University Press.

Pratt, Mary Louise (1992) *Imperial Eyes: Travel Writing and Transculturation*, New York: Routledge.

Puttenham, G. (1589) *The Arte of English Poesie; Continued into Three Bookes: the First of Poets and Poesie, the Second of Proportion, the Third of Ornament*, London, n.p.

—— (1936) *The Arte of English Poesie*, ed. Gladys D. Willcock, Cambridge: Cambridge University Press.

Quinn, D. B. (1979) *New American World: A Documentary History of North America to 1612*, New York: Arno Press.

Ralegh, Walter (1929) *Poems*, ed. Agnes M.C. Latham, London: Constable.

Retamar, Roberto Fernandez (1974) 'Caliban: Notes towards a Discussion of Culture in Our America', *Massachusetts Review* 15: 7–72.

Roediger, D. (1991) *The Wages of Whiteness: Race and the Making of the American Working Class*, New York and London: Verso.

—— (1994) *Towards the Abolition of Whiteness*, New York: Verso.

Róheim, Géza (1934) 'The Evolution of Culture', *The International Journal of Psychoanalysis*, Oct., 15 (4): 387–418.

Rose, Jacqueline (1996a) 'Introduction – Part Two', in Wulf Sachs *Black Hamlet*, Johannesburg: Witwatersrand University, 38–67.

—— (1996b) *States of Fantasy*. The Clarendon Lectures in English Literature 1994, Oxford: Clarendon Press.

Routh, H. V. (1941) *The Diffusion of English Culture outside England*, Cambridge: Cambridge University Press.

Rushdie, Salman (1984) *Shame*, London: Picador.

—— (1991) *Imaginary Homelands*, London: Granta Books.

—— (1995) *The Moor's Last Sigh*, London: Jonathan Cape.

Sachs, Albie (1994) 'Language Rights in the New South African Constitution', *English Academy Review*, 11.

Sachs, Wulf (1933) 'The Insane Native: An Introduction to a Psychological Study', *South African Journal of Science*, October 30: 706–13.

—— (1934) *Psychoanalysis: Its Meaning and Practical Applications*, London: Cassell & Co.

—— (1937) *Black Hamlet: The Mind of an African Negro Revealed by Psychoanalysis*, London: Geoffrey Bles.

—— (1947) *Black Anger*, Boston: Little, Brown & Company.

—— (1996) *Black Hamlet,* Johannesburg: Witwatersrand University Press.

Said, Edward (1975) *Beginnings: Intention and Method*, New York: Basic Books.

—— (1978) *Orientalism*, London: Penguin.

—— (1995) 'East Isn't East: the Impending End of the Age of Orientalism', *The Times Literary Supplement*, February 3, 3–6.

Salih, Tayeb (1991) *Season of Migration to the North*, London: Heinemann.

Salingar, L. (1994) 'The New World in *The Tempest*', in J. Maquerlot and M. Willenis (eds) *Travel and Drama in Shakespeare's Time*, Cambridge: University of Cambridge Press, 209–22.

Salmond, Anne (1991) *Two Worlds: First Meetings between Maoris and Europeans 1642–1772*, Auckland: Viking Books.

Samoff, Joel (1994) 'Crisis and Adjustment: Understanding National Responses', in Joel Samoff (ed.), *Coping with Crisis: Austerity, Adjustment and Human Resources*, London: UNESCO/ILO.

Sanyal, Bikas C. (1987) *Higher Education and Employment: An International Comparative Analysis*, Brighton: The Falmer Press.

Schoenbaum, S. (1977) *William Shakespeare: A Compact Documentary Life*, Oxford: Oxford University Press.

Schuurman, Franz, J. (ed.) (1993) *Beyond the Impasse: New Directions in Development Theory*, London: Zed Books.

Scott, H. S. (1937) 'Educational Policy in the British Colonial Empire', *The Yearbook of Education* 8: 411–38.

Sedgwick, E. K. (1985) *Between Men: English Literature and Male Homosocial Desire*, New York: Columbia University Press.

Seshadri-Crooks, Kalpana (1994) 'The Primitive as Analyst: Post-colonial Feminism's Access to Psychoanalysis', *Cultural Critique*, Fall, 28: 175–218.

—— (1995) 'At the Margins of Post-Colonial Studies,'*Ariel*, 26: 3.

Shakespeare, William (1944) *A New Variorum Edition of Shakespeare: The Sonnets*, ed. Ryder Edward Hollins, 2 vols, Philadelphia and London: Lippencott.

—— (1954) *The Tempest*, ed. Frank Kermode, London: Methuen (Arden Edition).

—— (1960) *Henry IV, Part 1*, ed. A. R. Humphreys, London: Methuen (Arden Edition).

—— (1966) *King Henry IV Part II*, ed. A. R. Humphreys, London: Methuen (Arden Edition).

—— (1968) *The Tempest*, ed. A. Barton, London: Penguin.

—— (1972) *King Lear*, ed. Kenneth Muir, London: Methuen (Arden Edition).

—— (1974) *The Riverside Shakespeare*, ed. G. Blakemore Evans, New York: Houghton Mifflin.

—— (1977) *Shakespeare's Sonnets*, ed. Stephen Booth, New Haven and London: Yale University Press.

—— (1984) *Henry V*, ed. Gary Taylor, Oxford: OUP (Oxford Shakespeare).

—— (1987) *The Tempest*, ed. Stephen Orgel, Oxford: OUP (Oxford Shakespeare).

—— (1988) *The Rape of Lucrece*, in *The Complete Works of William Shakespeare*, ed. Stanley Wells and Gary Taylor, Oxford: OUP (Oxford Shakespeare).

—— (1989) *Hamlet*, ed. Harold Jenkins, London and New York: Routledge (Arden Edition).

—— (1995) *Henry V*, ed. T. W. Craik, London: Routledge (Arden Edition).

—— (1997) *The Norton Shakespeare*, ed. S. Greenblatt, W. Cohen, J. Howard and K. E. Muns, New York: W. W. Norton.

Shapiro, James (1996) *Shakespeare and the Jews*, New York: Columbia University Press.

Sherman, W. (1995) *John Dee: The Politics of Reading and Writing in the English Renaissance*, Amherst: University of Massachusetts Press.

Shohat, Ella (1993) 'Notes on the "Post-colonial"', *Social Text*, 31/32: 279–98.

Shole, J. Shole (1990/1) 'Shakespeare in Setswana: An Evaluation of Raditladi's *Macbeth* and Plaatje's *Diphosophoso*', *Shakespeare in Southern Africa*, 4.

Silverblatt, Irene (1995) 'Becoming Indian in the Central Andes of Seventeenth-Century Peru', in Gyan Prakash (ed.) *After Colonialism, Imperial Histories and Postcolonial Displacements*, Princeton, NJ: Princeton University Press.

Simon, David (ed.) (1995) *Structurally Adjusted Africa: Poverty, Debt and Basic Needs*, London: Pluto.

Sinfield, Alan (1992) *Faultlines: Cultural Materialism and the Politics of Dissident Reading*, Berkeley: University of California Press.

Singh, Jyotsna (1989), 'Different Shakespeares: The Bard in Colonial/Postcolonial India', *Theatre Journal*, 41(4): 445–57.

—— (1996), *Colonial Narratives/Cultural Dialogues*, London: Routledge.

Sinha, T. C. (1966) 'Development of Psycho-Analysis in India', *The International Journal of Psychoanalysis*, 47: 427–439.

Skilliter, S. (ed.) (1977) *William Harborne and the Trade with Turkey*, Oxford: Clarendon Press.

Skura, M. (1989) 'Discourse and the Individual: The Case of Colonisation and *The Tempest*', *Shakespeare Quarterly*, 40: 42–69.

Smith, Anthony D. (1991) *National Identity*, Harmondsworth: Penguin.

Smith, B. (1991) *Homosexual Desire in Shakespeare's England: A Cultural Poetics*, Chicago: University of Chicago Press.

Sole, Kelwyn (1994) 'Democratising Culture and Literature in a "New South Africa": Organisation and Theory', *Current Writing*, 6(2): 1–37.

Soobrayan, Bobby (1995) 'Banking on Education: A Critical Assessment of the World Bank's Involvement in Education in the South', *Perspectives in Education* 16(1): 5–32.

South African Dept. of Education (1995) 'Towards a Language Policy in Education'. Discussion document.

Spencer, Terence (1954) *Fair Greece, Sad Republic: Literary Philhellenism from Shakespeare to Byron*, Bath: Weidenfield & Nicholson.

Spiro, Melford E. (1988) 'Is the Oedipus Complex Universal?', in George H. Pollock and John Munder Ross (eds) *The Oedipus Papers*, Madison: International Universities Press, 435–73.

Stallybrass, P. (1986) 'Patriarchal Territories: The Body Enclosed', in M. W. Ferguson, M. Quilligan and N. Vickers (eds) *Rewriting the Renaissance: The Discourse of Sexual Difference in Early Modern Europe*, Chicago: Chicago University Press, 123–42.

—— (1993) 'Editing as Cultural Formation: The Sexing of Shakespeare's Sonnets', *Modern Language Quarterly*, 54(1): 91–103.

Starobinski, Jean (1989) *The Living Eye*, trans. Arthur Goldhammer, Cambridge, Mass., and London: Harvard University Press.

Stewart, Larry (1976) 'Freud before Oedipus: Race and Heredity in the Origins of Psychoanalysis', *Journal of the History of Biology*, 9(2): 215–28.

Stone, L. and Stone, J. C. (1984) *An Open Elite?: England, 1540–1880*, New York: Oxford University Press.

Strong, R. (1986) *The Cult of Elizabeth*, Berkeley: University of California Press.

—— (1987) *Gloriana: The Portraits of Elizabeth I*, London: Thames & Hudson.

Taylor, Gary (1989) *Reinventing Shakespeare*, London: Hogarth Press.

Todorov, Tzetlan (1982) *The Conquest of America: The Question of the Other*, New York: Harper & Row.

Tokson, Elliot H. (1982) *The Popular Image of the Black Man in English Drama, 1550–1688*, Boston: G.K. Hall & Co.

Traub, Valerie (1992) *Desire and Anxiety: Circulations of Sexuality in Shakespearean Drama*, London: Routledge.

Traversi, D. A. (1969) *An Approach to Shakespeare*, vol. 2, Garden City, NY: Doubleday.

UNDP (1996) *Human Development Report*, Oxford: Oxford University Press.

University of Witwatersrand (1995) 'Proposed Masters by Coursework in the Field of English Education', English Dept, Johannesburg.

Van Wyk Smith, Malvern (1990/1) 'Othello and the Narrative of Africa', *Shakespeare in Southern Africa*, 4.

Van Zyl, Susan (1990) 'Explaining Violence in South Africa: Some Psychoanalytic Considerations', *Project for the Study of Violence*. Seminar paper no. 8, Department of Applied Psychology, Johannesburg: University of the Witwatersrand.

Van Zyl, Susan and Bowyer, Allan (1994) 'Culture and Psychoanalysis: Hamlet, Prospero and Caliban'. Unpublished paper, Department of Applied English Language Studies and Department of Comparative Literature, Johannesburg: University of the Witwatersrand.

Vaughan, A. (1988) 'Shakespeare's Indian: The Americanization of Caliban', *Shakespeare Quarterly*, 39: 137–53.

Vaughan, Alden T. and Vaughan, Virginia Mason (1991) *Shakespeare's Caliban*, Cambridge: University of Cambridge Press

—— (1997) 'Before *Othello:* Elizabethan Representations of Sub-Saharan Africans', *The William and Mary Quarterly*, 3rd series, 54(1): 19–44.

Vaughan, Megan (1991) *Curing Their Ills: Colonial Power and African Illness*, Cambridge: Polity Press.

Vickers, Nancy (1982) 'Diana Described: Scattered Women and Scattered Rhyme', in Elizabeth Abel (ed.) *Writing and Sexual Difference*, Chicago: University of Chicago Press, 98–110.

Viswanathan, Gauri (1987) 'The Beginnings of English Literary Studies in India,' *Oxford Literary Review* 9: 2–26.

—— (1990), *Masks of Conquest: Literary Study and British Rule*, London: Faber.

Vitkus, Daniel (1997) 'Turning Turk in *Othello*: The Conversion and Damnation of the Moor', *Shakespeare Quarterly*, 48(2): 145–76.

Walcott, Derek (1986) *A Branch of the Blue Nile* in *Three Plays*, New York: Farrar, Strauss, Giroux.

Wall, W. (1996) 'Renaissance National Husbandry: Gervase Markham and the Publication of England', *Sixteenth Century Journal* 27/3: 767–85.

Watson, Keith (1982) 'Colonialism and Educational Development', in Keith Watson (ed.) *Education in the Third World*, London: Croom Helm.

Weimann, Robert (1978) *Shakespeare and the Popular Tradition in the Theatre: Studies in the Social Dimension of Dramatic Form and Function*, Baltimore and London: Johns Hopkins University Press.

Wettinger, Godfrey (1985) *The Jews of Malta in the Late Middle Ages*, Valetta, Malta: Midsea Books.

Whitehead, Clive (1982) 'Education in British Colonial Dependencies, 1919–1939: A Re-Appraisal', in Keith Watson (ed.) *Education in the Third World*, London: Croom Helm.

Whitney, Lois (1922) 'Did Shakespeare Know Leo Africanus?', *PMLA* 37: 470–83.

Williams, Gwyn A. (1985) *When Was Wales?*, Harmondsworth: Penguin Books.

Williams, Raymond (1979) *Modern Tragedy*, London: Verso.

Willis, D. (1989) 'Shakespeare's *Tempest* and the Discourse of Colonialism', *Studies in English Literature 1500–1900*, 29: 277–89.

Wilson, R. (1997) 'Voyage to Tunis: New History and the Old World of *The Tempest*', *ELH*, 64: 2.

Wilson Knight, G. (1951 [1931]) *The Imperial Theme*, London: Methuen.

—— (1932) *The Shakespearean Tempest*, Oxford: Oxford University Press.

Wind, Edgar (1967) *Pagan Mysteries in the Renaissance*, revised edn, Harmondsworth: Penguin Books.

Wolpe, Harold (1972) 'Capitalism and Cheap Labour-Power in South Africa: From Segregation to Apartheid', *Economy and Society*, 1(4): 425–56.

—— (1975) 'The Theory of Internal Colonialism: The South African Case', in I. Oxaal, T. Barnett and D. Booth (eds) *Beyond the Sociology of Development*, London: Routledge & Kegan Paul, 229–52.

The World Bank (1995a) *African Development Indicators 1994–95*, Washington: The World Bank.

—— (1995b) *Priorities and Strategies for Education: A World Bank Review*, Washington: The World Bank.

Wright, Laurence (1990/1) 'Aspects of Shakespeare in Post-colonial Africa', *Shakespeare in Southern Africa*, 4: 31–50.

Yates, Francis (1975) *Shakespeare's Last Plays*, London: Routledge.

Yeats, W. B. (1950) *Collected Poetry*, London: Macmillan.

Young, Robert (1990) *White Mythologies: Writing History and the West*, London: Routledge.

—— (1995) *Colonial Desire, Hybridity in Theory, Culture and Race*, London: Routledge.

Zarrilli, Philip B. (1984) *The Kathakali Complex*, New Delhi: Abhinav.

—— (1992) 'For Whom Is the King a King? Issues of Intercultural Production, Perception and Reception in a *Kathakali King Lear*', in Janelle G. Reinelt and Joseph R. Roach (eds) *Critical Theory and Performance*, Ann Arbor: University of Michigan Press, 16–40.

Zhiri, Oumelbanine (1991) *L'Afrique au miroir de l'Europe: Fortunes de Jean Léon l'Africain à la Renaissance*, Geneva: Librairie Droz.

Index